A History of the
City of Warsaw, Indiana

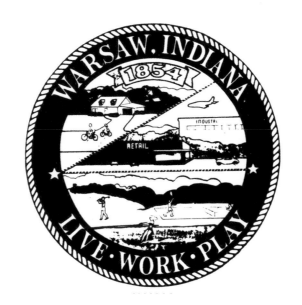

Preserving the Past for the Future

by
Michelle J. Bormet

Footnotes were not used in this book in order to facilitate the flow of the text. Contributors of information and photographs are listed in the acknowledgements.

Every effort has been made to ensure the accuracy of the information herein. However, the author and the Kosciusko County Historical Society are not responsible for any errors or omissions which may have occurred.

The 3rd Annual Twins Convention was held August 26, 1934, at the Center Lake Pavilion. The boys wearing dark sweaters in the second row, Doyle and Devon Smith of Warsaw, won first place. The Smith twins were born March 4, 1918. The cute girls standing in front are Carolyn and Marolyn Cook also of Warsaw. They were born August 2, 1931.

Copyright © 2001 by Michelle J. Bormet
Published by Kosciusko County Historical Society

International Standard Book Number: 0-9617301-1-0

Library of Congress Control Number: 2001092235

Edited by Marjorie Priser and Chelsea LeCount Stover
Designed by Sue Noppert

Printed in the United States of America by
Harmony Visual Communications • 113 N. Main Street • Bourbon, Indiana 46504

This book is dedicated

to those who so graciously shared

their priceless memories and photographs,

for without them,

it would not have been possible.

Foreword

Although for many a morning over many a coffee we sat across that round table from one another, we were still worlds apart. It was the hat that first caught my eye. That old, gray, sweat-stained fedora. But it was like a crown to him, in some strange way, a badge of legitimacy when he lived among the surface people.

I think he took a liking to me because, as he said, "The good Lord gave us two ears and one mouth for a reason". . . I honed my listening skills . . . really had no choice . . . the table was populated with "old sages," with bodies that were shutting down, but mouths that made up for the loss. It was maybe the best of all classrooms, for me anyway.

But each day he seemed to struggle a bit more, trying to figure how his lifetime in the Kentucky hills and coal mines had any value to a new world he said seemed "shallow as a creek in summer." "What good was I," he would lament "when there ain't nothin' the same? It's all changed . . . way too soon, though, to know for good or bad."

For more than ninety years this old man, like so many others, had authored a simple moment in history; his creases, scars, and stains a testimony to a life of unforgiving toil, now lost in time. His stories were but another window on one more "lost world." Nobody has just one teacher. From Blacky, I learned a lot about priorities. I really loved the old guy.

With no special fanfare his life ended, no doubt much as it began. I always kinda thought that going back underground, for him, was an especially welcomed escape, even though I heard the fedora went with him. I think about him often, but I know his address. He took great pride in proclaiming that "all miners go to heaven, 'cause the good Lord knows we spent enough time next to hell." I miss him and his tales about that foreign time. . . .

I always meant to record his stories. I wanted to protect this snapshot of history from the eraser of time, but I failed myself, as well as the future. Why is it that there is never enough time to do what we should do, but more than enough to do those things that contribute to nothing?

I've always been thankful that there are those among us, a few rare and impassioned souls, who command nothing less than a missionary spirit when it comes to preserving a record of the past for some future use. They seem driven by a fear that unless for their efforts, something of great value may be forever lost; for they see times past increasingly ignored and histories being rewritten to suit some new "bias," or discounted in value, as we bask in the glow of the newest "enlightenment."

This book is of unique value, the fruit of long hours of dedicated effort. My contribution, in meager comparison, is limited to offering but a few thoughts on our regard for times past and what I fear to be the growing ease with which some are turning out the guiding lights of history.

I fear that the greatest danger in our accelerated pace of technological development is the increasing disregard we seem to have for anything "past" or "old." With misplaced arrogance, some among us stamp huge chunks of our past "irrelevant" and "obsolete." We are victims of our own vanity, believing as we do that with all of our creations and advancements it should be quite obvious that we are living in the dawn's first light on a new world, unmatched in history, with few meaningful links to the past. Too many of us live our lives in houses of mirrors, as if the "march of time" commenced with our birth.

For an increasing number, less and less of the past seems to apply to the future. Everything is changing so fast. The distances between invention and obsolescence are shorter and shorter. But none of this is justification for discounting the value of history.

The past is more than a timeline of inventions. History is a record of lessons learned and errors repeated, and sadly enough, a testimony, to date, of man's morality and civility lagging sorely behind his creativity.

History is more than a record of man's applied intelligence; the creation of marvelous new "things" at a record pace. The true value of history may have little to do with "creations." Its value, I believe, is as a textbook on the "nature of man," his actions, reactions, light sides, dark sides, and never-ending efforts to achieve a truly civilized state. Some of life's greatest discoveries come from looking backward, not looking forward.

Despite all of man's discoveries, inventions, conquests, and perceived progress, the nature of man has changed very little, like it or not. This truth alone makes any past record an invaluable guide for living life now and in the future; for again, it is not intelligence that defines the level or degree of civilization, but our ability to live in fruitful peace with one another, without depravity in any form. History is full of man's good moves and bad moves in this direction, even on a local level.

Life is not as shallow as we live it. It is we who lack depth, not life itself. If tomorrow, all who have ever lived returned and walked among us, not only would the crowds be suffocating, but the reality of the event would be humbling to the extreme. For squaring off with the reality that we are but one more sedentary layer, one more small entry in the parade of history, not really much when compared to it all, would underscore the attention that history may deserve and make us, perhaps, a bit more generous with our humanity.

Those who acted upon the stages of times past were not always right, not always wrong, and they wrestled with life, as do we. But my guess is they had a bit more respect for history. Perhaps they had more in common with the past. For the most part, life in our over-privileged culture is not the survival contest it once was.

Some seem to believe we're a lot smarter now, more advanced, maybe even more civilized than many of those who came before. After all, look at us. We can travel to the distant stars, examine the smallest particles of life, and build a living thing in accordance with our own formulas. We command incredible power and limitless potential. It is only ourselves we cannot control . . . only our children we cannot reach.

It is wrong . . . and it is damaging for each new generation to reinvent the way life is lived, as if the past contains nothing but backward practices and beliefs. There are moral and ethical constants, and in our vain efforts to stand for everything, we run the risk of standing for nothing. It should be obvious that there is not a direct correlation between intelligence and moral/ethical enlightenment. In fact, more often than not, success numbs the conscience of man.

Yes, we need to teach the children that all ideas have not yet been thought, that all dreams have not yet been dreamt, and that all sights upon which future eyes will one day gaze have not yet been imagined. Yes, they must know there is yet great room for contribution and for differences to be made . . . but at the same time, they must be taught of lessons from the past . . . of successes, failures, rights and wrongs, what really counts, and things that never change . . . of heroes, villains . . . of work and play . . . what they had, what didn't exist, and what we really need . . . of families and fears and far-off lands . . . of love, and wars and tears.

History is the light which illuminates our way. It can make life easier to live. It can make decisions better ones. It can sharpen our judgment and order of things. It can make us more rightfully responsible to the future. History is who we are, what we are, and what we stand for. It cannot be rewritten by each new generation. It is history that gives depth to our existence, meaning, and purpose to many a cause, identity and enthusiasm for the future . . . and when honored, a consciousness that can protect us from ourselves. If you wish to see the future, then explore the past; for the constant is man, in all his glorious fault and frailty.

Any factual record that focuses on our roots is a bit of treasure, too often ignored . . . then discovered anew. Yet, too often, written historical record targets only important major events, with local histories lost to the closing of each generation. History seems to assume greater value as we grow older . . . perhaps because we wish we could live parts of life again . . . perhaps because we can see ourselves about to join it.

So to whom is the greatest tribute due? Those who lived the eventful past . . . the heroes we applaud . . . those who created history . . . or those who have labored tirelessly to record it . . . to give it immortality and breath of life? Without question, Michelle and her contributors are heroes, too.

— Jeffrey W. Plank

Preface

This history of the City of Warsaw evolved from my original research about the twenty-two mayors who have led the progress and growth of the City since 1875. The short biographies of the mayors are what inspired me to continue gathering information. As I learned about the businesses mayors were involved in over the years, my interest grew, and I went on to assemble historical information regarding many Warsaw businesses.

While talking with one person about a specific topic, another business or subject would be mentioned. I would then seek out yet another contact name for follow up, and the "snowball" began. In addition to researching information at the Warsaw Community Public Library and Jail Museum, the stories are composed with details from the *Northern Indianian*, *Daily Times* and *Times-Union* newspapers. Historian George A. Nye's bound typewritten notes and Daniel L. Coplen's books about Kosciusko County were also used as reference.

I have always lived in Marshall County, but I have worked in Warsaw since 1973. It was not until I accepted the position of secretary to the mayor in 1991 that I truly began to "know" Warsaw. After contacting many local residents and former residents across the United States during this research, I now feel like I've always lived here.

Just as time does not stand still, neither does history cease. Information was compiled as accurately as possible with the recollections and precious memories of current and former Warsaw residents and relatives. This book includes many "pieces to the puzzle." However, there are and always will be many pieces still missing.

Without a doubt, there are numerous businesses and people not noted who also greatly contributed to the development of the City of Warsaw throughout the years. I have attempted to include as many topics as possible, but the history of such a vibrant community is endless.

Michelle J. Bormet

Acknowledgements

I am especially grateful to the many wonderful people I have met and "reminisced" with over the past eighteen months. In addition to those sharing pertinent details about Warsaw businesses, items loaned to me for this project included priceless photographs, stereoscope cards, old postcards and newspapers, Warsaw High School Tiger annuals, scrap books, memorabilia items, and video tapes. I appreciate everyone's willingness to share their memories with me, and it is their input which makes this book so special.

This entire project was a "team" effort. Al Disbro, a local well-known photographer who is seldom seen without a camera draped around his neck, is the Winona Lake Branch Manager for Lake City Bank. He invested many hours in making copies of the photographs and negatives loaned to me for this project. Al's photographic expertise and avid interest in history most certainly confirms the phrase "a picture is worth a thousand words." Each year he takes hundreds of photographs throughout our community. Al Disbro is to still photography what former Warsaw movie theatre owner Ralph Boice was to recording local community events on 16mm film.

Marjorie Priser, a retiree of R.R. Donnelley & Sons, guided me through the procedures for printing a quality book. Being a devoted historian herself, Marge's research experience and wealth of resources was invaluable. Chelsea Stover, a staff member at Grace College, is a genealogist and also has an avid interest in county history. I owe both Marge and Chelsea a debt of gratitude for their knowledge, input, adept editing and proofreading skills. Their efforts greatly enhanced the quality of this book, and I whole-heartedly appreciate their time and talents.

Thanks also to local historian Jerry Gerard. He has extensive knowledge about the history of Warsaw, and he was a wealth of information leading me to key people about specific topics. Having lived in the 200 block of W. Center Street as a child and being involved with his father's shoe store just two blocks to the east, Jerry has a vivid recollection of Warsaw's "days gone by." Jerry has been a volunteer at the Old Jail Museum for twenty years, and I appreciate his enthusiasm and assistance in helping me locate information and photographs.

Lastly, and most importantly, I want to thank Jeff, my best friend and husband of 25 years, for his continued patience and support this past year while I spent the majority of my personal time completing this book.

Cherish yesterday, Dream of tomorrow, Live today!

Many people contributed information and/or photographs for this book. I apologize for any inadvertent omissions.

Joe Adams	John Crum	Jack Helvey	Jean Lucas	Lela Salman
E. Mazie Alexander	Sally Denney	Dave Hillery	Isadora Mann	Ray Salman
Barbara Anderson	Jean Ann Dennie	Marge Himes	Evelyn Marsh	Gary Salyer
Dr. James L. Baker	Harold Derry	Sally Hogan	Leslie Martin	John Sanders
Lois Baker	Linda Dilling	Keith Horn	Lanny Mauzy	Robert Sanders
Kimberley Baney	Al Disbro	Pauline Hoskins	Jody Maxwell	Sylvan Schwegman
Phil Barkey	Cindy Dobbins	Judge Duane Huffer	Jim Maze	Bruce Shaffner
Bill Bartlemay	Irene Dome	William D. Huffer	James E. McCleary	Dennis Sharp
Dr. Wallace Bash	Jane Edmond	Mack Jordan	Jane McGuire	Ronald Sharp
Sue Ann Beattie	Esther Edwards	Bess Joyner	Elizabeth McMillan	Karen Sheetz
Joe Beeson	Don Engle	Irene Kaufman	Jake Menzie	Jon R. Shively
Elaine Bell	Larry & Betty Engle	Peggy Keeton	Kate Metzger	J.C. "Mac" Silveus
Jack Bilz	Janet Essig	Doug Kehler	D. Blaine Mikesell	Charles Simpson
Laura Bixel	Edna Evers	Vereen Kelley	Mary Miller	Devon Smith
Jon Blackwood	Jeff Fackler	Donna Keough	Mallory Miniear	Howard "Chub" Smith, Jr.
Timm Bledsoe	Jacque Ferguson	Jeff Keough	Pat Molebash	Rex Snyder
Bob Blosser	Pam Flory	Doris Kesler	J. Alan Morgan	Louise Sponseller
Randy Boice	Peggy Fox	Weldon "Cy" Kincaide	Elaine Morrow	Jo Anne Star
Harold Brown	Phyllis Fribley	Barb Kintzel	Gael & Herberta Munson	Connie Stavropulos
Robert E. Brown	Eugenia Fulkerson	Dave Kintzel	Bob Murphy	Robert Steele
Steve Brown	Kim Fuller	John Kleeman	Phil Neff	Charlotte Stempel
Geneva Brumfield	Ken Gable	Chanda Kline	Nanette Newland	Wallace Stouder
John Bruner	Paul Gadson	Terry Klondaris	Sally Nichols	Chelsea Stover
Gordy Bumbaugh	Dave Gast	Tom Knoop	Gary Nieter/*Times-Union*	Don Sweatland
Burleigh Burgh	Frank Gatke	Ralph Konkle	Rene Nine	Warren Tatter
Judge Robert Burner	Jerry Gerard	Arleen Koors	Sue Noppert	Becky Thomas
Sheila Burner	Wilbur J. Gill	Bob Korth	Mark Norrell	June Thomas
Darwin Call	Richard Glover	Betty Kratzsch	D. Jean Northenor	Michael L. Valentine
Vernon Campbell	Doug Gooch	Esther Lackey	Becky Notestine	Russell Van Curen
Neal & Joy Carlson	Barb Goon	Keaton Landis	Fred Olds	Dr. Thomas Van Osdol
Teddy Carnegis	Diane Grose	Mary Belle Latta	Jerry Patterson	Roger Vore
Gwen Carter	Paul Grossnickle	Jerry Laurien	J.C. Paxton	Juergen Voss
Jeannine Cavell	Gerda Haack	Dewey Lawshe	David Peffley	Maynard Wade
Ford Chinworth	Gordon Hackworth	Mark Leiter	Janet Petro	Marge Warren
Robert H. Clarke	Norm Hagg	George Lenke, Jr.	John Petro	Jeanne Weirick
Sharon Clay	John Hall	Howard Levin	Doris Pittenger	Lucy Whiteneck
Bob Clendenen	Don Hanft	Bob Lichtenwalter	Agnes Jane Plummer	Rex Wildman
Sue Cole	Bob Hardin	Pat Likens	Marge Priser	Candy Wiley
Priscilla Conley	Linda Harman	Tony Lloyd	Joe Prout	Jenny Wilkins
Jon Couture	Ernest & Merl Hauth	Carmen Lock	Dennis Reeve	Chandler Williams
Michael Cox	Max Hay	Ken Locke	Robert Richmond	Barbara Wilson
Carol Craig	Dr. George M. Haymond	Marian Longenecker	Barbara Ringer	June Wimer
Bette-Jo Creighton	Dick Heagy	Dan Lowman	Wendell Sadler	Lyn M. Windsor

Introduction

The initial intent of this book was to preserve as much historical data as possible, but interesting and sometimes humorous memories and past events have been intermingled with the "facts and figures." Much of the information is in chronological order according to when businesses were started or lists the establishments in sequence that have been located in prominent buildings and locations over the years.

Readers will be introduced to many companies, organizations, and people who have helped make the City of Warsaw so special. I hope the stories and photographs will lead you on an enjoyable journey through Warsaw's history, development, and growth into the wonderful community it is today.

A view from atop the wooden toboggan slide at Center Lake in the 1930s. Water was piped to the top and continuously trickled down the slide to keep it wet for easy gliding of the wooden sleds.

I invite you to turn the page and "plunge" into Warsaw's history!

City of Warsaw

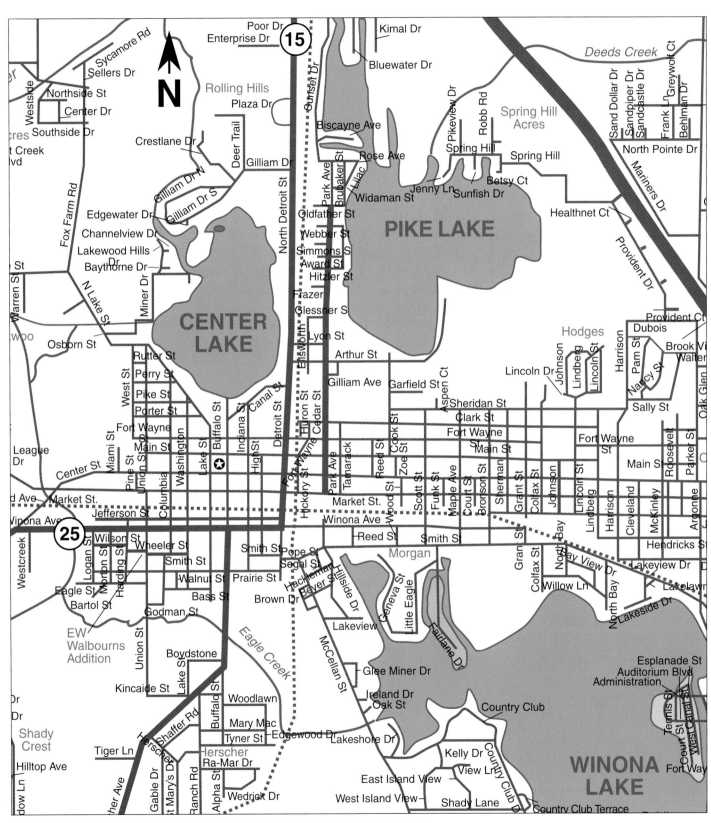

Courthouse Square

Provided by Anchor Graphics

x

Contents

This view from atop the toboggan slide in the 1930s shows a large crowd at Center Lake.

A view of the courthouse looking northwest in the 1930s.

Chapter 1

The Early Years

In the Beginning

In 1834, the original settlement was called "Red Brush." The first house/tavern was made of tamarack poles by Matthew D. Springer and located on what is currently the southeast corner of Center and Hickory Streets. A Potawatomi Indian camp was situated on what is now N. Lake Street.

In 1835, William J. Pope built the first store of tamarack poles at the corner of Lake and Market Streets and put in a stock of general merchandise. The town of Warsaw was laid out in 1836 and six families comprised the settlement in 1839. By 1850, the town boasted a population of 250. George Moon (future mayor) took the 1850 census and John B. Chapman (attorney and legislator) named the county and selected the site for the county seat.

During the first years of Warsaw's existence, all the fires that occurred in the village were put out by throwing water on the fire with a bucket or other suitable utensil. As soon as a fire was discovered, a bucket brigade was formed. Later, there was one hose cart house on W. Market Street at the Lesh factory. Another was the central station at the Town Hall, and the east end hose house was near the site where the East Ward School was later located.

Street Names

The following outline about Warsaw's streets is from newspaper excerpts written by Edwin C. Aborn in 1932 and has been included for documentation with Warsaw's history.

When the town site was platted in 1835 by John B. Chapman, three students in civil engineering were engaged to assist in the work of survey. Although their names had long since been forgotten, it was known that their home cities were **Buffalo**, New York; **Detroit**, Michigan; and Columbus, Ohio.

Looking north on Buffalo Street, this is the earliest known photo of Downtown Warsaw in 1868 before the Courthouse Square was established (the tree area). Phillipson's clothing store, which began in 1864, can be seen on the west side of S. Buffalo Street.

Upon completion of the survey work, a gathering was held at the "Shot Tower" tavern located on the northwest corner of Detroit and Main Streets. It was suggested streets be named in honor of the students' hometowns—thereupon Buffalo and Detroit Streets came into being. However, to give a street the name of Columbus would be too similar to Columbia Street. The man who lived in Columbus, Ohio lived on **High** Street; hence, Warsaw's High Street was established.

The street called **Main** is said to have been the first regular thoroughfare established when the original plat of the village of Warsaw came into being. In early days, it was the location of the post office and principal stores, including wagon, blacksmith, and harness shops.

Lake Street very appropriately received its name by reason of its meandering along the west shore of Center Lake and the outlet into the Tippecanoe River. As a tribute to the union of

The California gold rush began in 1849.

1

George W. Polk's South Side Livery had locations at 117 W. Center Street and 205 W. South Street. They advertised safe horses and careful drivers. Cabs, carriages, open and covered buggies were available day or night.

Well-dressed drivers posed with their horses and carriages in front of the Polk's Livery & Feed Barn on South Street (now Winona Avenue). Barbara Anderson states that her grandfather, Noble Wolford, was employed by Polk's at one time and most likely is in this photo. She remembers him talking about picking up passengers and packages when they arrived at the railroad depots.

states, a short trail on the west was named **Union** Street. **Columbia** Street was so named in honor of the Goddess of Liberty, recognized as the emblem of freedom. Derived from the name of our first president and "Father of Our Country," **Washington** Street extended from its junction with Lake Street southward to Prairie Street.

Indiana Street was so called in recognition of the Hoosier commonwealth. **Hickory** Street is said to have derived from the fact that a grove of

trees of that variety had to be removed in order to construct the so-named street. **Cedar** Street gets its name from the large cedar trees that once adorned the home of Rev. John Hatfield on that street.

Scott Street was one of the first thoroughfares to be opened in East Warsaw and was originally known as "Scott's Road," because on one of the corners at the Center Street intersection lived a man by the name of George Scott, one of Warsaw's leading businessmen at the time. Extending a distance of two blocks from Center Street south through the old fairground area, **Funk** Street is named in honor of the pioneer family of that name.

Maple Avenue was known as Card Street until the platting and opening of the old fairgrounds addition in the late 1890s and the opening of Oakwood Cemetery. **Bronson** Street derives its name from the early days when, in East Warsaw, a man named Rush Bronson owned a large tract of land in that vicinity. **Sherman** Street perpetuates the memory of the gallant William Sherman of Civil War fame.

Grant Street commemorates Ulysses S. Grant, commanding general of the Union Army during the Civil War and twice elected to the presidency of the United States. **Colfax** Street was named for Schuyler Colfax, an Indiana statesman and vice president of the United States during Grant's first term. And, of course, **Lincoln** Street takes its name from President Abraham Lincoln, the Great Emancipator. Other streets which derive their names from former presidents include: **Cleveland, Harrison, Garfield** and **McKinley**.

Market Street was so named because it is said that early settlers had in mind a project to provide a market space on this street for farmers who brought their produce to town for sale. **Center** Street is known to have been given its name for the same reason that Center Lake is so called— namely, it is the geographical center of the county. As such, Center Street traverses the entire length of the city from east to west, also the route of the Lincoln Highway (U.S. Road 30).

Tamarack Street gets its name from the fact that when first constructed it ran most of its length through a dense growth of tamarack trees. A.T.S. Kist named **Reed** Street after one of his sons. The next street east, only one block in length, bears the name of his daughter, **Zoe**.

Cook Street gets its name from an early pioneer family. **Wood** Street was so named to perpetuate the memory of A.G. Wood, former mayor and Union Army captain in the Civil War. **South** Street was so called because it was the town's southern-most street.

Jefferson Street gets its name in commemoration of Thomas Jefferson, third president of the United States and author of the Declaration of Independence. **Fort Wayne** Street derives its name from the fact that in pioneer days all of the travel between Warsaw and Fort Wayne was directed over that route. **Clark** Street was named for S.B. Clark, for many years one of Warsaw's most highly respected citizens.

Canal Street extends in a somewhat irregular course from Buffalo to Detroit Streets and passes the south boundary of Center Lake, paralleling the canal constructed years before as a waterway to connect Center and Pike Lakes. **Pike** Street originally extended to the shore of Center Lake. Where the street met the lake, it is said great quantities of fish of the pike variety were unusually abundant.

Perry Street was so named in honor of Commodore Perry, who so heroically defeated the British forces in the battle on Lake Erie during the War of 1812. **Arthur** Street was named in honor of former President Chester A. Arthur.

Pope Street was named after a pioneer resident who conducted a general store at the location of the old Post Office on S. Lake Street. **Godman** Street was named to commemorate a former city engineer who lost his life in a sewer tragedy in 1904. **McClellan** Street was named in honor of Civil War General George B. McClellan. **Segal** Street also derives its name from an officer who achieved fame during the Civil War.

Durbin Street and **Hendricks** Street were both named in honor of former governors of the Hoosier commonwealth, Winfield T. Durbin and Thomas A. Hendricks. **Roosevelt**, **Taft** and **Adams** Streets were named respectively for former presidents.

An October 1935 article discusses changing the name of **South Street** to **Winona Avenue**. It appears the street known as "South" never had a name legally bestowed upon it. It was the southern street of the original plat of the Town of Warsaw and was just referred to as "South Street." While under that name, it absorbed two other streets—**Hays** Street on the west and **Baker** Street on the east. From Scott Street east to **Bronson**, it was known as Baker Street until

The first courthouse that was built on the Courthouse Square in 1848.

1930, at which time it was extended to intersect Smith Street at a point opposite Dalton Foundries.

When a petition was circulated requesting a change of name, all residents of the street were invited to suggest a name. The fact that the Beyer interests donated right-of-way 60 feet wide through their extensive tract east of the Big Four Railroad for the street extension, was largely responsible for the City Council's decision in the selection of the name, as the Messrs. Beyer favored Winona Avenue, and it quickly became one of Warsaw's major residential thoroughfares.

Courthouse and Jail

The first Courthouse, a one-story 20-foot x 30-foot frame building, was built in the spring of 1837 on the northeast corner of Center and Indiana Streets. It burned just a few months later, and a two-story structure was built during the fall of that same year in the same location. That building was used until 1848 when a larger two-story courthouse was built on the Courthouse Square facing Buffalo Street at a cost of $4,200. The present courthouse was constructed between 1881 and 1884 at a cost of almost $200,000.

The first jail, constructed of brick, was located on the southwest corner of the Courthouse Square. By 1871, a larger facility was needed, and a new county jail was built on the southwest corner of Main and Indiana Streets. That jail served the county for 110 years.

When the Justice-Jail Building was completed in 1981 on the southwest corner of Lake and Main

The first American World's Fair was held in 1853 in New York City.

The Kosciusko County Jail on the southwest corner of Indiana and Main Streets was built in 1871 and served as a jail for 110 years. Since 1981 this structure has been known as the Old Jail Museum, operated by the Kosciusko County Historical Society.

There were 44 physicians living in the county in 1911, of which 29 were members of the Society.

Meetings were first held in the Superintendent of Schools' office in the courthouse; by 1917 the group met at the Public Library. The Society held its annual banquets each December at the Hotel Hays. For each meeting, a member or visiting physician would give a lecture about a particular disease, illness, or medical updates for the group to discuss.

During the 1920s, the society somewhat declined, and some members left town in the 1940s to serve in the military during World War II. In 1947, a meeting was called in an attempt to revive the organization. Regular meetings were scheduled to be held at the Camel Club, which at that time was located above the former Hall Hardware on S. Buffalo Street.

The Kosciusko County Medical Society continues today with about forty county physicians as members, plus there are numerous medical specialists from surrounding cities who come to Warsaw.

First Brick Building

The first brick building was built in 1849 on the southwest corner of Center and Buffalo Streets by George Moon and William Cosgrove, both future mayors of Warsaw. That structure was razed in 1913 so a building could be constructed for the Indiana Loan & Trust Company, which later was the site of the First National Bank of Warsaw.

Independent Order of Odd Fellows

In 1849, the Independent Order of Odd Fellows (IOOF) was represented by two lodges—an encampment and a women's auxiliary. Kosciusko Lodge No. 62 was granted a charter January 9, 1849. Charter member George Moon was elected its first noble grand. Meetings were initially held on the third floor of the building on the northwest corner of Market and Buffalo Streets, occupied by the Sons of Temperance. By 1850, the third story of Moon and Cosgrove's brick building was secured and beautifully finished for the Lodge's use for the next eight years.

The members then formed a stock company with the idea of providing a hall of some permanence. The Empire Block on the northwest corner of Market and Buffalo Streets was completed about 1859 and for nearly twelve years served admirably for the Lodge's work and affairs. When a fire in 1871 destroyed the building, funds were raised to build a new hall which was dedicated in 1873.

The Civil War, 1861-1865.

Streets, the century-old structure was named the Old Jail Museum and has been occupied since by the Kosciusko County Historical Society.

Shot Tower

In 1840, the "Shot Tower" tavern/hotel was built on what is now the southwest corner of Detroit and Main Streets. So named because of its height, the Shot Tower was originally built to be used as a hotel. However, A.T.S. Kist purchased the property in 1851 and removed one story from the structure.

It was suspected that in the early days this building was used to manufacture counterfeit coins and bills. At a time when it was unoccupied, someone searched through the building and did find a number of engraving items, including a seal that stated "This is genuine," complete with a banking firm's name.

This corner was later occupied by the First Church of Christ Scientist, and is now part of the public library parking lot.

Kosciusko County Medical Society

The Kosciusko County Medical Society, incorporated January 21, 1847, was one of the first organizations in Warsaw. Early records were not found, but the first meeting with available minutes took place on January 31, 1911, with eight members in attendance. The physicians present were: president M.S. Yocum, C.C. DuBois, L.W. Ford, J.W. Heffley, W.L. Hines, A.C. McDonald, J.E. Potter, and secretary C.N. Howard.

The three-story Masonic Temple was constructed in 1924 on High Street between Center and Main Streets.

A view of the third floor Masonic Lodge room during a lodge meeting.

Masonry Lodge No. 73

In 1849, a charter was granted to William Parks and fourteen other Masons to establish the Free and Accepted Masonry Lodge No. 73 in Warsaw. Meetings were first held in the Empire Block. By 1864 the membership had grown to 69.

A new Masonry Lodge, Lake City Lodge No. 371, received its charter in 1868. When the Empire Block burned in 1871, the lodge met in the Wright building on the northeast corner of Center and Buffalo Streets. The lodges then consolidated in 1887 under the name of Lake City Warsaw Lodge No. 73.

The second story of the Wright House (now the Saemann Building) served as the Masonic Lodge until the early 1920s. The Masonic Temple was used almost every night of the week by one of its organizations: the Blue Lodge, York Rite Bodies, Eastern Star, and Rainbow Girls. In fact, the Masonic light bar remains today on the southwest corner of the Saemann Building, where one of the lights used to be lit to represent which organization had a meeting that particular night.

A three-story neoclassical brick Masonic Temple was built in 1924 on High Street between Center and Main Streets (now the west side of the Warsaw Community Public Library parking lot). The dining room was on the first floor, which was partially underground, the second floor had the office and recreation areas, and the lodge room occupied the third floor. Maurice DePoy was the custodian of the High Street building and served

The Warsaw Masonic Lodge #73 had a centennial celebration in 1949. Officers in front, left to right: Samuel F. DePoy, Robert S. Zimmer, Worshipful Master Joe C. Paxton, and James E. Lambert. In back, left to right: Harold R. Clingenpeel, William C. Harvuot, James A. Sarber, Maurice C. DePoy, and John E. Cantwell.

as secretary. The building was vacated in 1988 when the Lodge moved to Boggs Industrial Park. The High Street building was demolished a couple of years later for expansion of the Library.

J.C. Paxton notes that Grand Master Bruce Carr helped lay the cornerstone of the present Courthouse in 1882. Paxton also relates that his father, Joe C. Paxton, was the Worshipful Master when the organization celebrated its 100th anniversary in 1949, and as a child J.C. spent many evenings at the Masonic Temple with his parents.

Union School sat on the southwest corner of Detroit and Market Streets from 1872 to 1916.

West Ward School was built on N. Union Street in 1872. This site is now occupied by the Madison Elementary School.

The Town of Warsaw

Not much information was recorded in the early days. However, in 1850 Warsaw was the largest village in the county with a total population of 304. There were 64 residential homes in Warsaw, most valued at less than $1,000. Charles W. Chapman, a lumber merchant, was the wealthiest with $9,000 worth of property. Druggist George R. Thralls was second with property valued at $4,900. Warsaw had a population of 752 when it was incorporated as a town on March 25, 1854.

Community Schools

Early records show that Joseph A. Funk was teaching pupils in Wayne Township by 1844 at a salary of $17 a month. Classes were held in a small 18-foot x 28-foot structure on Fort Wayne Avenue where it joins Fort Wayne Street.

In 1851, Robert and Jane Cowen came to town and first opened school in a frame building on the southeast corner of Buffalo and Jefferson Streets. The two-story Cowen Seminary, also referred to as the Grove School, was later built on the east side of S. Detroit Street, extending from Winona Avenue north to the Pennsylvania Railroad tracks (current location of The Rental Shop and Town & Country Feed & Seed).

The Cowen Seminary was a social and educational center for the community. Desks could be stacked in one corner to make room for big parties and plays. The private school cost about $5 per term of 10 to 12 weeks and had 150 students during its busiest times. The primary classes occupied the main floor and the older pupils were upstairs.

The first piano brought to Warsaw arrived at the Cowen Seminary on February 12, 1860. Thus, the school was able to offer music lessons. All classes at the school were taught by Mrs. Cowen until her death in 1876. The building was destroyed by fire in 1884.

The earliest free public school, known as the Union School, was built in 1858 on the southwest corner of Market and Detroit Streets just north of the railroad tracks. D.T. Johnson was the first principal. Following stories in the early 1870s that the three-story building was unsafe, especially during storms, the building was demolished in the spring of 1872.

Warsaw built three schoolhouses in 1872. A new high school, known as Center Ward School, was built at a cost of $37,000 on the former Union School site. The East Ward School, constructed on Scott Street between Main and Fort Wayne Streets, and the West Ward School, on N. Union Street near what was then called Thrall's picnic grounds, were built at a cost of about $18,000 total. Both schools were occupied by the elementary grades.

As the number of pupils increased, the schools filled to capacity, and in 1904 a new high school was erected on the northwest corner of Main and Washington Streets. The building faced Main Street between Washington and Columbia Streets, and the first classes were held in 1905.

West Wayne Township School was located on S. Union Street. This is now the site of Washington Elementary School.

East Wayne Township School was located on Kings Highway in Winona Lake. This is now Jefferson Elementary School.

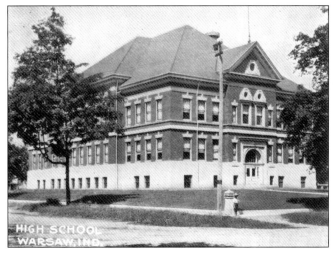

This High School was built in 1904 on Main Street between Washington and Columbia Streets.

Additions were eventually built on to both sides of the High School on Main Street to extend the full block between Washington and Columbia Streets.

Workers posed for this photo in 1916 during the construction of the Center Ward School on E. Main Street.

The Center Ward School on E. Main Street was completed in 1917.

McKinley School, formerly known as East Ward School, faced Scott Street between Main and Fort Wayne Streets. It closed in 1978.

Farewell gathering at the close of McKinley School in 1978. Left to right: third grade teacher Jim Morrison, school board member Charlie Ker, Mrs. Dorothy Hogan, former principal Floyd Hollar, principal Vernon Campbell, and fifth grade teacher Charles Hunter.

The elementary grades remained at the East and West Ward Schools. As years passed, they became very crowded and unsanitary, and the old Center Ward School building on the corner of Market and Detroit Streets was condemned by 1916. (L.M. Neher bought that property and built a two-story brick structure for a Ford garage and sales room. That building has been occupied by Schrader Auto Parts since 1976.)

Six lots were purchased at the north end of High Street along Main Street and a new school was built at a cost of $56,000. The three-story building, with its first floor below the street level, opened for school in January 1917. Classrooms and offices were on the first and second floors, and the third floor had classrooms and a large auditorium with a stage. Stairways on the east and west ends led to a large playground on the north side of the school. (The Center Ward School was demolished about 1990 and the Zimmer corporate headquarters was completed on this site in 1992.)

When the Center Ward School on Main Street opened in 1917, the school board consisted of: W.F. Maish, president; William Crist, treasurer; and Flint Bash, secretary. The superintendent was James M. Leffel. Principals were: R.W. Townsend, high school; James E. Blue, Junior High and Center Ward; Miss Penelope Shoup, West Ward; and Mrs. Alice Biggs, East Ward.

About this same time, the East and West Ward Schools only had room for grades one through five. Therefore, the east end of the new Center Ward School housed grades one through six for the Central District and also sixth grade students from the other districts. The west end was known as the Junior High School for grades seven, eight and nine, as the High School on Main Street was not large enough to include freshman students.

When Dwight Eisenhower became president of the United States in 1953, Doug Kehler recalls that Thames Mauzy, owner of Home Furniture Mart, took what was then considered a "huge" television (probably a 16-inch screen) to the Center Ward School and placed it in the study hall so the students could watch the inauguration. At that time, only "rich" people owned televisions, so that particular school day was very special to many of the kids.

With the community rapidly growing, more schools were built to accommodate additional students. Effective January 1, 1966, Plain Township was annexed and became a part of the Warsaw School system. At that time, all the schools were renamed after former presidents of the United States.

The East Wayne Township School on Kings Highway in Winona Lake was renamed Jefferson School. Now known as Washington Elementary, the former West Wayne school was built on S. Union Street in 1957. An addition was built on to the school in 1979.

Groundbreaking for a new West Ward School on N. Union Street took place in 1953, and the first classes were held there in 1954. William Farrar was a teacher at West Ward School when it opened.

This school was renamed Madison Elementary, and Farrar was the school's principal from 1959 to 1986.

Across town was the East Ward School, between Main and Fort Wayne Streets, which became known as McKinley School. Vernon Campbell served as principal from 1960 until it closed in 1978. After the school was demolished, a city park and playground was constructed and appropriately named McKinley Park.

Lincoln Elementary was built in 1959 at the corner of Lincoln and Main Streets, and Edgewood Middle School was built in 1975 at 900 S. Union Street. Both Eisenhower Elementary at 1900 S. County Farm Road and Harrison Elementary at 1300 Husky Trail were completed in 1991.

The High School remained located on W. Main Street until a new building was completed on Smith Street in 1962 at a cost of $1.8 million. At that time, the Main Street facility became the freshman high school, housing only ninth graders. A gymnasium was later added to the west end of the school.

When the current Warsaw Community High School was completed south of town in 1989 at a cost of nearly $25 million, the facility at 848 E. Smith Street became the Lakeview Middle School.

The former High School on W. Main Street was torn down and the Retired Tigers apartment building was constructed in its place.

Armory / Community Building

A Community Building was constructed in the 400 block of W. Center Street in 1902. In addition to being used for basketball tourneys, the building was also used as a military arsenal for Company L, 152nd Infantry, 38th Division. A new Armory was built in 1928 east of Center Ward School on E. Main Street. The Armory had a rifle range in the basement that extended underneath the sidewalk on Main Street, and the gymnasium was used to perform drills.

By the 1940s, the Armory had offices and a large room on the west end of the building to store equipment and uniforms, and the east end was used as the administration office for the Warsaw Schools. When the rifle range was closed, that area was converted into a locker room with showers. The gymnasium was used for school basketball games and other community events until the new high school on E. Smith Street (now Lakeview Middle School) was built in 1962.

Center Ward School on E. Main Street opened in 1917. The east end housed grades one through six, and the west end was for the Junior High students.

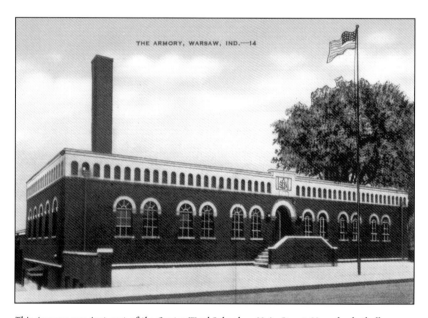

This Armory was just east of the Center Ward School on Main Street. Many basketball games were held in the gymnasium, and the School Administration Office was located in the building until the mid-1980s.

The school administration office remained in the Armory on Main Street until the mid-1980s. The building went into disrepair and was eventually demolished. The National Guard Armory relocated to a new building on County Road 350 N, where dances and other social events are still occasionally held.

Shane's Corner

A brick building was constructed on the southeast corner of Center and Buffalo Streets in 1854. It was originally two stories and a third story was

The county fair held on the Courthouse Square was well attended in 1919.

President Abraham Lincoln signed the Emancipation Proclamation on January 23, 1863.

added in 1858. (One story remains today.) Henry Shane ran a grocery store at this location for over 40 years, thus the nickname "Shane's Corner."

From the early 1900s, Shane's Corner was the site of the Warsaw Candy Kitchen for almost 50 years. The building was then leased to the Judd Drug Store for about ten years, until it moved to 1775 E. Center Street. The corner building and next door (now Crownover Jewelry) was renovated and housed Paul Barney's men's clothing store for a number of years. The Le Gourmet Chocolate Shoppe has been located on this corner since 1993.

Pierce Hotel

The Pierce Hotel, later known as the Central Hotel, was located in the 200 block of S. Buffalo Street on the north side of the alley. In the early 1840s, the land was owned by George Moon. The property changed owners several times, but Rowland Willard bought it about 1854 and built a hotel.

Hattie M. Pierce purchased the building in 1874, and it became known as the Pierce Hotel. When the building was no longer used as a hotel by the 1890s, it was a bicycle store, and later George H. Jordan managed the American Express office there. The old hotel building was demolished in the early 1900s to build a laundry facility.

Kosciusko County Agricultural Society

The Kosciusko County Agricultural Society was organized June 2, 1855, for the purpose of inaugurating county fairs. Officers at that time were: David Rippey, president; M.A. Bierce, S. Hoppus and John Makemson, vice presidents; George Moon, secretary; and Samuel H. Chipman, treasurer.

The first county "street fair" was held on the Courthouse Square in the fall of 1856. The entire downtown area was involved and the carnival show was a highlight. Merchants built booths in front of their stores to sell their wares. The midway was down Buffalo Street from Center to Market Streets, and there was a big parade of livestock.

Platforms were placed on prominent corners from which free live entertainment was provided. An hour-long concert by the Merchants Band of Warsaw on the platform at Shane's Corner was usually the first event of the festivities. The day's program ended with a balloon ascension from the Hotel Hays corner. On Wednesday night, a grand water carnival was held on Center Lake with the band on a raft and hundreds of boats loaded with musicians playing beneath the lights of Roman candles and fireworks.

A committee was later formed to consider purchasing fair grounds. The committee purchased, fenced and cleared six acres of land owned by A.T.S. Kist just south of the Tippecanoe River Bridge west of the West Ward School. These grounds were used until 1861, when the committee purchased ten acres for $1,000 in East Warsaw owned by Abner Baker.

The buildings and fence were moved to the new grounds and two additional buildings were erected. The society held the first fair on the new grounds October 2-4, 1861. A racetrack of one-third mile was constructed for training and racing horses. In 1874, the society purchased five adjoining acres from Dr. Jacob Boss so a larger, half-mile track could be built to attract finer horses from a distance.

This 15 to 20 acre tract was bounded on the north by Center Street, on the east by Bronson Street, on the west by Scott Street, and on the south by the Pennsylvania Railroad right-of-way.

Following the demise of the Kosciusko County Agricultural Society in 1885, no fairs were held in the county for a number of years. However, in 1906 a group of enthusiastic citizens combined efforts for a free fair. Officers then were: Charles Ker, president; Capt. C.W. Scott, vice president; W.S. Rogers, secretary; Ben Phillipson and Conrad Schade, directors; and Gordon Rutter, manager of amusements.

The first fair held at the present fairgrounds along the shore of Winona Lake was in the fall of 1946. The next year four buildings were constructed,

General Reuben Williams (1831-1905), founder of the Northern Indianian newspaper, takes a moment to relax.

including the Merchants Building, the 4-H Building, the Grandstand, and the Petrie Band Camp. The Women's Building was erected in 1948. The racetrack at the new location was only one-fourth mile.

The main entrance and the dairy barn were constructed in 1960, followed by the horse barn and sheep barn in 1961. Between 1962 and 1963, the fish fry building, the hog barn, and the Shrine Building were added.

Northern Indianian Newspaper

The *Times-Union* is the third oldest family-owned newspaper in Indiana and is also the oldest continuous business in Kosciusko County. The publication is in its fifth consecutive generation of ownership by the Williams family.

This chronology focuses mostly on those family members. The generations are: first, General Reuben Williams; second, Logan and Melvin Williams; third, Raymond B. and Charles Reuben Williams; fourth, Michael R. Williams and Lane Williams Hartle; and fifth, Christopher R. Williams, Chandler M. Williams, Cooper L. Williams, Ashley Williams Rettig, and Craig Norrell.

General Reuben Williams (1831-1905) was born in Tiffin, Ohio. His father, Reuben Williams, Sr. (1793-1851), was a soldier in the War of 1812 and his grandfather, Jeremiah Williams, fought in the Revolutionary War of 1776.

Reuben Williams came to Warsaw in 1844 at age 13 and attended Mrs. Cowen's Seminary for a short time. He was first elected to a Lieutenant's post in the Indiana 12th Infantry Regiment of volunteers for the Union Army in 1861 and received numerous promotions thereafter. During his military service, he was captured three times and held prisoner. In 1865 Williams was promoted to Brevet Brigadier General for his meritorious service during the war, and led the victory parade in Washington, D.C.

To acquire a practical knowledge of the printing business, Williams began as a journeyman printer and traveled through several states, paying his expenses by setting type in newspaper offices while en route. After learning the printing trade, General Reuben Williams returned to Warsaw in 1856 and with George W. Fairbrother began publication of the *Northern Indianian* newspaper.

The inaugural publication of 250 issues appeared on January 10, 1856, and was printed in a frame building at 116 N. Buffalo Street (now

Reuben Williams as Captain of Company E in 1862 during the Civil War.

Raymond B. "Ted" Williams (1891-1981)

Charles R. "Reub" Williams (1910-1987)

The publishing staff of Williams & Sons Publishing in 1911. Left to right is William C. Cronon, K. Fred Weick, Rollin Teel, Ralph O. Nusbaum, George Ungerer, Logan H. Williams, Bram Williams, Daniel Gallentine, Ed D. Line, Ralph W. Bartol, and Charles W. Argerbright.

the site of Dig's Diner). By the early 1860s, the *Northern Indianian* was published on the third floor of Shane's Corner on the southeast corner of Center and Buffalo Streets.

The offices were moved down Buffalo Street in 1866 to the Phoenix Block where the presses were first powered by steam. Following a fire that destroyed the Empire Block on the west side of S. Buffalo Street, General Williams constructed the Indianian Building at 114 S. Buffalo Street for Williams & Sons Publishing.

Publishers of the *Northern Indianian* started the *Warsaw Daily Times* in 1881, and the two merged in 1919. In 1938, the *Warsaw Daily Times* bought out the *Warsaw Union*, a newspaper founded by Henry C. Rippey in 1854. That consolidation formed the current *Times-Union* daily newspaper. For half a century, General Reub Williams, a staunch Republican, was editor of the politically influential publication.

General Williams wrote at length about two subjects—early county history and his Civil War experiences. Late in 1901, he started a series of articles titled "Early Times in Kosciusko" that ran in the *Warsaw Daily Times* for over a year. The articles were full of firsthand experiences of pioneers in this area. Shortly after coming back from the war, General Williams wrote a series of articles titled "Reminiscences of the Civil War." Years later, he then expanded on that series and wrote another long series titled "Incidents of the War."

General Reuben Williams married Jemima Hubler in 1857, and they had one daughter and five sons. The General's son, Logan Howard Williams (1867-1950), married Estelle Wahl in 1889 and the couple had two sons, Raymond Bramwell "Ted" (1891-1981) and Charles Reuben "Reub" (1910-1987). Raymond was nicknamed Ted because as a child he often wore Teddy Roosevelt "rough rider" military uniforms. All five of the General's sons worked at the newspaper at one time or another.

General Williams was elected as Kosciusko County Clerk in 1866 and again in 1870, serving for a total of eight years. In 1875 he was appointed Deputy Second Comptroller of the United States Treasury, but resigned after seven months to resume his editorial work in Warsaw. Williams was an intensely patriotic, noble man. Even as a strong political figure, he was highly respected by all and was an acquaintance or friend of almost everyone in town and throughout the county.

General Williams was held in high esteem by members of the press on account of his ability, long service and kindness. His bravery, loyalty and fidelity gained him the respect of Governor Morton and members of the military. When General Williams died, Rev. D.H. Guild conducted the funeral service. A quite lengthy article appeared on the front page of the January 19, 1905, edition of the *Northern Indianian*, in which Rev. Guild was quoted as saying, "He is as generous as he is brave and the number of his friends is limited only by the extent of his acquaintance among men."

The Times Building was erected in 1924 on the northwest corner of Market and Indiana Streets for the publication of the newspaper. For a time, extra office space was leased to other businesses. Occupants in 1925 included: Suites 1 and 12, Drs. Copper and Olds, Osteopaths; Suite 2, Clark Hat Shoppe and fine millinery; Suite 3, C.E. Strouse, Chiropractor; Suite 8, Mrs. Emma Linder, Modiste; Suite 9, T.U. Franklin, general salesman for motor brushes; Suite 10, Justin O. Zimmer, sales manager for DePuy Splint Manufacturing Company; Suite 11, Indiana Farm Bureau, Onion Exchange department and headquarters.

Raymond B. "Ted" Williams married Ruth Harmon in 1932 and they had one daughter, Martha Lane (1936). Lane Williams grew up in Warsaw and Sarasota, Florida. She married Horace Avery Norrell, Jr. in 1956 and they had three sons. Their son, Craig, is currently a computer systems manager with the *Times-Union*.

Charles Reuben "Reub" Williams married Helen Smith in 1937, and they had one son, Michael Reuben (1938). Following their grandfather's death, brothers Ted and Reub became co-publishers of the *Times-Union* newspaper. In 1948, they also started and owned the radio station WRSW 107.3 FM and added WRSW 1480 AM in 1952.

In the spring of 2001, author Jack Kneece published a book titled *The Ghost Army, WWII*, which includes Charles Reuben Williams' military service during World War II. Williams served in the 12th Army's 23rd Special Forces Unit and was one of several officers commanding a top-secret combat deception unit that was credited with saving thousands of allied lives. Williams retired from the military with the rank of Lieutenant Colonel.

The Indianian building was located on the south side of the alley in the 100 block of S. Buffalo Street.

Michael Reuben Williams married Nancy E. Morgan, daughter of Robert E. Morgan and Betty Zimmer, in 1960. Michael, the current publisher of the *Times-Union*, and Nancy had three sons and one daughter. Their son, Chandler, is currently an owner and business manager with the *Times-Union*. Chandler's son, Reuben Zimmer Williams, is the seventh generation bearer of the name Reuben.

Now in its 147th year of publication, the *Times-Union*, an independent Republican newspaper, continues to be the main source of local news and current events for the entire county and beyond.

Formerly known as the Kirtley Hotel, this view of the White House Hotel on E. Center Street was taken in 1892. This site is currently occupied by the old Eagles Building.

A Pennsylvania Railroad employee looks out the watchman's tower which was located on the north side of the tracks by the Warsaw Overall Company.

Early Hotels

A leading hotel in the mid-1800s was the Wright House on the northeast corner of Buffalo and Center Streets. The hotel was started by brothers Benjamin P. and E. Rigdon Wright in 1856.

This was a popular corner, as the Wright House was a stopping point for stagecoaches that ran every day from Warsaw to Goshen. On April 7, 1866, the first trip for the street car commenced along Center Street in front of the Wright House. Four horses driven by Sam Wharton were hitched to the decorated car, and anxious citizens paid as much as $5 for the first ride.

The building burned in 1867, a new four-story structure was built by 1869, and that building burned in 1883. The present three-story brick building was then constructed in 1883, and is now known as the Saemann Building.

At the time of the fire in 1883, William Kirtley owned the building and had changed the name to the Lake View Hotel. The fire occurred during the term of Mayor Ed Greene, who wired Fort Wayne for assistance. A company of fire fighters, a pumper and necessary equipment was ordered to come to Warsaw, and arrangements were hurriedly made for the Pennsylvania Railroad to send a special train to rush the Fort Wayne department to Warsaw's aid.

Businesses on the first floor in the building at the time of the fire included George Pringle's saloon and the Richardson & Moran dry goods store. The Gottsman sisters had a millinery emporium in the third room. On the Buffalo Street side was a cigar and tobacco store operated by George Crebbs.

William Kirtley also managed the Kirtley House one-half block east on Center Street. In the 1890s, the Kirtley House was known as the White House. The Rigdon Building was later constructed at that site, but was demolished in the late 1920s so the current Eagles Building could be constructed in 1930.

Railroads

In 1856, the east/west railroad was built through Warsaw (Pittsburgh, Fort Wayne & Chicago Railroad). The first depot was on Union Street, and when it burned, a replacement was quickly built. A large gristmill and two hotels were built nearby. There was also a stockyard near the early depot, and Warsaw's west side was quite a lively area. Cattle, hogs and sheep were driven through town to the stockyard and held in pens until shipped out on trains.

In 1892, the current depot was built several blocks east between Lake and Washington Streets. John Gill owned and operated the Victory Hotel for many years, which was on the south side of the tracks adjacent to the Pennsylvania Railroad Depot. Railroad workers often stayed there, and trains stopped so passengers could get food from the restaurant. The Miller Hotel was just to the north of the depot facing Lake Street (now site of Wolford Cleaners).

The north/south railroad was built through Warsaw in 1870 by the Cincinnati, Wabash and Michigan Railway. A house on the southwest corner of Center and Hickory Streets was the first Warsaw passenger station. The C.W. & M. Railroad leased their tracks to the Big Four Railroad in 1891. A merger later followed and eventually became the New York Central Railroad.

In 2001, the north/south railroad line through Warsaw is owned by Norfolk Southern Railroad, and the east/west line is owned by CSX Transportation.

Fire Department

The Warsaw Fire Department began evolving as early as 1858 when the town had quite an array of frame structures and some had already been scorched or more seriously damaged by fire. By that time, the volunteer bucket brigade had been outgrown, so a meeting was called to discuss a means of organizing a regular fire department.

Since the town treasury had no excess funds available to purchase equipment, a joint stock company was formed which issued fifty shares at $5 per share. Shortly after, enough money was raised to purchase a second-hand engine.

The Independent Protection Engine Company No. 1. was organized in 1859 with 38 charter members and Joseph A. Funk as the chief engineer. A hand-pumping engine with 500 feet of hose was bought for $300. The company leased a strip of land on the corner of Center and Buffalo Streets and erected an engine house.

Warsaw suffered a serious blow on January 24, 1861, when the block on the northeast corner of Buffalo and Market Streets burned. Although that building was destroyed, surrounding structures were saved. The company's success at containing the fire brought such credit to both engine and firemen that the town trustees purchased the stock of the citizens' company. Thereafter, the name was changed and Hose Company No. 1 was organized.

Sheriff Charles Moon is sitting to the right of the driver in front of City Hall at 205 E. Center Street (c. 1919-1922). Sheriff Moon is Warsaw Police Department Sergeant Doug Brumfield's grandfather. The man standing on the fire wagon's step is former WPD Officer Eugene C. Brown's father, Everett Brown.

A bicycle was two-term Mayor John Hansman's key mode of transportation. Hansman, left, posed with a cycling friend by a fire truck in front of City Hall on E. Center Street.

In April 1861, in response to the call for troops at the beginning of the War of the Rebellion, 39 members of the Warsaw Fire Department enlisted for the national service and Company No. 1 was almost disorganized. However, recruitment in the community soon brought the department to its original strength and the high standard of the organization was maintained.

The department expanded during the following years and in 1876 when Warsaw had been a city for one year, its fire department was as follows:

A crowd gathered to see Horace Tucker's prize-winning triplet calves. They were born February 4, 1868, and were shown at the Centennial Exposition in Philadelphia that year.

Clark W. Mumaw purchased a newsstand in 1902 and operated Mumaw's Newsstand in Downtown Warsaw for about 50 years.

Protection Company No. 1, 26 members and Hose Company No. 1, 13 members, in one organization; Never Fails No. 2, 18 members, and Hose Company No. 2, 12 members, in another organization; Lake City Hook and Ladder No. 1, 15 members; Independent Hose Company No. 1, 16 members. Records show that the first full-time paid fireman was hired in 1912.

To date, the City of Warsaw has lost only one fireman in the line of duty. Fireman Harold Shepler, age 42, died October 10, 1930. Shepler was on duty at the time of a fire at a residence on E. Center Street and drove the pumper to the scene. The house was filled with smoke by the time he got there. Shepler and several other firemen went into the basement of the house to search for the fire's origin. Dense smoke soon forced the other fire fighters out. Shepler finally left the basement and as he stopped in the yard to report to Chief Moon, he collapsed and fell to the ground. Despite emergency efforts by Dr. Samuel Murphy, Shepler never regained consciousness.

In 2001, Fire Chief Matt Warren reports that the Warsaw Fire Department has a staff of 27 paid full-time fire fighters whose shifts are 24 hours on duty, followed by 48 hours off duty. The Warsaw Fire Department also has 17 volunteer fire fighters.

Hitzler, the Carpenter

Robert H. Hitzler, a German carpenter who made furniture and coffins, came to Warsaw in 1858 and entered the employ of Richard Loney as a cabinet maker. Hitzler continued in that capacity until 1863, when he went into business for himself, starting the Warsaw Hitzler Furniture Factory. His first building on the southeast corner of Center and Lake Streets burned and he replaced it with the current two-story brick structure about 1883.

Hitzler was known as both a designer and manufacturer of fine furniture, and was hired to do the fine interior of the courthouse. The building on the southwest corner of Buffalo and Market Streets, which was occupied by the State Bank of Warsaw, also had nice interior furnishings of native walnut made by Hitzler.

East Warsaw

In the 1860s, the area located in the vicinity of East Center and Bronson Streets, then known as East Warsaw, was considered a separate town because the low, swampy land isolated it from the remainder of the Town of Warsaw. The "Huckleberry Marsh" which lay between Warsaw and East Warsaw was so densely covered with trees and brush that children gathering berries often got lost. Water stood from a few inches to a foot or more in depth, and for a time celery was grown in that area.

By the 1880s houses had been built all along East Center Street, and East Warsaw was merged into the Town of Warsaw. The high ground in the area south of Center Street and east of the railroad tracks was commonly known as "The Island."

Wall Street

In the 1860s, "Wall Street" was the name given to the very narrow alley in back of The Globe clothing store. It began at Foster's Drug Store on Market Street from the south and ended at Jim White's restaurant on the north. Area businesses on Wall Street included Ed Hall and Frank Breading's saloons, and the Wall Street Exchange. The saloons all closed at 11:00 PM.

Book Stores & Newsstands

Book stores have always been at the service of the reading public in Warsaw. The Moon & Cosgrove store and Thralls & Pottenger's drug store were selling books and newspapers by the time the town was ten years old.

B.Q. Morris had a bookstore in the 1870s and 1880s that became a popular loafing place for retired men. After the Civil War, General Reub Williams and John Rousseau started a corner bookstore that carried a full line of children's school books. The store later moved to S. Buffalo Street, and by the 1930s was known as Goshert's Book Store.

Today, avid readers can still find a good selection of books in downtown Warsaw at Readers World on N. Buffalo Street. In the spring of 2001, James Bishop opened Bishop's Books, a store at 114 S. Buffalo Street that carries both new and used books.

Newsstands: Clark W. Mumaw was first engaged in the bakery business with his brother and later was employed at the Hotel Hays. In 1902 he purchased a news and confectionery stand. A 1903 city directory lists Mumaw as the proprietor of a newsstand in the White House Hotel at 113-115 E. Center Street.

Mumaw's Newsstand moved to 112 W. Center Street in 1909 and then for a number of years was located at 123 E. Center Street in the Interurban Station next to the Centennial Theatre. The Interurban Railway had a track siding just around the corner on Indiana Street where passengers boarded, so the newsstand was a convenient place for people to go while waiting for the next train.

By 1947, Mumaw's Newsstand was at 112 N. Buffalo Street. The store sold newspapers, magazines, and sheet music, along with cards, stationery, pens and inks. Mumaw's also carried a full line of domestic and imported cigars, in addition to cigarettes, candy, soft drinks, and ice cream. Larry Engle worked at the newsstand when it was owned by the Mumaws and later by the Ramseys. He recalls that Mr. Mumaw never owned a car and always walked to work.

In the 1940s, Bill and Buthene Ramsey established Ramsey News Company at 1128 E. Winona Avenue. In 1960, they acquired the newsstand from the Mumaw estate. The Ramseys' son-in-law, Marcus Kosins, and grandson, Eric Kosins, eventually were involved with the daily operations of the Ramsey Newsstand. The business was sold in 1992 to the Majerek family from Niles, Michigan, and the name was changed to Readers World.

Empire Block

The three-story Empire Block was built in 1860 on the west side of Buffalo Street between Center and Market Streets. It extended from the alley on the west side of the 100 block of S. Buffalo Street south to Market Street. The lower floor was six store

Phillipson's clothing store in the Chapman Block building on the northeast corner of Buffalo and Market Streets. The awning of Foster's Drug Store can be seen hanging over the sidewalk on E. Market Street.

rooms and the second floor was used for offices. The top floor was used by lodges, including the Odd Fellows, Masonic, and Good Templar's rooms. A large room at the north end of the third floor, known as "Empire Hall," was used for community events.

The Empire Block burned January 14, 1867. At the time of the fire, it was the largest building in town and one of the largest in northern Indiana. General Reuben Williams constructed the Indianian Building at 114 S. Buffalo Street after the fire.

Phillipson's Clothing Store

Marcus Phillipson opened Phillipson's clothing store in 1864, and his son, Benjamin, eventually joined him in the business. Although the business began on the west side of the 100 block of S. Buffalo Street, the store moved several times. Phillipson's moved to the northwest corner of Buffalo and Market Streets in 1888, but for many years was located on the northeast corner of Buffalo and Market Streets in the Chapman Building.

The Phillipson's store was widely known as a "meeting place" and had a table and some chairs in an alcove beneath a balcony that stretched out over the first floor. The downtown streets were always bustling with people on Saturday nights. Like other stores in that era, Phillipson's stayed open until 11:00 PM on Saturdays, the busiest day of the week.

President Abraham Lincoln was assassinated on April 14, 1865.

BAPTIST CHURCH, WARSAW, IND.

The First Baptist Church was built in 1866 on the northeast corner of Center and Indiana Streets. Its bell was used to alert the town when fires occurred.

Phillipson's had a unique system of handling sales transactions. Instead of having cash registers scattered around the sales floor, the only cash drawer was in the balcony. When a sale was made, the clerk would put the customer's money and a sales slip in a cup-like container and send the container to the balcony on a little track made of wires. Mrs. Rosbrugh, the store's bookkeeper for

nearly 20 years, would calculate the change, place the money in the container, and return it by way of the wire track. The Phillipson's store closed December 31, 1958.

James Whitcomb Riley, the famous Indiana poet, was known early in his life as a painter. He painted a sign for the Phillipson's store that says "A deposit of one third required down on goods before cut." Penciled on the back is "Spring 1867." After the store closed, the employees presented the sign to the Warsaw Community Public Library for safekeeping and display. The sign now hangs in the Indiana Room at the Public Library.

The Hull House clothing store, operated by Max and Francis Hull, was first opened in 1947 behind Phillipson's clothing store on E. Market Street where a clothing alteration shop had been previously located. The Hull House, which carried upscale lines of suits and professional attire for men and women, expanded into the corner building when Phillipson's closed.

After the Hull family's Warsaw Feed Store closed, Max Hull's brother, Stanley, worked in the clothing store for twenty years, until 1975. John Kleeman began working at the Hull House in 1960. John and his wife, Nancy, bought part of the business in 1974, and then purchased the remainder in 1976. The Hull House closed in 1991.

The well-known Phillipson's building was occupied by the Champs Sporting Goods store from 1992 to 1998. Following the euphoria of the Warsaw High School boys' state basketball championship in 1984, Eugenia Fulkerson started the Champs store in November of 1984. The store was first located in the Town Center Mall on E. Center Street, and in 1989 moved across the street to the Elks Arcade for another five years.

The business then moved into the Phillipson's building, which Fulkerson bought in 1991. Although a fire on April 8, 1993 required some renovation, Champs operated there until 1998. Fulkerson relates there were seven dedicated employees who remained involved with the business over its entire 14-year span.

Fulkerson notes that she is the third owner of this building which was built in 1888. Ben Phillipson inherited it from his father, Marcus. Max and Fran Hull owned it from 1948 to 1991.

Church Bell serves as Fire Bell

The First Baptist Church was built on the northeast corner of Center and Indiana Streets in 1866. Not only did the church's bell call the congregation to worship from the belfry, it also alerted citizens of fires in town.

When the building burned in 1871, the bell was found warped and cracked among the ruins. The church was rebuilt in 1874, and members donated coins, silverware, jewelry, and other items to make the additional metal needed to repair Warsaw's only bell at that time.

The property was sold to the City in 1915 and the building was demolished. The First Baptist Church constructed a new building two blocks away on the northeast corner of Center and Detroit Streets. The bell was positioned in a belfry on top of the church. During some remodeling in 1953, the bell was mounted in a stand and placed on the south side of the church.

The last service at the church on Detroit Street took place April 30, 1995. The church was demolished to make way for the CVS Pharmacy. A new Baptist Church was built on Patterson Road, where Warsaw's first bell is currently placed.

Loveday Tailors

Thomas Loveday originally came to Warsaw to work for Marcus Phillipson. Known as "Tommy the Tailor," in the 1890s he had a shop at 8 W. Market Street in the State Bank building. At that time, the Charles F. Nye Clothiers store was around the corner at 204 S. Buffalo Street, and provided Loveday with additional business.

Loveday's popular shop was where the well-dressed went to buy their tailor-made suits, and an exceptionally good suit could be purchased for about $30 to $50. His son, George D. Loveday, also became a tailor and their shop was later located just east of Phillipson's on Market Street.

Lake City Bank

Founded in 1872, Lake City Bank is the third oldest of the State Chartered banks in Indiana. It commenced business May 14, 1872 as a private bank with assets of $60,000, and was located on the town square next door to Wynant's Drug Store. Prominent businessman James McMurray was the bank's first president.

Lake City Bank was located in the Indianian Building at 114 S. Buffalo Street from the late 1920s until 1961.

In October, 1875, Lake City Bank was reorganized and incorporated as a State Bank. The bank later moved into the Indianian Building at 114 S. Buffalo Street. The second floor was occupied by the bank's attorneys, Rasor & Rasor. William B. Funk, a prominent member of the community, held several positions during his employment at Lake City Bank and was elected president in 1885. His son, Elmer B. Funk, who joined the bank in 1895, later also served as president.

The 1920s were thriving years, as industry was booming in Warsaw. There were five banks in Warsaw at that time, but only Lake City Bank was able to survive the Great Depression in the 1930s.

Judge John Sloane was president of Lake City Bank during the Depression and for a total of 23 years. Sloane's niece, Mildred Radatz of Fort Wayne, lived with him as a child and recently told Al Disbro about an incident she recalls happening in the early 1930s.

The first commercial typewriter was introduced in 1867.

Looking south in the 1950s along the 100 block of S. Buffalo Street. The sign for Mable Hile's beauty salon can be seen on the left, and Lake City Bank's stately clock can be seen on the right.

Judge John A. Sloane was president of Lake City Bank and from 1921 to 1925 served as Warsaw's mayor.

After many banks had closed following the "bank holiday" during the Depression, people lost their trust in banks and wanted their money. Lake City Bank was eventually the only local bank still operating. Sloane arranged with a large corresponding bank in Indianapolis for enough cash to give all depositors their money if they requested it.

Driving to Indianapolis and back during the night, Sloane returned to Warsaw before the bank opened the next morning. As expected, there was a large crowd gathered outside the bank's front door, and the people were talking about getting their money out of Lake City Bank and where they would put it.

When the doors opened, the lobby was immediately filled with patrons. Not stating that he had just returned from Indianapolis with a car full of cash, Sloane announced that anyone wishing to withdraw funds could readily do so. Just then a woman's voice was heard over the clamor of the crowd: "John Sloane, if I can't trust my money with you, I don't know of any man I can trust!"

The chatter quickly came to a halt. Whether they didn't know where they'd hide their money if they did withdraw it—bury it, put it under a mattress, or someplace else—the people gave their money back to the cashiers, the crowd disbanded, and Lake City Bank carried on business as usual.

That evening when Sloane got home and sat down, Mildred recalls him saying, "That lady saved our skin today." So if it were not for the well-known integrity and righteousness of one honest man and one voice that spoke up, it is quite possible that Lake City Bank would not be as we know it today.

The banking community stressed that money should be saved first if a major purchase was desired. The automobile's greatest effect upon the American economy was the introduction of the "Time Payment Plan." The automobile finance industry evolved due to bankers of the era thinking that a loan to an individual to purchase a car was unsound and had no business in a bank's portfolio. Banks saw the finance companies prospering and becoming large depositors. Attitudes began to change in the banking arena; however, it took another ten years before car loans became an acceptable part of banks' loan portfolios.

Lake City Bank hosted the first annual Egg Breakfast in 1970 to emphasize the importance of the egg industry in the local community. When Lake City Bank celebrated its 100th anniversary at the Egg Breakfast in 1972, president Bruce Wright presented a key to the bank to Robert Ellison, president of the Greater Warsaw Area Chamber of Commerce.

Now in its 129th year, with its main office on the former location of the Hotel Hays at the southeast corner of Buffalo and Indiana Streets, Lake City Bank has a total of 45 branch offices in communities throughout northeastern Indiana. The one-story main office building was erected in 1961, with the second story being added in 1972.

Lake City Bank purchased the original Kline's Department Store building at 113 E. Market Street on the north side in 1984 and developed it into their Operations Building. Then they renovated the second Kline's building on the south side at 114 E. Market Street in 1998 for their Trust and Investments Division. Lake City Bank also has a Training Center at 107-109 S. Buffalo Street.

Ara Parseghian, Notre Dame head football coach from 1964 to 1974, chats with Pete and Fay Thorn at a Lake City Bank egg breakfast (c. 1987).

Lesh Manufacturing

Gabriel B. Lesh started one of the most successful woodworking businesses in 1870 in Pierceton. Lesh moved to Warsaw in 1872, and built a bending factory in 1876. The bending department had a capacity for 4,000 plow handles per day, besides large quantities of wagon materials. Lesh also manufactured beams and bobsleds.

A band sawmill was added to the factory which had the capacity to saw 25,000 feet of hardwood lumber daily. The factory was located south of Market Street on the west side of Washington Street next to the Pennsylvania Railroad. It employed about 100 men and boys, who were paid $1.50 for a 10-hour workday.

Knights of Pythias

A meeting was held at the Milice Art Gallery in January of 1874 for anyone interested in joining the order. The only Knights of Pythias in Warsaw at that time were H.C. Milice and J. Silbers. A petition for membership was instituted and on May 22, 1874, the Forest Lodge, No. 4, Knights of Pythias, was chartered with 36 members.

The lodge occupied rooms in the Moon Block for many years, but in 1912 purchased the W.H. Gibson home on the northeast corner of Center and High Streets. They transformed it into an elegant Pythian lodge, and by 1912 the Pythians had about 200 members.

Purdue University started classes in 1874.

This chapel in Oakwood Cemetery was donated by Samuel Chipman in 1902. It was demolished in the 1970s, and a new chapel was erected on the west side of the cemetery entrance in 2000.

One of the unique gravesites in Oakwood Cemetery is the Brock monument that features the full music score of the gospel hymn "Beyond the Sunset." The song was written by Virgil and Blanche Brock, and Virgil designed the monument in memory of his wife when she died in 1958.

Oakwood Cemetery

A tamarack swamp encompassed about 55 acres immediately east of Hickory Street and south of Fort Wayne Street. On the south edge of the tamarack swamp was Warsaw's first cemetery, about two acres of property deeded to the town in 1848 by Richard L. Britton for the purpose of providing a public burying ground.

This small tract of land was where the Conrad factory was later located on Smith Street just south of the gas works at the intersection of Country Club Road. (At one time, the business on this property was known as Big Boy Products.)

This small plat of ground was becoming overcrowded, and in 1874 Warsaw purchased what is now known as Oakwood Cemetery on the east shore of Pike Lake from Dr. Jacob Boss for $2,000. Coincidentally, Dr. Boss was the first person buried in Oakwood Cemetery on August 6, 1874.

While digging a grave at Oakwood Cemetery in 1892, Billy Bowen came across the skeleton of a full-grown person. The probabilities are that the skeleton was that of an Indian, as there are plenty of indications that what is now Oakwood Cemetery was at one time used by Native Americans as a burial ground.

In 1893, improvement was needed around the grounds of the Soldiers' Monument at Oakwood Cemetery. The problem was realized by local citizens, and money was raised to remodel and beautify that area to recognize it as a special burial place of deceased veterans.

Oakwood Cemetery contains the memorial to the youngest Civil War veteran, Thomas Hubler (1851-1913). Five months before his tenth birthday, "Little Tommy" joined the 12th Indiana Regiment as its drummer boy and was present for some 26 battles. He returned to Warsaw and learned to be a printer under General Reuben Williams. Dale Hubler, a cousin three times removed, has been employed with the *Times-Union* since 1998.

One of the unique gravesites at Oakwood Cemetery is the Brock monument which features the full music score of the gospel hymn, *"Beyond the Sunset,"* written by Virgil and Blanche Brock. The monument was designed by Virgil in memory of his wife who died in 1958.

Chapter 2

1875 to 1899

Warsaw Becomes a City

On April 19, 1875, the Town of Warsaw voted to incorporate as a city. There were 278 votes for and 200 against incorporation.

A few weeks later on May 4, 1875, Warsaw's first city election was held with Hiram S. Biggs elected as the mayor. Other officials from the first election were: Charles H. Ketcham, clerk; Edward J. Greene, city attorney; S.B. Clark, treasurer; and Joseph A. Wright, marshal. There were three wards with six councilmen elected: 1st Ward - T.C. Stuart and S.W. Chipman; 2nd Ward - D.R. Pershing and A.J. Bair; 3rd Ward - J. McMurray and N. Nutt.

On May 7, 1875, the City Council met for the first time at the office of Mayor Biggs. Mayor Biggs and all the members of the Council were duly sworn into office and bonds for the treasurer, assessor, marshal and clerk were approved.

The Council determined by ballot the length of time each member should serve, and the results were: Chipman, Bair and Nutt, one-year terms; Stuart, Pershing and McMurray, two-year terms. Councilman Pershing and the City Clerk were appointed to obtain a corporate seal and the necessary books for the use of the city.

The first and third Friday evenings of each month were set as the time for regular meetings of the Council. Before 1900, offices of the mayor, clerk, and treasurer were located in the Court-house. By 1910, City Hall was established at 205 E. Center Street.

Notes of Interest

Newspaper excerpts, circa 1875: Too many hogs were running at large about town, so the City Council passed an ordinance to remedy the situation. • July 31, 1875: John Robinson's "Big Show" gave an exhibition in Warsaw that included 40 cages of

Harry Oram's Carriage and Wagon Works on the northwest corner of Center and Lake Streets in the early 1900s. Note the kerosene street lamp, upper left, which had to be lowered, filled, and lit each evening.

wild animals. •There were 524 students in the grade schools and 72 students in the high school.

Andy J. Bates was Justice of the Peace and later had a law office. He was 6' 8 1/2" tall. • A silver dollar would buy a basket of groceries. • Rent was $3 per month and the best houses rented for $100 per year. • The City had dirt streets and wooden plank sidewalks.

A Large Rally

One of the biggest ever combined Centennial and Republican rallies took place in Warsaw the first Tuesday in October of 1876. Former Governor Oliver P. Morton and Thomas A. Hendricks, Democrat candidate for Vice President, then Governor of the State, both spoke at the rally. Cavalcades of horsemen and floats of all kinds

Alexander Graham Bell invented the telephone in 1876.

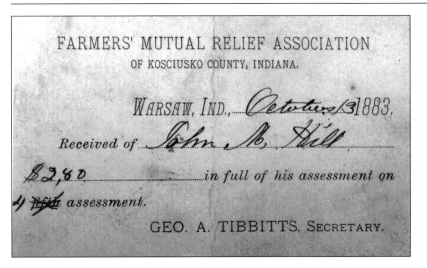

An assessment receipt issued by Farmer's Mutual Relief Association to John M. Hill in 1883.

Thomas A. Edison invented the phonograph in 1877.

paraded through town, and wagons and buggies could be seen at all the hitching posts and livery barns. The ladies of the Methodist Episcopal Church served dinner for 25 cents in a room in the Moon Building.

The two-mile grand parade began to move along Center Street promptly at noon, headed by the Centennial escort — a delegation of men dressed in the costumes of 1776. Next came the Warsaw Silver Cornet Band led by Col. Bronson, then the drum corps of boys led by Dr. Olney. Behind them marched the Warsaw Scalpers and the Harrison Guards led by Captain A.S. Millice. The parade also included a wagon carrying about thirty women wearing dresses in fashion at the time when Martha Washington lived.

The Central Block

The Central Block was built in 1877 by Samuel Chipman and Dr. Jacob Boss on the southwest corner of Market and Buffalo Streets. It was also known as the Boss Block and was originally occupied by the State Bank. The former State Bank building is currently the studio of Bob List Photography.

Ladies Benevolent Society

The Warsaw Ladies Benevolent Society was organized in October of 1878, with the wife of Warsaw's first mayor, Mrs. Alice Biggs, as president. The society consisted of members of nearly all of the churches, contributing to the community at large, for the purpose of ministering to the needy "without causing them to feel the cold charity of the world."

Farmer's Mutual Relief Association

A small group of farmers met in Claypool to discuss forming an insurance association and on December 16, 1878, the Farmers' Mutual Relief Association was organized with the following officers being elected: John Parker, president; J.W. Garvin, secretary; John Garman, treasurer; and directors W.D. Ring, David Smith, and A. Knoop.

In the beginning years, the business was operated from the secretary's home. June Thomas states that minutes are on file for every meeting since the association started. Records show that the first office was established in Warsaw in April of 1917 on the second floor of the Indiana Loan & Trust Building and the rent was $10 per month.

The association later had an office in the bay window area above the Boice Theatre, before moving to its current location at 118 W. Market Street in 1962. With the exception of a few minor revisions, farm mutual insurance companies still operate under state laws that were set in 1923.

The first policies provided fire and wind coverage, but by 1900 the wind coverage was dropped and fire policies were extended to insure against damage from smoke and lightning. People did not pay insurance premiums in those days; when someone had a loss, every policyholder would be billed a percentage to help cover that expense. In 1951 an agreement was made with the Indiana Farmers Mutual Insurance Company to provide wind coverage for the association on a joint policy arrangement. A Multiple Peril endorsement in 1957 added theft, vandalism, water damage and overturn to the coverage.

In the late 1950s the joint policy arrangement was discontinued and the Farmers Mutual Relief Association assumed coverage for wind liability and other perils under its policies. This led to a reinsurance program to insure that the association always has enough surplus to pay all claims.

An Indiana statute prohibits the association from writing liability insurance directly, so the Home & Farm Insurance Company was established in 1985 by several Indiana farm mutuals. It is through that relationship that Farmers Mutual Relief Association was able to expand its coverage to include liability and other lines.

Loyd C. Miner served as secretary from 1953 to 1981. Since then, June Thomas has been the secretary-treasurer of the association and was the founding president of Home & Farm Insurance

Company. Thomas explained that in the early days, secretaries ran the company and a president's position was like the chairman of the board is today. Maurice Dorsey, a former county commissioner, served as the association's president from 1983 to 1998, and Fred G. Powell has been the president since that time.

Gas Service

Gas street lights were lighted for the first time on August 12, 1880. The Chapman house at the southeast corner of High and Center Streets was one of the first homes to be lighted by gas. In 1897, electric street lights replaced the gas lights.

In early 1917, the Warsaw Gas Company, along with many other gas and electric companies, was bought and combined by an Eastern syndicate. The company laid new pipe lines in different parts of the city to accommodate growing needs, in addition to laying a new and entirely separate pipeline to Winona. By 1918, over 1,500 consumers in Warsaw and Winona were being served.

A Canal

In 1880, workers began to dig a canal between Pike and Center Lakes. There were "camel" bridges built at Arthur, Parker and Detroit Streets. The canal, which cost $2,200 to dig, was intended to give Center Lake steamers access to Pike Lake, but it was not successful.

In 1886 the steamer called the "Norman Beckley" arrived from Chicago. It had too much draft for the canal and was able to make only one round trip with all men helping. A smaller boat then tried but couldn't make it either, and the canal was abandoned.

The old canal bed became a stagnant mosquito breeding pond, and in 1926 some 2,000 yards of dirt was used to fill in the canal. Thereafter, the east-west street on the south side of Center Lake was appropriately named Canal Street.

Oram's Carriage & Wagon Works

Harry Oram was born in London, England, and came to America in 1863. He worked at Conrad's Wagon Factory on the southwest corner of High and Center Streets during the 1870s. In 1880, Oram started his own shop in a small building on the northwest corner of Center and Lake Streets.

With business growing, in 1884 Harry Oram erected a two-story brick building on that same

Owner Harry Oram, in the center of the doorway, with employees of his wagon shop (c. 1880).

corner. Oram's Carriage and Wagon Works turned out some of the best wagons, buggies, and general woodworking in the area. The business also had a horseshoeing department with several forges, and advertised horseshoeing stocks for vicious or wild horses.

When his son, George M. Oram, joined the business, the name changed to Oram & Son. Upon Harry's death in 1915, George and his mother continued operation of the successful business. A room to the north was later added for the blacksmithing department, and the building was also extended to the alley on the west to allow more room for woodworking.

George convinced his mother that the introduction of the motor car would change the direction of their business, and a garage was added that same year so they could start an agency for the Dodge Brothers Motor Car. By 1917, the expansive facility included a paint department, trimming and rebuilding department, all under one roof.

So in addition to general blacksmith work and horseshoeing, Oram's also did general repair work for cars and carried a full line of automobile parts and accessories.

Isadora Mann recalls that Harry Oram, her grandfather, was called "Bone Dry Harry" because he never used a piece of wood that wasn't bone dry. She states all of his wagons were painted red, and some wagons and buggies are still in use today. Oram buggies are still used by some Amish, and they can occasionally be found at area auctions.

Born in 1880, Helen Keller was blind and deaf from infancy, and yet became a world-renowned writer.

A view of Oram's Garage during the early days of the automobile. This entire half block is now the site of the new county jail.

Employees at Harry Oram's Garage (c. 1920), left to right: Rex Hartsock, unknown, Frank Hartsock, Vernon Smith.

In addition, Oram wagons can sometimes be seen in local parades.

The landmark Oram's Wagon Works building was demolished in early 2000 to construct a new county jail.

Reading Clubs

Mark Twain published "Huckleberry Finn" in 1884.

The Warsaw Reading Club was organized on October 8, 1880, with the motto "Redeeming the Time." The club held its 50-year celebration in 1930 at the Centennial Theatre, and a 100-year celebration was held at the Methodist Church in 1980.

The late Esther Pfleiderer, a long-time math teacher at Warsaw High School, was a member of the Warsaw Reading Club for almost 70 years. Connie Miller, founder of Miller's Merry Manor, was also a member for many years.

Ms. Pfleiderer used to tell about her grandmother discussing the early years of the club when members met each Monday for the entire day. In the 1800s, most members were the wives of doctors, lawyers, and teachers. However, the club is now open to anyone.

Meetings were held in members' homes, as most clubs still do today. As the original group became too large, other reading clubs were formed. The original Warsaw Reading Club currently has 19 members and four honorary members.

The Zerelda Reading Club was started in 1886. Emma Haymond served as the first president from 1886 to 1888. Mary Ettinger is currently president of the Zerelda Reading Club, which has 20 members.

The Clio Reading Club was organized in 1888. Present member Margaret Reafsnyder is the oldest member, having joined in 1935. Mildred Boley is the current president of the Clio Club which has about 25 members.

The Telephone

Telephone lines were first installed in 1882 and the first telephone office was in the Moon Building on the southeast corner of Market and Buffalo Streets. It is reported that Dr. Eggleston had the first phone. Interestingly, he also was the first to have an automobile in Warsaw.

By 1898, the Van Vactor Telephone Company had an office in the Moon Building, and in 1900 Van Vactor Telephone Company was taken over when the Commercial Telephone Company was organized in Warsaw.

In 1918, the Commercial Telephone Company purchased the building on the southwest corner of Center and Indiana Streets from the missionary society of the Methodist Church. Its central office was located upstairs, and the top of the building was covered with a row of 8-foot cross arms, four high, to which was fastened many telephone wires radiating in all directions. The main floor was rented as a store and office space.

There were about 300 subscribers in 1903 when J.W. Scott became manager of the company, and by 1918 there were 1,600 within the city and rural districts. Officers of the Commercial Telephone Company in 1918 were: Simon J. Straus, president; John D. Widaman, vice president; Joseph S. Baker, secretary; A.O. Catlin, treasurer; and J.W. Scott, manager. At that time, the telephone offices often consisted of a corner in someone's living room, where the switchboard was an integral part of the family's life.

Cleyson L. Brown started Brown Telephone Company in 1899 in Abilene, Kansas. In 1925, he formed a holding company called United Telephone and Electric, in order to purchase stock in subsidiary companies across a wide geographical area. Brown purchased 18 companies in 1931 and formed United Telephone Companies of Indiana, which was headquartered in Warsaw.

Between 1940 and 1970, United Telephone of Indiana acquired 17 additional companies. Then in 1986, U.S. Telecom, United's long-distance division, merged with GTE Sprint, GTE's long-distance division, and became known as U.S. Sprint. Soon after, the name changed to Sprint Corporation.

While Sprint has become a worldwide telecommunications giant and earned the top honor in the telecommunications category of *Fortune* magazine's 1999 list of "America's Most Admired Companies," it has continued to be a substantial corporate citizen to the Warsaw area community.

Additional Sprint divisions in Warsaw are Sprint North Supply on Crystal Lake Road, which is a warehouse for Sprint's telephone supplies, and Sprint Publishing & Advertising, the yellow pages section. Sprint currently has over 200 employees and 145 retirees living in Kosciusko County.

Myers Brothers Lumber & Coal

Myers Brothers Lumber & Coal, on the north side of Market Street between Washington and Columbia Streets, was founded by Fredrick Myers in 1882. Fred's sons, George W. and Silas Myers, succeeded him in 1890.

Jerry Gerard's grandfather, David A. Peterson, and Silas Myers later became co-partners and the business was known as the Myers & Peterson Lumber Company. In the 1940s, the business was known as Talbert-Schaab Lumber Company, owned by H.E. Talbert and C.E. Schaab.

After the lumber business closed and before the structure was torn down, part of the building was used as office space. The Republican Headquarters was located there for a time.

Water and Electricity

In 1884, the Warsaw Water Company facility was built at the foot of Buffalo Street on Center Lake. In 1886, the Winona Electric, Light & Water Company was organized and subsequently erected an electric light plant near the water works. It furnished illumination only to the business district,

The Myers & Peterson Lumber Company (c. 1900) was on the northwest corner of Market and Washington Streets, now site of the Owen's Supermarket.

Lakeside Park on the southwest side of Pike Lake before 1900. Note the intricate sculpture designs of the plants in the foreground.

cutting off the electricity at 10:00 each night. The two companies were eventually combined and many improvements were made.

Prior to the building of the water works plant, the city's fire protection consisted of large cisterns constructed beneath the surface of the streets and located at a few of the principal street intersections. These cisterns were filled with water from the town pumps located within convenient distances from the cisterns.

Summer Resort Association

The Warsaw Summer Resort Association was founded in 1885 for the purpose of improving and developing the natural advantages of Warsaw as a summer resort. Former mayor Hiram S. Biggs was president of the association.

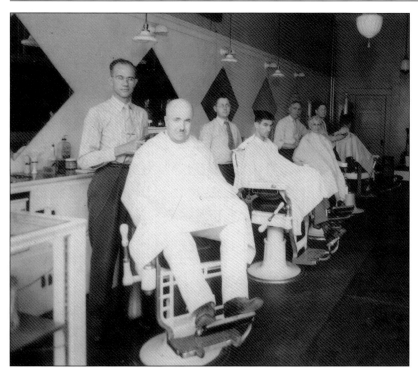

In the early 1940s, Russell Knoop had as many as six barbers working in his shop. In this photo are, left to right: Knoop, Gerald "Jerry" Rosbrugh, Ora Stamper, unknown.

Barbers at Knoop's Barbershop in the basement below Breading's Cigar Store in 1973, left to right: Terry Runkle, Russ Knoop, John Kinsey, Jim Barnhart.

Then known as Lakeside Park (the entire area between Park Avenue and what is now Lucerne Park), it was described as "a cool and delightful place for recreation." The park is said to have had several flowing wells, a greenhouse, and an amphitheatre/pavilion with seating for 3,000 people. In addition, the park had a roller coaster, boathouse, a restaurant that sold sandwiches for a nickel, and a zoo with bears, deer, wolves, geese and other animals.

By 1895, Lakeside Park had been divided into lots and houses were eventually built on much of the property. The park area was further diminished by the construction of a building that was first used as a canning factory and then as a furniture factory. The building no longer stands.

Pike Lake also had a park named Mineral Beach which was located across the lake from Lakeside Park. It also featured several flowing wells. Mineral Beach is now the site of the Springhill Acres Subdivision.

Clothing Stores

In the 1890s, there were three main men's clothing stores in town. The Globe, Phillipson's, and Charlie Nye's American Clothing Store were all located on S. Buffalo Street. Suit prices started at $2.45. Those tailor-made at Phillipson's cost $11.75 and up.

Frog Town

Dennis May made barrels and kegs in a red frame building just east of S. Columbia Street that overlooked the marshes of what people of the village called "Frog Town." On the east side of S. Washington Street, water would stand several months of the year, and a small lake would sometimes extend to Buffalo Street. Ice skaters used this area in the winter, and in the summer most of the marsh was a cow pasture.

History of a House

Orval Johnston, who lives at 625 W. Center Street, states that he was told his house was built in 1890 by Marcus Phillipson, founder of Phillipson's department store, for his tailors to live in. Some of the wood used to build the house was from the first railroad depot.

Gorton Machinery

A letterhead and envelope dated March 21, 1891, states: W.E. Gorton, milling engineer and manufacturer of Gorton's Machinery for flour, oat and corn meal mills, Warsaw, Indiana. David Gorton, a distant relative who tracked his family's history, notes that William Eddy Gorton had patents for grain milling machines, and by 1907 was president of the Pawnee & Ingalls Mills Companies in the Oklahoma Territory.

Barbershops

Years ago, barbershops were very plentiful in downtown Warsaw. For 32 years, from 1892 to 1924, George A. Essig operated a barbershop at the corner of Buffalo and Market Streets in the basement under the Phillipson clothing store.

W.H. "Effie" Wainwright was a partner with Essig in 1903, and by 1910 Edwin Curry was a partner.

Essig moved his shop in 1924 to 102 S. Buffalo Street in the basement of the Indiana Loan & Trust Building. At that time, barbers Roy G. Sprigg and Ross L. Baker were in the Elks Arcade on E. Center Street.

A newspaper excerpt reports that on November 21, 1925, Martin Durkin, a Chicago bandit who had shot seven policemen and for whom there was a nation-wide manhunt, was seen in Warsaw with his female consort. They stepped into the Arcade Barbershop where Durkin stood at the mirror and shaved himself, while watching for rear attacks. He politely paid proprietor Sprigg for use of the razor and materials before fleeing.

Well-known barber Russell V. Knoop was born in 1905. One day after Russ quit attending Manchester College in 1927 due to a lack of money, he read a newspaper advertisement that caught his interest. Because of that, Russ moved to Cincinnati, Ohio, to live with his sister and attend a barber school. After graduation, he returned to Kosciusko County and worked in an Akron barbershop for two years.

In 1937, Russell Knoop opened the Black & White, his first barbershop, where three barbers worked with him. When the Black & White was destroyed by fire in 1939, Knoop bought the Arcade barbershop from Roy Sprigg. During that time, Russ had as many as six barbers working with him, including Pierre Underhill and George Sauder.

There were large windows in the barbershop facing Center Street so people could see inside. Being located on the ground floor of the Elks Lodge, the Arcade Barbershop got a lot of business from Elks members.

In 1952, Russell Knoop moved his shop to the basement of Breading's Cigar Store. From the 1960s to the mid 1970s, Knoop's barbershop was located on W. Center Street just east of the Warsaw Dry Cleaners. Barbers who worked with Knoop over the years include: John Kinsey, Bill Bartlemay, Rex Woodruff, Bob Swanson, Lowell "Rusty" Valentine, and part-time barber Larry Hoffer. Bill Bartlemay, who now resides in Florida, recalls that haircuts cost $1 in the 1960s.

When Knoop retired in the early 1970s, John Kinsey bought the business. He later sold the shop to Merlin Fish and the name was changed to Merlin's Barbershop. For a number of years, the barbershop

The Huffer Bros. Feed and Livery was located on the northwest corner of Center and Indiana Streets before the Widaman-McDonald building was constructed in 1916 for the Centennial Theatre. The man in the center holding the harness is Noble Wolford.

was located in the back of the Centennial Theatre building, and the name changed to the Razor Stop in the 1980s. John Kinsey currently operates the Downtown Barbershop at 110 N. Buffalo Street.

Forrest Bouse worked with Art Gibson before opening his own barberhop at 110 N. Indiana Street about 1948. Dee Wagner, who had worked with Bouse for a number of years, bought one-half interest in the business in 1968. When Bouse retired in 1972, Wagner started a barbershop in his home, but closed it several years later.

Dewey Lawshe had a barber shop in the Opera House on E. Market Street when the building was destroyed by fire in 1967. Lawshe then worked at other barbershops in town for a while before entering the trucking business for a number of years. Since 1980, Lawshe has operated a barbershop in his home at 1210 E. Center Street.

Huffer Bros. Livery

The Huffer Brothers Livery Barn, established in 1893, was well-known throughout Northern Indiana. It was operated by Jacob D. and Horton C. Huffer until 1911. The livery barn was located on the northwest corner of Center and Indiana Streets, now site of the Town Center Mall. Jacob was the Kosciusko County sheriff from 1912 to 1917, and "Hort" was a deputy sheriff for his brother.

P.T. Barnum merged with James A. Bailey in 1881 to form Barnum & Bailey Circus.

Revra DePuy (1860-1921) founded DePuy Manufacturing in 1895.

The first roller coaster was opened in 1884 at Coney Island in New York.

DePuy Manufacturing

Revra DePuy pioneered the orthopedic industry when he started DePuy Manufacturing in 1895 to make wire mesh and wooden splints, becoming the world's first commercial manufacturer of orthopedic appliances. During his early career, DePuy was also a chemist, having invented the formula for sugar-coated pills.

For some time, Mr. DePuy resided and conducted business at the Hotel Hays. By 1898, the DePuy splint factory had moved its headquarters to the rear of a building at 213 S. Buffalo Street, over the State Bank. The business was moved to Michigan for a few years at the turn of the century. DePuy then returned to Warsaw in 1904, beginning production in a building near Center and Columbia Streets, at the location formerly known as the M.M. Syphers Ice Cream Factory.

Revra DePuy hired Justin O. Zimmer in 1905 as a splint salesman. Earl Longfellow joined DePuy in 1906 as an errand boy. Over the course of 52 years, by the time Longfellow retired in 1958 he had moved up to vice president and general manager. Zimmer, however, broke away from DePuy in 1927 to start his own orthopedic company, Zimmer Manufacturing.

By 1925, Mr. DePuy had constructed a new two-story brick building at 407 W. Market Street (now occupied by Hardesty Printing), where the company remained for the next 50 years. Continued growth led to construction in 1955 across the street on the northwest corner of Market and Columbia Streets of a general office building (now occupied by Dahms & Yarian). DePuy moved to its current location on U.S. 30 East in 1975.

A long-time friend of the DePuys recalled that they ate out most of the time because Mrs. DePuy did not like the smell of food cooking in her house. She was particular about everything, doing housework with gloves and a hat, and she wore diamonds every day.

Mr. DePuy had also been a director of the Warsaw Investment Company and the Braude-Pierce Furniture Company. Revra DePuy died in 1921. As sole owner, DePuy's wife assumed management of the company. In 1924 she married Herschel Leiter, a salesman for DePuy. Leiter then held the position of executive president until his death in 1950.

Six investors bought DePuy in 1965, and in 1968 the company was sold to Indianapolis-based Bio-Dynamics, a blood diagnostic business. Also in the late 1960s DePuy acquired exclusive U.S. marketing rights to the Müller Total Hip, which changed the company's image from that of a soft goods company to a contender in the implant market. The company was purchased in 1974 by Boehringer Mannheim, a German pharmaceutical company, and was then acquired by Johnson & Johnson in 1998.

J. Keaton Landis played a key part in the progress of DePuy. Landis joined the firm in 1955 as sales manager, and as president from 1965 to 1971 directed the company's continued growth and development. He also held executive positions following the company's acquisitions, and retired in 1981. Long-time employee Pat Sisk started at DePuy in 1957 as a secretary, was promoted to sales manager, and currently serves as the administrative supervisor.

M.M. Syphers

Maynard M. Syphers came to Warsaw in 1896 and established the first business in Kosciusko County to manufacture pure ice cream and high-grade soft drinks. M.M. Syphers was also a dealer in fine flavoring extracts and New York and Baltimore oysters in season.

Agnes Jane Plummer, age 87, states that her grandfather's first establishment was in a small frame building on W. Center Street. The M.M. Syphers business then moved to 112 S. Washington Street. When Syphers retired, the ice cream portion of the business was sold to Ed Collins, an employee, who moved the business to a building on N. Cedar Street.

Sometime in the mid 1920s, the soda pop portion of the business was sold to five brothers from Adams County—Harvey, John, Philip, Irvin, and Lester Davis—and the bottling company remained at 112 S. Washington Street. A glass pop bottle with the name "M.M. Syphers" is on display at the Pound Museum in Oswego.

Syphers constructed the one-story brick building at 110 S. Washington as an investment. It was used many years as a storage business. Harold Derry operated a body shop there and a glass business was located in the building at one time. Since 1982, however, it has been occupied by Tarkio Road, owned by Rob and Nancy Gast. Tarkio Road sells bicycles and skateboards, and rents cross-country skiing equipment in the winter.

M.M. Syphers in his truck in 1911, ready to deliver the pure ice cream and high grade soft drinks that he manufactured.

Drug Stores

J.B. Watson had been clerking in a pharmacy since 1886 until he purchased the A. Woolley and Son's store on E. Market Street in 1897 and changed the name to J.B. Watson's Drugs. Watson carried a wide variety of items, including novelties, art goods, photographers' and physicians' supplies, and the store became the largest in the county. This business was later owned by Glenn Dewitt Dufur and known as Dufur Rexall Drugs.

Following his experience in the 1930s as general manager for J.B. Watson's Drug Store and Dufur Drugs on the corner of Market and Buffalo Streets, Frank Brennan purchased the business when Watson Drugs lost its lease at 110 E. Market Street. Brennan Drugs opened for business the day after Thanksgiving in 1948 with four full-time employees.

Frank's son, Robert, joined the firm in 1951. Frank purchased the adjacent building at 112 E. Market Street in 1964 and expanded the business. Upon Frank's death in 1979, Robert Brennan

became president, and in 1983 Brennan Drugs opened a second pharmacy in Owen's Supermarket on E. Center Street. Bob's son, Jim, was involved with the business from 1990 until it was sold to Horizon Pharmacy in 1999.

Downtown Amenities

In the 1880s, curbside water pumps, where people could stop for a drink, were located on the northwest corner of Market and Buffalo Streets and another on the southeast side of the Courthouse Square. The watering trough for horses on the Courthouse Square was used from 1886 until about 1937. Dating from about 1857 until the 1930s, hitching posts for horses were located on all four sides of the Courthouse.

Ringle Furniture

After being in the retail grocery business for eight years in Emporia, Kansas, Amos Ringle returned to Warsaw in 1889. He worked in the furniture factory of R.H. Hitzler prior to engaging in his

The Statue of Liberty was dedicated in New York Harbor in 1886.

Employee Charles Mauzy talks with a driver for Ringle's Furniture Store before a delivery is made to a customer.

Amos Ringle, founder of Ringle Furniture Store, in 1940 at age 86.

Brigadier Brice Phillipson (1881-1974) was an active officer with The Salvation Army for 47 years.

own very successful furniture business in 1898. The three-story Ringle Furniture Store was located at 207 S. Buffalo Street.

In the early days, Ringle could be seen throughout the county in the early morning hours making deliveries of furniture with his horse and wagon, and then returning to Warsaw in time to open his store.

Amos' son, Benjamin F. Ringle, took over the business after World War I and ran it until about 1955, when Leslie C. Noggle and Lester Johnston bought the business. The store's name remained the same. Noggle sold his interest in the business to Johnston in 1965, and Johnston then closed the store about 1968.

The Salvation Army

The Salvation Army was established in Warsaw and Kosciusko County in 1898 by two women from Chicago. The first meetings were held in a building not far from the Nye grocery. In the summertime the Salvation Army would stage parades and have outdoor meetings at Shane's Corner on the southeast corner of Buffalo and Center Streets. The organization held regular services until about 1901 when it ceased operation.

Twenty years later in 1921, Captain and Mrs. Fred Harvey headed the Salvation Army's return to Kosciusko County. J.C. Schade served as chairman of the county-wide Advisory Board, which met in the mayor's office in 1922 to establish a goal of $3,015 to support the local Army's work. Mr. & Mrs. Elmer Funk were strong supporters of the Army from its beginning, and Mr. Funk was named a Life Member of the Advisory Board.

After surviving the Depression and World War II, the Salvation Army purchased a building in 1939 for $4,500 on the southeast corner of Detroit and Main Streets, to provide a center to serve those in need. After an extensive capital campaign in 1957 headed by Brigadier Brice Phillipson raised $40,000, the present facility was built at 501 E. Arthur Street.

The Salvation Army and Rotary have had a lasting relationship since 1921. Brigadier Phillipson was a long-time member of the Warsaw Rotary Club, and J.C. Schade and W.R. Thomas were also Rotarians. The Rotary Club established "Rotary Toy Day" in 1927 to collect gifts for children in need, an event that continues today.

In the mid-1960s, N. Bruce Howe, Jr. established "Brice's Day," in honor of Brigadier Phillipson, to raise funds for the annual "Tree of Lights" campaign. In 1990, Rotary Club president Don Clemens asked that the event be renamed "Phillipson/Howe Day" in honor of Bruce's many years of service.

In 1999 the Rotary Club raised a record $30,000 for the Army's outreach to those less fortunate, and Mr. Howe was awarded the "William Booth Award," the highest recognition a volunteer can receive, for his efforts in supporting the Army.

The Salvation Army became a charter member of the United Way of Kosciusko County in 1958. Mazie Alexander, Marge Gast, and a number of other women formed a Women's Auxiliary in 1968 to support the Army's mission, with the annual holiday "nut sale" being one of their main fundraising projects.

Phillipson's daughter and son-in-law, Colonels Anita and Loyd Robb of Winona Lake, served over 42 years as active Salvation Army officers, retiring in 1977. The Robbs celebrated their 65th wedding anniversary in March 2001.

On June 29, 2001, Anita received the "Order of the Founder," the highest award presented by The Salvation Army. She is just the eleventh person in the central states to receive this award since 1917, and only 210 individuals worldwide have been bestowed with such an honor.

Cols. Loyd and Anita Robb actively served as Salvation Army officers for 42 years.

This building on the southeast corner of Detroit and Main Streets was purchased in 1939 by The Salvation Army. Standing near the door are Lt. Edward Deretany, Corps Officer, and Lt. Warren Johnson, Corps Assistant.

The 1972 Salvation Army advisory board members included, left to right: Marge Gast, Robert Gephart, Martha Taft, Freeland "Flip" Phillips, Christine Kelly, Charles R. "Chick" Lamoree, E. Mazie Alexander, Captain Homer Fuqua, Georgia Kaufman, Milo Lightfoot, Charlotte Mikesell, Lester Davis, Esther Pfleiderer, Alex Shealey, Don Brown, and John Hall.

Allan Saine constructed a two-story brick building in the 100 block of S. Buffalo Street in 1877 on the north side of the alley.

Two cannons from Fort Royal in South Carolina were placed on the southeast corner of the Courthouse Square in 1897 as a memorial to the soldiers of the War Between the States. Left to right: Jap Frush, A.G. Wood, Jim Cisney, Gib Furlong, S.D. Hathaway, Irv Sharp, N.N. Boydston. The cannons and cannon balls were removed November 16, 1942, to be melted down for ammunition during World War II.

Smith Grain & Milling Co.

As early as 1899, the Smith Grain & Milling Company was located in a four-story brick building by the railroad tracks on the corner of Union and Jefferson Streets. The business was owned and operated by brothers Daniel E. Smith and Floyd Smith. Daniel's son, Howard, also worked at the gristmill which ground wheat and flour.

The mill supplied people in Kosciusko and surrounding counties with their popular flours. Howard "Chub" Smith, Jr. recalls that his father and grandfather sold "Sunshine" biscuit flour and another flour named "None-Such," because there was none such like it anywhere else. The Smiths' flour was said to be milled from the best wheat grown and its bread-producing qualities were of the highest.

The Depression forced Smith Grain & Milling Company to close in the early 1930s. However, the Smith family is still in the grain business, as Daniel Smith's son, Floyd, later took over operations of the Leesburg Elevator. Floyd's son, Doug, continues to manage the elevator.

Chapter 3

The Mayors

Hiram S. Biggs

Biggs' parents were among the earliest settlers of Kosciusko County, having located in Prairie Township in 1836. His father died in 1847, and at an early age Biggs was obliged to assist in maintaining his widowed mother and younger brother. He attended school during the winters for three or four months and worked on the farm in the summer, until about age 20 when he entered the college at Valparaiso.

For the next five years, he attended that college and the Northern Indiana College at South Bend. His studies were interrupted to teach school three months each winter in order to pay the necessary expenses for the rest of the year.

Biggs entered the law office of Frazer & Frasier in 1863. He was admitted to the bar in 1865 and entered into partnership with his preceptor, George W. Frasier, which ended due to the death of Frasier in 1872. He was admitted at the bar of the Supreme Court of Indiana in 1869 and at the bar of the U.S. Circuit and District Courts in 1875.

Biggs was elected to represent Kosciusko County in the Legislature in 1870-1872. He was elected as Warsaw's first Mayor on May 4, 1875 and re-elected in 1877. He served as the City Attorney from 1889 to 1895, and was a judge with the Kosciusko County 54th Circuit Court from 1896 to 1904.

Biggs was one of 14 people who formed the Warsaw Summer Resort Association in 1885. He erected the two-story brick building at 121 West Center Street in 1883, which is adorned with a concrete-embossed marquee that bears his name. He became a member of Kosciusko Lodge No. 62, IOOF in 1863 and filled all the elective offices and represented it in the Grand Lodge of the State, of which he was also a member. *(Born January 15, 1838 in Kosciusko County / Died July 20, 1911)*

William Cosgrove

Cosgrove went to Dayton, Ohio, at age 16 to begin work with a carpenter to learn that trade. He moved to South Bend in 1837 and continued working at his trade, contracting for the erection of houses and other buildings. When the Kosciusko County Commissioners advertised for bids for the construction of the Courthouse in 1843, Cosgrove and his brother, Bradford, were successful in securing the contract. They immediately commenced work on it, with completion in 1845. Being an architect and builder, he owned the "Cosgrove Block" on the south side of the courthouse.

In 1844, he was a candidate for Sheriff of St. Joseph County on the Whig ticket, and was defeated by one vote. Moving then to Warsaw, from 1844 to 1851 Cosgrove was in a business partnership with George Moon. At various times, he engaged in businesses of different kinds, selling books, dealing in grain and pork, and for a number of years he owned the brick flouring mill near the depot of the Peru, Fort Wayne & Cincinnati Railroad. Cosgrove was one of five directors when the Warsaw Gas, Light & Coke Company was organized.

He was treasurer on the Board of Trustees for the school system. Cosgrove held a number of town and township positions at different times, including Trustee of Wayne Township, before being elected Mayor in 1879.

Cosgrove was a member of the Warsaw Masonic Lodge No. 73, AF & AM; Warsaw Chapter No. 48, RAM; Warsaw Commandery No. 10; Knights Templar; and was a long-time member of the Kosciusko Lodge No. 62, Independent Order of Odd Fellows. He held the highest positions in each of the organizations of which he was a member, and served many years during the 1860s as treasurer of Lodge 73 . *(Born November 25, 1812 in New Jersey / Died November 2, 1883)*

Hiram S. Biggs
Mayor, 1875-1878

William Cosgrove
Mayor, 1879-1880

Edward J. Greene
Mayor, 1881-1884

Lemuel W. Royse
Mayor, 1885-1890, 1920-Resigned

John H. Brubaker
Mayor, 1891-1895

George R. Moon
Mayor, 1896-1897

James H. Cisney
Mayor, 1898-1900

Edward J. Greene

Greene was the first city attorney, serving in that position from 1875 to 1880. He was then elected mayor from 1881 to 1884.

Lemuel W. Royse

Royse began teaching school at age 18. He taught for eight winters and worked on a farm during the summer. While teaching, he also studied law and was admitted to the Bar in 1873, entering the office of Frazer & Encell. He was later a senior member of the law firm of Royse & Shane. He was elected Prosecuting Attorney in 1875-1876 for the 33rd Judicial Circuit of the State of Indiana, composed of Kosciusko and Whitley Counties.

In 1884, Royse served as an elector in the Blaine-Cleveland Presidential Campaign. Royse interrupted his legal career by serving three successive two-year terms as Mayor of Warsaw (1885, 1887, 1889). He served a fourth time in that capacity and was named by the City Council to fill the vacancy due to the death of Mayor Rigdon in 1919; however, Royse resigned in 1920.

Royse served two terms in the U.S. House of Representatives, 1895-1899. He was elected to represent the 13th Congressional District in the lower house of the national legislature. Royse was a member of the Republican State Central Committee from 1886 to 1890, and served as a delegate in 1888 to the National Convention at Minneapolis, which nominated Benjamin Harrison the second time for the Presidency.

Under an appointment from the Governor, he served as Judge of the Kosciusko Circuit Court from 1904 to 1908, and sat on the bench for a total of sixteen years. Royse had a continuous association with the Kosciusko County Bar for 45 years, and was still working as a lawyer at the age of 92. In 1919, L.W. Royse wrote a two-volume set of historical books about Kosciusko County. *(Born January 19, 1847 near Pierceton; Died December 18, 1946)*

John H. Brubaker

Brubaker began his law practice in 1881 with Andrew Wood at Wood & Brubaker. In the early 1900s, the J.H. Brubaker & Son partners were lawyers, loan agents, and abstractors. Brubaker was treasurer for the town when George Moon was mayor. Brubaker was active in civic life and generous of his time and means in promoting any cause for the improvement of the community. He also served as secretary of the Warsaw School Board of Education. *(Born May 20, 1853 in Wakarusa, Indiana / Died October 16, 1934)*

George R. Moon

Moon came to Pennsylvania from Ireland in 1836 and arrived in Warsaw in 1837. He first engaged in the service of Metcalfe Beck, Esq., with whom he remained until 1840, when he entered into partnership with George R. Thralls in the grocery trade. That relationship was dissolved in 1843 and Moon then formed a co-partnership with William Cosgrove, with whom he was associated until 1850. The Moon & Cosgrove's store was regarded by the people in the county as the emporium for everything in the line of general merchandise.

He took the census in 1850, at which time the population was 250. He owned the Moon Block on the southeast corner of Market and Buffalo Streets (now site of a one-story building occupied by the Kosciusko County Foundation). When a charter was granted for the Kosciusko Lodge No. 62 IOOF (Odd Fellows) in 1849, Moon was its first Noble Grand. He was the first secretary of the Kosciusko County Agricultural Society when it was organized in 1855.

In 1852, Moon was elected County Treasurer and re-elected to a second term in 1854. In 1856, he was elected as a Representative of the State Legislature and was chairman of the Committee of Ways and Means. Being an old line Whig, Moon naturally gave his loyalty to the then-rising Republican party. He was chairman of the first Republican Convention. In 1860, he was sent as a delegate to the Republican National Convention in Chicago that nominated Abraham Lincoln as President.

In 1884-1886 Moon was elected to the State Senate, and served two terms representing the counties of Wabash and Kosciusko. Retiring from the Legislature at the close of his term, Moon became the agent at Warsaw of the Pittsburgh, Fort Wayne & Chicago Railway. He later was appointed Internal Revenue Collector in 1869 by the 10th Collection District of Indiana. In the 1880s, he was an agent for the German-American Insurance Company located in the Moon Building. Being held in such local high esteem, Moon was elected Mayor in 1896. *(Born July 11, 1816 in Ireland / Died April 15, 1902)*

James H. Cisney

Cisney left school at an early age and entered an apprenticeship with a harness maker, with whom he learned the trade. He came to Warsaw in 1860 and was employed in his trade until 1861 when he enlisted in Company B, 30th Regiment, Indiana Volunteers, where he was held in the highest esteem by his comrades and superiors. Mustering out of service in 1864, upon his return he engaged in the harness business in Leesburg.

Cisney was elected Sheriff of Kosciusko County in 1867 and re-elected in 1870, retiring in 1872. It was during his term when they moved into the new jail on Christmas Eve of 1870. Cisney was elected to the City Council in 1877 and was the originator of a project which was ultimately successful for funding the debt of the city at a reduced rate of interest, which resulted in a net savings to the taxpayers of more than $1,200 per annum. Cisney also served as chairman of the Republican Party.

In the 1890s, he was one of the prominent people involved in the ice business on Center Lake, and he also had an auction store on South Buffalo Street (Phillipson's store location). *(Born August 19, 1841 in Richland County, Ohio / Died February 10, 1901 while in office as Mayor)*

Benjamin F. Richardson

As a young man, Richardson clerked in a feed store and drove a dray in Toledo, Ohio. When he located to Warsaw in 1883, he embarked in the retail dry goods and shoe trade. Richardson's Dry Goods store on S. Buffalo Street became one of the leading establishments in Warsaw. It was during his tenure as a member of the City Council (1891-1900), with his public spirit and vision of a better and greater Warsaw, that the city acquired substantial improvements such as paving streets and establishing a sewer system.

Richardson was appointed Mayor in 1901 to fill out the unexpired term of Mayor Cisney, at the close of which he was then elected to a full term. It was during his administration that the Winona Electric Light and Water Company was granted its franchise in 1903 to provide utility service to the community. The citizens of Warsaw sought his leadership again and elected him as Mayor in 1910. *(Born August 9, 1851 in Monroe County, Michigan / Died September 28, 1924)*

Andrew G. Wood

Wood first headed the legal firm of Wood & Bowser. Responding to the first call for volunteers in 1863, Wood enlisted as a Union soldier in the Civil War, earning a captain's commission. He returned to Warsaw in 1865 to practice law as head of Wood & Brubaker Bros. From 1866 to 1867 Wood was editor of the *Warsaw Union* newspaper.

Wood was a charter member of the Odd Fellows Lake City Lodge in Warsaw. During his 54 years of membership, he passed all the chairs and served as financial secretary for seven years and then trustee for seven years.

In the Masonry, Wood also reached an eminent position in this organization as a Scottish Rite Mason. Wood was a charter member of the Henry Chapin Post G.A.R. in 1868 and served as Post Commander. He also joined the Encampment at South Bend and was the first Chief Patriarch of Hackelman Encampment at Warsaw.

He was an active and popular member of the Democratic party, serving as delegate to county, state, district and congressional conventions. For 30 years Wood was chairman of the Democratic County Committee and also a member of the state committee. Wood served two terms as a member of the City Council and one term as mayor, and was the first Democrat that had that honor.

He took a leading part for many years in the development of the agricultural resources of the county and was a member of the first Library Board. For more than 40 years, he acted as a Trustee of the Winona Agricultural Society. Wood practiced law for half a century in Warsaw, and served as Dean of the Kosciusko County Bar. He was in partnership with Francis E. Bowser (Wood & Bowser), a circuit judge, for about 23 years. Wood served as the county attorney, and resigned in 1910. *(Born January 16, 1835 in Marysville, Ohio / Died May 4, 1924)*

Charles A. Rigdon

Rigdon began his dentistry schooling at age 16. In 1878 he opened a dental depot for the sale of dental supplies and surgical instruments, employing two traveling selemen. He began publication of *The Dental Student* in 1884, a journal devoted to dental literature. Rigdon was a member of Warsaw's first fire company and the Warsaw saxophone band. He was also a professional photographer,

Benjamin F. Richardson
Mayor, 1901-1903, 1910-1917

Andrew G. Wood
Mayor, 1904-1906

Charles A. Rigdon
Mayor, 1907-1909, 1918-1919

John A. Sloane
Mayor, 1921-1925

*John G. Hansman
Mayor, 1926-1929, 1938-1942*

*Lewis J. Bibler
Mayor, 1930-1932*

*Dr. C. Clifford DuBois
Mayor, 1933-1937*

an optometrist, restaurant owner, and owner of the Rigdon Jewelry Store.

Notes also show that he bought a chair factory and turned it into a bowling alley, and he was a leading bicycle dealer. Rigdon acquired much real estate in the downtown area, as well as land by Center Lake. His property on the south side of Center Lake, then known as "Rigdon Row," was purchased by the City in 1919 and renovated into what is now Center Lake park, beach, and the pavilion. The Rigdon Building was in the 100 block of Center Street that also housed the Interurban Street Car Depot.

In 1884, he was the first president of the Central Union Telephone Company of Kosciusko and Marshall Counties, and during the same year was elected secretary of the Warsaw Building, Loan & Savings Association. Rigdon was also one of the lessees and managers of the Warsaw Opera House. He was a Grand Master of IOOF Kosciusko Lodge #62 and High Priest of Hackelman Encampment #37, and was involved in founding the Eagles Lodge in 1907. *(Born September 16, 1857 in Warsaw / Died September 11, 1919 while in office as Mayor)*

John A. Sloane

Sloane worked in the John D. Widaman law firm for five years, then for a major part of his law career was a partner of Sloane & Eschbach, and later a partner of Sloane & (Everett) Rasor. He was attorney for the Strauss Bros. Co. in Ligonier for three years and Prosecuting Attorney for the county, 1905-1906. Sloane was the city attorney in 1919 when the City purchased "Rigdon Row," and continued practicing law until 1936 when he was elected judge of the Kosciusko Circuit Court, serving two six-year terms.

Sloane was also a teacher and express agent, and was one of the founders of the Presbyterian Church on the southwest corner of Market and High Streets, where he was honored with the title of elder emeritus. He was a charter member of the Warsaw Kiwanis Club and served as lieutenant governor of the Indiana Kiwanis organization. The eminent jurist was a member of the Kosciusko County and American Bar Associations.

Sloane became a stockholder and director of Lake City Bank in 1915, and then beginning about 1930 served 23 years as president of Lake City Bank. He was appointed to fill out an unexpired term left by Mayor Rigdon and was then elected for a full term. *(Born October 25, 1872 in Missouri / Died April 12, 1953)*

John G. Hansman

Hansman worked at Harry Oram's wagon factory at the turn of the century, and later was employed as an inspector at the Warsaw Foundry. For a time, he was the ticket taker at the Centennial Theater, and his wife sold popcorn at the newsstand next door. Hansman always rode a bicycle to work. He was a member of the City Council prior to being elected mayor in 1926, and was elected to a second term in 1938.

One Halloween Hansman's wife, Annie, called to tell him she was serving sauerkraut and weiners for lunch. That being one of his favorite dishes, he hurried to his bike, only to discover that it was not in its usual parking place. Assuming it had been stolen, he called every city, county, and state police officer and demanded that they immediately start looking for the bicycle. In just a few minutes Hansman's bicycle was spotted at the top of a nearby flagpole swaying gently in the breeze hanging just below the flag. The bicycle is now stored at the Kosciusko County Jail Museum. *(Born January 15, 1884 in Peru, Indiana / Died August 9, 1950)*

Lewis J. Bibler

From 1898 to 1900, Bibler was associated with J.M. Stinson in the undertaking business and then worked briefly at the Shane grocery. He joined R.C. Smith's undertaking business in 1902 and three years later founded Bibler Funeral Home at 124 W. Main Street.

Bibler was also an agent for the S.A. Karn Music company. An undated advertisement states his store was opposite the Opera House on Market Street, where he sold pianos, organs, and sewing machines.

By 1925, the Bibler Funeral Home was located in the two-story brick house on the northwest corner of Lake and Fort Wayne Streets. After Bibler's death, his wife, Vera, and son, Lewis, continued the funeral business until the late 1960s. *(Born August 5, 1867 / Died November 30, 1932 while in office as mayor)*

Dr. C. Clifford DuBois

Orphaned at the age of eight, DuBois became a highly respected physician, mayor, and civic leader. He was a physician in the Warsaw community for over fifty years, beginning in 1907. He attended the University of Missouri at Columbia, where he majored in biology and received his bachelor of arts and master of arts degrees, staying on as an assistant in the Department of Anatomy.

At his graduation, he was handed his diploma by the famous humorist and author, Mark Twain from Hannibal, Missouri. In 1925, DuBois published the book *Bringing Up The Baby*, which received much local acclaim and added to the standard of pediatric care. His office was over the J.B. Watson Drug Store (now Horizon Pharmacy) on East Market Street.

Dr. DuBois had many firsts to his credit in the medical profession: the first doctor to use the blood pressure instrument in this area; the first doctor in Kosciusko County to give vaccine immunization for Typhoid Fever and Tetanus; and the first doctor in the area to use insulin. He held every honor the county and state medical societies could bestow upon him. He served as a captain in the Medical Corps during World War I, and in World War II he served as Medical Examiner for the Selective Service Board.

Always a public servant, DuBois served as secretary of the City Board of Health 1910-1915 and 1944-1948. He cared for county home residents and inmates needing medical help at the county jail, and also served as acting physician in Warsaw when the Fort Wayne Bloodmobile was in Kosciusko County.

One of his greatest public services to the citizens of Warsaw was when he agreed to become Mayor in the depth of the Great Depression in 1932. It was by his keen guidance and astute business ability that Warsaw managed to ride out the Depression without closing schools and doing away with many necessary services ordinarily provided by the City.

DuBois was appointed mayor in 1932 by the City Council to fill the vacancy created by the death of Mayor Bibler. The following year, all city offices were extended by Governor Paul McNutt because there was no money to hold city elections. In November 1935, Dubois was elected to continue as Mayor for another term. *(Born March 30, 1878 in Liberty, Indiana / Died January 6, 1978)*

Frank O. Rarick

Rarick, whose nickname was "Slats," was the first baseman on a pro baseball team in the 1920's. He was employed by the Pennsylvania Railroad, Fort Wayne Division, as a telegrapher for 39 years. In 1928, Rarick founded the Warsaw Dry Cleaners, which he owned and operated for 30 years, and was appointed Postmaster at Warsaw 1954-1968. He served as a state representative to the Indiana

General Assembly, 1950-1956; Kosciusko County Republican chairman for four years; and City Councilman, 1939-1942.

In 1965 Rarick, a 33rd degree honorary member of the Supreme Council of the Northern Masonic Jurisdiction, was the first of only three from Kosciusko County to ever be installed as Potentate (top position) of the Fort Wayne Shriners Mizpah Temple. Among his contributions to the Fort Wayne Scottish Rite was the organizing of the Kosciusko Co. Scottish Rite Club and serving as its president for 25 years. The famous comedian Red Skelton was in his Shriners class at Boston. Rarick was also active in the Shrine Band. *(Born March 29, 1894 in Prairie Township / Died April 28, 1976)*

Charles H. "Bush" Rice

Rice played football, basketball and track at Warsaw High School and played football at Battle Creek College. He also played fullback on the semi-pro football Warsaw "Fighting Tigers" Elks Team in the 1920s.

Rice served with the local National Guard as commander, was a member of the "Company L" of Kosciusko County, and with the rank of colonel served with the U.S. Army during World War II in the Philippines. Both before and after the war he was employed by DePuy Manufacturing. About 1939-40 Rice was a Warsaw police officer and won many pistol shooting medals in the state.

He was employed for a time as the Veteran's Advocate for Kosciusko County and at one time owned a service station on the northwest corner of Center and Lake Streets. During his term as mayor, Rice also worked at the Ford Auto Supply Store on Indiana Street just south of the old Jail (now the Jail Museum).

Parking meters were installed in the downtown area during his term. Following his tenure as mayor, Rice moved his family to California in 1953, where he was employed as the Director of Safety for Bertea, Inc. which produced airplane parts. He retired in 1968, and having always been athletic, Rice turned to playing golf. Six years later, he suffered a fatal heart attack on a golf course. *(Born August 30, 1906 in Warsaw / Died September 9, 1974 in Upland, California)*

Paul E. "Mike" Hodges

Although not consecutive, Hodges served five full 4-year terms as Warsaw's Mayor. Hodges was owner of a local construction company (1941-1954) and was the general contractor for constructing the

*Frank O. Rarick
Mayor, 1943-1947*

*Charles H. "Bush" Rice
Mayor, 1948-1951*

*Paul E. "Mike" Hodges
Mayor, 1952-1955, 1960-1963,
1968-1975, 1980-1983*

Andrew G. "Jack" Engle
Mayor, 1956-1959

Joseph J. Johnson
Mayor, 1964-1967

H. Dale Tucker
Mayor, 1976-1979

following buildings: Kosciusko County REMC, Lakeland Motor Sales, Lake Theater, Mellencamp Furniture, Elks, Breading's Cigar Store, Shine Shoe Store, Service Electric, Jomac factory. His firm was also responsible for the remodeling of: Lake City Bank, First National Bank, Eagles Lodge, Brennan Drug Store, Widaman Building, McKown Garage, Kimble Glass, and Union Tool. He also built the Warsaw and Winona Lake disposal plants.

Hodges was involved in acquiring property for the city airport, and spearheaded a movement to get an 18-hole golf course (Rozella Ford) built on the southwest side of Warsaw. He was elected president of the golf club's board of directors and served two years as its president during construction. He was also a member of the Murphy Medical Center advisory board (formerly located on the southwest corner of Buffalo Street and Winona Avenue).

Hodges was a fireman at the time John Dillinger raided City Hall on April 13, 1934. The fire station was the first floor of City Hall; the Police Department, Mayor's Office, and meeting rooms were upstairs. Hodges was sleeping in the fire station when Dillinger and one of his henchmen burst up the stairs at 1:00 a.m., where they stole three bullet-proof vests and two revolvers from a cabinet in the Police Department. *(Born February 9, 1909 in Warsaw / Died October 20, 1990)*

Andrew G. "Jack" Engle

Engle was employed by the Winona Railroad from 1920 to 1934. From 1934 to 1936 he worked for the Cox Brothers Grocery at 1002 E. Center Street (current location of Blosser's Camera & Video). He opened his own grocery store in 1936 at 805 E. Fort Wayne Street. The store was closed in 1943 during World War II and Engle took a job at Bendix Corp. Defense Plant in South Bend, Indiana.

After the war he opened another grocery store at 2226 E. Market Street in partnership with his two sons who had returned from the Navy and Army Air Force. The partnership was dissolved in 1955 and the store was sold to Laddie Hoffer.

From 1956 to 1959, Engle served as Mayor. After leaving the Mayor's office, he bought back the store at 2226 E. Market Street and operated it until 1963. In the following years Engle worked for some other grocers, the Lake City Candy Company, and Robert Hall Insurance Agency. Engle was then employed by the City as assistant city engineer until he retired in 1979. *(Born August 12, 1900 in Akron, Indiana / Died July 4, 1989)*

Joseph J. Johnson

Johnson owned the Flagpole Drive-In, known for its delicious frozen custard, at the corner of Winona Avenue and Bronson Street for 27 years. He worked at Gatke Corp. on Winona Avenue right after high school, before obtaining a job with General Electric in Fort Wayne. A tool and die maker, Johnson worked for Clausing, Inc. in Chicago for five years making equipment and materials for World War II, and then came to Clausing's Warsaw plant on East Center Street.

Johnson served one term as councilman-at-large on the City Council, was a Council representative on the Park Board and Board of Works, and member of the Planning Commission. He was also a precinct committeeman for four years. In 1963, the closest mayoral election in Warsaw history brought a demand by incumbent Mayor Hodges (who ran as an independent candidate) for the city's first mayoral recount, the results of which cut Johnson's victory margin from 95 to 73.

Mayor Johnson had the honor of placing the first "switchover" call using the new U-touch, push-button telephone with musical sounds for each number "touched," when he dialed the first direct distance dialed call through United Telephone Company's new Warsaw switching center.

A side note: Johnson's wife was given a recipe for fudge by an aunt in California who operated a candy store. But the women in the family couldn't cook the fudge to taste as creamy and delicious as her aunt's. One day Johnson tried his hand at the fudge recipe, and the end result was perfect. Thereafter, family members and friends looked forward to Johnson's special fudge at Christmas. *(Born March 5, 1910 in Warsaw / Died May 31, 1977)*

H. Dale Tucker

Tucker served in the U.S. Army Air Force from 1941 to 1946 and instructed Air Force Cadets. He was a sales manager and corporate pilot for Orthopedic Equipment Co. in Bourbon (1946-1953), owner of Tucker Realty and Insurance (1955-1981), owned a retail store in Jeffersonville, Indiana (1981-1986), and was manager of the Indiana Department of Transportation Warsaw Subdistrict (1989-1993).

Prior to his term as Warsaw's Mayor, Tucker served one term on the Mentone Town Board (1948-1951). The airport underwent a major expansion project, the old High School on the northwest corner of Main and Washington Streets was purchased and renovated for the Retired Tigers Apartments for senior citizens, and the North Park Avenue area saw major rehabilitation during his mayoral term. *(Born March 11, 1922 in Warsaw)*

Jeffrey W. Plank

Plank served one term as Councilman and was then elected to four consecutive terms as Mayor. He resigned March 1, 1997 in his fourth term to return to the private sector as vice president for Instrumedical Technologies, Inc. January 1, 2000, Plank became co-owner of Midwest Rake Company.

Plank was a teacher at Warsaw Community Schools (1969-1974), a graduate teaching assistant at Indiana University (1971-1972), and a long-time insurance representative. Plank was the key force in both the creation of Warsaw's beautiful Central Park downtown (through the use of Tax Increment Financing and the construction of a $20-million world headquarters for Zimmer, Inc.) and development of the 65-acre City-County Athletic Complex on the west side of Warsaw.

Plank was instrumental in the construction of six new neighborhood parks; the creation of Kiddieland play area at Center Lake; implementing the DARE and SCUBA programs in the Police Department; and establishing the Haz-Mat and Residential Smoke Alarm programs and instituting the Squad 70 Fire Investigation Team for the Fire Department. He was also instrumental in getting the ILS and AWOS systems installed at the Municipal Airport, complete restoration of the Oakwood Cemetery entrance area and land acquisition for expansion, and creation of the Planning & Building Department in 1984. *(Born September 9, 1947 in Elkhart)*

Ernest B. Wiggins

Wiggins was elected Mayor of the City of Warsaw on March 1, 1997, following the resignation of Mayor Jeffrey W. Plank. Prior to this appointment, Wiggins had served as the 3rd District Councilman since 1983 and was president of the City Council.

Mayor Wiggins has been a Certified Public Accountant since 1980 and is a partner of Ramsey, Wilson & Wiggins, Inc. Since 1986, he has been a member of the Warsaw Rotary Club, helps deliver Mobile Meals for the elderly, and rings the bell each Christmas season for the Salvation Army. He is also a board member of the Kosciusko County Solid Waste Management District. *(Born July 9, 1949 in Warsaw)*

Jeffrey W. Plank
Mayor, 1984-1996

Ernest B. Wiggins
Mayor, 1997-Present

Warsaw elected officials in 2001. Seated, left to right: council member Trish Brown, Mayor Ernie Wiggins, Clerk-Treasurer Elaine Call. Standing, left to right, are councilmen George Clemens, Dr. Joe Thallemer, Jeff Grose, Jerry Patterson, Charlie Smith, Bill Rhoades.

The three-story brick Opera House was built in 1874 on the southwest corner of Market and Indiana Streets. Six stores were located on the first floor and a wide stairway led to the large theatre hall. Note the vacant corner in the foreground, which has been occupied by the Times Building since 1924.

The only known view of the interior of the Opera House during the late 1800s, as depicted on a stereoscope card obtained by the Historical Society in 2000. "Warsaw Band" is painted on the drum sitting on the floor to the right of the stage.

Chapter 4

Landmark Buildings

The Globe Building

"Cosgrove's Big Brick," the three-story brick building at 113 S. Buffalo Street, was built in 1861 by William Cosgrove (Mayor, 1879-1880) and his brother. Mr. Cosgrove took title to the property in 1862 with Dr. James H. Carpenter. The first floor was originally occupied by the Cosgrove and Popham Exchange, a retail emporium that carried a wide range of goods. The second floor was used as the law office of Lee K. Stookey for many years, and the third floor was a photography studio for Henry C. Milice. Stereoscope cards by Milice Photography date from as early as 1856 through 1893.

In 1886, Jacob Rosenstock and Jacob Shields purchased the property and opened the main floor as The Globe Clothing House. Both were Jewish merchants from Chicago who had come to Warsaw to operate another clothing business at 113-115 W. Center Street known as The Enterprise. When The Enterprise closed, they were well-prepared to open their own retail store. The Globe established a reputation for a full line of merchandise, including grocery items.

Shield conveyed his interest in The Globe to Rosenstock in 1896, and Rosenstock sold the business and leased the real estate to The Globe Clothing Company, which was then owned by Charles H. Ker and William S. Felkner. Ker sold his interest to Felkner in 1917, and The Globe continued in business until 1938, when Felkner changed the operation to a retail shoe store known as Fashion Shoes.

A major remodeling took place at that time, and extensive interior and exterior changes were made to the building. Dahms & Yarian, an accounting firm, occupied the second floor from 1943 to 1954, and the third floor was used for storage.

In 1960, B & B Shoe Corporation purchased the property. At that time, aluminum siding was installed around the perimeter of the structure and

This three-story brick building at 113 S. Buffalo Street was built in 1861. It was occupied for many years by The Globe clothing store. Center Title Services has occupied this building since 1993. Note the covered stairway by the alley leading to the second floor.

These men are standing at the entrance to John Grabner's Hardware at 108 N. Buffalo Street (c. early 1900s). The L-shaped store also had an entrance at 107 E. Center Street.

the upper story windows were covered and the outside stairway removed. The B & B Shoe store ceased operation in 1988, and the building was occupied for several years after by an appliance store and a resale shop for consignment merchandise.

The property was acquired by Jon R. and Deborah K. Shively in January 1992, and the building was renovated as office space for their real estate appraisal and title insurance company known as Center Title Services.

The Grabner Building

Grabner Hardware originated when John Grabner purchased a small hardware known as the "Thrift" in 1865 and with a partner changed the name to Grabner & Adams Hardware. Following a fire in 1867, Grabner purchased the lot at 107 E. Center Street in 1869 and constructed a building to house Grabner Hardware. A retail hardware operation occupied the main level of the structure for the next 100 years, 75 years under the direction of a Grabner family member—thus, referred to as the "Grabner Building."

The Grabner Building was erected on a site previously occupied by a wood frame structure that was destroyed by a fire that spread from the Wright House in 1867. The Wright House corner and three other buildings were rebuilt with brick rather than wood to reduce fire risks. The hotel was destroyed again in 1883 by a fire that threatened the same buildings. However, the firewall in the Grabner Building stopped the spread of the blaze that threatened the adjacent Post Office and Johnny Rousseau's saloon.

Aaron Montgomery Ward issued his first mail order catalog in 1872.

John Grabner operated the hardware until the early 1900s when his son, Charles, became the general manager. The Grabner store sold everything from farming implements, machinery and wire fencing to Angus cattle, stoves, tin and granite ware.

Charles ran the operation and lived above the store until 1931 when Royal and Thurl Pottenger, grandsons of John Grabner, took control of the operation and changed the name to Pottenger Brothers Hardware. In 1871, the upper level was occupied by N.B. Shoemaker, a Warsaw photographer. By 1900, the Houser Photography Studio occupied the second floor at 107½ E. Center Street.

The Grabner Building was designed as a four-story structure and after construction was joined with another building at 108 N. Buffalo Street. The retail hardware store was then an "L" shape for many years and also had an entrance on E. Center Street. The building underwent a major renovation in 1946 and the top quarter of the building was removed.

It was about this time when the Ace Hardware franchise was obtained. The Pottengers sold the business to Ronald O. "Andy" and Lewis Goshert in 1949, and the business became known as Ace Hardware. Ned Maze worked with the Gosherts in the 1940s and became a partner about 1950.

By the late 1950s Ace Hardware included Skelgas. The business was later divided, with Gosherts taking Skelgas and Maze operating the Ace Hardware store with his sons, Jim and Tom. A major fire in 1962 necessitated some remodeling and the business moved to 1701 E. Center Street in 1966. Ned retired in 1975, leaving his two sons to continue the hardware business.

After Ace Hardware vacated the 107 E. Center Street building, Avco Finance became the first occupant in nearly 100 years that was not hardware related. Frank I. Saemann purchased the building in 1978 as part of a major renovation project along E. Center Street. Occupants during the following years included a clothing store, cookie business, and the Wayne Township Trustee's Office.

The property was condemned by the City in 1995 due to structural problems with the front facade of the building. Jon R. Shively and Michael "Mick" Welborn purchased the property in 1997 and following extensive renovation, the site has since been occupied by Merrill Lynch on the first floor and Greg LeBarron has a photography studio on the second floor.

After Phillipson's clothing store closed in 1958, Charlie Miller started his own men's and boys' clothing store in the Opera House on E. Market Street. Miller is shown behind the table during a Pioneer Days sidewalk sale (c. 1960).

Opera House

On March 25, 1873, a group of men met in the room over the Post Office of John N. Runyan and organized themselves into a company for the purpose of constructing an Opera House. Officers were: Andrew J. Bair, president; John N. Runyan, secretary; and Thomas Woods, treasurer. H.F. Berst, A.T.S. Kist, and A.F. Ruch were also members of the organization.

B.G. Cosgrove drew up the plans for a three-story, all-brick Opera House. The building was completed on the southwest quarter block of Market and Indiana Streets in 1874 at a cost of $45,000, and was the showplace of Warsaw for over 40 years. The building was 130 feet long by 60 feet wide. Inside at the east end, an elaborate stairway led to the ticket booth in the second-floor lobby.

The auditorium was capable of seating over 1,000 people, and the gallery seated two-thirds that many more. The floor in the auditorium sloped to the west toward the huge stage which

had a curtain painted with various scenes and business advertisements of that time.

Outside a wooden plank sidewalk stretched across the front of the building to give access to the half-dozen stores on the street level. Ruch & Sheffield originally occupied the east room with a wholesale and retail paint store, in addition to a sign writing establishment. The other five rooms were first occupied by N.D. Heller's department store.

Numerous businesses occupied the six stores on the first level for the building's entire 93-year existence. In 1903, Bertha E. Nye had a millinery shop there and Otto A. Fisher manufactured fine cigars in one of the stores. The Winona cigar cost five cents. John D. Kutz, a steam fitter and manufacturer of the Winona radiator and the Kutz boiler, had a shop in the Opera House.

In 1911, Mrs. L.O. Oyler's Opera House Millinery Store offered the latest designs in trimmed and untrimmed hats. In 1912, Evans & Polk's grocery and meat market was in the Opera House block. Their store sold everything from lettuce,

Harriet Beecher Stowe wrote "Uncle Tom's Cabin" in 1852.

When the Opera House building was destroyed by fire October 13, 1967, the Moose Lodge occupied the second and third floors, and businesses occupied the street level storefronts.

The Ferris wheel premiered at Chicago's first World's Fair in 1893.

parsnips, Spanish onions and solid cabbage to sweet oranges, jumbo bananas, fancy lemons and cranberries. In addition to lake herring and fancy mackerel, Evans & Polk also offered all kinds of fresh, smoked and cooked meats.

The Opera House was the center of public gatherings for social entertainment and civic activities, high school commencements, caucuses, political rallies and conventions. According to George Nye, James Whitcomb Riley, Indiana's most noted poet, was known to dance with the local belles in the huge ballroom. In the 1890s, the Opera House was a very interesting place. Stock companies would come to town for a one-week stand. Sometimes a medicine show would be the week's attraction, and good vaudeville stunts entertained the audience between shows.

In December 1900, the Opera House was featuring "Uncle Tom's Cabin." The cast included fifty women and children, a double band, an orchestra, and a pack of genuine bloodhounds. The cost of seats for adults was 30 cents on the main floor and 20 cents up in the gallery. Children attended for 10 cents.

A newspaper excerpt states that the Opera House opened "under new management" on November 23, 1914. An experienced showman by the name of Harman from Kalamazoo, Michigan, who had leased the theatre, brought four vaudeville acts to Warsaw. Act one was a young lady whose singing and yodeling received a hearty applause. She was followed by a group known as the Ridges, who had a comedy act. Fritz Christian, a talented

man who played the violin, was a big hit for the third act, and the evening closed with an exciting performance by a group of Australian gymnasts known as the Aldeans.

Charles A. Rigdon (Mayor, 1907-1909 and 1918-1919) also managed the Opera House for a number of years. However, as moving pictures began to emerge, the Centennial Theatre was built on Center Street in 1917 and the interest no longer centered so much around stage plays. The upper level of the Opera House was then converted to a gymnasium until about 1920.

County high school basketball tournaments were held there, and Jerry Gerard remembers his father, Al, talking about when the Warsaw team played in the county tourney. During practice the players would bounce the ball off the high ceiling and try to make a basket.

Roller-skating promised to become popular in 1919 when Norval C. Yarger and Loren Stokes opened a roller skating rink in the Opera House. New flooring was added and 100 pairs of skates of various sizes were purchased. Peggy Fox, now 95, recalls what fun it was roller-skating there with her friends.

The Moose Lodge purchased the building in the early 1920s and closed off the gallery area to form a third floor. The lodge used the second floor for its business and social activities, and the third floor mostly for storage. During that time, five of the six 22-foot storefronts on the first floor, and their land, were owned by Bill Chinworth. The sixth, the entrance to the Lodge (formerly the grand staircase to the opera house) was owned by Reuben Williams.

Terry Klondaris recalls the story when the Moose Lodge wanted to obtain a liquor license, which was prohibited within 200 feet of a church. With the Methodist Church being just across the street, someone with a "creative mind" measured from the church, across the street, and up the stairs to the bar on the second floor which was occupied by the Moose Lodge, and determined that the distance was more than 200 feet. Therefore, the Moose was allowed to serve liquor.

In the early 1940s, Samuel G. Cook had Sam Cook's Café at 118 E. Market Street on the main floor of the Opera House. James and Daisy Chapman later operated the Square Deal Café at that location, and in the 1960s, Devon Smith had the Calico Kitchen there. In addition, Wayne W. Wertenberger had an accounting office in the Opera House during the late 1950s. Other occupants over the years included: the Post Office in the mid-1920s, the Red Cross office in the late 1940s, Waco Supply Company, Strayer's Insurance Agency, and Robinson's Supermarket.

A massive fire on October 13, 1967, destroyed the entire Opera House building. At the time of the fire, occupants on the ground floor were as follows: Wayne Fribley's Market was on the west end of the building by the alley. Lawshe's barbershop was on the east end by the Moose stairway to the second floor. Charlie Miller's Men's & Boys Clothing and the Lowery Sewing Center were in between. Fortunately, the firemen were able to save the offices of Dr. J.R. Baum and Dr. Winton Thomas, located in a separate building facing Indiana Street south of the Opera House. The Local Finance Corporation was west across the alley at 112 E. Market (now Horizon Pharmacy), and that building was also saved.

Dewey Lawshe was on the Volunteer Fire Department at the time of the fire and and his barber shop had been located in the Opera House since 1963. Lawshe's mother had sent him a barber pole from Dublin, Ireland, which was taken off the wall and saved. He recalls watching the Moose Lodge's slate-top pool tables tumble through when the floor collapsed. Over 125 volunteer firemen joined in the battle to fight the raging fire with flames that shot as high as 150 feet and could be seen for nearly twenty miles. More than 1.5 million gallons of water were poured on the Opera House, with hundreds of gallons also poured on the Times Building across the street in an attempt to prevent the fire from spreading.

The following spring when excavation was begun to clear the debris, Harold Lowery, whose sewing center was destroyed in the fire, asked workmen to watch for an old steamer trunk that was in the basement of his store. He soon received a call that the trunk was found. The top of the trunk had been burned off, as well as a few paper items, but many of his valuable papers, although still water-soaked, were saved.

Subsequent to this fire, the City passed an ordinance that required business structures in Warsaw to be faced with brick. In addition, when William J. Chinworth planned to construct a new building on that site, the structure was required to be capable of sustaining a second story because the Moose still had "air rights" at that location. Chinworth did construct a new building on the lot and the first occupant, Gamble's department store, signed a 15-year lease.

The cornice of the building at 121 W. Center Street constructed in 1883 by Hiram S. Biggs, Warsaw's first mayor.

Hiram S. Biggs Building

During Warsaw's earliest years, a small frame, one-story building was located at 121 W. Center Street. It was occupied by T.J. Quick, a silversmith and jeweler, who also sold watches, clocks, and spectacles. Quick, who has the largest monument in Oakwood Cemetery, was Dr. J.M. Bash's brother-in-law, having married Mrs. Bash's sister, Jennie Wallace.

Hiram S. Biggs, Warsaw's first mayor, constructed the current two-story brick building at 121 W. Center Street in 1883. It is believed that Biggs had his law office on the second floor at one time.

In 1903, J.M. Cook and John Hall were dealers in staple and fancy groceries, and smoked and

Warsaw Police Patrolman Marian "Mush" Warner is issuing a ticket to a horse and buggy tied to the "No Parking Bus Stop" sign located in front of the Hotel Hays (c. late 1940s). Warner, a Times-Union reporter at one time, is Warsaw Police Detective Mike Speigle's great-uncle. City Hall is the first building across the street.

The key for guest room #39 at the Hotel Hays.

Shown are three types of small bars of soap that were used by guests staying at the Hotel Hays. The middle soap was used during the time that Homer B. Smith was the proprietor.

H.J. Schrader & Co. occupied both the Biggs Building at 121 W. Center Street and the Hitzler Building at 123 W. Center Street in the 1940s. Later, Cumberland Hardware also occupied both buildings.

By 1949, the H.J. Schrader housewares and furniture department was still at 121 W. Center Street; however, the automotive department had moved west across the street to 201-203 W. Center Street.

Montgomery Ward had a catalog store in the Biggs Building around 1970, and from 1987 to 1993 Sue Cole operated the 121 Yogurt store at that location.

Hotel Hays

The Hotel Hays was built by Elijah Hays in 1884 on the southeast corner of Center and Indiana Streets. The hotel opened with 44 rooms for overnight guests and two conference rooms, and was later expanded to 54 guestrooms. In addition to the marble-floored lobby, the main floor had a gift shop, two dining rooms, a kitchen, and several small offices available for rent.

When Revra DePuy was first establishing his orthopedic company in 1895, he had an office in the Hotel Hays. In the 1930s, optometrist Otis R. Hale had an office in the Hotel Hays, followed by optometrist Dr. Lysle Willits in the 1940s. During the 1940s, the Elite Shop, which sold baby clothes, and a knit shop were located in the hotel, and Western Union had an office in the Hotel at that time. Also in the 1940s, The Beauty Box salon was located there, along with the Seaboard Finance Company in the 1950s.

In the early days, a standing rule was that men would not be admitted to the dining room unless they wore a coat that covered their suspenders. The tables in the elegant dining room were covered with white linen cloths, topped with sparkling china and polished silverware.

A December 9, 1947 menu lists four main entrees: swiss steak or fried halibut for $1.00, roast loin of pork for $1.10, and baked premium ham for $1.25. The meals included a choice of two vegetables, rolls, and coffee. À la carte items for 15 cents each were chopped salad, escalloped potatoes, steamed potatoes, buttered corn, and creamed onions. A dish of ice cream cost 10 cents, a slice of pie was 15 cents, and a pineapple sundae cost 20 cents. A cup of coffee cost 5 cents, and a glass of milk or cup of hot tea cost 10 cents.

Elijah Hays died in 1907 at age 86. W.W. Reed owned the Hotel Hays for a few years until Homer B. Smith became the proprietor in 1921. Smith also owned the Miller Hotel on S. Lake Street. When

salted meats, and their store was in the Biggs Building. In 1910, Marcellus Thompson operated Thompson School of Music on the second floor. The Biggs Building was occupied in 1925 by the Goshert & Ward Grocery, owned by Charles N. Goshert and George Ward.

The Hotel Hays, built in 1884, was located on the southeast corner of Center and Indiana Streets.

Homer Smith died in 1945, his son, Stanford "Stan" Smith, assumed the ownership.

Randy Boice, a boyhood friend of Fred Smith (Stan's son), recalls the days when Fred would get a room at the hotel on Friday nights so their group of buddies could stay there after the ballgames. In fact, Fred was known to use his skills to beat the pinball machine in the hotel lobby, and the boys would have as much as twenty dollars to go "out on the town," which was quite a bit of money in those days.

B.W. Ferguson was one of the early head chefs at the Hotel. During the busy summer seasons, black men came from Indianapolis to work at the Hotel Hays. For the winter months, Mr. and Mrs. Ferguson traveled to Florida where "BW" cooked for fine restaurants in the larger cities. Joan Miner recalls working as a waitress at the Hotel Hays in the late 1940s when Marie Lursen and Fayne Waterson ran the dining room.

J.C. "Mac" Silveus states that he delivered milk to the Hotel Hays when he was employed by the Winona Dairy. At one time, Glen Long washed dishes and Clarence Cook was a porter. Randy Boice remembers asking his parents after church each Sunday if they could eat at the Hotel, because the cooks there made the best bean soup.

Former president Herbert Hoover stayed at the Hotel Hays in 1939 when he was in town for a Republican Editors meeting. Before St. Anne's Episcopal Church constructed their building on W. Center Street, the members held services in the bar area at the Hotel.

A three-story building across the street at 207 E. Center Street was referred to as the Hotel Hays Annex in the 1940s. The second and third floors had additional guestrooms to use when the main hotel had full occupancy.

Former police officer Ralph Konkle recalls the night of February 20, 1957, when he helped fellow officer Don Snyder remove a distraught man from the third floor of the Hotel Hays. The unemployed man first broke into the Sears, Roebuck store and stole three .22 caliber revolvers and some ammunition. He then robbed two guests at Gill's Motel and less than an hour later, he robbed the Kaufman service station. The man then fled to the Hotel Hays, where police forced the man out of his room with tear gas.

After the hotel closed, the building sat vacant for a few years. The Hotel Hays was purchased in 1959 by Lake City Bank and demolished to construct a new bank building.

Travelodges were introduced in the 1940s to offer homelike accommodations for weary travelers.

The Elks Building at 118-120 E. Center Street was built in 1907. The first floor was known as the Arcade, and there were small offices and shops on each side. The Elks club rooms were on the second floor and the lodge hall was on the third floor.

The Elks Lodge/Arcade

The local Brotherhood Protective Order of Elks was chartered in August of 1902 with 64 members. For the first five years, the organization was quartered on the third floor of the building on the northeast corner of Center and Buffalo Streets (known then as the Red Men Building, now the Saemann Building).

The three-story Elks Building at 118-120 E. Center Street was completed in 1907 at a cost of $30,000. D.A. Peterson, a former lumber dealer,

owned the first floor; the second and third floors were owned by the Elks Lodge.

The first floor, which was sold several times over the years, had an open, wide hallway through the building with stores and offices located on both sides. The Elks owned and operated the entire building from 1926 until 1952. There was a beautiful stairway that led upstairs to the Elks Lodge. The second floor was used as clubrooms, and members also played poker and used slot machines. The third floor was the Lodge Hall, where banquets and special events were held.

In 1904, Dr. Lydia Notre Copper, an osteopathic physician, started her practice in Warsaw. Her office, with a corps of assistants, was located in room 12 of the Elks Arcade. Dr. Copper moved her office to the new Times Building in 1925.

In 1911, C. Melville & Co. in the Elks Arcade advertised "everything electrical," and Miss Leedy's Beauty Parlor was in rooms 14 and 16. Optometrist M.B. Knouse was also located in the Arcade at one time, as well as the Diddel Insurance Agency.

There were various businesses on both sides of the arcade hallway that came and went over the years. The Carnegis Confectionery, owned by brothers Angel and John Carnegis, was in the Elks Arcade beginning in the early 1920s for nearly the next thirty years. The store was on the main floor and the candy and ice cream were made downstairs. Russell Knoop's Barber Shop was on the other side from the late 1930s until 1952.

Conkle's Tot & Teen children's shop was in the Arcade for a time and then it moved across to the north side of Center Street. In the 1940s, the License Bureau was also there for a number of years. Dayton Paxton and Benny Herscher had a realty office there, where they sold mostly farmland. In 1954, Merle Mock was manager of the Owners Discount Corporation in the Arcade, and D.H. Lessig Engineers was in room eight.

By 1952 the Warsaw Elks Lodge No. 802 had 650 members. Gael D. Munson and his son, Gael D. Munson, Jr., Warsaw automobile dealers, purchased the Elks Building just before the Elks moved into their new lodge March 1, 1952, at 310 E. Center Street (former site of the H.H. Leiter home).

In 1997, the old Elks building was purchased by Jon R. Shively and Mick Welborn, who restored the façade and renovated the interior for office use. Attorneys Daniel H. Hampton and Brad Voelz moved into the second floor in March 1999, and the Farmers State Bank Trust Company has occupied the first floor since October 1999.

Chapter 5

1900 to 1909

"City of Warsaw" Steamer

In the early 1900s, the 124-foot double-decker steamboat named "City of Warsaw" was navigated on Winona Lake. The steamer would go along the Beyer Canal from the Winona Hotel to the Railroad Depot where the Pennsylvania and Big Four Railroads crossed. Another steamer on Winona Lake named the "Daisy" was captained by Frank Pine. A round trip on the steamers from the Winona Hotel landing to the Big Four Depot on the Beyer Channel cost fifteen cents.

The Dutch Grocery

There were numerous groceries and dry goods stores in the early 1900s. The Dutch Grocery at 206 S. Buffalo Street carried staple and fancy groceries, and had the largest selection of teas and coffees in town. The grocery also sold a variety of nuts, including English walnuts, pecans, Brazil nuts, and Filberts.

The Dutch Grocery was originally owned by Ed E. Nye. A.A. Mendel was the proprietor in 1910, and C.U. Lowe was the owner by 1912. In the 1920s, the proprietor was Merl Ringgenberg.

Mail Delivery

Free city mail delivery via the carrier system was instituted in Warsaw on November 1, 1900, with two carriers and one substitute. Carriers were permitted to sell stamps and envelopes in limited quantities, but their deliveries or collections could not be delayed in making change. Whistles were used by carriers in the residential portion of the city to give notice of their coming, so that residents would know the carrier had mail for them.

It was considered quite an increase when the cost of local letter postage was doubled, from one cent to two cents. One hundred years later, with the current cost of a one-ounce letter at 34 cents,

Driver Ed Sterling parked his truck in front of the Center Ward School on E. Main Street (c. 1918). Car dealers Gael and Burr Munson are shown with a new Allen car. The banner states that C.U. Lowe was proprietor of The Dutch Grocery at that time.

it is still considered a bargain compared to foreign postage costs.

The Ice Business

In the early 1900s, the ice business was one of the largest industries in Warsaw. There were two local leading ice companies, Warsaw Ice Company and Collins Ice Company. Warsaw Ice, operated by Ernest Clase and Dr. W. L. Hines, was located on Center Lake at the north end of Buffalo Street. The Collins Ice plant, owned by John Collins, was on the east side of Center Lake near the site of Band City Oil Company.

It took approximately seven to ten days for one icehouse to pack ice, usually around the end of February. An ideal block of ice was about 10 inches thick x 22 inches square. In early years the ice was scored by horse-drawn cutters, and later scored by a gasoline-driven saw designed and built by Ernest Clase. Each of the three rooms in

The first baseball World Series was held in 1903.

Men harvesting ice on Center Lake. The elevator was used to get the blocks of ice into the Warsaw Ice Company building on the left.

Warsaw Ice Company employees, left to right: George Nine, Howard Hines, Irwin Nine, Ed Gray, Ernest Clase, John Shroyer, and Bill Munson.

the Warsaw Ice Company plant held approximately 1,000 tons of ice. After the room was filled, the ice was packed with Timothy hay to keep it from melting. Clase's son-in-law, Herman Frauhiger, Sr., bought Warsaw Ice Company in the early 1940s.

A wholesale ice company was also located in Warsaw, owned by Henry Kithmer of Indianapolis, which shipped to all parts of southern Indiana year-round. Icehouses were also located on the west side of Pike Lake and the west side of Eagle Lake (now Winona Lake). Warsaw Ice Company, the last in business, closed in 1944.

John R. Lucas was also involved in the ice business. He served the Warsaw hotels, Boys Club, and Winona Lake, as a distributor for the Goshen Ice Cream Company. The business, known as the

Independent Ice Company, was first located at 419 E. Fort Wayne Street. Jean Lucas recalls that her father later moved the business to Winona Avenue, where the company operated until the late 1960s.

The Collins Ice Company was later owned by Ed Collins, who made his own ice cream and also sold strawberry, orange, and root beer soda. After World War II, Alex King and Charles Hughes bought out Collins and established K & H Distributing. By the early 1960s, they also sold beer. K & H Distributing was located on N. Cedar Street beside the railroad tracks for many years.

Jerry Nelson purchased K & H Distributing in 1983 and changed the name to Nelson Beverage. The business moved to its current location at 255 W. Bell Drive in 1992, and is now solely a distributor of beer.

Era of the Automobile

There have been many automobile dealers in Warsaw over the years. This section chronicles the ownership and location of some of the principal dealerships.

A 1902 newspaper excerpt states: "Warsaw, for its size, is certainly leading off in the number of automobiles owned in the area. The number has now reached six, and it is nothing at all uncommon to hear and see the new vehicles whiz through the streets. What is somewhat odd is that no two of them are of the same build; consequently, the variety is as great as the number of autos. There is every appearance that the automobile has come to stay and there can be no doubt that when they can be procured at a much less price than is now possible, they will become quite general."

A 1915 newspaper ad for A.J. Wiltrout's Overland car dealership stated that the Model 81, five-passenger touring car sold for $850, f.o.b. Toledo, Ohio.

In 1916, hardware store owner John Grabner was struck by a car driven by Keith Hankins at the intersection of Center and Buffalo Streets, and became the first auto fatality in Warsaw.

Ford

Neher: In 1911, L.M. Neher of Milford signed the first contract with the Ford Motor Company of Detroit to sell Ford automobiles in Kosciusko County. He came to Warsaw in 1913 and established an office in the Polk buggy rooms on W. Center Street. In 1914, Neher moved into the Widaman garage on W. Main Street, and when the business required more space, the old Dalton Foundry property on W. Market Street was remodeled to serve as a garage.

Three years later, Neher bought the property on the southwest corner of Detroit and Market Streets occupied by the old Center Ward School. The school was demolished and a new two-story brick building with 21,000 square feet of floor space was completed in December 1917. The entire front of the first floor of the new Neher Ford facility was plate glass windows for the display of cars in the sales room. By 1928, this building at 314 E. Market Street was used by the Power King Tool Company. It has been occupied by Schrader Auto Parts since 1976.

Overmyer: The Overmyer Ford Motor Company was opened in 1920 at 527 E. Winona Avenue by Gerald D. Overmyer. From 1929 through the 1940s, Overmyer was selling Ford, Lincoln-Zephyr, and Mercury vehicles at 102-106 W. Main Street.

Schaefer: Overmyer sold his dealership to Herm Schaefer and the business became known as Schaefer Ford Company, and he was a dealer for Ford, Falcon, and Thunderbird cars and Ford trucks. Schaefer played basketball for Indiana University and became a professional basketball player for the Pistons.

Smith: Schaefer sold the Ford dealership in 1966 to M.R. Smith and his son, Robert D. Smith. The location remained the same, but the name was changed to Smith Ford. The Smiths built a new facility on State Road 15 N. in 1977, at which time Robert Smith assumed operations of the business.

Rice: The dealership was sold in 1985 to brothers Dan and John Rice, and the name was changed to Rice Ford-Lincoln-Mercury.

Chevrolet

Munson: In October 1916, brothers Gael and Burr Munson announced the opening of Munson Motor Sales and their new garage business, following negotiations for the Allen automobile agency. They bought out the Rabbit brothers' combination livery stable/carriage-auto repair business which was in an old frame building then known as the Botkin barn located on N. Indiana Street just south of the county jail (later site of Ford's Auto Supply).

The Allen was a small four-cylinder car made in Fostoria, Ohio. The first in Warsaw to purchase this car was Bob Emmons, a painter, who bought a

A view of the first Munson Motors garage (c. 1916). Owner Gael Munson, Sr. is second from the left. The employee on the far right is Fred Richmond.

The Munson Motors staff (c. 1946 to 1951). Front, left to right: unknown, Pat Lowery, Paul Diefenbaugh, unknown, Mel Miller, Gerald Thomas, Gail Howard, Mrs. Pearl Munson, and Gael Munson, Sr. Back, left to right: Bill Ladd, Bill "Jake" Jacobs, Frank Gilworth, Tommy Mosher, Lonus Wise, Gael Munson, Jr.

touring model. In 1917, during World War I, the business moved into its location on Main Street across from the Courthouse.

They held the Hudson-Essex agency for only four or five months. However, following the War's end, the brothers decided to sell the Willys-Overland. John D. Widaman purchased the first Willys-Knight car in town, a sedan.

During a two-month-long nationwide contest by Willys-Overland in November and December of 1925, the Munson brothers pitted their selling

Fred McKown, Sr., right, passes keys to Capt. Jack Olds in front of the McKown dealership on E. Winona Avenue in 1948. Olds worked for McKown after he left the service.

Posing in 1952 with this early car are six Kosciusko County automobile dealers. Each were honored at an Indianapolis state auto convention for owning dealerships for 25 years or more. Standing, left to right: Gerald Overmyer, 35 years in the auto business; Fred McKown, 32 years; Russell Kerlin of Silver Lake, 26 years. At the wheel is Gael Munson, Sr., an auto dealer for 36 years, and the passenger on the right is Donald Poulson of Etna Green, 29 years.

prowess against the country's best for the sale of new and used cars. They sold 81 new cars and 134 used cars, for a record sale of 215—an average of 3.5 cars per day. Their younger brother, Albert, was hired as a salesman at that time. Unfortunately, the Depression forced the closure of the Willys-Overland plant in Toledo.

In 1934, Gael Munson signed a franchise for Chevrolet. Chalmers Dome was Munson's chief mechanic for many years, and Bob Richmond's father, Fred, was in the mechanical department 22 years, along with Lyda Stokes who served 16 years in the accounting department.

The business grew to include a warehouse at the corner of Fort Wayne and Washington Streets and a used car lot on the southeast corner of Lake and Fort Wayne Streets. The body shop was behind the used car lot at 223 W. Fort Wayne Street.

During their first year in business, they sold only six automobiles. However, they sold 9,600 cars in their first 22 years, and estimated a total of 11,000-12,000 had been sold by 1947. Gael Jr. joined the firm about 1947 as general manager and then took over the business when his father died in 1952.

Munson Motor Sales built their garage into one of the finest automobile service departments in the state and maintained one of the largest automotive parts and accessory inventories in northern Indiana. Munson's was appointed an official service station for members of the Chicago Motor Club and for many years the garage maintained a 24-hour, 7-days-a-week wrecker service for motorists.

The business closed in February of 1980. The building at 108-110 W. Main Street was later renovated into office space and has been the location of Three Rivers Title Company since 1993.

Smith: In the 1920s, Howard S. Smith, Sr. operated Smith Chevrolet at 216 S. Columbia Street. He also sold Peerless, Viking, and Oldsmobile vehicles. Smith owned the entire half block on S. Columbia Street between Market Street and the railroad tracks. He also had a gas station and garage, coal yard, and bulk fuel business (now site of Gast Fuel & Service).

His son, Howard "Chub" Smith, Jr., remembers pumping gas from the visible pumps during the Depression, ten gallons for a dollar. Chub recalls some of his father's "tricks" to sell cars. Smith, Sr. would chain one of the rear wheels up and drive a Chevrolet around town on three wheels. Another time a car was driven around 24 hours a day for seven days to prove the longevity and dependability of the Chevrolet.

At that time dealers, not finance institutions, had to take cars back if customers did not pay for them. Banks had closed during the Depression and when Smith had to take 129 cars back in one month, he was forced to close the dealership.

Others: For a time in the 1980s, Steve Ross had the Chevrolet dealership in Warsaw, which was then assumed by Kelley Chevrolet in Fort Wayne. Robert H. Kesler purchased the Warsaw

Kelley Chevrolet dealership at 2249 N. Detroit Street in November 1988 and the business became known as Lakeside Chevrolet. The dealership moved into its new facility on State Road 15 N. in June 2000.

General Motors

Polk: In 1918, George W. Polk and his sons, Lawrence and Norman, operated a Buick garage east of the Post Office. By 1925, Polk had moved the agency to the southeast corner of Lake and Market Streets, which was later occupied by Sears, Roebuck & Company for nearly 50 years.

McKown: In 1929 Fred McKown, who had the Ford dealership at Silver Lake, acquired Warsaw's Buick agency, in addition to Pontiac, Oldsmobile and Cadillac. McKown moved the business to the old Chinworth Building at 114-116 W. Main Street on the north side of the Courthouse Square. That building was destroyed by fire in the early 1930s and a new structure was then built. McKown was selling Pontiac, Oldsmobile, Oakland, Buick, LaSalle, and Cadillac cars in the early 1930s, in addition to GMC trucks.

Kaufman/Bledsoe: In 1946 the Buick agency was acquired by Ethan Allen Kaufman, who moved it to the southwest corner of the Courthouse Square in the old Oram Building. Kaufman Motor Sales was sold in 1950 to H.E. "Bus" Bledsoe, who had grown up in the auto business and had been a factory representative for several of the major manufacturers.

Bledsoe enlarged the garage to include a paint and body shop, and expanded into an adjoining building on Lake Street on the west side of the Courthouse Square. In 1954, Bledsoe sold the Oldsmobile and Cadillac franchises to Anthony Hames, a resident of Chicago, and moved his Buick-Pontiac dealership to a new building at 1075 N. Detroit Street just north of the Standard Oil station.

Petro: Bruce and Janet Petro acquired the Oldsmobile, Cadillac, and GMC franchises from Hames in 1972. The Petros also had a used car and storage lot on the northwest corner of Center & Columbia Streets (for many years later the site of Jane McGuire's beauty shop).

In 1973, the Petros bought 28 acres on State Road 15 N. from George Bowser, and moved into their current facility in 1976. The Petros acquired the Buick-Pontiac franchise from Timm Bledsoe in 1981.

Warsaw Police Chief Don Snyder, left, accepts the keys for a new squad car from "Bus" Bledsoe, owner of Bledsoe Buick on N. Detroit Street, as Mayor Mike Hodges looks on.

Bruce Petro sponsored a car show when his dealership was located on the west side of the Courthouse Square (c. 1975). That was just the beginning, as the dealership has sponsored an annual car show to benefit the Big Brothers/Big Sisters organization since 1991.

Employees of Hartsock's Studebaker dealership with new cars in the late 1930s, left to right: Norman Banghart, who later became fire chief; salesman Gene Foresman; employees Forrest Huffer, "Smiley" (proper name unknown), Harold Derry; salesman Al Bowman; Mrs. Blanche Hartsock; and owner Frank Hartsock.

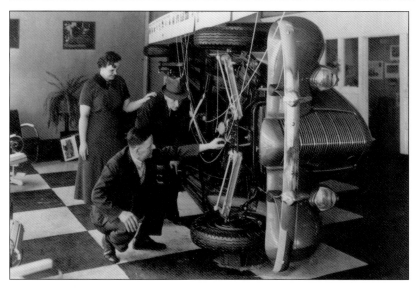

Owner Frank Hartsock, kneeling, points out some features of a 1938 Studebaker to a potential customer as daughter Elvira looks on. Former employee Harold Derry states that the motor, transmission, differential, brake lines, and steering were always color-coded for the showroom display cars. He knows, because he painted them!

Employees at the Hartsock Studebaker garage in the early 1940s, left to right: Ernie "Plunk" Osborn, Harold Derry, owner Frank Hartsock, and Donald Snyder, who later became chief of police.

Warsaw Police Chief Roy Adams, left, with officers Eugene Brumfield, center, and Eugene Kinch, right, in front of the Hartsock Studebaker Agency.

At the time their son, Bob, graduated from college in 1979, Jake Menzie, the former Chrysler dealer, had retired and the Smith Ford dealership had just moved into a new building. This offered the opportunity for brothers Steve and Bob Petro to buy the Chrysler franchise, and they rented the building on E. Winona Avenue vacated by Smith Ford to start Petro Brothers Chrysler-Dodge. Their current facility was constructed in 1986 on State Road 15 just north of the GM dealership.

In 1988, Bob changed positions to general manager of Petro's GM Showplace, and upon his father's retirement became owner of that dealership. Steve remained owner of Petro Brothers Chrysler-Plymouth-Dodge-Jeep & Eagle.

Steckhan: In addition to McKown and Bledsoe in the 1940s, Robert F. Steckhan operated Steckhan Pontiac Sales & Service in the 200 block of E. Center Street in the former Conrad garage. By 1952, Steckhan Pontiac was located at 322-324 N. Detroit Street.

Studebaker

In the 1920s, Forrest S. Deeter was proprietor of the Studebaker sales, service and garage. It was located on the corner of Main and Buffalo Streets in 1925. H.J. Outcelt was proprietor of the Studebaker garage at Buffalo & Main Streets in 1928.

Frank R. Hartsock then owned the Studebaker Agency in Warsaw for nearly 30 years. Hartsock signed his Studebaker franchise on July 8, 1934, and was one of the few agencies that consistently sold 100% above national average. The agency was located in a two-story brick building on the southwest corner of Lake and Main Streets, now site of the Kosciusko County Justice Building. (The Blue Bell factory was upstairs, where they manufactured Wrangler blue jeans.)

Having spent his youth in his father's blacksmith shop tinkering and helping repair wagons and mechanical gadgets, Frank attained a mechanical background. He worked as a mechanic apprentice in the Premier Motor Manufacturing plant in Indianapolis for eight years. At that time Premier employed 1,500 men and turned out about 30 cars per week. Touring cars at that time sold for $5,000—tops and windshields were extra.

Frank was then employed by the Harry Oram & Son garage for 18 years, selling and repairing automobiles. During that time, he designed, built and obtained U.S. patents for several tools that were used in connection with the repair of cars. For some time these tools were in great demand and were sold the world over. They were also used by the U.S. Army and Navy during World War I.

However, with the fast changing design of automobiles, these tools became obsolete, with the exception of one tool that continued to be used by a Chicago firm under the Hartsock patent. Hartsock retired in October of 1962 at age 70, just before Studebaker ended production in 1963.

Howard "Chub" Smith, Jr. recalls buying eleven Studebaker Champs from Hartsock over the years. In fact, Smith bought three in one year when he didn't like the color of the first one, he didn't like the body style of the second one, but then found the third one to be a "keeper."

Wayne Love moved his Studebaker dealership from Bourbon to Warsaw at 310 Argonne Road in the early 1960s. Wayne Love Motors also provided sales and service for Rambler and Datsun vehicles. American Motors bought out Rambler during that time. Sonny Nellans, an employee since 1965, bought the business from the family when Mr. Love died and moved it to 1075 N. Detroit Street, changing the name to Nellans Motors. Nellans sold Jeep, Eagle, and Nissan until the early 1990s, at which time he then sold the Jeep-Eagle dealership to Petro Brothers and the Nissan dealership to Max Capel.

Chrysler-Dodge

Homer T. Menzie started Menzie Motor Sales in 1929, and his son, Maurice Jacob, joined him working in the garage. The dealership salesroom and service center were located at 110 E. Main Street (behind the County Jail). "Jake" later opened a used car lot on the southeast corner of Indiana and Main Streets (now a parking lot).

Menzie first began selling Auburns in 1929, added Chryslers and Plymouths in 1932, and Dodge cars and trucks in 1967. The business also sold Imperial and Lancer automobiles. When his father died in 1940, Jake continued operations until he closed the 50-year-old business in 1979.

Dry Cleaners

The dry cleaning business was a viable means of income as far back as the early 1900s. Most coats were made of wool at that time, along with men's and women's suits. Some dresses and suits were

Kring Auto Sales was located at 1421 N. Detroit Street in the 1930s. The dealership sold DeSoto and Plymouth automobiles. This was the site of Miller & Sons Lumber Co. for many years and is currently occupied by Glamour Pools & Spas.

Homer T. Menzie started Menzie Motor Sales in 1929 at 110 E. Main Street. His son Jake joined him, and the dealership was in business for 50 years.

made of silk or serge, which also required dry cleaning. Back then, individual wardrobes were quite small and people wore their limited selection of clothing for many years. The following information depicts the change in business names and ownership over the years of some of the dry cleaning establishments in Warsaw.

Shrock Dry Cleaners was established in 1906 at 209 S. Buffalo Street. By 1910, Shrock's was located at 407 W. Market Street, and from about 1925 through the 1960s, the business was located at 114 W. Market Street. Although the founder's name is unknown, Lawrence L. Dunkleberger and Herschel Campbell owned Shrock Dry Cleaners for many years.

Employees at Wolford Dry Cleaners (c. 1957), left to right in front: Lucille Clase, Agnes Smith, Stella Marshall, Judy Childers. In back, Geneal Wolford, Dean Hoover, Carol Price, Harold Wolford.

Wolford Dry Cleaners was first located at 116 W. Market Street in the early 1960s.

Early details about the origination of the Troy Laundry is not available. However, a 1901 newspaper ad states the Troy Steam Laundry, located at 407 W. Market Street, was operated by proprietor Zeal Baringer. By 1903 it was at 213 S. Buffalo Street on the south side of the alley, and a 1911 ad states the Troy Laundry Company, owned by Stark and Kemp, was managed by W.F. Hamm.

In 1920, Homer Lewis constructed a new building at 211 S. Buffalo Street on the north side of the alley, and the laundry business moved to that site. John W. Whiteneck had previously operated a big laundry in Marion, Indiana, and moved his family to Warsaw in 1925 to manage the Lewis Troy Laundry. By 1932, Whiteneck owned the business.

Whiteneck changed the name to Warsaw Laundry Company and in 1944 his sons, Jack R. and Robert E. Whiteneck, bought the business. Jack's wife, Lucy, recalls that they sold the company in 1962 to C. Max Myer and Harvey Welty.

Myer had been the manager of the laundry department for the previous ten years, and Welty owned and operated the Central Dry Cleaners in Bourbon. The business did not do well and went back to the Whitenecks. Jerry Smith then leased the business for awhile before buying it, and the name was changed to Warsaw Laundry & Dry Cleaning.

In 1928, Frank and Ethel Rarick started Warsaw Dry Cleaners on W. Winona Avenue where the Animal Medical Center is currently located. To

Frank Rarick started Warsaw Dry Cleaners at 207 W. Winona Avenue in 1928. This building was located where the Animal Medical Center is today. Ethel Rarick, on the left, and her husband Frank are standing in the doorway, with two employees in front.

the south of this site today is Rarick Park along Washington Street, named after Frank Rarick who was elected mayor from 1943 to 1947. The Raricks moved their business to 119 W. Center in the early 1930s, where it was known as Warsaw Dry Cleaning & Shirt Laundry.

Evelyn Rarick Marsh recalls that her parents' business was located between the H.J. Schrader store on the west and a barbershop on the east. Easter was a very busy time and Evelyn remembers dealing with the many, many trousers with cuffs. The tacking on the cuffs would be cut to clean the trousers, and then Evelyn helped tack them again before customers picked them up.

Frank did the actual dry cleaning at the back of the building. Across the alley to the west, facing Lake Street, was the home of wagon maker Harry Oram. Evelyn remembers her father telling about the time Oram's granddaughter, Isadora Mann, was playing in her grandparents' back yard.

Isadora thought Mr. Rarick was always a nice, friendly man, but one particular day he stepped out in the alley and saw her standing under the tree. He sternly said, "Isadora, do not move!" She knew something was wrong, because Mr. Rarick never spoke to her like that, so she stood very still. Mr. Rarick went in to his store and returned with a shotgun. Known as somewhat of a "sharp shooter" at that time, Rarick precisely shot a rattlesnake out of the tree right above Isadora's head!

Harold Wolford had been working at George East's Dry Cleaners, at 211 W. Center Street, when Shrock Dry Cleaners on E. Market Street offered him more pay. Wolford also worked a couple years for a dry cleaning business in Bowling Green, Ohio, before returning to Warsaw where he was hired by Frank Rarick at Warsaw Dry Cleaning.

When Rarick decided to sell the cleaners after thirty years in the business, Harold Wolford and Henry "Hank" Nyenhuis bought it in 1958. By 1961, Wolford wanted to start his own business. Rex Wildman bought Wolford's interest and the Warsaw Dry Cleaners was then owned by Rex Wildman and Nyenhuis.

Wolford bought the building at 116 W. Market Street, formerly occupied by Joy's Lunchroom. Barbara Anderson remembers that her father was going to remodel the building to be more appropriate for a dry cleaning business. However, when Wolford found the front walls were covered with painted cardboard nailed to the frame structure, he decided

An early view of Wildman Laundry Company on S. Buffalo Street.

to demolish that building and construct a new one.

In the early 1960s, Wolford bought the old Miller Hotel at 216 S. Lake Street, demolished it, and constructed a new facility. In 1964, Wolford Dry Cleaners opened for business on S. Lake Street, where it remains today. Wolford retired in 1978 and sold the business to David and Maria Henderson, who chose to retain the Wolford name with the business. Their son, Vincent, bought the dry cleaners in July 2000.

In 1972, Jerry Smith's Warsaw Laundry & Dry Cleaning merged with Rex Wildman's Warsaw Dry Cleaning & Shirt Laundry to form Warsaw Laundry & Dry Cleaners, Inc. at 211 S. Buffalo Street. The business was also known as Buffalo Street Cleaners for a time.

Wildman bought the former Korth Furniture property at 800 S. Buffalo Street in 1986. Today, Wildman's son, Brent, and his grandson, Josh, are both involved in the business, now known as Wildman Uniform & Linen. The company provides uniform rental and sales, dust control products, shop and ink towel services, executive and image programs, and leather glove reconditioning services.

Phillip and Elizabeth Blue operated a dry cleaning business in Mentone during the 1940s. When they sold that business in the mid 1950s, they purchased East Cleaners in Warsaw at 211 W. Center Street, owned by George East, and the name was changed to Deluxe Cleaners.

The Blues then sold the W. Center Street dry cleaners to Bob Leiter in 1962 and bought the Vogue Cleaners at 2020 E. Winona Avenue. After

Named after President Theodore Roosevelt, the Teddy Bear was introduced in 1902.

50 years in the dry cleaning business, the Blues sold Vogue Cleaners to Fort Wayne-based Peerless Cleaners in January 1996.

Leiter sold his business to Claude Smith in 1970, and the dry cleaners closed a short time later. The 211 W. Center Street location has since been used as the Republican Headquarters.

Greenhouses & Flower Shops

Anderson Greenhouse: William Terrell started a greenhouse and flower shop on State Road 15 N. in the early 1900s. By 1910, his son, George E. Terrell, had joined in the business. A Mr. Gibson bought the greenhouse about 1916, and then sold it to Leroy G. Anderson in 1927. Anderson Greenhouse has grown in size over the years, including the addition of silk flower arrangements, candles, and other gift items, and continues to be owned and operated by the Anderson family.

Maple Avenue Florist: Ralph C. Fifer started the Maple Avenue Florist at 403 N. Maple Avenue in the 1920s. Agnes R. Sparks took over the business in the early 1930s and operated it for nearly 30 years. Two women then owned the flower shop for a time.

In 1983, Dennis Reeve, who also owned the Nursery Stop Garden Center, took ownership of Maple Avenue Florist for several years. Bob Martin operated the flower shop from about 1987 to 1993, when Lea Derbyshire purchased the business.

Dederick Greenhouse: Willard Wright Dederick, born in 1869 to William and Elsie Dederick, first worked at his father's sawmill in Roann with his two brothers. Willard and his cousin, Edson Colt, then built the first bandsaw mill in Indiana and operated that for several years.

About the turn of the century, they disposed of the mill and Willard went to work for the Wabash Railroad as a florist. He was responsible for growing plants for station yards and dining cars. Conductors, motormen and other employees of the railway wore carnations, roses, and other flowers both in and out of season. Wishing to operate for himself, Willard built a greenhouse on State Road 15 N. in 1906.

The Winona Interurban Railway tracks went directly in front of the greenhouse, which was located a short distance from the Jeremiah Herrin residence. Willard married Jeremiah's oldest daughter, Eva Marie, in 1908. Their son, Forrest Thorald Dederick, was born in 1913. Due to financial problems during the Depression, Forrest was forced to quit college. He returned to Warsaw, where he operated the greenhouse with his father until 1943.

A boiler, which was a key operating component of the greenhouse, malfunctioned and due to wartime priorities, the Dedericks could not get it

Wilbur and Orville Wright's first airplane flight took place at Kitty Hawk, North Carolina, on December 17, 1903.

The W.W. Dederick Greenhouse on State Road 15 North. It was purchased by Sun Metal Company in 1959 and demolished to make a parking lot.

replaced and were forced to close. Forrest found work in the shipyards at Van Port, Oregon, where he helped build 156 tankers for the U.S. Maritime Commission. He returned to Warsaw at the end of the war, and with his father worked toward re-opening the greenhouse.

The greenhouse did re-open in 1946, but unfortunately, Willard died in June of that year. Forrest then bought the greenhouse from his mother and operated it until 1959, when he sold it to Sun Metal Products. The greenhouse was demolished so the property could be used as a parking lot.

Following in the tradition of her family, Mallory Dederick Miniear, daughter of Forrest, opened Miniear Flower and Gift Shop in the Lakeview Shopping Center on Winona Avenue in 1972. As a third generation florist, she ran a full-service flower shop featuring FTD, Teleflora wire services, and Hallmark cards. Mallory's grandfather, Willard, was a charter member of Florist Transworld Delivery.

Located near Grace College, a special synergy was developed with Grace College students working part time at the shop. In addition, her husband, Gary, and three children made this fun family operation a successful enterprise.

Mallory was later inspired to create the Wagon Wheel Mall at 2517 E. Center Street next to the Wagon Wheel Playhouse. Through the mid-1980s, these friendly environs enabled theatre patrons to enjoy the upscale shopping boutique she had designed.

After the theatre and building that housed the mall were sold, Mallory chose to relocate downtown at 215 E. Center Street. Still featuring the main floral services, Miniear Flower Shop expanded its line to include balloons, candy, and gourmet coffee. Soon to follow was a catering kitchen which blossomed into a petite lunch café called The Good Stuff. In the 1990s, strong public demand for her Good Stuff Swiss Dill Turkey Salad garnered her awards and placement in cookbook publications.

The flower shop was sold to Lisa Robinson in 1995 and the name was changed to Iris Trails Florals. By 1998, increasing demands for custom catering and the lunchtime turkey salad trade was "gobbling" up all of Mallory and Gary's time, so after 25 years of service industry entrepreneurship, they chose to retire and spend time with their family and to travel. Iris Trails closed in 2001.

The walls and shelves of the W.R. Thomas Store were loaded with merchandise in this 1904 photo. Left to right: Fanny Thomas; Emma Durbin; Mrs. Stoneburger, a customer; Mr. W.R. Thomas, standing at the back; and a salesman, far right.

Richardson Dry Goods

The Richardson Dry Goods Company, started in 1900, was owned by two-term mayor Benjamin F. Richardson. The store was first located on the east side of the 200 block of S. Buffalo Street. By 1903, it had moved to 117-119 S. Buffalo Street and was called Hafer & Richardson's, owned by Frank H. Hafer and B.F. Richardson. The store sold everything from shoes and suits to carpets and wallpaper.

W.R. Thomas Store

In 1900, William R. Thomas established Warsaw's first variety store in the Opera House block on Market Street. It was first called the Notion Store. By 1903, the W.R. Thomas 5¢ to $1 Store had moved to the Moon Building on the southeast corner of Buffalo and Market Streets. By 1933, a chain of the variety stores had spread throughout Indiana, Ohio and Michigan, with headquarters in Warsaw. The W.R. Thomas chain consisted of 13 stores by the late 1970s, including five in Indiana.

In 1937, the W.R. Thomas Store moved to 115-117 S. Buffalo Street. Philip G. Spear began working at the local store in 1940 and became president in 1960. In 1954, Miss Emma Durbin was recognized for her 54 years of faithful service as an employee of Mr. Thomas.

Albert Einstein developed his theory of relativity in 1905.

Interurban officials, left to right, Charles Sigler, George Boone, Theodore Frazer and John Motto standing by the Interurban car known as the "Tooner Trolley," as it stopped on Market Street in front of the Times building in 1933.

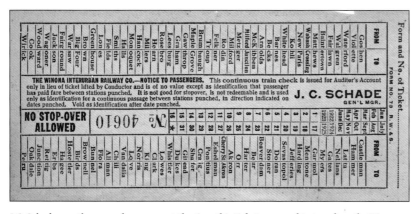

J.C. Schade was the general manager at the time this ticket was used to travel on the Winona Interurban Railway.

The W.R. Thomas store closed about 1993. For a short time after, a furniture store was at this location, and since 1995 the building has been occupied by a restaurant.

Houser's Studio

Houser's Studio, a popular photograph gallery, was established in 1900 above Pottenger's Hardware by G. E. Houser at 107½ E. Center Street. The studio later moved to 212½ S. Buffalo Street (current site of Dennie House Country Collectables).

Houser's work, shown at the State Photographic Association at Winona Lake in 1905, received the highest rating and was awarded the

Gold Badge. That same year Houser was issued an award of merit at the National Convention of Photographers in Boston, Massachusetts. Houser maintained a complete picture framing department which offered the latest and prettiest designs in frames. By 1925, the studio had moved to 107½ S. Buffalo Street.

Millinery Shops

In 1900, Mrs. Ed "Hattie" Poulson established Poulson's Millinery and Bazaar at 112 E. Market Street in the Opera House. Her specialties were fine millinery and ladies' undergarments. She also carried an artistic stock of china and cutglass ware.

Also in the early 1900s, Clara Ellen "Nell" MacConnell had a millinery shop at Shane's Corner above the grocery, and she was still there when the Candy Kitchen was on the first floor. Nell designed and made hats for the ladies of the community, and her hats were mentioned around town even thirty years after her shop had closed.

Traveling the Interurban

The first street paving bricks were laid in 1903, and the Winona Interurban trolley car system was completed in Warsaw. It was first powered by overhead electric lines. The Interurban was a direct result of Samuel Insull's innovations. Insull, who came to the United States from Great Britain in 1881 to be Thomas Edison's private secretary, went on to become an American public utilities magnate.

The Winona Interurban Railway was developed in our community to transport people from Warsaw to the assembly grounds at Winona Lake. By 1910 it had grown to about seventy miles of track, running from Goshen to Peru, Indiana. The trolleys went east on Center Street to McKinley Street, then turned south and reached Winona Lake by passing under a viaduct near its power plant. Having first been powered by overhead electric lines, by 1938 the Interurban had switched to diesel engines.

The first power plant was located in a building that later became part of Litchfield Creamery on Argonne Road. The second, a larger power house, was built where Gatke Corporation was later located on Winona Avenue. At the height of the summer, as many as 15,000 people a day rode to Winona. However, the Winona directors insisted that a strict observance of the Sabbath be followed; as a consequence, the railway cars were not permitted to operate on Sunday.

The normal schedule allowed for two cars to operate simultaneously so that a car checked in every 15 minutes at the gates of Winona Lake. Passenger service was available on the Interurban until 1938. A farewell ceremony was held on May 31, 1952, when the last freight train traveled the Winona Railway line between Warsaw and New Paris.

Little Crow Foods

Little Crow Foods was founded in 1903 by Wilbur F. Maish, Sr. The company's original flour mill was located on the west side of the courthouse square and within five years was making American food products. Following a fire at that location, the Kinsey Elevator on the southeast corner of Detroit and Market Streets was torn down in 1924 to build the new home of Little Crow Milling Company.

Clarence L. "Red" Maish later assumed the presidency and his brother, Wilbur, Jr., also worked at the company. About 1960 Clarence was appointed chairman of the board and his son, Robert D. Maish, became president. Bob's daughter and son-in-law, Kim and Dennis Fuller, joined the company in 1983, and Dennis became president in 1991.

Now in the fourth generation of continuous family ownership, Little Crow Foods is best known for its Coco Wheats, the first flavored hot cereal (1930); Miracle Maize corn bread and muffin mix (1939); Fryin' Magic all-purpose seasoned coating mix (1953); and FastShake pancake mix in a bottle (1985).

Warsaw Investment Company

Warsaw Investment Company, Inc. was established in 1903 by William Felkner and Ben Phillipson at 202 S. Buffalo Street in the State Bank building. The insurance office was in the front, and the building and loan division was in the back. When Pauline Lowry started working there in 1955, the name was still the same, but was changed to Warsaw Insurance Agency sometime in the late 1950s. At that time, the major agents were Donald Hogan (from 1955 to 1984) and Ray Dryer (from about 1960 to 1982). John Holm and Lester Ball were also associated with the firm.

The business moved to the southeast corner of Winona and Buffalo Streets about 1965 (now site of Ramsey, Wilson & Wiggins, Inc.). For a time, Dick Riedel was managing broker of the company's real estate department and Doris Bloom was a real estate agent. The business was purchased by

A group of men riding in a Pennsylvania Railroad gondola as it traveled west on Center Street during a celebration.

An early view of the Little Crow Milling Company.

Beauchamp & McSpadden in 1982, who then dissolved the real estate part and acquired just the insurance business. Beauchamp & McSpadden had previously acquired Strayer Insurance at 311 S. Buffalo Street, the business' current location.

Sporting Goods Stores

In 1903, Joseph S. Campfield opened a sporting goods store at 108 E. Center Street. Campfield was a dealer for Rival and Ben Hur bicycles, and also carried guns and ammunition, baseball supplies, and fishing poles and tackle.

Joe Campfield's Sporting Goods Store at 108 E. Center Street in 1912. Campfield is behind the counter on the left, Charles Mauzy is in the center, and John Wainwright is on the right.

Joe Campfield's Sporting Goods Store became Mauzy's Sporting Goods Store in 1919. Pictured are owner Charles A. Mauzy, his son Thames, and John Wainwright.

Robinson Motor Sales on the southeast corner of Market and Lake Streets. In the early 1900s Cook's Motorcycle and Sporting Goods Store was on this corner, and Sears, Roebuck & Co. was located there for about 50 years. Note the Interurban tracks in the center of the street.

In 1919, Charles A. Mauzy purchased the business and changed the name to Mauzy's Sporting Goods. In 1940, Raymond "Sport" Essig had Essig's Sporting Goods at that location until 1965. Essig carried a full line of hobby supplies and Lionel trains.

Burke C. Cook started Cook's Motorcycle and Sporting Goods Store about 1909 on the southeast corner of Market and Lake Streets. By 1915, Cook advertised that he carried the largest stock of motorcycle parts and accessories in northern Indiana. Cook was a dealer for Excelsior, Harley-Davidson, Indian and Wagner motorcycles. (This corner was later occupied by Robinson's Garage.)

A Civil War Reunion

A conference that drew an extremely large crowd in Warsaw was the reunion of Civil War veterans in June of 1904. So many old soldiers turned out that all the rooms in town were filled and some of the veterans slept on the Courthouse lawn. A highlight of the week-long reunion was a parade of soldiers more than a mile long. Warsaw's downtown streets were abundantly decorated with bunting and over 1,000 incandescent lights.

Chamber of Commerce

A group of local businessmen formed the Warsaw 10,000 Club in 1904 for the purpose of promoting the growth and development of Warsaw. The group incorporated in 1911 as the Warsaw Chamber of Commerce. Members at that time included: Judge L.W. Royse; attorney W.D. Fraser; Charles Ker, owner of The Globe clothing store; L.H. Lones, agent for the Pennsylvania Railroad; grocery owner E. Alleman; insurance agent J.W. Coleman; W.W. Reed, proprietor of the Hotel Hays; D.H. Lessig, president of Lake City Bank; A.O. Catlin with the State Bank; and Postmaster L.C. Wann.

On January 7, 1925, a mass meeting was held at the Hotel Hays, in which a proposal was presented to reorganize the Warsaw Chamber of Commerce. Rotary and Kiwanis Club members and all businessmen interested in the welfare of the city were encouraged to attend. The meeting was led by Attorney J.E. Headley, president of the Chamber of Commerce, and the discussion focused on a proposal to organize the Chamber on a larger, more active scale to bring factories to Warsaw and improve overall betterment of the community.

A parade in 1904 of Grand Army of the Republic soldiers marching south on Buffalo Street and turning east on Market Street.

Little information was found about the days of the Chamber of Commerce in the 1940s and 1950s. However, 1959 was the first year the Chamber named a man and woman as its "Man of the Year" and "Woman of the Year," to recognize their contributions in our community. L.N. "Pete" Thorn and Mrs. Hazel Murphy were the first honorees. Each year since, two special people have been chosen and honored at the Chamber's annual banquet.

By 1961, an Industrial Division of the Chamber of Commerce had been organized and Robert M. Ellison served as the executive secretary. It was through his efforts that an annual industrial fair was held at the fairgrounds for about ten years. Many local companies set up exhibits to display their products. The Industrial Division was responsible for R.R. Donnelley & Sons coming to Warsaw.

About 1971, the Chamber consolidated with the Industrial Division under the directorship of Sam Dungan. The Chamber office was located on the northeast corner of Lake and Market Streets from about 1969 to the late 1970s, and then moved to its current location at 313 S. Buffalo Street.

Deb Wiggins succeeded Dungan as executive director of the Chamber of Commerce in 1979. Following her resignation in 1991, the position was held by a couple of individuals over the next several years.

Since 1998, Joy McCarthy-Sessing has been the executive director. The Kosciusko County/Warsaw Chamber of Commerce has continued to grow stronger each year and in 2001 has a membership of 500—a large Chamber for the size of the area.

Kellogg first sold Corn Flakes in 1906.

Mayor Charles Rigdon built this three-story brick building on the east side of the alley in the 100 block of E. Center Street. The Rigdon Block was later razed so the Eagles Building could be constructed in 1930.

The Huff Sanitarium

The Dr. E. A. Huff Sanitarium, formerly known as the Warsaw Sanitarium, was located at 428 S. Indiana Street in 1905. Dr. Huff overhauled and renovated the facility and added modern improvements to provide pleasant guest rooms and bathrooms lit with gas and heated with steam.

On the grounds of the sanitarium was the celebrated magnetic medical well, whose water for years had a noted reputation for its wonderful medicinal qualities. The 700-foot-deep well flowed a constant stream of 1,000 gallons of magnetic mineral water each hour.

An excerpt from the *Northern Indianian* states, "In the medical world, this is an age of progress and the works of man are many. The present generation has become so accustomed to wonderful operations and surgery and achievements in medicine, that they look upon them more in a matter-of-fact way than in a sense of vital importance, not comprehending their startling magnitude."

The article further noted that patients at the Huff Sanitarium were constantly under the careful scientific observance of Dr. Huff and his assistants, who directed the patients as to their daily diet, exercise, and amusements, which they felt had so much to do with the patients' advancement to good health. It stated that a change from business and social surroundings would work wonders with

"Mutt & Jeff," the first daily comic strip, remains the longest running (1907-1981).

the afflicted, and in chronic ailments especially, the sanitarium was an acknowledged place to go for treatment and thought that in nearly all cases better results would be obtained.

Kathy (Plew) LeCount remembers growing up in this house from 1953 to 1963 after the sanitarium ceased operations. The house, with a big front porch, was converted into two living quarters. The building deteriorated over the years and was condemned, and the Warsaw Fire Department burned the structure during a training session in 1964.

Fraternal Order of Eagles

The Kosciusko Aerie No. 1339, Fraternal Order of Eagles, was organized in Warsaw on March 8, 1906. The Eagles originally met on the third floor of the Indiana Loan and Trust Building on the southwest corner of Center and Buffalo Streets. They had an auditorium, a kitchen and social room, and a secretary's office.

In 1917, the national organization of the Fraternal Order of Eagles announced that the Order would buy $1-million worth of Liberty bonds. The Warsaw Aerie, being one of the wealthiest per capita aeries in the country, was required to take a large proportion of the bonds, as the Warsaw Lodge had over $10,000 on deposit in a local bank at that time.

Robert M. Hickman joined the Eagles in 1911 and in 1915 secured the first life membership. He made a provision that the Hickman Building, located just west of the Indiana Loan & Trust Building, would become the property of the Eagles at the time of his death, upon payment of $7,000 to his estate.

By 1918, membership had grown to 225 and the Eagles had $12,000 cash on hand. Annual dues of $10 entitled members and their families to the services of a physician, $75 death benefits, and $6 per week sick benefits for twelve weeks.

Mayor Charles Rigdon and businessman Charlie Nye were instrumental in erecting the Eagles Lodge on the north side of Center Street in 1930. The Lodge bought the property and demolished the old Rigdon Building, to construct the current three-story brick Eagles Building. A large ballroom with a stage located on the second floor was used for dances and other social events. The Eagles meeting rooms and a kitchen were on the third floor.

The members rented out the first floor, and over the years some of the businesses to occupy that location at 113-117 E. Center Street were: E.W. Gresso's Department Store, Child's Department Store, Burr Department Store (c. 1944-1947), and Phipps Department Store in the 1950s. Since then it has been home to Compton Furniture, Anderson Furniture, and an antique mall. In June 2001, Jon Blackwood opened the Downtown Mattress Showcase at this location.

The Eagles moved to their current lodge on W. Center Street in Boggs Industrial Park in 1992. Total membership of both men and women in recent years has remained between 900 and 1,000.

Billiards

Billiards has always been a popular pastime. J.H. Scollard established The Brunswick Billiard and Pool Parlor at 210 S. Buffalo Street in 1907. It was the largest of its kind in the county, and his brothers, Patrick and Thomas, assisted with the business.

By 1910, Ed F. Hall had a billiard parlor at 113 E. Market Street, and the Princess Billiard Hall was located at 107 W. Center Street.

A 1925 city directory lists four billiard halls. Beebe & Bumbaugh, owned by Earl S. Beebe and Gerard M. Bumbaugh, was located at 104 S. Buffalo Street in one of the small store spaces on the east side of the Indiana Loan & Trust Building. Gordy Bumbaugh states that his father's business had pool tables both on the main floor and in the basement. When the bank needed to expand, the "Recreo" pool hall moved across the street into the basement under the W.R. Thomas store, where they also operated a lunchroom.

Also in 1925, Walter L. Brant had a billiards room at 107 W. Center Street. Nick Gores and George Stavropulos offered billiards at 115 E. Center Street in their Liberty Café. Charles B. Hearn's South Side Billiard and Lunchroom was at 210 S. Buffalo Street.

In 1947, billiards could be played at Breading's Cigar Store, 114 E. Center Street, and Gordy Bumbaugh's uncle, George Deerwester, had a billiard parlor in the basement below the Roxy Café at 123 E. Center Street.

The Suffering Papas Club

Although no local resources were found to document the following story, this somewhat humorous excerpt of an Indianapolis newspaper article in 1908 describes the dilemma of the "Suffering Papas Club of Warsaw" which was organized for the purpose of rebelling against the husband's traditional bondage.

The Miller Hotel was located at 216 S. Lake Street just north of the Pennsylvania Railroad Depot. It was demolished in the early 1960s when Harold Wolford purchased the property to build a new facility for Wolford Dry Cleaners.

The twenty-plus members were all prominent business and professional men in Warsaw. Their concern was that the wife of nearly every business and professional man in town belonged to various clubs or societies, with many wives being members of more than six organizations.

One of the leaders explained that year after year the husbands had been forced to stay at home while wives, mothers and sisters attended club and lodge meetings or social events. Charter members of the club included: F.E. Bowser, D.H. Lessig, Bertram Shane, Charles Grabner, W.F. Maish, Dr. C.N. Howard, Charles H. Ker, Elmer B. Funk, C.W. Chapman, and Dr. John White. An excerpt of the Suffering Papas Club stringent oath of allegiance follows:

"I promise and agree to fully perform my sacred duties as a husband at all times. I shall ever love, cherish and obey and carry wood, water and ashes and mow the lawn whenever the state of my wife's health will not permit her to do so. I will faithfully and regularly build the fires in the furnace and heating stoves whenever required between the first day of July and the first day of September of each and every year and further deponent sayeth not.

"I will never scowl, scold or swear within the sacred confines of my sweet home if my wife doesn't first; or if she doesn't make me carry the baby at night, get the baby a drink, go for the doctor, build a fire in the furnace, button her new dress, go out calling, burn the chicken, get the

Bakelite, the first completely synthetic plastic, was invented in 1909.

In 1909, Robert E. Peary became the first man to reach the North Pole.

pie crust too wrong, the fried potatoes too short or the applesauce too sweet, lend my pipe and tobacco to the laundry boy, tell me of her other beaux, how her mama wants things done, what troubles she has with the hired girl, washwoman or butcher; how tired she is of the humdrum of country life; how she would like to have a sealskin coat, Parisian gown or net hat a la mode, or do any of the ten thousand other things which it is said that some women do."

Miner Lumber Company

In 1909, William Miner opened Miner Lumber Company at 731 W. Jefferson Street, and by 1915, it was one of the largest employers in Kosciusko County. Miner sold the business to his four sons (Ray, Russ "Bus," Deke and Albert) about 1920.

The lumber company sold wood to hardwood lumber manufacturers, including AMF Corporation in Warsaw, which made bowling alleys and gymna-

sium floors. Chris Craft Boats bought solid walnut to decorate their launches, and furniture manufacturers bought a lot of walnut and maple wood.

The lumber company was destroyed by fire in 1956, but within one year was completely rebuilt. In the early 1970s, the Miner brothers sold the business to Robert Wollfrum, who in turn sold it to an out-of-town warehouse in late 1999.

Undertakers

After working with funeral directors in Peru and Plymouth, in 1909 C.C. Dukes purchased the old R.C. Smith undertaking stand in Warsaw and continued alone until C.R. Zimmerman joined him in partnership and Dukes & Zimmerman was formed. This business was located at 207 W. Center Street. As was common for funeral directors and embalmers in those days, Dukes & Zimmerman was also a dealer in the sale of pianos, organs, and sewing machines.

A Templar Conclave in 1908 marching west on Center Street past the Courthouse and turning north on Lake Street.

Chapter 6

Prominent Physicians

Dr. J.M. Bash

Dr. John Marshall Bash (1847-1909) built the Bash mansion on the northwest corner of Lake and Market Streets in 1881, shortly after he married Elizabeth Wallace. With its fine interior wood finishing, Brussels carpets, expansive stairway and elaborate decorating, it was by far one of the finest houses in Warsaw.

When the masons were erecting the limestone Courthouse around 1882, Dr. Bash contracted with them for a limestone fence at a cost of over $4,000—one of the most elaborate boundary lines that has ever existed in the city. The elaborate home adorned that corner for almost half a century, until 1930 when the mansion was sold to Uncle Sam for $10,000 and demolished to construct a new Post Office.

Simultaneously with his practice, Dr. Bash enjoyed raising some of the finest trotting horses in the country. A very nice barn for the horses was just to the northwest of the house, and he had a stock farm on State Road 15 south of Warsaw. His trotters and brood mares were mentioned in a historical volume entitled "Memorial Record of Northeastern Indiana."

Dr. John Bash devotedly practiced his profession for 32 years. His son, Flint E. Bash (1886-1931), although not a doctor, was very active in the community, including his involvement on the library board and school board. The 1931 Warsaw High School Tiger Annual included a page dedicated to Mr. Bash, who had been a member of the Board of Education for 16 years.

The massive desk from Dr. J.M. Bash's office became a prized possession of his grandson, Dr. Wallace E. Bash (b. 1917), who practiced pediatrics in Fort Wayne for 37 years. He is now retired and resides in Florida. His sister, Janet Bash Balsbaugh (b. 1913), who married a doctor, lives in North

Dr. J.M. Bash by the large, elaborate desk in his office (c. 1900) that has since been used by his grandson and great-grandson. Dr. Wallace Bash currently possesses the tall secretary/bookcase shown sitting against the wall.

Dr. J.M. Bash built a home on the northwest corner of Lake and Market Streets in 1881. When the limestone courthouse was being built the following year, Dr. Bash hired the workers to construct an elaborate limestone fence around the mansion.

The main entrance to the Bash mansion faced Market Street. This house was demolished in 1930 so the limestone Post Office could be built on that corner.

Dr. T.J. Shackelford

Dr. Tiffin J. Shackelford was a successful physician who resided in a large house at 216 S. Buffalo Street. His small office was located next door at 214 S. Buffalo Street, which was later used as Dr. James L. Baker's dental office for 49 years. Dr. Shackelford studied medicine in Baltimore, Maryland, and returned to Warsaw in the fall of 1883. Over the years, he built a well-stocked library of medical books written by the most prominent practitioners. Amos Ringle's furniture store was across the street and his son, Frank, was known to drive Dr. Shackelford to see patients.

Dr. Shackelford was active in civic affairs, serving on the county health board for four years and as secretary on the city health board for several years. He also held the positions of president, vice president, and secretary of the Kosciusko County Medical Society. Shackelford was prominent in fraternal orders and served as a director of Lake City Bank. He also was the organist at the Methodist Church for many years.

In 1877, Emma Grabner, the daughter of prominent merchant John Grabner, married Seth Irland, a minister in Ohio. The couple had two daughters; Bunny was born in 1878 and Grace was born in 1880. The parents divorced and Emma returned to Warsaw. Unfortunately, the young girls died five days apart in 1882.

Dr. Shackelford married Emma Irland in 1902. Mrs. Shackelford taught water color and china painting classes in the basement of her husband's office, where students painted vases, dishes, and cups and saucers. Mrs. Shackelford's hand-painted items are signed "Emma G. Irland." A former student gave Jean Lucas a painted tea set and tray, which led to her interest in collecting the china. Others in our community also collect Mrs. Shackelford's painted china.

Like her husband, Mrs. Shackelford was involved in the community, such as serving as president of the Warsaw Reading Club from 1912 to 1915, and being active with the missionary program at the Methodist Church.

Dr. Shackelford often found time to indulge in his literary interests, and wrote many verses and poems, some of which were printed. For a time the Doctor's poems were printed in the *Warsaw Daily Times* under the name of "Skipling." The *Indiana Writers of Poems and Prose* published in 1902 included selections from not only John

Manchester. Janet donated the wedding dress to the Jail Museum that her grandmother, Elizabeth Wallace, wore when she married Dr. Bash in 1881.

Dr. Wallace Bash's son, Stephen (b. 1941), became a physician and practiced with his father for eleven years. He is currently a pediatric cardiologist in Peoria, Illinois. It is in his office that the heirloom desk continues to serve the Bash family. A fourth generation physician, Dr. Stephen Bash's daughter, is currently practicing in California.

Dr. Tiffin J. Shackelford
(1855-1915)

Dr. and Mrs. T.J. Shackelford with Dr. Shackelford's mother, far right, at the entrance of their home at 216 S. Buffalo Street. His office was in the building on the right.

Emma G. Shackelford
(1858-1925)

An interior view of the Shackelford home shows the intricately carved stairway and several ornate rockers in the sitting room.

*Dr. Angus C. McDonald
(1865-1944)*

Hay, James Whitcomb Riley, and Lew Wallace, but also a poem by Warsaw's own Dr. Shackelford.

In the 1940s the former Shackelford home was the site of the Shera Funeral Home, operated by Glen G. Shera. It later became the Kelly Funeral Home, owned by Robert L. Kelly, and in the early 1960s Lucy Upson had her law office there. The house was demolished in the early 1960s.

Dr. A.C. McDonald, Dr. J.R. Baum & McDonald Hospital

Dr. Angus C. McDonald came to Warsaw immediately following his graduation from the University of Pennsylvania School of Medicine in 1892. For forty years he worked diligently in ministering to the health of the people of the community and was an outstanding physician, as well as a leading citizen. His office was on S. Indiana Street between the Opera House and the railroad tracks.

In 1916, Dr. McDonald and John D. Widaman built the Widaman-McDonald building on the northwest corner of Center and Indiana Streets, which housed the Centennial Theatre. Dr. McDonald was the first president of the Baker Boys' Club, and was always identified with movements toward the welfare and improvement of the community. When he retired from active practice, he gave his full

*Dr. John R. Baum
(1898-1979)*

McDonald Hospital was built on the northeast corner of Center and Parker Streets by Dr. John R. Baum to honor his mentor, Dr. Angus C. McDonald. The hospital was in operation from 1936 to 1956.

*Daisy Lou Baum
(1900-1979)*

Irene Dome, in the "drug room" at the medical clinic on S. Indiana Street, where she worked with Dr. Baum for 46 years.

attention to the management of his extensive realty holdings of business and residential properties.

When Dr. McDonald was planning his retirement in 1927, Dr. John R. Baum, then living in Bloomington, Illinois, was handpicked from a long list of applicants to join McDonald's practice. Dr. Baum practiced 46 of his nearly 50 years in medicine in Warsaw. During World War II when many doctors were called to the service, Dr. Baum was one of the few doctors in the county. He was known at times to average 16-hour work days, seven days a week.

In 1934, Dr. Baum nearly mortgaged his life to build the city's first modern hospital on the hill at 2501 E. Center Street, at the intersection of Center Street and Argonne Road. The facility was completed in 1936 and named the McDonald Hospital, in honor of his highly respected predecessor. Dr. Baum operated the hospital for twenty years prior to selling the building to Frank Wilson, a nursing home operator, who started the Alfran Nursing Home. After selling his hospital, Dr. Baum joined the medical staff at Murphy Medical Center, in addition to maintaining his office, known as the Warsaw Clinic at 212 S. Indiana Street along the alley behind the Opera House.

The dedicated doctor was on call from 1927 through 1946 before he and his wife, Daisy Lou, enjoyed their first vacation. Mrs. Baum, a nurse at the McDonald Hospital, received the Chamber of Commerce's "Woman of the Year" award in 1963. The Chamber honored Dr. Baum in 1967 as "Man of the Year."

Irene Dome worked for Dr. Baum for 46 years. The Baums adopted two baby girls who were born just days apart. When the girls were 20 months old, Irene was initially hired to help take care of the girls in their home, but also worked at the clinic and hospital as needed. Irene recalls that at one time Dr. Baum had nearly $500,000 recorded on his books that patients had not paid. When she asked about having a collection agency help recoup payment, he replied, "I don't need the money that bad." In appreciation for her faithful dedication, the Baums gave Irene a life-long lease on their house at Winona Lake, where she still lives today.

Carlyle and Mildred Mason purchased the former McDonald Hospital in 1977 and it was called Mason Health Care Facility. In 1994, Mason's residents and staff moved into a new nursing home facility at 900 Provident Drive. The

tan brick building on Center Street was then renovated into 31 living units for senior citizens and was known as Mason Residential Care. It later closed and the building was bought by Kosciusko Community Hospital and used for its MedPark Center. The former hospital is currently occupied by the KCH Financial Department.

Dr. Samuel G. Murphy & Murphy Medical Center

Dr. Samuel G. Murphy began practicing medicine in Claypool in 1911 and came to Warsaw in 1914 to specialize in surgery. When he returned from military service following World War I, Murphy worked at the Emergency Hospital at the top of Prospect Hill on the southeast corner of Winona Avenue and Union Street, which Mrs. Frank (Margaret) Randall had operated since 1916.

Dr. Sam Murphy, Dr. Norman L. Reynolds, Dr. C.Clifford DuBois and Dr. Orville H. Richer added surgical facilities to the seven-bed hospital, and in 1935 Dr. Murphy purchased the Emergency Hospital from Mrs. Randall. In the early 1920s, Hazel Jameson began working at the hospital. With no prior training, Hazel worked hard and learned quickly under Dr. Murphy's direction. In time, her hard work and dedication led to her becoming Dr. Murphy's head nurse and dependable "right arm." Murphy was a good physician and expert surgeon, and welded by a common compassion for people and dedication to saving lives, easing suffering and comforting the sick, the two made a great team. Dr. Murphy was also deeply interested in civic affairs and personally covered the City's payroll many times during the Depression.

Murphy and Jameson had a mutual dream of building a new hospital. The first stage of that dream began in 1939 when Dr. Murphy used over $100,000 of his own funds to construct a 25-bed hospital on the southwest corner of Buffalo Street and Winona Avenue. However, the stress of continuing his practice and building a new facility at the same time took its toll, sending Dr. Murphy to the Mayo Clinic in 1940 where he was diagnosed with an ulcerous stomach. Although ignoring his illness, Murphy thought the Mayo Clinic was a terrific facility and came back to Warsaw to revise his own plans.

The Murphy Medical Center opened February 16, 1941, with 3,000 people touring the new facility with the finest surgical and x-ray equipment and

Dr. Samuel G. Murphy (1885-1945)

Hazel J. Murphy (1908-1994)

The Murphy Medical Center on the southwest corner of Buffalo Street and Winona Avenue opened in 1941. A fourth floor was added in 1968. The hospital closed in 1977.

Clara Barton incorporated the American Red Cross in 1881.

state-of-the-art heating and ventilating systems. A reporter described the hospital as "a marvel of science and engineering, and one of only four of its kind in the United States." On February 18, Elmer Banghart was the first person to undergo surgery at Murphy Medical Center.

Dr. Murphy and his nurse worked happily and diligently, and even talked of the future when they would add an east wing and a west wing. Dr. Murphy was a dedicated perfectionist and his surgery work kept him quite busy with far too many patients. For Hazel, no chore was too menial or no detail unimportant. When she saw a job that needed done, she did it, and she found time every day to visit the patients and ask how they were doing. Another faithful employee, Mabel Rebman, was Dr. Murphy's office nurse.

Mayo surgeons had removed much of Dr. Murphy's stomach in 1940 and warned that he should reduce his workload. The sick needed him, however, and Dr. Murphy did not slow down. His fatigue deepened and symptoms began to appear. He eventually had to sit on a stool doing surgery because he couldn't stand very long, and by late 1945 he was diagnosed with cancer.

Dr. Murphy had lived most of his adult life with his mother, who persistently refused to let

him get married. But a year after she died—and just shortly before his own death—Dr. Sam Murphy married Hazel Jameson on January 7, 1945. Only the minister and closest associates attended the ceremony performed at the doctor's bedside in Murphy Medical Center, which united two people who had given their entire lifetime to the service of others.

Dr. Murphy faced the truth and began making plans to settle his affairs. His will included a trust fund to provide nursing scholarships for Kosciusko County high school seniors and college freshmen. He told Hazel the hospital belonged to the community, so he put it in her name to follow through with his wishes. When Dr. Murphy died February 10, 1945, at the age of 59, his will sparked litigation that froze the estate for eleven years. Therefore, in 1946 Hazel borrowed $200,000 to build a west wing, followed by another $150,000 in 1952 for an east wing.

Through Hazel Murphy's tireless efforts and extremely long work days seven days a week—in addition to her frugality, generosity and faith—by 1957 much of the hospital's debts had been retired and the estate was finally settled. As Hazel struggled to fulfill her husband's wishes, she offered the three-story hospital to the city and county. When both refused, she continued on the services of the hospital with the aid of Dr. George Schlemmer, a long-time associate of Dr. Murphy.

Under the ownership and direction of Hazel J. Murphy, by 1957 the Murphy Medical Center had increased its bed capacity to 50 and updated its surgical, maternity and emergency facilities. It was at that time the hospital incorporated and became a not-for-profit facility. Also in 1957, Dr. Baum sold the McDonald Hospital on E. Center Street and joined the staff at Murphy Medical Center. A covered ambulance drive and entrance was also completed. A fourth floor was added in 1968 for a new maternity ward and intensive care center, and the bed capacity increased to 70.

The hospital was Hazel's whole life, and when the board of directors discovered Hazel was drawing no salary, they insisted she receive a paycheck. But six months later the accountant discovered she had six uncashed monthly checks. In recognition for her continued service to our community, in 1959 Mrs. Hazel Murphy was named the Chamber of Commerce's first "Woman of the Year."

A rate schedule dated December 5, 1960, showed the following costs for patients at Murphy Medical Center: ward rooms, $11.50; semi-private rooms, $13.50; and private rooms, $14.50 per day. Operating and delivery room rates: major surgery cost $25 for the first hour and $5 for each one-fourth hour thereafter. The delivery room was $20 per hour, with labor induction costing $10.

Laboratory fees included: $3 for a cholesterol test, $4 for a blood sugar test, and $5 for a complete blood count. Ten dollars was charged for a pregnancy test. Fees for the x-ray department included: $10 for a foot and $15 for cranium or hip x-rays. A hand x-ray cost $7.50, elbow $10, and a shoulder was $12.50.

By the early 1970s, some of the doctors practicing in Warsaw wanted to build another hospital. Mrs. Murphy was very opposed to this idea and people in the community became very divided. Ultimately, Mrs. Murphy and the Murphy Medical Center filed a lawsuit against twenty people, including eight doctors, who had joined efforts to start planning for a new hospital.

The first human heart-transplant operation was performed in 1967.

These volunteer Candy Stripers were honored by the Murphy Medical Center in 1961. Front row, left to right: Kookie Burgh, Jeanne Klier, Betty Kaufman, LeEtta Ring, Gloria Butler, Rosemary Ring, Janet Mollenhour, Vicki Silveus, Karen Harp and Judy Frankle. The two Candy Stripers in the center, Claudia Fribley and Nancy Crum, were honored for the most hours of service. Back row, left to right: Martie Nelson, Becky Perry, Sue Hetler, Karen Dinneen, Jane Ring, Lilia Jacobs, Kathleen Noggle, Beth Pifer, Pam Hartman, Pam DeGood, Susie Gerard and Marilyn Clark.

William Mollenhour, a member of the Murphy Medical Center board of directors and master of ceremonies at the "Ball Parisienne," crowns Joy Carlson queen of the ball (c. late 1950s). Approximately 600 people representing the hospital's nurses, Gray Ladies, Candy Stripers, and Women's Service League attended the "appreciation ball" at the National Guard Armory.

Jonas Salk developed the first polio vaccination, which was introduced to the public in 1953.

These eight physicians—Dr. Hossein Hashemi, Dr. George M. Haymond, Dr. Thomas F. Keough, Dr. Harold Mason, Dr. Arthur Moser, Dr. William Parke, Dr. Roland Snider, and Dr. Wymond Wilson —purchased property on the east side of Warsaw and donated it for the purpose of building a new hospital. Other community leaders involved in the project included: Arch Bumgartner, Joe Boggs, Lawrence Castaldi, Robert Ellison, Darrell Frantz, Graham Kreicker, Thomas Lemon, George Lenke, Robert D. Maish, John Snell, Ralph Thornburg, and Bruce Wright.

Mrs. Murphy spent a lot of money in an effort to stop the building of Kosciusko Community Hospital, but subsequently an out-of-court settlement was reached wherein each of the defendants paid Murphy Medical Center $2,000 per person, or a total of $40,000, so construction of the new hospital could begin.

Murphy Medical Center closed July 1 1977, one year after Kosciusko Community Hospital opened its doors June 1, 1976. The Murphy Medical building was demolished in 1988, and Marsh Supermarket now occupies this property.

Lela Salman worked at Murphy Medical Center during the last 15 years of its existence and became a close friend of Mrs. Murphy. Lela recalls how Mrs. Murphy would sometimes call her and ask to go for a drive. Away from ringing phones and people, Mrs. Murphy would sit quietly, gazing out the passenger side window, as she contemplated problems and worries about the hospital. Lela would simply continue to drive until Mrs. Murphy had worked things out in her mind and would finally begin to talk. Sometimes they would be more than 100 miles from Warsaw when Mrs. Murphy would ask where they should stop for supper before they headed back home.

Lela also remembers the elegant annual balls Mrs. Murphy would host to honor the Red Cross Grey Lady hospital volunteers and the high school-age Candy Stripers. The Paris-themed balls were held each year at the National Guard Armory. A delicious buffet, complete with an ice sculpture centerpiece, was provided by a South Bend catering company.

The Candy Striper program was introduced at the Murphy Medical Center in 1961 by Hope Luckenbill, director of volunteer services. The program was formed to provide young people with an opportunity to learn the satisfaction that comes from community service, to develop an understanding of the nursing profession, and to help them develop initiative, poise, tact and responsibility. Requirements and standards were very high, and candidates had to be at least 15 years old, an average or above average student, well mannered, courteous, and loyal.

The girls were responsible for serving trays, delivering mail and flowers, and reading to patients. They also helped with clerical work. Candy Stripers were not eligible to wear the identifying white blouse and red and white striped pinafore until they had served 24 hours of duty.

Candy Stripers had rules with a demerit point system, in addition to a daily inspection by Mrs. Luckenbill. A demerit was recorded if a girl failed to show up for her assigned hours or didn't get a substitute when she was scheduled to be absent. Demerits were also given if the girls left the hospital while on duty, smoked in uniform, wore an incomplete uniform, or were cited for misconduct. However, very few demerits were issued and there was a waiting list of applicants. Many girls went on to nursing school to become RNs and then returned to work at Murphy Medical Center.

Chapter 7

1910-1919

Robinson's Market

Jack Robinson founded Robinson's Market in 1910 at 114 E. Market Street in the Opera House. Jack's brothers, Charles and Richard, worked at the store, and his son, Herbert B. Robinson, continued its operation over the years. Herb's children also helped at the store. On Saturday nights they would sweep the sawdust from the floor and sort through it to find change that customers had dropped during the past week, which served as their pay for helping.

Robinson also had a grocery store at 112 N. Buffalo Street, now site of Reader's World. He served an apprenticeship as a sausage-maker with Swift and Company in Chicago at an early age, and he was one of the early innovators in food handling and food processing.

In 1938, the grocery was sold to Owen Emerick and William Chinworth, who later started Owen's Supermarket on W. Market Street. The sale of the grocery also included a slaughterhouse one-half mile south of Warsaw on Country Club Drive. M.C. "Red" Metz, a butcher, headed the Owen's meat department and Donald Lynch, a former employee of the Robinson Market, handled the grocery department.

Robinson's Market was owned by Jack Engle and Wally Kirkendall in the early 1960s. When Wayne and Phyllis Fribley bought the business in 1967, the name was changed to Fribley's Market. The Fribley's business was short-lived, however, due to a fire that destroyed the Opera House building in October of that year.

Hugro Manufacturing

The Hugro Manufacturing Company was moved from Marengo, Illinois, to a factory in Warsaw in 1910. Hugro produced various models of hand-pushed vacuum and carpet sweepers, oil mops

In 1954 Robinson's Super Market was located on E. Market Street in the former Opera House. At that time, the Moose Lodge occupied the second and third floors.

Workers in Tool Department #7 at the Hugro Manufacturing Company on N. Detroit Street in 1925.

Sweep Easy
WITH THE

Hugro India Broom

GUARANTEED FOR ONE WHOLE YEAR

HUGRO

The lady on the front of this brochure is holding the Hugro Manufacturing Company's India Broom, which was guaranteed for one year and claimed to outwear other types of brooms.

with a red cedar handle, and their popular Red Bird and Blue Bird indoor clothesline reels. The company claimed to have sold 200,000 cleaners in 1916, reaching an annual sales volume of $500,000.

One year later with a floor space of 60,000 square feet, the sales volume had increased to over $1 million. As business grew over the years, including a $500,000 contract with the Jewel Tea Company, the facility was expanded and the building became quite large, extending between the 400 and 500 blocks of N. Detroit Street. At that time, the Hugro Company was the largest employer in Warsaw and significantly contributed to its progress. For instance, in 1910 there were 138 empty houses in Warsaw. However, by 1917 those residences were filled and over 200 more houses had been built to accommodate the city's growth.

The company had initially employed about 30 men, but as the volume of business increased, by 1916 the number had increased to over 300, and reached as high as 375 during the war. Hugro Manufacturing eventually closed and the building was occupied for a short time by a box manufacturing company. By 1938, however, the facility was occupied by Playtime Products.

Dalton Foundries, Inc.

Dalton Foundries, Inc. was started in 1910 by Donald J. Dalton on Warsaw's west side, in the former Werntz Foundry & Machine Works building at 513 W. Market Street (later Fitzpatrick Paints) to produce one product—a home cobbler set for repairing shoes. The manufacture of gray iron castings for cobbler kits continued through the early 1920s when the firm began taking contracts to furnish castings for other manufacturers.

The foundry moved to its present location at the corner of Lincoln and Jefferson Streets in 1913. Their production in 1917 was keyed to the war effort. In 1918, Dalton acquired and moved the equipment of Sunderland Pump Manufacturing Company to Warsaw to enter the auto tire pump manufacturing field. Dalton Malleable Casting Company was founded in 1923 and later that year, the Gray Iron Foundry and the pump business were consolidated under the name The Dalton Foundries, Inc.

Over the years, the Dalton "manufacturing complex" was comprised of the Dalton Foundry (producing gray iron and malleable castings), the

Endicott Church Furniture Division (a leading supplier of custom quality church seating and chancel furnishings), and Big Boy Division (which manufactured trailer hitches for all types of lightweight trailers and travel trailers).

Donald Dalton passed away in 1947 and his son, Bill, then headed the company until his death in 1952. At that time, Charles H. Ker became president, followed by W.M. "Matt" Dalton in 1959. Eugene Paul became president in 1968 when Matt Dalton became CEO.

The company was sold to the salaried employees in 1985 under the "Employee Stock Option Plan," and Kenneth L. Davidson was appointed President and CEO. Dalton Foundries was acquired by Neenah Foundry Company in 1998, and the current president is Joseph DeRita.

Electrical Businesses

As early as 1910, Ray R. Henderson operated an electrical business. His brother-in-law, Earl W. Parker joined him in 1920 and the business was called Henderson & Parker Electric Company. It was first located in the Rigdon Building at 113 E. Center Street.

By the 1930s, Parker operated his own business, E.W. Parker Electric Co., in a small building opposite the Masonic Temple on N. High Street (later occupied by the Royal Cab company). Parker's business was located in the Opera House on E. Market Street for a few years, until 1942 when he built a new shop at 315 E. Fort Wayne Street.

Earl Hatfield started an electrical and refrigeration business in 1929. His son, Eddie, however, chose to work for Earl Parker. When Parker decided to retire in 1961, Eddie and his wife, Kay, bought the business and the name was changed to Hatfield Electric Service. The Hatfields operated at that location until McDonald's purchased the property to build a restaurant in 1973. Hatfield Electric Service has since been located at 314 S. Harding Street.

Hardware Store

Vern Frantz and his brother, John, bought a hardware store in Claypool in 1906 and named it Frantz Brothers Hardware Company. A few years later they purchased an adjoining grocery and dry goods store.

As early as 1910, George F. Liebrock and Harvey B. Gerard owned the Liebrock & Gerard

Earl Parker and his bookkeeper/assistant, Mrs. Francis Blackford, at Parker Electric Company in 1960.

Hardware store at 113 W. Market Street in Warsaw. In 1928, Vern Frantz and R.A. Anglin bought Liebrock's interest in the business, and with Gerard's one-third interest named it Warsaw Hardware Company.

In those days, a corner of the back room of the store was a stable, complete with a haymow, for the team of horses used to make deliveries. Large items in stock then included wood and coal cook stoves, heating stoves, windmills, hand-turned cream separators, kerosene lamps and lanterns. Warsaw Hardware sold Oliver, John Deere, and New Idea horse-drawn machinery. The store was a favorite loafing place for men in the wintertime, as they would sit around the stove visiting and telling stories.

When Anglin's health began to fail in 1934, his partners bought him out. That same year Vern Frantz's daughter, Vena Myerly, joined the staff as a clerk and office person. She then bought in as a partner in 1942 when Gerard left the business.

Earl Parker chats with "Blue Boy" at the Parker Electric Company. The parakeet was given to Parker in 1951 by his daughter, Charlotte.

Dr. Ernest F. Van Osdol, second generation dentist (1879-1925)

Dr. Cortes Dean Van Osdol, third generation dentist (1903-1960)

Dr. Thomas D. Van Osdol, fourth generation dentist (b. 1940)

Frantz' son-in-law, Jack H. Beebe, who married his daughter June, joined the business in the late 1940s, but later sold his interest back to the Frantz family. Following Vern's death in 1966, his wife, Mandilla, and daughter, Vena, continued operating the business until the doors closed December 2, 1967.

Brian Szalai started Warsaw Tool Supply in 1986 at this long-time hardware location. When the two-story brick building was damaged by a fire in September 1998, Szalai removed the debris and built a new one-story structure for his tool business.

Fourth Generation Dentist

Ernest Flemming Van Osdol was the son of Dr. Charles Lee Van Osdol (1854-1930), a dentist who practiced from 1890 to 1915 in Dillsboro and Aurora, Indiana. Dr. Ernest Van Osdol acquired his degree of dental surgery in 1899 and practiced in Aurora for seven years. In 1906 he moved to Rushville, and in 1910 moved his practice to Warsaw. His dental parlor was located on the southwest corner of Center and Buffalo Streets above the F.P. Bradway grocery.

Ernest's son, Cortes Dean Van Osdol, graduated from Indiana University Dental School in 1934. He practiced six months with an uncle in Tiffen, Ohio, before moving to Warsaw. His dental office was first located above the United Telephone Company, but for most of his 25 years in Warsaw the office was at 216 E. Center Street.

Dean and Marjorie Van Osdol had seven children. Van Osdol died unexpectedly in 1960 of a heart attack at the Warsaw school armory while watching his son, Bill, play during the final minutes of a Tiger basketball game.

When Dean's son, Tom, graduated from high school in 1958 he had not decided on a profession. However, following a family "tradition," he went on to graduate with honors in 1964 from the Indiana University School of Dentistry. Following two years of service with the U.S. Army, Dr. Thomas Dean Van Osdol operated a dental office in the professional building at 600 E. Winona Avenue from 1966 to 1976. He was located in the Kosciusko Professional Arts building (now site of Grossnickle Eye Center) from 1976 to 1986, and since 1987 his dental office has been at 2283 Provident Court.

Shoe Repair Businesses

There have been numerous shoe repair businesses in Warsaw over the years. Glenn G. Smith owned the Smith Shoe Hospital at 108 N. Buffalo Street from about 1910 through the 1940s. V. Zehner had the Quality Shoe Repair at 213 S. Buffalo Street from around 1925 through the 1940s. In addition, the Warsaw Shoe Shop at 122½ W. Main

In the early 1900s, F.P. Bradway had a grocery store on the northwest corner of Center and Buffalo Streets, now site of National City Bank. On the far left is part of a sign showing Dr. Ernest Van Osdol's dental office on the second floor.

Street was owned by John W. Bough from the early 1930s through the 1950s.

Herb Kehler owned the Modern Cobbleries Company at 116 E. Center Street, next door to the Elks Building. Doug Kehler relates that Herb, his distant cousin, also had a stand that sat in front of the Elks Arcade along the edge of the street. The Interurban delivered leather to the stand for Herb to make and repair shoes.

This property sat vacant for a time, but at some point Herb Kehler deeded his property to Louis Breading, who then built the current Breading's Cigar Store in 1950. Norman Nine, a blind man, had a trailer with a popcorn stand that he often parked on the vacant lot in the late 1940s. Doug Kehler and his friends were always amazed that the man could give them the correct change when they bought popcorn.

In 1967, Larry Momeyer started a shoe repair business at 219 E. Center Street. When the Greyhound Bus Station moved in 1982, Momeyer relocated around the corner to 111 N. High Street, where his shoe repair shop has been ever since.

Harold E. Biltz was manager of the Shine Shoe Store on E. Center Street from 1960 to 1968. Since 1973, he has operated his own shoe repair business in his home at 1102 E. Center Street.

For a number of years, Frank Firestone operated a taxi service out of the former Greyhound Bus station at 111 N. High Street. Ed See replaced batteries and performed other minor car repairs there in the 1930s, and it was later occupied by Earl Parker's electrical business.

Saga of the Chinworth Stores

The first Chinworth connection to Warsaw was the purchase of a farm by Robert Chinworth about 1872. His second oldest son, William H. Chinworth (1837-1894), spent some time working on that farm. Upon William's death, his wife and their three youngest children—Robert, Irene and Augustus—struggled to make a living on the Warsaw farm. The farm later devolved to the Chinworths' son, Robert.

About 1910, Robert and Gus formed Chinworth Brothers Hardware, a plumbing supply, farm implement and hardware retail business located at 114 W. Main Street. William J. Chinworth came to Warsaw in 1918 to work for his uncles, Bob and Gus. Although destined to be a downtown merchant for 43 years and a Warsaw businessman and

The Elks Building in the 100 block of E. Center Street was decorated in 1916 for a patriotic celebration. Herb Kehler owned the Modern Cobbleries business which had the small building in front to store leather for repairing shoes.

community leader for 60 years, Bill started as a plumber's helper to Bob who installed windmills. He then took a business course at Valparaiso University and became the store's bookkeeper.

In 1920, Gus incorporated the partnership as the Warsaw Farm Supply Company, with Bill Chinworth and Harry Oram as officers. (Oram was also owner of the well-known Oram Wagon & Carriage Works on the northwest corner of Center and Lake Streets.) Gus and Bob ended their involvement with the Chinworth Hardware store about 1926, and Bill closed the operation shortly thereafter.

1927-c. 1930 Harry Oram again became a partner with Bill Chinworth, and they entered into another business relationship. The Chinworth-Oram store was initially located at 114 W. Main Street, but relocated prior to that building being destroyed by fire in 1932.

c. 1930-1933 The second location of Chinworth's appliance store was on the southeast

Ray Harroun won the first Indianapolis 500 race in 1911 with an average speed of 74 mph.

The Chinworth-Oram store on W. Market Street (c. late 1920s). Posing with a Maytag washer are, left to right: salesman Glenn Miller, who distributed to Mr. Chinworth for many years, William J. Chinworth, bookkeeper Susie J. Chinworth, original partner Harry Oram, Dave Miller, unknown, S.F. "Jim" Jordan, unknown.

Jimmy Durante, best known for his song "Inka Dinka Do," started his career in 1911 as a rag-time piano player and bandleader.

corner of Market and Lake Streets at 115 W. Market Street, later occupied by the Sears, Roebuck store. By this time Bill's sister, Susie J. Chinworth Hamman, became the store's book-keeper, and Harry had left the business.

c. 1933-1939 Chinworth's third location was at 205 S. Buffalo Street, the second storefront to the south of Market Street. By this time, Jungers furnaces and space heaters were included in the product line, in addition to Majestic ranges and refrigerators. Philco radios were also a long-time product sold at Chinworth's, and the neon "Philco" sign was transported from building to building as the store moved.

c. 1939-1948 The Chinworth store then moved to 109 S. Buffalo Street in the second storefront north of the alley on the east side of the street. Appliances continued to be the focus of the business, but at this location furniture was added to the product mix. This required buying trips to the Merchandise Mart in Chicago, and a storage shed was built about 1946 on the back of 532 E. Center Street. The sale of bottled propane gas was also began at this location and grew to be the primary focus of Chinworth's.

The 109 S. Buffalo store was where a gift and housewares shop was introduced. Ownership was vested in Bill's wife, Louese Chinworth, who did work in the store, but the initial operator was Hilda Hardman. Louese and Hilda also made regular buying trips to Chicago. The store featured

furniture out on the sidewalk, on display to attract attention, but with a note on the furniture that said "please do not sit." It is reported that the Klondaris boys, Terry and Peter, were known to wander down the sidewalk (from their family's Candy Kitchen just north on the corner) to sit on the furniture. An employee would come out of the store to chase them off and they'd go scampering and laughing down the sidewalk.

c. 1948-1952 Situated at 118 E. Market Street, this was the first storefront owned by Bill. It was third from the west in the old Opera House building. To the west was Robinson's Market. Chinworth purchased five of the six 22-foot store-fronts on the first floor, along with the land. The sixth area was the entrance to the Moose Lodge, formerly the grand staircase to the Opera House on the second floor.

c. 1952-1961 The Chinworth's location at 116 S. Buffalo Street was just south of the Lake City Bank and north of Haffner's Five and Ten. As one entered, this store featured appliances on the right and the gift store was on the left. By this time, Mary Moon had become the manager of the gift shop. In the late 1950s, Bill purchased the Village Gift Shop from Mr. and Mrs. Fred Myers, merging the stock of the Chinworth's gift store into it. The store was located on W. Market Street.

The transport of propane had become an added feature of Chinworth's. The business was incorporated about 1958 as a separate operation and was known as Chinworth-Holly. A retail dealer in Rochester by the name of Holly formed the partnership with Chinworth, but he died shortly after the business was formed.

c. 1961-1963 The Chinworth's store at 970 W. Lake Street was built to accommodate the then-dominant LP gas business. It was the first location that Bill actually built as an appliance store, and was next to the LP gas tanks that were used to service farm and industrial customers. The masonry building and appliance operation was sold to Redi-Gas, Inc. in 1963, however, the trans-port of liquid petroleum gas to dealers throughout Indiana continued by Chinworth.

At the height of operations, Chinworth-Holly had five transport rigs. Bill's brother-in-law, R.L. "Teak" Erwin, and long-time, faithful employee Earl Ketrow had bought in as equity partners by that time. Having been scaled down considerably, the operation was dissolved after Bill's death in 1978.

The primary products sold over the years by the Chinworth store included: Philco, Gibson and Amana household appliances, Jungers furnaces and Perfection stoves, and Maytag laundry equipment. Perfection stoves used kerosene for fuel and required a disposable wick for operation, which Chinworth's was still selling in 1960. Bill continued as a Maytag retailer until he sold the appliance business in 1963. The propane gas operations continued to grow, with the retail distribution then focused on bulk delivery for heating purposes.

Interestingly, although Bill operated out of seven different locations over the years, the phone number was always 419, until seven-digit dialing replaced it in the late 1950s.

Other Chinworth Ventures

William J. Chinworth was also involved as a silent partner with Owen Emerick in purchasing the Jet White Grocery at 111 S. Buffalo Street. Emerick had been a meat cutter for the grocery and wanted to purchase the business. This represented the first example of Bill's involvement as a silent partner, but most often maintaining a 51% ownership.

Herbert Robinson owned a competing grocery in the Opera House building on E. Market Street. Robinson's son was killed in action during World War II. Devastated by the loss, he decided to sell the operation. Thus, Bill Chinworth and Owen Emerick expanded their relationship by buying Robinson's Market. It remained at that location until Emerick built a new store in the 200 block of W. Market Street. The Robinson's Market name was used until Emerick bought out Chinworth's interest in the late 1950s and the grocery became known as Owen's Supermarket.

John Snell was a young buyer and salesman for Stephenson's department store on Center Street. In the late 1940s, Snell explained to Chinworth his interest in starting his own business. That conversation led to a partnership that lasted until Snell bought out the Chinworth interest in the late 1950s. The John Snell Ladies Apparel store originally opened on E. Market Street, but relocated to 109 S. Buffalo Street in a swap of locations with the Chinworth's appliance store.

About 1955, Donald Youse was manager for a prefabricated door manufacturer in Warsaw. Seeking to purchase the business and increase the capital stock, Youse approached Bill Chinworth as a

Looking east on W. Main Street across from the Courthouse Square, cars were parked in front of the Chinworth Building (c. 1940).

potential investor. Bill gathered in his close friend, Thomas Walter, owner-operator of the Walter Drug Stores, and they established the Champion Door Corporation of Indiana. Chinworth and Walter each owned 25%, with Youse owning the remaining half. The business was sold in 1968.

Bill Chinworth also owned various real estate in downtown Warsaw. The building at 114 W. Main Street, which depicts his name, has been occupied by the Kroger supermarket, Glover Furniture Store, and currently by Reinholt's Town Square Furniture.

During the 1950s and 1960s, Chinworth owned the buildings at 117-119 W. Center Street. When the Opera House at 114-122 E. Market Street was destroyed by fire in 1967, Chinworth built a one-story building for a new tenant, the Gamble's hardware store. Kline's Department Store occupied this building for many years. When the store closed, Lakeland Financial Corporation purchased the property.

Bill Chinworth also owned the Conrad building at 215-219 E. Center Street, one of the oldest properties in the downtown. It was originally the Conrad Wagon Works location, and for many years was occupied by the Kimm Paint Company.

About 1940, Bill purchased a 12-acre wooded lot on Old Road 30 east of Warsaw. He built a modest house for his father on a front corner of the property. Following his father's death in 1949, the house became the broadcasting studio of WKAM radio, owned by Joe Autenreith. The small house still sits nestled beside the woods on the

The 882-foot-long Titanic luxury ship hit an iceberg and sank on April 12, 1912.

Employees of the Warsaw Overall Company outside the factory in 1915 with owner William S. Felkner, center, wearing white and a straw hat.

The sewing area of the Warsaw Overall Company, June 13, 1913.

World War I, 1914-1918.

north side of Old Road 30 (Division Road) just east of new U.S. 30. The Chinworth heirs sold the property in 1993.

Portions of the Beyer Farm, located along Parker Street on the northeast side of Warsaw, was purchased by Bill Chinworth and Tom Walter in 1941. Several subdivisions were platted for residential development over the years, and when the U.S. 30 right-of-way was purchased for a bypass of downtown Warsaw, the property was bisected on a diagonal. Thus, the property was re-platted as Wayside Terrace to the north and Oak Glen Estates to the south of the highway.

An additional note of interest is the bridge that was built across the Tippecanoe River in the

1890s on the Robert Chinworth farm west of Warsaw. Appropriately referred to as the Chinworth Bridge, it provided a means for residents in towns to the west, such as Atwood and Etna Green, to cross the Tippecanoe River and not have to travel a long distance to get to Warsaw. The Chinworth Bridge was closed to automobile traffic in 1975, and it has since been placed on the National Registry of Historic Landmarks.

Warsaw Overall Company

At the turn of the century, partners William S. Felkner and Charles H. Ker owned The Globe clothing store. Felkner had been employed as a traveling salesman for an overall business. In 1911, Felkner founded the Warsaw Overall Company to manufacture overalls and coats for the railroad trade throughout the Midwest.

The Warsaw Overall Company began operations with 22 machines on August 1, 1911, in a room above Widaman's garage on Main Street. After being in business for about a year, Felkner constructed a 44-foot x 132-foot brick building with a full basement on the north side of the railroad tracks between Buffalo and Indiana Streets (now the municipal parking lot).

The cost to erect the new factory was $12,000, plus an additional $11,000 for machinery and fixtures. The following year a second story was added as the new sewing room. The main floor was occupied by offices and shipping and cutting rooms, and the basement was used for storing goods. At one time Warsaw Overall had as many as 200 employees.

In 1917, Ker sold his interest in The Globe and joined Felkner at the overall factory as vice president. When Felkner died in 1927, Ker and Flint Bash purchased the entire stock of the company. Warsaw Overall closed about 1932, prior to American Brattice Cloth occupying this building.

Warsaw Cut Glass

Oscar Johnson and John Carlson, owners of the Johnson-Carlson Cut Glass Company of Chicago, built a two-story brick structure in Warsaw on the southeast corner of Detroit and Smith Streets. Warsaw Cut Glass opened July 17, 1912, with expert cutters from Chicago. Turry Johnson, Oscar's brother, was appointed president of the Warsaw company.

Although the business closed in 1930 for a short time during the Depression, it reopened in 1933. Warsaw Cut Glass was sold to Jackson Dobbins in 1957, who started working as an apprentice cutter in 1914 at the age of 14, and by 1957 was considered a master glass artisan. He became known as the "Lone Cutter," working day and night to keep up with the demand for elegant hand-cut crystal.

In 1964, Randy Kirkendall started his apprenticeship under the direction of Dobbins. In 1980, Dobbins sold the business to Randy and his wife, Linda.

Free-hand design and a preservation of the art of glass cutting makes each original piece as desirable today as it was during the early 1900s to upscale department stores and hotels across the nation. Warsaw Cut Glass was accepted into the National Register of Historic Sites in 1984. In 2000, Warsaw Cut Glass opened a second shop in The Village at Winona (Lake).

Rozella Ford

Miss Rozella Ford farmed from 1912 to 1958 and was considered the county's "most successful lady farmer." She lived on a 400-acre farm southwest of Warsaw and also had a 226-acre farm near Burket. George Creakbaum was Miss Ford's right hand man during her last 17 years in operation, and his sons grew up helping on the farm.

At one time she had 100 head of cattle, 100 hogs, and raised corn, oats and hay. Always keeping farm interest before self-interest, in the late 1950s, Miss Ford once debated whether to buy a new television or a corn mulcher—and chose the mulcher.

In 1960, some area golfers formed the Lakeland Golfers Association. They purchased 200 acres of Miss Ford's farm for $50,000 to build the nine-hole Rozella Ford Community Golf Course. At the time of Miss Ford's death in 1964 at age 88, Dr. Virgil McCleary was secretary of the golf association. Upon payment of the remaining $25,000, the association received the deed to the property. The second nine holes were added a few years later.

"Firsts" for Ettinger

Joe J. Ettinger (1895-1974) had several "firsts" in his life. He was editor of the first Warsaw High School Tiger Annual in 1912. He was a member of the founding board of directors for the Greater Warsaw Community Foundation, now known as the Kosciusko County Foundation.

In addition, Ettinger was a key player in the founding of Zimmer Manufacturing in 1927. It was in the basement of Ettinger's home on Prairie Street that he and Justin O. Zimmer began making their own line of splints and orthopedic equipment that evolved into today's Warsaw-based Zimmer, Inc.

The staff members for publication of the first Warsaw High School Tiger Annual in 1912: Glennie Sellers, art editor; Joe Ettinger, editor-in-chief; Madeline Ruse, literary editor; Ed M. Andereck, athletic editor; Clem G. Michael, business manager; Francis Aller, local editor.

The boys' basketball team for the 1911-1912 season : Seated, left to right, Ed M. Andereck, Clem G. Michael (captain), Kenneth Berst, Frank M. Conklin (substitute). Standing, George Franklin, Frank Lucas, Coach Fred L. Rouch.

The girls' basketball team for the 1911-1912 season: Rose Schloss, Edith Garner, Gertrude Boyd (captain), Roberta Spencer (substitute), Marguerite Carroll, Madeline Ruse. The team's coach was Miss Frances M. Elder.

The Three Stooges first appeared in vaudeville shows in 1912.

The Zimmer Manufacturing Company was founded with Zimmer as president, W.S. Felkner as vice president, Ettinger as secretary, and W.S. Rogers as treasurer. When Zimmer died in 1951, Ettinger served as the company's president until he retired in 1954. The Chamber of Commerce named Ettinger "Man of the Year" in 1962.

An undated note in the *Times-Union* in the early 1970s states former president and chairman of the board at Zimmer Manufacturing Co., Joe Ettinger, raised a howl at Murphy Medical Center. In traction to relieve pain from what was believed to be a "slipped disc," Ettinger found that the pelvic traction belt used was one manufactured by a competing medical supply firm.

Still loyal to the firm where he was a fixture for so many years, Joe complained loud and clear to his physician that he wanted a Zimmer-made pelvic traction belt. A call to president J. Alan Morgan, and the company went into action to see that Joe was fitted with one of their own models. Ettinger was then reported to be resting comfortably in his room and enjoying chats with his friends.

License Bureau

From 1905 to 1912, individuals with automobiles purchased small silver seals for $1 at the local Chamber of Commerce office, which served as vehicle registrations. Owners were responsible for making their own license plate on which to affix the seal. Plates could be made of cardboard, wood, or tin.

The State of Indiana first began issuing license plates in 1913. In the 1920s, auto licenses were available at 113 E. Center Street in R.R. Henderson's electrical supply store. While the history of the Warsaw Branch of the Indiana License Bureau is not complete herein, the office was located in the 1930s at 116 N. Indiana Street in a building that faced the Centennial Theatre. The Bureau was in the Elks Arcade in 1942 through at least 1949, when Marie Stokes was the manager.

Ernest L. Hauth was manager from 1951 to 1956 when the Bureau was located at 301 W. Market Street. Hauth was responsible for setting up the Syracuse Branch. Mrs. Hauth recalls that in the 1950s, all plates had to be issued by March 1st and the License Bureau closed at noon on Wednesdays so the staff could go to factories and sell plates to the workers.

In 1961, under the direction of branch manager Nell Reed, the License Bureau moved to 2022 E. Winona Avenue in the Lakeview Shopping Center where there was a larger parking area. About 1971 the Bureau relocated to 120 W. Market Street (now site of Allstate Insurance).

Following a fire at that location about 1980, the License Bureau moved to the Arnolt Building on E. Center Street (a two-story building which sat at the current site of the Key Bank drive-thru), which was next door to City Hall at that time. Around 1983, branch manager Barb Eastlund moved the License Bureau to the southeast corner of Center and Lake Streets, and in 1996 the office was moved to the current location at 215 S. Lake Street.

Hodges Construction

In 1913, M.P. "Brick" Hodges started building houses and then branched into heavy construction. He was construction foreman for building the Westminster Hotel in Winona Lake. Hodges Construction built the original Dalton Foundry buildings, the Hugro plant on N. Detroit Street, the Braude-Pierce Furniture Factory (later Kimble Glass) on W. Market Street, and Little Crow Milling Company. The Center Ward School and the Junior High addition, and also the Gatke plant and old Winona Power Plant were built by Hodges, in addition to the Times Building and Joe Foote's restaurant on Center Street.

Brick Hodges was killed in 1936 at the construction site of the Plymouth school gymnasium. His sons, Al, Mike and Bob, completed the gym and also went on to construct the Farm Bureau Co-op building on the southeast corner of Market and High Streets (current site of City Hall) and an addition to Warsaw High School.

Some of the construction projects P.E. "Mike" Hodges completed from 1941 to 1954 included: the Kosciusko County REMC building, the Lake Theater, Mellencamp Furniture, the current Elks Building, Breading's Cigar Store, and Shine Shoe Store.

Savings & Loan Association

The Warsaw Building, Savings & Loan Association was founded as a state chartered association in 1913. It was converted to a federal association in 1974 and became the Warsaw Federal Savings & Loan Association. In 1981, the Warsaw association was acquired by well-established Mutual Home Federal Savings & Loan Association of Muncie, Indiana, which was founded in 1889. Leo Pfister oversaw the Warsaw branch of Mutual Federal Savings Bank when it opened in 1981. Max Courtney, now vice president regional manager, succeeded Pfister in 1983.

Public Library

The early history of the public using books in the community is rather vague, but people were known to loan and borrow books from each other. An organization in the 1850s known as the McClure Workingmen's Institute was founded by William McClure. A somewhat wealthy man, McClure enjoyed helping to improve the conditions of the working classes through the Workingmen's Institutes.

WARSAW AND WAYNE TOWNSHIP PUBLIC LIBRARY, WARSAW, IND.—1

The Warsaw Public Library opened April 1, 1917, with approximately 5,000 books.

About the time of the Civil War, a county library was established in Warsaw, although the location is unknown. After 1858, however, Warsaw had a three-story brick schoolhouse on the southwest corner of Market and Detroit Streets, and it is quite likely that the first library open to the public was started there.

The first reported "reading room" was started by Captain John N. Runyan in 1867 after the Civil War. The reading room was on the second floor of the Phoenix Block, located below the publishing rooms of the *Northern Indianian.*

The Warsaw Public Library was established in 1881. Books formerly belonging to a county library or held elsewhere were turned over to the Warsaw Public Library by 1885 and housed in the basement of the old Center Ward School on the southeast corner of Detroit and Market Streets.

In March of 1914, twelve women's organizations in the city coordinated a meeting at the Methodist Church to discuss plans for a separate library building. A representative from the Indiana State Library Commission explained the procedures needed to obtain a Carnegie Library. The School Board turned over the old library to the City Council and a resolution was passed February 19, 1915, to levy a library tax which would generate about $2,000 income. Those funds would be used to secure a Carnegie building.

Prizes were first put in boxes of Cracker Jack in 1912.

The first Library Board was appointed in 1915. Officers were: Mrs. William Conrad, president; Mrs. W.W. Reed, vice president; and Flint E. Bash, secretary; along with members A.G. Wood (Mayor 1904-1906); Mrs. Emma Shackelford; T. Wayne Anglin; and H.S. Kaufman.

A grant of $15,000 was received from the Carnegie Corporation in 1916, and the lot on the northwest corner of Center and Detroit Streets was chosen as the site for a new library. The house that stood there had several owners over the years, and had also been used as the McCoy Sanitarium.

The citizens wanted to acquire both lots occupied by the sanitarium, but didn't have enough funds. Mayor B.F. Richardson was able to purchase the other lot, with the understanding that the library board would purchase it when they were financially able to do so. The Warsaw Public Library opened in April of 1917 with about 5,000 volumes and 1,936 borrowers. Miriam Netter was the librarian, and her assistant was Anna Fitch.

In the early 1990s, the Warsaw Community Public Library began making plans for a major expansion and the entire block was eventually purchased. The Glenn Dufur home and First Church of Christ Scientist along Detroit Street, the Reed & Earhart law office (formerly Titus Funeral Home) facing Main Street, and the Masonic Lodge facing High Street, were all demolished for this project.

The Library celebrated the opening of its new facility in September of 1998. The library's book volume in 2000 reached 91,241, with a circulation of 409,118. Ann Zydek has been the library director since 1985.

Myer Levin & Sons, Inc.

In 1914, Myer Levin & Sons, Inc., scrap iron and steel processors, was located on the east side of North Detroit Street slightly north of Fort Wayne Street. After a fire destroyed the building, the yard was moved to the west side of Detroit Street at the canal by Center Lake. Myer and Rosa Levin donated a part of their property to the City for establishment of the public tennis courts.

When World War II ended, Howard Levin joined his father's business. After years of negotiations, the City purchased the scrap yard property and in 1980 the business moved to its present location at the intersection of State Road 15 North and U.S. 30. In 1986, the property beside Center Lake was converted into the Warsaw Biblical Gardens which includes plants named throughout the Bible.

Norman Rockwell's paintings graced the covers of the Saturday Evening Post from 1916 through 1963.

Mellencamp's Furniture

Brothers Fred and Jesse Mellencamp pooled their resources of $8,000 in 1915 to buy out the Albert Powers Furniture Store located on the southwest corner of Center and Indiana Streets. The telephone company maintained its offices and switchboards above the furniture store.

Mellencamp's Furniture Store struggled through its first year with about $17,000 in sales. Fred and Jesse worked both day and night as their own sales force, delivering merchandise by horse and wagon, and maintaining their bookkeeping.

Mellencamp's first employee was Harold Shepler, and Miss Vera Cook was then hired as the company's first bookkeeper from 1917 to 1931. Fred bought out Jesse's interest in 1932 during the Depression and continued to operate the business with his wife. The store's ice boxes were made by Crosley and Kelvinator, with the first line of appliances added in 1935.

In December of 1947, Fred moved the business to a new store at 113-115 E. Market Street, directly west of the Times Building. The two-story structure with a basement (currently occupied by Lake City Bank offices) provided nearly 17,000 square feet of floor space. With the exception of one very large firm in Fort Wayne, at that time Mellencamp's offered the largest assortment of rugs and carpets of any retail store in northern Indiana.

Fred Mellencamp was described as a spirited, hard-working man with a clean, wholesome way of life and a strong will to progress. He was a fine connoisseur of sweets who bought only the finest of milk chocolates, which he was known to generously give to friends and associates each holiday season.

East Center Street Stores

George M. Stephenson was a salesman for Marshall Field & Co. in Chicago. About 1915, he came to Warsaw and opened Stephenson's dry goods and millinery store on the second floor at 111 E. Center Street (west side of the alley). Eventually he occupied both the first and second floors, expanding the business to include ladies and children's clothing. The store closed a short time before Stephenson died in 1953.

The location of 113-115 E. Center Street (east side of the alley) where the current three-story

Looking west from the middle of the 100 block of Center Street in the 1950s. The Cox Studio sign on the Stephenson's building directed customers to their studio in the basement.

Looking west on Center Street in the 1950s from the southeast corner of Center and Indiana Streets, one could clearly see the Boice Theatre. Next door was the Phipps department store on the first floor of the Eagles building.

brick Eagles Building sits has quite an extensive history. During the mid- to late 1800s, the Kirtley House hotel was situated on this property, and by 1890 the hotel was known as the White House.

That frame building was removed sometime around 1900 so Mayor Charles Rigdon could construct a three-story brick building. The popular Liberty Café was first located in the Rigdon Building when it opened during the 1920s. The Rigdon building was demolished in the late 1920s to construct the current three-story brick Eagles Building.

The E.W. Gresso store, which was started in the 1920s, first had stores at 115-119 S. Buffalo Street and 107-111 W. Market Street. The store was owned by E. Williard Gresso, president; Calvin E. Gresso, vice president; and Irvin E. Gresso, secretary. In the 1930s, the store was still located on S. Buffalo Street, but by the 1940s E.W. Gresso had moved to the first floor of the Eagles Building on Center Street.

The Burr Department Store then occupied the space at 113 E. Center Street during the late 1940s through the mid-1950s, eventually expanding to include all of the storefront space to 117 E. Center Street. The Burr Department Store carried a large selection of nationally advertised lines of merchandise.

The Phipps department store was then located at 113 E. Center Street for several years, but by 1959 the Sengers store occupied this site. The Sengers store, which carried draperies, bedspreads, luggage, lawn furniture, and other related merchandise, then moved across the alley to 109-111 E. Center Street.

By the late 1960s, Falvey's clothing store occupied the first floor of the Eagles Building. Don E. Childs was manager of Falvey's men's department in the early 1970s. By the late 1970s, the name of the business had been changed to Childs'. Don Childs managed the men's and boys' clothing department, and his wife, Diane, managed the ladies and children's department.

Since Childs' closed, the Eagles Building has been occupied by the Compton Furniture Store, followed by the Anderson Furniture Store. In the late 1990s, it was used as an antique mall, and in June 2001, Jon Blackwood opened the Downtown Mattress Showcase at 113-115 E. Center Street.

In 1916, the first Hallmark retail greeting card store opened in Kansas City.

"Sarge" Lichtenwalter

With thirty years in military service, Ralph C. Lichtenwalter rightfully earned the nickname "Sarge." Bob Lichtenwalter states that his father was a first sergeant for 28 years. At age 21 in 1915, Ralph was with the Mexican Border Campaign. In 1918 during World War I, he was stationed in France. Lichtenwalter also served during World War II. From 1943 to 1945, he was assigned in the South Pacific, New Guinea and the Philippines, and fought the Japanese in the Battle of Zig Zag Pass.

Sarge was like a father to every serviceman he knew. Having served with Company L 152nd Infantry, he was still active with the local National Guard after he retired. Following his military service, Lichtenwalter was a Warsaw mail carrier for eleven years and also worked at the Sheriff's Department.

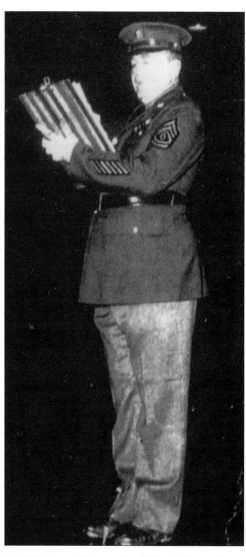

Ralph C. "Sarge" Lichtenwalter (1894-1983) served thirty years in the military.

The Richmond Family

Fred and Thelma Richmond moved to Warsaw from Lebanon, Tennessee, about 1915. Over the years, Fred worked at the Oram, Munson and McKown garages. The Richmonds lived on N. Buffalo Street near the Center Lake boat launch.

Their son, Robert (born in 1918), recalls catching his first fish at Center Lake and remembers the toboggan on the east side of the beach. Bob states that when there was high water, the entire area on the south side of Center Lake would flood and they had to use a rowboat to get to the shed where their firewood was stored. During high water in the mid- to late 1920s, Fred Richmond would take his son to the Center Ward School on Main Street in a rowboat.

As a youngster, Bob participated in boxing at the Boys Club, under direction of the well-respected and admired Pete Thorn, and is honored to be listed on the "Pete's Boys" plaque at the Club. Later, Bob was in the Welter Weight class (134-140 lbs.) when he was in the Army, winning 15 of 16 bouts. Bob described Mr. Thorn's technique of teaching kids to swim. As the boys would attempt to swim across the lake, Thorn would be giving them encouragement from a rowboat alongside them.

When Bob Richmond returned to Warsaw in 1947 following his military service in France, his deep voice and bubbly personality was introduced to our community via his Saturday afternoon radio show. Called "Melody Morgue," the program aired on the local WKAM radio station owned by Joe Autenreith. Richmond's program featured big band music from the jazz era, including the popular Duke Ellington and Count Basie bands.

From the mid 1950s and during the 1960s, Bob had a program on WRSW Saturday mornings from 10:00 a.m. to noon. Richmond also had a one-hour program on Sunday afternoons called "Twilight and Strings." He played semi-classical music and would speak to his listening audience, telling jokes and talking about the bands, as soft music played in the background.

Harvey Miller, the morning news commentator at that time, recalls his part in the program when "The Old-Timer" came to visit Bob. Harvey would bang doors and stomp around to make noise as "The Old-Timer" (aka Richmond with a voice change) arrived to disrupt Bob's program. "The Old-Timer," who referred to Bob as "Sonny," was always up to something and always giving Bob a hard time.

In the late 1940s, Bob Richmond hosted a radio program called "Melody Morgue" each Saturday afternoon on local station WKAM.

During a musical career that spanned 50 years (1947-1997), the "Bob Richmond Band" was comprised of trios, quartets and quintets. In early years, Richmond played the stand-up drum in his quartet that included Jim Yeazel (current mayor of Plymouth, Indiana), bass player; Kenny Ranard, piano; and Dick Bibler, alto sax. He formed another band later that included Paul Russell, piano; "Blacky" Eherenman, alto sax; Johnny White, drums; and Richmond, trumpet. The band had many engagements at the Warsaw Elks Club and Holiday Inn, in addition to many New Year's Eve and private parties throughout northern Indiana.

The Richmond family had many wonderful friends in Warsaw over the years and Bob has fond memories of growing up in our community. He recalls one incident, however, when his cousin Rosemary and her date went to the Centennial Theatre. Even though there were vacant seats on the main floor, the manager made them sit in the balcony. When Rosemary came home after her date and told Bob where they had to sit, he called his friend, Nick Mallers (then owner of the Centennial Theatre), and explained what had happened. The manager admitted he had sent the young couple to the balcony, and Mallers fired him that same evening.

After retiring from United Telephone Company, Bob Richmond was elected to three terms on the City Council (1984-1995) and served ten years as president of the Council. He continues to be active in the community, serving on the Warsaw Parks Board and Multi-Township EMS Board. Bob is a

Leaders of the Big Bands of the 1930s and 1940s included Count Basie, Fats Weller, Tommy and Jimmy Dorsey.

Chef Bishop Waymond "BW" Ferguson and his wife, Viola, rest outside one of the restaurants he worked at (c. 1920s).

BW was one of the early head chefs at the Hotel Hays. Bob Richmond recalls his uncle being smartly dressed in his white chef's uniform. During the busy summer months, black men came from Indianapolis to work at the Hotel Hays, and for the winter months, BW and his wife, Viola, would travel to Florida where he cooked at fine restaurants in the larger cities. Ferguson was later employed as a chef at Joe Foote's restaurant on Center Street.

The Fergusons had ten children, eight sons and two daughters. One son and one daughter died as children. When he retired as a chef, BW pushed a cart with big wheels around town that held the supplies he used to sweep sidewalks and wash windows.

Some of his sons worked at Dalton Foundries for a while. Pete and his wife, Oweeda, worked at the Hotel Hays for a time with his parents. Oweeda then had her own restaurant on N. Detroit Street called Oweeda's Place, where brother-in-law Arnold helped out and Bob Richmond washed dishes for a while. Richmond recalls that everyone would rave about Oweeda's potato salad when, in fact, his mother, Thelma, was the one who actually made it. Oweeda also worked at the Camel Club and had a catering business.

A music enthusiast himself, Bob Richmond fondly remembers the famous "Fats" Waller, one of the finest jazz pianists ever. In the early 1930s, Fats came to Warsaw for a week to perform in a tent at the downtown street fair. Mr. Waller stayed with the Fergusons during that time, and as a young boy Bob recalls the enjoyable time he had visiting with him.

Hardware Stores

R. Gordon Rutter owned Rutter Hardware at 113-115 W. Center Street in the early 1900s. Harry C. Hall purchased Rutter Hardware in 1945 and moved the business to 119 S. Buffalo Street. The name was changed to Hall Hardware.

When Hall died in 1955, Norman "Laddie" Hoffer, who married Hall's widow, continued operation of the hardware store. Lester "Bud" Vandermark owned the business from 1971 to 1987. Mark Bishopp took over management until January 1998, when Hall True Value Hardware was sold to Mike and Dawn Burgess. The store moved to the former Rocket TV building on E. Winona Avenue in the fall of 2001.

past president of the Warsaw Optimist Club and one of only five individuals to achieve the designation of Distinguished Member. He has also been involved with Toastmasters for many years and is a Distinguished Toastmaster.

The Ferguson Family

When the Bishop Waymond Ferguson family first came to Warsaw, they shared a large house on N. Buffalo Street with the Richmonds. Thelma Richmond was a sister to "BW." Ferguson was a personal friend of Indiana poet James Whitcomb Riley, who lived in Warsaw during his early years, and the two were known around town as "Whit and Fergie."

After founding Sharp Hardware in Milford in 1905, about 1915 Harlan Sharp opened his Warsaw hardware store at 113-115 W. Center Street next to the Indiana Loan & Trust Company. In addition to hardware items, Sharp sold paints, sporting goods, Westinghouse appliances, and McCormick-Deering farm equipment.

His son, Jack, worked at the store from 1956 to 1971. Jack's brother-in-law and sister, Harry and Esther Gawthrop, were also involved in the business. The Sharp building was sold in 1971 to First National Bank who demolished it for their current parking lot.

Harlan and Jack built the brick building at 2307 E. Center Street for their Sharp's Farm Store, which sold International farm equipment. Sharps operated the farm store until 1957 when they sold the building. It was then occupied by Tractor Supply Company for a time, and since 1994 has been the site of Executive Office Products.

Author Theodore Dreiser

American author Theodore Dreiser (1871-1945), who lived in Warsaw about 1884-1886 during his early teens, wrote *A Hoosier Holiday* in 1916 which describes his travels back to Warsaw years later. In 1931, Dreiser titled his autobiography *Dawn*, which describes in greater detail his years in Warsaw. Excerpts of his books include:

"Most of the cities and towns of America, to say nothing of the Middle West, have always seemed to me to be deficient in both individuality and charm. . . But Warsaw remains in my memory as one of the most agreeable minor residence towns it has ever been my pleasure to know. . . At that time it lay in the very centre of three small but beautiful lakes, two of them so close that they formed an integral part of the town, its streets and houses following their nearer shore lines. The third—Eagle—was only two miles distant from the public square. . . And I was possessed of a sense of peace as well as beauty here—such sylvan and idyllic beauty as rarely elsewhere I have met.

"In spring, summer and fall here—quite as much so in winter, really—the lakes, the Tippecanoe River, and the woods were delightful. Though one might not own a rowboat, one could fish and swim from the banks or the public and private piers, the owners of which did not object to their use. Also boats were to be hired for very little—twenty-five cents for an afternoon or evening.

"In regard to the bicycle, the first one I ever saw was in Warsaw in 1884—a high-wheeled one . . . and the first pair of roller skates I ever saw was in the same place in 1885, when some adventurous amusement provider came there and opened a roller-skating parlor.

"The first ice cream soda fountain I ever saw, or the first ice cream soda I ever tasted, was served to me in Warsaw, Indiana, at the corner bookstore, opposite the courthouse. That was in 1885. It had just succeeded a drink known as the milk shake, which had attained great popularity everywhere the preceding year.

"Warsaw was an idyllic town for a youth of my temperament and age to have been brought to just at that time. It was so young, vigorous and hopeful. I recall that never-ending delight the intense sense of beauty its surrounding landscape gave me . . . People were always coming to Warsaw to shoot ducks in the marshes about, or to fish or summer on the lakes.

This photo was taken just before the three-story building on the south side of the Courthouse Square, occupied for many years by Sharp Hardware, was demolished for the First National Bank's parking lot.

The Crystal Dairy Bar on S. Buffalo Street served delicious malts, sundaes, sodas, and ice cream.

Crystal Dairy owner Norm Kelly prepares to make deliveries. The Crystal Dairy sat back off the road at 701 S. Buffalo Street.

"The principal streets, Centre, Buffalo and South, were better built than in my time, and actually wider than I had recalled them as being. Only on the southwest corner of Centre and Buffalo Streets (the principal street corner opposite the court-house) where once had stood a bookstore, and next to that a small restaurant with an oyster counter, and next to that a billiard and pool room, the three constituting in themselves the principal meeting or loafing place for the idle young of all ages, the clever workers, school boys, clerks and whatnot of the entire town, and I presume county—all this was entirely done away with, and in its place was a stiff, indifferent, exclusive look-ing bank building of three stories in height, which gave no least suggestion of an opportunity for such life as we had known to exist here.

"Warsaw was becoming famed at this time for its scenic beauty. Railroads offered excursions to Warsaw from Fort Wayne, Indianapolis, South Bend, and even points farther off. A great new pleasure park was opened on Eagle Lake, and the stores and shops generally began to look more prosperous. The variety and beauty of the craft on the several lakes increased at a great rate. A canal was cut between Pike and Center Lakes, so as to provide a longer water trip for visitors."

Excerpt from *DAWN* Copyright © 1931 by Theodore Dreiser and reprinted with the permission of Black Sparrow Press.

American Red Cross

The American Red Cross of Kosciusko County was chartered in 1917 by the American National Red Cross to provide Red Cross services in Kosciusko County. Judge F.E. Bowser was the first board chairman (1917-1920), followed by John Shoup (1920-1946). The first Red Cross office was located in the Boice Theatre on E. Center Street, and by 1949 had moved into two rooms in the Opera House at 124 E. Market Street.

The Red Cross office then moved to the northeast corner of Detroit and Market Streets in 1955 and in 1967 relocated to 501 N. Lake Street in the former North Side Grocery building. The Red Cross office has been at its current location at 320 N. Buffalo Street since 1995.

The first bloodmobile was held February 13, 1951, and collected 127 units of blood. The need for nursing assistant volunteers was discussed in 1953, and the "Gray Ladies" were formed in 1955 to meet that need, with them donating 1,631 hours in 1957. Lucy Whiteneck states that she is the only "Gray Lady" who, after nearly 50 years, is still helping with the Red Cross blood drives.

During 1968, the Red Cross handled eight to ten military-related calls each day due to the Vietnam War. The Welfare Department asked the Red Cross in 1972 to furnish volunteers to help establish the Well Baby Clinic and Big Brothers/Big Sisters. The Red Cross coupon book fundraiser was started in 1992.

The Red Cross served 13,250 Kosciusko County residents in 2000. Services provided include: aquatics classes, first aid/CPR, blood services, disaster services, and Armed Forces emergency services. There are currently 247 vol-unteers that help with the Red Cross programs.

Crystal Dairy

In 1918, the Crystal Dairy was founded by local dairyman Floyd Kelly at 701 S. Buffalo Street. Products included milk, coffee and whipping creams, chocolate milk, cottage cheese, yogurt, butter, and orangeade. In addition, the Crystal Dairy Bar restaurant next door carried a full menu including steak, pork chops and chicken. The fountain service offered malts, sodas, and sundaes.

Marvin Weirick and Walt Sutherland were plant managers, and Lyda Stokes was the office manager. Lewis Dobbins delivered milk for the Crystal Dairy from 1948 to 1956 and recalls passing out tickets to dairy customers for a free matinee at the Centennial Theatre. Upon Floyd's death, his wife and son, Norman, continued operation of the Crystal Dairy until the business was sold in 1956 to Sunshine Farms of Lafayette.

Another business venture, Crystal Preforming, was started by Norman and his mother in 1953 to supply preformed cartons for the dairy industry. Production lines were first installed in a building on State Road 25 at the city's west edge.

The business began with two employees and one Pure-Pak pre-forming machine. The Pure-Pak Milk Carton Division served over 100 dairies in a five-state area. At that time, Crystal Dairy was a primary supplier of milk to community retail outlets.

The business expanded, and in 1957 the Visual Plastic Packaging Division introduced three ways to package hard-to-wrap items for other industries. This service included bubble pack, skin-pack and vacuum forming of cartons and packaging for retail items such as hardware, curtain rods, cosmetics and vitamins. The Preforming Division developed the first Pure-Pak paper carton used for the distribution and display of apple cider on a national basis. By the 1960s, however, this division had converted to the plastic coated Pure-Pak milk carton, and Crystal Preforming had six pre-forming machines working in its production line.

Jet White Groceterias

John H. Hall purchased the Thomas Grocery at 111 S. Buffalo Street in 1918, did some remodeling, and re-opened the store ten days later as the Jet White Groceteria #1. Hall established neighborhood grocery stores in towns throughout northern Indiana during the 1920s. Winona Lake, Leesburg,

The Crystal Dairy Bar's sign on S. Buffalo Street invited patrons for lunch.

As early as 1903, J.M. Cook and John H. Hall were owners of the Cook & Hall Grocery located in the Biggs Building at 121 W. Center Street. In those days, groceries were delivered to the customer's door.

Syracuse, Ligonier, Nappanee, Elkhart, and Columbia City also had Jet White stores. Hall had a warehouse along the Pennsylvania Railroad tracks and was able to purchase large quantities of inventory.

Jet White #1 was operated by John's son, Harry C. Hall, and William S. Felkner. Beginning in the early 1930s and for almost the next 38 years, Glen and Velma Emerick were proprietors of Jet White #1. Mike Weirick and Jim Mayer owned the business in the early 1970s. Jet White #1 closed about 1975 after a fire.

Family members believe this is John H. Hall or his son, Harry C. Hall, in the Jet White #1 grocery (c. 1920).

In the early 1900s, a grocery on the southwest corner of Market and Union Streets was known as The Golden Rule. The store was owned by Jefferson M. Hankins and his son, Marvin. The business was later sold to John Hall and became known as the Jet White #5. In the mid-1920s, the grocery was managed by Fred Walton.

George W. Bruner began driving a delivery truck for John Hall about 1929 and eventually married his daughter. Hall and Bruner were co-owners of the Jet White #5 in the 1940s, and Bruner was the sole proprietor from 1950 until the store closed in 1964.

For a time, Jet White #9 was located at 1314 E. Center Street, and Charles Anglin was the manager of that store in the 1920s. There was also a Jet White store on the southwest corner of Lake and Market Streets for a number of years.

The first Goodyear blimp debuted in 1912.

Warsaw Rotary Club

After its initial organization in 1905 in Chicago by lawyer Paul P. Harris and three friends, an organizational meeting was held in 1919 to establish the Warsaw Rotary Club. In the 1920s, the club helped to form the local Chamber of Commerce, and in 1927 started "Rotary Toy Day" to help children in need during the holidays through The Salvation Army. The club sponsored its first exchange student in 1952 from Germany and sponsored many others almost annually until the mid 1990s.

The club has supported Mobile Meals for many years through the leadership of Bob Gast, and provides scholarships for students and funds in support of numerous efforts. The Warsaw Biblical Gardens, Shrine Building at Kosciusko County Fairgrounds, YMCA, and Baker Boys Club are some of the other projects the club has sponsored.

In 1971 John Snell and Bill Chinworth became the first "Paul Harris Fellows" of the Warsaw Club, sending $1,000 each to the Rotary Foundation. Since then, the club has given over $100,000 to the Rotary Foundation to support many efforts of Rotary International to address needs around the world.

Three local members have had the distinction of serving as District Governors of Rotary International: Arthur Raabe (1942-1943), William Chinworth (1948-1949), and John Snell (1969-1970). The club presents an annual "Pete Thorn Achievement Award" to recognize a person who has served the community in the spirit of former Rotarian, L.N. "Pete" Thorn.

Rotary Club membership currently consists of about 80 men and women. Meetings continue to include "Louie in the News," in remembrance of another long-time member, Lewis H. "Peanuts" Breading, who for many years read the current local and world events during the meetings.

City Improvements

The City initiated a plan in 1919 to clean up Center Lake and improve the sanitary conditions around the lake, by purchasing land on the south shore for a city park. At that time, junk vehicles and trash had accumulated in the area, along with homes in disrepair. The first step in the Council's cleanup program was for the city to acquire the ground bordering the south shore of Center Lake between Buffalo and Detroit Streets, including the property at the foot of Buffalo Street, and also part of the ground then owned by the Big Four Railroad.

The city had already acquired a number of lots in that section a few years before from the Haas brothers. "Rigdon Row" was owned by Mayor Charles A. Rigdon. The Rigdon Row and other land south of the lake was acquired through condemnation proceedings.

An agreement provided for the appointment of three appraisers—one named by the Council, one named by Mr. Rigdon, and those two to name a third. The construction of a park and playground, in turn, created the need for a city park board, which was soon established.

Chapter 8

Aviation in Warsaw

The history of aviation in Warsaw dates back to the early 1900s, not long after the Wright Brothers made their famous flight at Kitty Hawk, North Carolina, in 1903.

Irene Dome fondly recalls her uncle, Chalmers Dome, and his interest in flying. Nicknamed "Domie," he and other local mechanics pooled their skills and resources to build a "flying machine." The group included Henry Anson, who later worked at Cook's motorcycle garage; Frank Conklin, a mechanic at Oram's garage; and Marion Hart and George Mowrey, who worked in other local garages.

The "airplane" was powered by a 20-horse-power, two-cylinder automobile engine. About 1915, the plane was wheeled to the west side of Winona Lake for a test flight. Although it did leave the ground on several occasions, it was not very high, nor did it fly very far.

About 1922, brothers Wilbur and Raymond Zimmer acquired a Standard bi-plane and opened their airstrip on the Zimmer farm west of Warsaw between the Pennsylvania and Winona Railroad tracks (now the site of Gill's Auto & Truck Parts). D.H. "Jerry" Lessig recalls taking his first plane ride there in 1927 at age five.

There was also an airfield on the east side of town around 1931-32 called Beyer Field, where the Lincoln Elementary and Sacred Heart Schools are now located. Barnstormer Harold Preston had a plane powered by a Liberty engine and a Model T Ford radiator. He could sometimes be seen flying from the vacant lots along Argonne Road in East Warsaw.

The farm on the northwest corner of State Road 15 and Monoquet Road was originally owned by Daniel E. Smith, then by his son, Howard S. Smith Sr., and currently by his grandson, Howard "Chub" Smith, Jr. With a hangar, an aircraft franchise

An aerial view in 1946 of the Smith farm on the corner of State Road 15 N. (bottom) and Monoquet Road going west. The large plane on the left sitting at the corner was used by an aero club to hold meetings. The Smith Airport grass landing strip is shown just above the long, narrow building in the foreground.

Smith brothers Robert, left, and Wilbur, right, with their aluminum Luscomb plane, one of the first all-metal airplanes. Robert was one of the first from Kosciusko County lost in World War II, when his boat was torpedoed in the North Sea.

Warsaw pilot Raymond Zimmer in 1927.

Jake Menzie, Raymond Zimmer, and Bill Snyder built this car about 1930 with a 4-cylinder engine from a Henderson motorcycle. It was painted to commemorate the celebration July 25, 1948, to name the municipal airport "Memorial Field" in honor of soldiers who died during World War II.

and a will to fly, Howard Smith, Sr. and his sons, Robert and Wilbur, made a grass strip runway and started Smith Airport in 1938 on their farm. Chub remembers helping his father cut the timber from their woods to build the original hangar, which still stands today, although it is now surrounded by Fahl Manufactured Homes.

Sky-borne clients in the 1930s included Paul Lowman, Jake Menzie, Ray Zimmer, Bill VanDoran, Wilbur Hoppus, Bill Bailey, Bob Murtaugh, and Francis Brown. About 1945, some of these men joined forces with air-minded young men from Goshen and formed the Warsaw Aero Club with about 25 members.

About the same time, Fred Strauss, Jr. flew in a large Curtis C-46 cargo airplane. It sat on the corner of the Smith farm for several years. The plane seated about 30 people and the Aero Club used it as their meeting room. Chub Smith still has the cowbell the club used to call their meetings to order.

Over the years vandals took the control panel and other parts from the cargo plane, and in 1950 after the Aero Club disbanded, a private firm in Miami, Florida, bought it. Chub recalls that a crew worked two weeks to get it running again so it could fly to Florida. However, the pilot and co-pilot still had no instruments that worked, no lights and no radio, and they carried only a partial load of gas.

A couple pressure gauges mounted on the wings were the only aid they had, other than the years of flight experience of both men. In fact, the landing gear would not go up, which probably also slowed their speed. The crew got the plane in the air, and much to the amazement of local flyers, they were successful in getting the plane to its destination.

Some of the members of the former Aero Club secured a lease on a parcel of land four miles northeast of Warsaw (approximate site of the current airport) and Sportsman's Field was born. However, strict rules during World War II required an armed guard at airports around the clock, which caused both Smith Field and Sportsman's Field to close.

Bob Smith and Bob Burden, both pilots at Sportsman's Field, were among the first from Kosciusko County lost in World War II when their submarine was attacked in the North Sea. After being closed three years, Howard Smith, Sr. and his other son, Wilbur, re-opened Smith Field in 1945 by leasing it to Rev. Paul C. Hartford. Known as "the flying preacher," Hartford operated a flying school for ministers and missionaries, and the airport was called "Victory Field."

The State Commander of the Civil Air Patrol spoke at a meeting held at the Warsaw Masonic Temple. He talked about airplanes and airports, with those in attendance showing great enthusiasm.

Contributions came from interested citizens in Warsaw and surrounding towns to assist in raising the funds to purchase land. When $11,000 had been raised, it was turned over to the Chamber of Commerce for the purpose of acquiring some property.

State engineers chose land three miles north of Warsaw, east of the Big Four Railroad and State Road 15. The 117-acre tract was held by three owners who were contacted, and eventually all agreed to sell for the purpose of an airport. The landowners deeded their properties to the Chamber of Commerce in 1945.

The Warsaw City Council passed Ordinance No. 170 on February 18, 1946, establishing the Warsaw Board of Aviation Commissioners. Mayor Frank Rarick appointed William Chinworth, John Widaman, Tony Mathia, and Kenneth Stokes to the first Board of Aviation.

On June 5, 1947, the Chamber of Commerce deeded the three parcels of land to the City of Warsaw, creating what was then known as the Warsaw Memorial Airport, in memory of Kosciusko County soldiers who died during World War II.

Joseph F. Carlin, who became a civilian flight instructor in 1942, always wanted to have his own flight service so he, along with his wife, Dora, came to Warsaw and started Carlin Airways, Inc., based at Smith Airport. He had one airplane, a Tailorcraft. His work demanded long hours and soon the Carlins hired Kenny Linn, an aircraft and engine mechanic, who became their right-hand man. The venture became a family affair, with Dora doing the bookwork and anything else she could help with.

In 1947, the Carlins moved their business to the newly established airport. The runways were dirt at first. Getting off or on the ground during spring mud was difficult, and night flying without lights was nearly impossible. In addition to working with many student pilots, Joe oversaw the construction of an administration building and some T-hangars. By this time, the Carlins had three Tailorcrafts, two Cessnas, a young son named J.F. Carlin, Jr., and Dora had learned to fly.

On July 25, 1948, Warsaw's new $50,000 municipal airport officially opened with a thrilling air show, including acts with stunt pilots, crop-dusting demonstrations, and passenger rides all day. A helicopter built by Bell Aircraft amused the crowd by flying straight up and down, backward and sideways. The airport board was acknowledged for the success of the airport project. Engineer Donald Lessig and Robert Hall, of the Chamber of Commerce, were also recognized.

The scheduled hot air balloon ascension was postponed to the following Sunday due to high winds. However, the crowd received a special

Joe and Dora Carlin, owners of Carlin Airways, Inc., managed the Warsaw Airport from the late 1940s through 1961.

Airport manager Joe Carlin with his children, Fritz and Bette-Jo (c. 1952).

show that day by an Air Force F-80 jet plane that made repeated passes over the Warsaw Municipal Airport, sweeping the runways at 550 to 600 miles per hour.

The Carlins' second child, Bette-Jo, named by "Uncle" Kenny Linn, was born in November of 1948. Dora then took both small children with her to the airport so she could continue the daily tasks of the airport operations.

By the age of four the Carlins' son, known as "Fritz," could identify planes. There is a story that Joe and his young son visited another airport. Fritz visited all the hangars to inspect the planes. He returned and asked who owned the Fairchild.

A plane is fueled at the Warsaw Airport (c. 1950).

Mechanic Kenny Linn at the Warsaw Airport (c. 1950).

When told there was no Fairchild on the field, Fritz took the doubting person to the hangar where, sure enough, there was a Fairchild.

In 1950, Joe and Dora saw the fruits of their hard work materialize when a 2,400-foot x 75-foot North-South aggregate runway and a taxiway were constructed. Pilot Jerry Lessig was the first to land on the new runway. Jerry's wife was a sister to Dora Carlin. One year later, the Warsaw Aero Club helped install runway lights, and as an added convenience, indoor plumbing replaced the outhouses.

The City passed an Airport Zoning Ordinance to assure that no tall buildings could be built that might get in the way of planes. The airport got its

own snowplow so runways could be immediately cleared. Those safety factors, along with Joe's personal efforts toward air safety, earned him a Safety Award in 1959 from the Indiana State Aeronautics Commission.

Earl W. Parker, an aviation enthusiast, had been active in both flying and the administration of the airport since 1946. He was appointed to the Board of Aviation in 1952. Parker gave generously of his time and efforts over the years toward the growth and development of aviation and airport facilities for the City. Even though he had an interest in flying for most of his life, Parker first soloed on New Year's Day 1948 at the age of 60. He was only able to fly for twelve years, however, before poor eyesight forced him to give up his license.

Through negotiations with Washington, D.C., Parker was able to acquire an old beacon light that was along the former lighted flight trail (a series of lights) from Chicago to New York. Parker's daughter, Charlotte Stempel, recalls that members of the Warsaw Aero Club volunteered many hours to dismantle light #13, which was located in Wakarusa, and rebuild it at the Warsaw Airport. Parker numbered every part of the light and tower as it was dismantled to assure it would be reassembled properly.

The Warsaw beacon was the first beacon lighted in the new Indiana airport beacon program, wherein beacons abandoned by the federal government on the civil airways were relocated to Indiana airports. A special ceremony was held the evening of August 14, 1951, when the rotating beacon was first turned on at 9:30 p.m. The switch was thrown by Col. Clarence Cornish, director of the Indiana Aeronautics Department, at a signal broadcast over WRSW. Members of the aviation board, Warsaw Aero Club, Indiana Aeronautics Commission, and airport managers from across Indiana attended the ceremony.

Within two hours after the rotating beacon was turned on, it served its purpose by saving human lives and an expensive airplane. About 11:30 that evening, airport manager Joe Carlin; Bill Wagner, president of the aviation board; and Earl Parker, then president of the Aero Club, were standing at the airport preparing to go home when they heard the drone of an airplane engine.

Carlin recognized the motor—which sounded like it was cutting out—to be that of an Army plane. He said the aircraft appeared to be in real trouble, so the three men ran to get their cars and quickly parked them at the end of the runway so that the three sets of headlights formed a lighted arrow onto the runway.

Soon an Army plane carrying two young officers swept over the beacon, turned, and landed on the runway. The men were from Wright-Patterson airbase in Dayton, Ohio. They had been traveling from Biloxi, Mississippi, to Dayton when their radio equipment was damaged during an electrical storm, preventing them from transmitting or receiving any signals. Thus, they were blown off course and became lost.

The plane's fuel supply was running out and the men had just decided to make a blind parachute jump in the darkness and let the plane crash when they saw the flash of Warsaw's beacon twenty miles away. The officers were thankful to have landed safely, and Parker was very proud that the new beacon and their quick thinking saved the lives of two officers and prevented a plane from crashing.

In 1956, the municipally owned airfield was rated the most active small field in the state. It included five hangars, and the Carlins owned 28 planes and other operational slips. Carlin Airways provided air to ground Unicom radio, a flight school, commercial charter and cargo flights, and the sale of new and used aircraft. Carlin also employed three mechanics and a Federal inspector for aircraft repair.

In one of the hangars, Joe and Dora Carlin, along with Kenny Linn, started Carlin Manufacturing, a small business that produced bone screws, medical devices, and other innovative products for the local orthopedic industry. (This business became Warsaw Orthopedic, now known as Sofamor Danek.)

It was important to Joe that his children learn to fly. As a sixth grader, Fritz could pilot a plane and operate the dual controls when flying with his father. Bette-Jo learned to do the same three years later. Fritz went on to obtain his pilot's license and for a time operated a charter service as a sideline business. Unfortunately, he was killed in 1994 at the age of 46 in an airplane crash in downtown Sarasota, Florida.

Earl Parker had a vision into the future regarding the airport. He foresaw the need to eventually expand and lengthen the runways. When he learned that forty acres directly south of the airport were available to purchase, Parker sent a letter on

Dora Carlin, right, and an unidentified woman at the Warsaw Airport (c. 1950). Fritz Carlin is seated in the plane.

The staff of Carlin Airways in 1960. Seated, left to right: Jerry Arthur, owner Joe F. Carlin, Kenneth Linn. Standing, left to right: Tom Kerchenfaut, Fritz Carlin, Clayton Kerchenfaut, Vernon Rector.

October 25, 1956—that was actually dated October 25, *1966*—to a number of area businessmen.

Parker wanted to impress upon the local citizens the importance of guaranteeing the adequacy of the airport for the future. His letter explained that $15,000 was needed to acquire the adjacent property. An agreement was made that the City would pay back the purchase price over a three-year period. To start the drive, each member of the aviation board agreed to loan $500 for the cause. The letter asked for interested parties to also loan $500 toward the project.

Parker hoped that a number of men would be willing to loan $500 each to the airport. The very next day, however, Dr. Virgil McCleary stopped by the airport. He served as a city councilman from 1950 to 1953 and was involved in the construction of the airport administration building, a new maintenance building, and extending the runway. McCleary, who ultimately served as president of the Aviation Board from 1961 to 1969, loaned the entire amount to the City for the purpose of expanding the runway.

The project was implemented by the Federal Aviation Administration Program. It was through Earl Parker's untiring commitment to acquire the land south of the airport that a 1,200-foot extension was added to the runway, making it 3,600 feet.

In October 1960, the City Council—consisting of Charles H. Ker, Joseph S. Lessig, William E. Hadley, Joe J. Johnson, and G. Freeland Phillips—passed a resolution that designated the Warsaw Municipal Airport as "Parker Field," in honor of Earl W. Parker. The Warsaw Junior Chamber of Commerce, known as the Jaycees, planned a two-day dedication program and open house.

The event was held at the airport on October 8 and 9, 1960, with 10 new 1961 model aircraft by Beech, Piper, and Cessna on display. In addition, a helicopter gave a demonstration and the U.S. Air Force had an exhibit of military weapons and aircraft engines. A parade on the new runway and taxi strip featured county bands, the Civil Air Patrol Marching Unit, American Legion Color Guard, and new model convertibles carrying special guests.

Airport manager Joe Carlin and Parker's fellow aviation board members—Stan H. Arnolt, Forrest Bouse, and Henry A. Foy—were present for the

Bud Case, right, helped Earl Parker, left, build a fireplace at the airport, so the volunteers who helped build the beacon tower could cook meals while they were working.

Jake Menzie visits with friends as his plane is fueled in May 1951.

A group gathered at the Warsaw Airport in May 1952. The "C" on the window awnings refer to Carlin Airways, Inc.

ceremony. In addition, U.S. Air Force General Curtis E. LeMay flew to Warsaw for the dedication. Famed Colonel Roscoe Turner, who won several national air races and held the Distinguished Flying Cross at that time, gave the main address at the ceremony.

Charlotte Stempel was very fond of her father and noted that during the many years she lived in northeastern Illinois, he called her every Sunday morning promptly at 8:00 a.m. She recalls that Parker's faithfulness to the airport often took him there in the middle of the night during lightning storms. He wanted to be sure that the two red warning lights mounted on the barn at the north end of the airport were working, in case a pilot in trouble might need them.

Now 87, Charlotte vividly remembers an airplane ride she and her best friend, Ione Diddle Jonas, took when they were young girls. Ray Zimmer sometimes took Charlotte for short airplane rides. One day she and Ione were together when Ray asked if they wanted a ride. The two girls excitedly climbed into the front seat, with Ray in the second seat at the controls. Sitting in the open cockpit, the wind blew freely across the girls' faces.

After a few minutes in the air, Ione began to feel sick and Charlotte saw the look on her friend's face. She turned around to Ray and made a downward motion with her hand. The pilot misunderstood Charlotte's hand signal and thought the girls wanted a "real" ride. The plane went into a dive, and from there the girls got "the ride of their lives." Ione states she got so scared that day she forgot about being sick—but she has flown since.

The financial report for the year 1960 states that it cost $1.58 per night to light the airport from dusk to dawn and operate the beacon light. In 1960, the airport manager was paid $240, liability insurance cost $63, and snow removal cost $165.

Morrison Rockhill was on the original Indiana State Aeronautics Commission. He was replaced by William Mollenhour in 1946, who served in that position until 1959. The Warsaw Aviation Board in 1954 included William Chinworth, Dave Gast, Earl Parker, and Forrest Bouse. William Wagner, Al M. Hodges, and William Dalton were board members in the late 1950s. In December of 1960, at the end of Parker's term on the board, Mayor Mike Hodges appointed him a lifetime honorary member to the Warsaw Aviation Board as a consultant and advisor. Mike Light replaced Parker on the board.

This beacon light tower was dismantled in Wakarusa and rebuilt at the Warsaw Airport. Bill Mollenhour, Hank Henderson, and Bill Oakes climbed to the top when it was completed in August 1951.

Stan Arnolt had a warm friendship with General LeMay, who got him interested in the Civil Air Patrol, an auxiliary of the Air Force. In 1957, Arnolt was made Commander of the Indiana Wing, with the Warsaw Airport designated as the base. Arnolt held that position from April 1956 to November 1959. Jerry Lessig succeeded Arnolt as Commander. The headquarters was located on the third floor of the Arnolt Building (former Hotel Hays Annex) on E. Center Street. Warsaw was the Civil Air Patrol headquarters for the states of Indiana, Illinois, Michigan, Ohio, and Wisconsin.

Arleen Koors, who served in the Medical Corps of the U.S. Navy during World War II, received her

REMC employees Bill Oakes and Maurice Salman used their "cherry picker" truck to reassemble the beacon tower in 1951.

Arleen Dahl Koors received her pilot's license in 1951.

private pilot's license in 1951 under the G.I. Bill of Rights. She came to Warsaw later that year, but with a family by that time did not go on to obtain her commercial and instructor's ratings.

After passing the Civil Service test in 1957, Koors was given a GS-4 secretarial rating and was attached to the Air Force Liaison Office located on the second floor of the Arnolt Building. Koors was responsible for preparing and keeping records for the Air Force and coordinating matters between the Air Force and Civil Air Patrol.

The Air Force based a Beechcraft C-45 airplane in Warsaw, and that arrangement existed until 1965 when the headquarters was relocated to the Bunker Hill Air Force Base (now Grissom AFB) in Kokomo.

Wallace E. Stouder owned several airplanes during the 1950s, and beginning in the early 1960s, he served on the aviation board for about 20 years. His son, Wes, helped fuel planes at the airport in 1965 and 1966. For nearly four years Stouder worked with Phil Calvert and Mayor Dale Tucker to create a plan for the airport and its operation. Using his personal funds and own airplane, Stouder made many flights to Washington, D.C. and elsewhere to meet with senators and other prominent political figures in an effort to convince them of the importance of an airport in Warsaw and request financial assistance for improvements.

Stouder recalls flying with Birch Bayh and George McGovern during the years they were campaigning for governor. One night he will never forget is when he was attempting to fly into the South Bend Airport. On board were movie actors Dustin Hoffman and Paul Newman, who were campaigning for George McGovern. The weather was bad and ice had built up on the airplane's wings. There was no de-icing equipment in those days and Stouder was forced to land the plane at full throttle. It was a hard landing, but everyone was fine and there was no serious damage to the plane.

About the time funds had been raised for the airport, Mayor Tucker lost the next election to Mike Hodges. When Mayor Hodges told Wally Stouder he was going to scrap the airport project, Stouder contacted the presidents of local companies and urged them to call the mayor's office and give reasons why the airport was a worthy project. Within two hours, Mayor Hodges had contacted Stouder urging him to call off his "attack" and agreed to continue with the project.

Stanley H. Arnolt II, founder of Arnolt Corporation, was a pilot in the 1950s. When Arnolt had heart problems and lost his pilot's license in the early 1960s, he hired David Peffley to fly the company plane. Peffley states that following his employment with Arnolt Corporation, he was hired by J. Alan Morgan as Zimmer Inc.'s first pilot, a position he held for 14 years. Peffley was succeeded by Ken Gable, who was Zimmer's pilot from 1968 to 1981. Peffley states that he and Max Bumbaugh, who flew for Dalton Foundries, were the first two corporate pilots at the Warsaw Airport. Bumbaugh was Joe Carlin's first student to fly solo, and he went on to become a flight instructor.

Aviation board members in 1963 were: Mike Light, president; Lloyd Berkey, secretary; and members Dr. Virgil McCleary and Stan Arnolt. The airport did not have a snowplow in its early days and was practically closed during parts of winter; but when Stan Arnolt donated a truck and Dave Gast got the State Highway Department sub-district to contribute a plow, it was then able to operate as a 12-month airport.

In 1963, plans and financing were completed for the construction of a new administration building at the airport. An FAAP project in 1968 provided for additional land acquisition and the runway and parallel taxiway was extended to 4,300 feet. The City of Warsaw again lengthened the runway and taxiway in 1970 to 4,975 feet.

When Joe Carlin left in 1961, Eldridge Sheetz bought Carlin Airways, Inc. and changed the name to Warsaw Aviation. Other stockholders in the business were Wallace E. Stouder, Keith Horn, and Don Corl. For a time, Warsaw Aviation made daily flights to Chicago's O'Hare and Midway airports. Warsaw Aviation was sold to Skystream in 1973, which was managed by Phil Calvert.

Eldridge Sheetz served as part-time manager of the airport until he was killed in 1984 when the Lear jet he was in crashed while trying to land at Connecticut's Bradley International Airport. The City took over complete management of the airport at that time, including the governing of fuel sales. Karen Sheetz, Eldridge's niece, became the part-time manager, holding that position through 1991. Lance Ropte was the airport manager from 1991 to 1998. When he left, Karen served as interim manager through 1999, until David Beall was hired as the full-time airport manager in January 2000.

Chris Schenkel, a resident of Tippecanoe Lake, started Cheyenne Charter service at the

Earl Parker, right, shakes hands with U.S. Air Force General Curtis LeMay as he arrives at the Warsaw Municipal Airport for a dedication ceremony to rename the airport "Parker Field." Looking on, left to right: airport manager Joe Carlin, Stan Arnolt III, and aviation board member Stan H. Arnolt.

The Warsaw Junior Chamber of Commerce, known as the Jaycees, sponsored the two-day celebration October 8-9, 1960, when the airport was dedicated as "Parker Field." Front, left to right: Wayne Graff, Gordon Sands, Jack Helvey, Frank Kealey. Back, left to right: Leonard Bibler, W. James McCleary, Earl W. Parker, Tweed Robinson, Herb Mann.

Earl W. Parker, right, and his daughter Charlotte Stempel, left, with Col. Roscoe Turner, main speaker at the ceremony to rename the airport "Parker Field."

Earl W. Parker (1887-1967) during a solemn moment at the Warsaw Municipal Airport following a ceremony October 9, 1960, to honor his long-time involvement in the development of the local airport.

Warsaw Airport in 1978. Schenkel was a sports announcer for the New York Giants for 13 years and went on to become an emmy-award winning sports announcer for ABC, where he worked for 20 years. John Sanders first worked for Eldridge Sheetz at Warsaw Aviation when he came to Warsaw in 1969. Sanders, who was Schenkel's personal pilot since 1972, eventually bought Cheyenne Charter in 1985.

Cheyenne Charter networks with other charter services across the country. Sanders states that while he was flying Schenkel's plane he had the privilege of flying with the first and last men to walk on the moon. More recent celebrities he has flown across the country include Mohammed Ali, singers Tricia Yearwood and John Mellencamp, and current baseball players Alex Rodriguez and Derek Jeters.

As a side note, a special memorial is placed at the Warsaw Airport. James Lee Foreman of Warsaw was drafted into the U.S. Army in 1965 and was sent to Vietnam. Sgt. Foreman was the squad leader of a weapons platoon that the Viet Cong opened fire on while passing through a small river. Although hit in the thigh, he continued through sniper fire and made it to the other side. The squad's radio operator was wounded during the battle and when Sgt. Foreman made an attempt to save his fellow soldier, he was mortally wounded by sniper fire.

A plaque was dedicated in his memory and placed at Fort Benjamin Harrison in Indianapolis. Fort Harrison contacted James' brother, Mike Foreman, in 1994 to advise him that the base was closing and new locations were needed for memorials to fallen soldiers. Foreman contacted Mayor Jeff Plank, who arranged for the plaque to be moved from Indianapolis to the Warsaw Airport.

Coincidentally, the airport was chosen as the place for the memorial because the Foreman family once lived on some of the property. The plaque, which states, "In memory of Sgt. James L. Foreman who on May 18, 1967, gave his life in Vietnam while fighting to preserve our freedom," rests in the spot where James Foreman's bedroom once stood.

Chapter 9

1920 to 1929

Hall & Marose Agency

Believed to be Warsaw's oldest continuously operated, locally owned insurance business, the Hall & Marose Agency, Inc. is located at 122 W. Market Street. It was founded in 1920 by W. Robert Hall in the Rigdon Building and was first named the Hall-Spencer Agency.

In 1922 it became the Hall-Anglin Agency, James H. Anglin being the partner, and from the late 1930s through the early 1950s it operated in the back of the Elks Arcade on E. Center Street. In 1961, the agency moved to the First National Bank building in the 100 block of S. Buffalo Street.

Having joined the firm about 1958, Art Marose became a partner in 1964 when the business moved to its current location and became known as the Hall & Marose Agency, Inc. An agent since 1963, John Hall became a partner in 1968. New partners in 1998 were John's son, Mike Hall (agent since 1995) and Art's son, Kevin Marose (agent since 1990).

Warsaw Feed Store

Ernest E. Hull first started his feed business in the early 1920s in the building at 206 S. Buffalo Street. He sold vegetable and grain seeds in the front of the store and sold bales of hay and cleaned clover in the rear of the building.

Hull then bought the old feed mill on the north side of the railroad tracks on Lake Street about 1942. The Warsaw Feed Store continued to sell seeds and also milled corn. Ernest's son, Stan, took over the management prior to the business closing. About 1954, the abandoned grain mill was burned as a training session for the fire department, and has since been a parking lot.

Ernest Hull started the Warsaw Feed Store at 206 S. Buffalo Street in the 1920s. The Rainbow Café was the next business north.

The Warsaw Feed Store at 216 W. Jefferson Street was on the north side of the railroad tracks. This view is looking west from Buffalo Street.

Employees stand in front of the W.B. Yost Cigar Store at 114 E. Center Street in the early 1900s. Employee Robert Breading purchased the business and changed the name to Breading's Cigar Store.

A 25¢ token for Breading's Cigar Store.

Breading's Cigar Store

In the 1920s, Robert Breading, Sr. and his son, Lewis "Peanuts," started Breading's Cigar Store in a two-story wood frame building at 114 E. Center Street on the east side of the alley. The business then moved into its current location in 1950 at 116 E. Center Street.

The Breading's store was a popular gathering place for breakfast and lunch. Dominoes was such a favorite pastime there that tournaments were held. Some even played hearts, euchre, and other games with dominoes.

Opening at 5:00 a.m. and not closing sometimes until 2:00 a.m. the next morning, Breading's quickly became known as the place to call or stop by for the latest news and sporting event updates. When the Moose, Eagles, Elks, and other lodges closed after midnight, Breading's was where everyone went for an early morning breakfast.

The Breading men sold the business to Ray Deafenbaugh and Sam Holbrook in 1954, and Dick Heagy joined the business in 1955. Dick Kehoe was a partner for a short time. Burleigh Burgh bought Kehoe's interest in 1959, and when Deafenbaugh and Heagy decided to sell their interest in 1974, Burgh bought Heagy's one-third interest and Craig Smith bought Deafenbaugh's interest.

Although not open late at night like years ago, Breading's continues to be a favored downtown meeting place. The annual Breading's Christmas party "packs the house," and one can still stop by for an occasional game of dominoes.

This building was erected in the 1860s and was occupied by Yost's Cigar Store, where the famous "Bankable" cigars were made on the second floor. It later became Breading's Cigar Store. At the entrance is Terry Klondaris, left, and Paul Latta, right (c. 1940s).

Kiwanis Club

The Kiwanis Club of Warsaw received its charter April 4, 1921. The first meeting was held at the Hotel Hays with 58 charter members present, and dues were 50 cents. Charter officers were: J.E. Headley, president; Walter A. Kintzel, vice president; O. Reese Evans, secretary; and John F. Shoup, treasurer.

Over the years the club has met at various locations, including the Camel Club, which was located above Hall Hardware on S. Buffalo Street, and the Civic Center, which was on the northwest corner of Center and Lake Streets in the old Oram Building. Since 1963, the Kiwanis Club has met at the Shrine Building at the Fairgrounds.

J.E. Headley served as president of the organization during its first two years. Virgil "Doc" McCleary is the only other person who served two consecutive terms as president (1943-1944).

Current membership totals 65. Officers for 2001 are: Lowell Owens, president; Joy Lohse, president-elect; Suzie Light, first vice president; Bob Gephart, secretary; and Darrin Miller, treasurer.

Foundries

Warsaw Foundry Company was founded in 1923 by William Petro, Sr. The foundry began operations in a small building near the curve at the west end of Winona Avenue to produce aluminum castings. One of the company's first products was an aluminum brace for Zimmer Manufacturing. The property for the foundry's current site at 1212 N. Detroit Street was purchased in 1927.

By that time the firm was making step plates for automobiles and fabricating aluminum brackets for auto license plates, although aluminum castings were later discontinued. The foundry suffered a disastrous fire in 1945, which gutted the plant and caused it to cease operations for 13 months while a new facility was built.

William Petro, Jr. joined the business around 1950 and took over as president in the early 1960s. Following Bill's retirement in 1990, his son John has served as president and his other son, Mike, is currently vice president/secretary/treasurer.

Huffer Foundry: After six years of operating their own service station on N. Detroit Street from the ages of 18 and 16, brothers Morton and Norman Huffer constructed a building adjacent to their filling station. The Huffer Foundry Company began produc-

Mayor Ernie Wiggins, center in the white shirt and tie, enjoys a laugh with a group at the annual Breading's Christmas party in 1997.

Employees of the Huffer Foundry in 1961. First row, L-R: Steve Ross, Ed Huffer, Darrel Grindle, Lenzie Owens, Harold Holle, Curt Owens, Bruce Snell, Gerald Perkins, George Barnhart, Ridley Brown, Willie McKenzie. Second row, L-R: Herb Ross, Paul Draper, Bill Huffer, Harold Francis, J.C. Woods, Pete Grisso, Bob Mathews, Lanny Kelly, Henry Conley, Bruce Hyde, Clemens VanDyke, Charles Engle. Third row, L-R: ClaraBelle Demaree, Morton Huffer, Norman Huffer, Max Huffer, Ralph Byers, Arbie Francis, Roy Hatten, Estel Blanton, Danny Fenix, Valis Owens, Steve Bennett, Dale Ballentine, Bob Huffer.

tion in 1938 along the east shore of Center Lake. The foundry initially produced cast chilled plow points for farmers. The grey iron castings company was very busy during World War II when it received contracts from the U.S. Signal Corps and various sub-contracts from the Army and Navy.

The majority of the foundry's production was general job castings for automobile and farm machinery, but it also had a line of castings for farm dinner bells and boat anchors. Later, the

Huffer products included manhole covers for municipalities, some of which can still be found in Warsaw today. In 1960, the foundry began production of bar bell exercising equipment, which was marketed under the trade name "Champion Exercisers" and sold to retail sporting goods stores throughout the nation. The bar bell manufacturing building was just north of the foundry.

All of Mort Huffer's sons (Bob, Max, Ed and Bill) worked at the foundry, along with both of Norm's sons (Nolan and Duane). Norm sold his interest in the foundry in 1967 and the business was moved to Atwood. Huffer Foundry closed in 1969.

Other foundries in Warsaw over the years have included: Indiana Briquetting Company on Lindberg Street, where Donald A. Meroney was plant manager. This business produced cast iron briquettes which were sold to other foundries to melt for casting so they did not have to buy ore. Lakeside Foundry, a division of Hercules Motors in Ohio, was on S. Cleveland Avenue and produced gray iron castings. Pittenger Aluminum Foundry was founded by Alex Pittenger and was later operated by a husband-and-wife team, Vernon and Marna Hollar, who produced sand and yellow brass castings for local industries. It was located at 718 W. Center Street.

The 19th Amendment to the Constitution in 1920 extended voting rights to women.

Fitzpatrick Paint

As he recuperated in Plymouth from serious burns due to an industrial accident in 1909, Orth Fitzpatrick started making roof coatings, barn paints and house paints. In 1924, he moved to Warsaw and established Fitzpatrick Paint at 513 W. Market Street.

Long-time employee Russell Bixel bought the business from Fitzpatrick in 1938 and changed the name to Bixel Paint. His son, Donald, joined the firm in 1951 and took over full operation in 1970 until it closed in 1992.

The company had the ability to research and develop special purpose paints and special color paints. Its products were used by various industries throughout the Midwest in brushing, spraying and dipping to place tough, protective coatings on manufactured items.

Shoe Store for a Century

About 1886 the building at 106 E. Center Street was occupied by Beck & Metcalf's department store, followed by a number of shoe stores (Stout's, Rickett's, Viskniski). Clint Dedrick's shoe store was the last business at this location prior to Al Gerard opening Gerard's Central Shoe Store.

Having previously worked in the shoe department at Richardson's Department Store, Al Gerard started his own business in 1925. He carried the largest and most complete stock of shoes in northern Indiana.

Al's son, Jerry, ran the store from 1947 until 1983 when he sold it to several Grace College students who continued with the Central Shoe name. However, they went bankrupt in 1985, and Jim and Carol Craig then operated CJ's Shoe Store from 1986 to 1987.

After having been the site of a shoe store for nearly 100 years, the building at 106 E. Center Street received a new occupant. Joe and Joyce Conlon had started their business called Celebrations in 1988 at 109 E. Center Street. In 1989 they moved their store with cards and party supplies across the street to 106 E. Center Street and added Ape Over You, a costume rental business.

Making Music

In 1925, the Warsaw Conservatory of Music was located in the telephone building on the southwest corner of Center and Indiana Streets. In 1947, the Honolulu Conservatory of Music was located on

Gerard's Central Shoe store window display at 106 E. Center Street (c. 1930s).

the third floor at 102¹/₂ E. Market Street. The Worrell School of Music was located almost next door on the second floor at 106¹/₂ E. Market Street.

Paul Coffin owned Coffin's Music Shoppe at 217 E. Center Street in the 1920s. By 1936, the business was located in rooms 10 and 12 of the Elks Arcade.

In the 1960s, Trib and Patty Biddinger operated Biddinger Music Center at 123 E. Center Street. The store handled Lowrey organs and Gulbransen pianos, and also carried a wide selection of sheet music, instruction books, and other musical supply items. Biddinger's also offered music lessons and piano tuning. For a time, Mr. Biddinger, a professional musician, provided organ music nightly at Petro's Restaurant.

Car Wash

A common business in most towns today is a public facility for washing automobiles. As early as 1925, before there were many cars in Warsaw, Robert Ripple operated the Jiffy Car Wash on N. Indiana Street one-half block north of the jail. He advertised that cars were called for and delivered to any part of the city free of charge.

Warsaw Golf Course

During Prohibition in the 1920s, the homes along Country Club Drive were referred to as "Rum Row" because the residents in that area were notorious for drinking and having parties. In fact, to this day, the Country Club area residents continue to have an annual 4th of July parade and celebration.

In March of 1925, fifty Warsaw and Winona Lake golf enthusiasts met to begin planning a nine-hole golf course on the west side of Winona Lake with a clubhouse and caddy house. A.O. Catlin, John Shoup, T.C. Frazer, Frank Swihart, and Allan Widaman were named directors. Club memberships were sold for $100 with the privilege of paying $25 per year for four years.

A professional golf instructor from Fort Wayne was hired to lay out the course and select places for the greens. The holes were laid out so that afternoon play would not be against the sun. In addition, some 65 lakefront lots were offered for sale near the clubhouse for about $250 each.

On October 14, 1925, the wives of the club members sponsored a gathering to raise funds to purchase supplies for the clubhouse. Over 100 guests attended and enjoyed playing Bridge and Mah Jongg.

This 1930 photo shows the Country Clubhouse for the Warsaw Golf Course on the west shore of Winona Lake. When the golf course closed, Reub Williams remodeled it for his family's home. It is still owned and occupied today by the Williams family.

W. Robert Hall's membership card for the Warsaw Country Club's first season in 1925.

Jerry Gerard, Bruce Howe, and Paul Latta were among the caddies who worked at the Warsaw Golf Course in the 1930s. The Warsaw Golf Course existed until the early 1940s. The greenskeeper named Robinson died about that time, and many golfers had moved their membership to the 18-hole Tippecanoe Lake golf course.

Raymond B. "Ted" Williams purchased the entire golf course property for $5,000, including the clubhouse and Little Eagle Lake area. An April 1944 ad in the *Warsaw Daily Times* states that he then sold lakeshore lots for $350 each for "summer resort homes." John and Elaine Elliott currently reside at 1305 Country Club Drive which was where the 9th hole was located.

Ted's brother, Charles Reuben Williams, bought the clubhouse and remodeled it for his family's home. The home is presently occupied by the family of Reub's grandson, Chandler Williams, and his grandmother, Mrs. Betty Morgan. "Betsy," now 86, is the only child of Justin O. Zimmer, founder of Zimmer, Inc.

Tin Shops

As early as 1925, Blount L. and Paul H. Schlemmer operated Schlemmer & Schlemmer's Sheet Metal Shop at 213 S. Buffalo Street. The building was on the south side of the alley and a big advertisement was painted on the side of the building for the business.

In 1935, George Leiter worked for Schlemmer's Tin Shop, but by 1936 he was doing sheet metal work for a hardware company in Fort Wayne. In 1947, George and his son, Wayne, worked together in Elkhart doing sheet metal work.

About 1953, George Leiter purchased the City Tin Shop in Warsaw. The business phone number was 87, which had a major significance to the family. Both Arden Leiter, Sr. and Arden Leiter, Jr. numbered their stock cars 87, and they did quite well at the Warsaw Speedway.

The City Tin Shop was a family business, with sons, grandsons and cousins working there. When the buildings in that quarter block were demolished in 1967 for the city parking lot, the business was moved briefly to E. Fort Wayne Street. In 1969 as Boggs Industrial Park was getting started, George Leiter decided to construct a new building in the industrial park, and a street was named after him. Thus, the City Tin Shop was located on the northwest corner of Leiter Drive and W. Center Street.

George's son, Wayne, worked at City Tin for awhile and then left to start his own business. Wayne purchased the assets of his father's business in 1976 and moved his company, Town & Country Sheet Metal & Roofing, to the Boggs Park location. When Art, Mark and Ward Leiter purchased the Town & Country business in 1984, family attribution laws required that the name be changed again, so it was renamed Leiter Enterprises.

In 1992, Art and Mark Leiter purchased Ward's share of the business when he moved away. When Art and Mark decided to get out of the sheet metal business in 1997, they sold most of the larger business equipment and the building. Mark kept some of the equipment and has continued on under the business name of Leiter Roofing.

Babe Ruth hit 59 home runs for the New York Yankees in 1921, followed by 60 home runs in 1927— a record he held until 1961.

Circus Days

Dave Hillery fondly recalls the days when the circus came to Warsaw and operated on his grandfather's farm on the southwest side of Eagle Creek on S. Buffalo Street. The main show grounds were where the Kincaide roller skating rink was later located. When he was a kid, Dave remembers that someone lost a diamond ring valued at $10,000, and doesn't recall it ever being found.

Warsaw celebrated Independence Day in 1926 mostly at the lakes, boating and swimming. Thousands also attended the fireworks display and the opening of the Strayer Amusement Company's carnival, sponsored by the American Legion Post, which began at the Hillery property for a week's stay. On July 9, 1926, more than 1,000 people witnessed the wedding ceremony of two people who had been performing in the carnival for some time. Justice J.S. Cain performed the ceremony on an open platform at Hillery Park.

Dave Hillery notes that over the years the Ringling Brothers, Barnum & Bailey, and Robbins Circuses all performed in Warsaw. Clyde Beatty, the great lion tamer who lived in Rochester, performed quite often at Hillery Park. Warsaw resident Karl Hathaway joined the traveling circus shows and became general manager of the Ringling Brothers Circus.

Years later when sod was cut from the pasture fields previously used as the show grounds, Dave found many coins which had been dropped by patrons while attending the circus.

One of Dave's favorite memories of the circus days occurred in 1940 when Tom Mix, the famous cowboy, performed in Warsaw. Mix, a former Texas Ranger, appeared in over 300 Western movies and by the 1920s was earning $10,000 a week. Dave got to meet Tom Mix and ride his horse, but sadly recalls that just a few weeks after his appearance in Warsaw, Mix was killed in an automobile accident.

First Woman Attorney

Miss Lucy Upson was Kosciusko County's first female to practice law. She was a legal secretary from 1909 to 1926, first in Fort Wayne and then with the Warsaw firm of Stookey and Anglin. As she attempted to work with the firm's clients following the death of both attorneys, Upson decided to pursue her own law degree.

Miss Upson became a member of the American Bar Association in 1926. She was the last attorney admitted to the Bar by an oral examination. In the 1940s, she was in partnership with John J. Boyle. The Upson & Boyle office was located at 106½ N. Buffalo Street. In 1967, William M. Dalton II joined with Miss Upson to form Upson & Dalton at 109 Fourth Street in Winona Lake.

Miss Upson retired in 1976 at age 90, after fifty years of practicing law. Active in her community, Lucy Upson was a charter member of the Kosciusko County Historical Society and the Warsaw Business and Professional Women's Club.

Gatke Corporation

The Perfection Tire & Rubber Company began in 1905 with a plant in Fort Madison, Iowa, and a textile mill in Wabash, Indiana. Perfection Tire made "bald" automobile tires prior to when tires had treads. Those types of tires were not very reliable and motorists did not expect to travel long distances without having to change at least one flat tire. Recognizing that heat was the main cause of tire failure, Perfection began using an open weave, jute brattice cloth type fabric to manufacture tires.

Meantime, the Mikesell Brothers Company in Chicago was a "job shop" that handled the Perfection Tire & Rubber Company line. The Mikesell Brothers Company was operated by Harry S. Mikesell, president; Neal Mikesell, sales manager; and Daniel Mikesell, in charge of mine sales. The company sold a jute fabric, similar to burlap bagging, to coal mines in southern Illinois and Indiana.

In 1920, Mikesell Brothers took over the Wabash textile mill. Thomas L. Gatke was a sales agent in Chicago at that time. When he and his wife inherited some money, Gatke bought the Wabash company from Mikesell Brothers and changed the name to Gatke Corporation. In 1926, he moved the business to the former E. Winona Avenue location of the Interurban power plant.

The Warsaw firm began with 12 employees and 12,000 square feet and grew to 250 employees with over 125,000 square feet. Long-time employee Neal Mikesell held the position of superintendent at the Gatke Corporation from its inception until the day he died in 1946.

Gatke Corporation was also a job shop, and Thomas Gatke held in excess of 100 patents, one of his inventions being molded brake linings. Gatke Corporation produced thousands of different

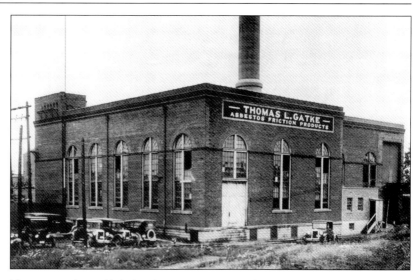

Thomas L. Gatke established Gatke Corporation in the former Interurban power plant on E. Winona Avenue in 1926. The factory closed in 1991.

parts for numerous companies associated with three main product lines: frictions, bearings, and gasket materials. There were few industries that Gatke did not serve, as they provided non-metallic bearings and friction products for the automotive industry, steel mills, and machinery manufacturers.

In fact, some of the parts that Gatke manufactured in Warsaw went to the moon on the Apollo space shuttle, and some of its products were used in the construction of the Empire State Building, the Golden Gate Bridge, and the Mackinac Bridge. Gatke Corporation provided a stable work environment in the Warsaw community for over 65 years. Since about 1991, however, the factory's buildings have been vacant.

American Brattice Cloth

American Brattice Cloth (ABC) was founded by Daniel B. Mikesell in 1926. The original stockholders—Mikesell, William S. Rogers, Ben Phillipson, and William S. Felkner—put together $10,000. ABC began in part of the old state highway garage on the corner of Cleveland and Jefferson Streets (now occupied by Quine Heating & Cooling).

Mikesell imported burlap at different widths, ran it through a tank containing a water solution of calcium chloride, then through rollers to remove excess water, put it into 50-yard rolls, and sold it to the coal mines through mine distributors and agents. The treatment made the cloth flame resistant, which was required by the mines. The cloth was hung in the mines, roof to floor, and guided the flow of fresh air to the working area of the mine.

The Grand Ole Opry radio program has been held every Saturday night on station WSM since November 28, 1925.

American Brattice Cloth occupied the former Warsaw Overall building from 1930 to 1959. This building was demolished in 1967 to make way for a municipal parking lot.

Stan Laurel and Oliver Hardy made their first silent comedy film together in 1927.

In 1930, the business moved to a two-story building along the railroad tracks (formerly Warsaw Overall Company) between Buffalo and Indiana Streets. Mikesell thought long and hard about renting the 15,000-square-foot facility, as rent at that time was $75 per month. He later bought the building for $8,000.

By 1935, the product line had expanded to include flexible ventilation tubing for mines and tunnels. As Mikesell continued making a profit and the business grew, the investors tried to gain control of the company by converting their preferred stock to common stock. Dan contacted his attorney, who helped him borrow enough money to buy out the three investors.

Dan Mikesell died suddenly in 1940. His son, Blaine, took over the company at age 25. When Blaine volunteered for the service in 1943, he left three valuable employees to run the company. The two men left the company while Blaine was overseas; however, Mary Edith Gerard stayed on the job and actually ran ABC. Although she left the company for a time and then returned, Mary Edith's service extended from 1936 to 1973.

Another dedicated employee was Jim Turner, who joined the company as a factory worker in 1946, soon advanced to foreman, moved into the office as production manager, and later became vice president. Turner retired in 1985. Larry Marshall, a chief mining engineer, joined the ABC team in 1958. He operated out of the company's Grand Junction, Colorado facility, and that working relationship lasted 32 years.

In 1959, ABC moved into a building on the west side of Argonne Road (formerly occupied by the Baughn & Zent Company, now the Warsaw Chemical property) until its new plant was completed on Kings Highway in 1961. Mikesell sold the company in 1972 to Peabody International and the name was changed to Peabody ABC. In 1973 Robert M. Ellison, who had joined ABC in 1967, was appointed president. When Ellison passed away in 1984, Steve Rufenbarger became president.

Salesman Bill Huffer has been with the company since 1968, and this author was a secretary for the sales department from 1973 to 1983. Bill would travel from state to state visiting the mines. As he traveled to his next stop, he would use a hand-held recorder to dictate information about his previous meeting.

During that time, singer Kenny Rogers had several popular songs. Bill knew I liked those songs, and as he was driving along, when a Kenny Rogers song came on the radio he would stop talking and record the song. Then back in the office, I would have the headset on to transcribe Bill's notes. Those in the office would hear the click of my typewriter keys, and then all of a sudden it would be quiet. When they looked over, I would be happily bobbing my head to the tunes of Kenny Rogers.

The Peabody organization underwent a couple of takeovers, but in 1989 the ABC management team, who are all stockholders, returned the company to local ownership. D. Blaine Mikesell re-joined the company, now known as ABC Industries, as a stockholder and is currently a member of the board of directors.

Pango Milk Chocolate Co.

In 1926, the Pango Milk Chocolate Company was a branch of the National Dairy Company. Its main function was the processing of milk chocolate for the ice cream industry, with evaporated milk as a means of absorbing the surplus. The plant moved into the old Winona Lake car barns at the base of the hill on Argonne Road (later the AMPI building).

In place of the vacuum pan method, Pango used its patented centrifugal pan process. Winona and Jerzee were two of the significant brand names in the early days, although at one time 33 different labels were used. The plant operated successfully for several years, but a falling economy during the Depression caused the company to close in 1935. The Litchfield Creamery Company took over the plant in 1936.

Baker Boys' Club / Pete Thorn

The Baker Boys' Club originated from a Kiwanis Club's Friday lunch meeting when in 1926 the Boys' Club National Convention was held in Winona Lake. Bramwell Baker's family from Boston summered at Winona Lake. "Bram" went to the meeting and told the members that if they raised $1,000 he would give them $1,000 every year. In 1927, Lee Norman "Pete" Thorn was hired as the first director and the organization was named the Baker Boys' Club. Dr. A.C. McDonald was the organization's first president.

An iron stairway along the alley on the outside of the Sharp's Hardware building (on the south side of the Courthouse Square) led to the second floor meeting place where kids could play basketball, ping-pong, checkers, carom, and other games. The Club moved to the west end of the old high school building on W. Main Street and met there until the 1970s, when they began meeting in the old Armory building on E. Main Street. Many will remember the softball games at the Fort Wayne and Indiana Street diamond where boys would "choose up" and Pete would pitch for both sides.

The Korth family had donated property along the southwest shore of Pike Lake (now Lucerne Park) to the St. Meinrad's Academy in southern Indiana, who then sold the land to the City in the late 1970s. A grant was written and approved for a building, and the Pete Thorn Youth Center was built at 800 N. Park Avenue in 1979.

Robert Lichtenwalter, executive director of the Baker Boys' Club, receives a car from Bledsoe Buick-Pontiac owner H.E. Bledsoe. The station wagon was donated to the local club for transporting boys to various activities.

Lee Norman "Pete" Thorn (1896-1990) and his wife, Fay. Thorn was executive director of the Baker Boys' Club from 1927 to 1963.

Pete Thorn retired in 1963 after 36 continuous years of devoted service to the youth of Warsaw as executive director of the Baker Boys' Club. Since 1927, hundreds of boys literally grew up under his watchful eye to become outstanding men in our community.

A 1924 graduate of Wabash College, Pete Thorn is the first and only four-letter freshman in Wabash College history to win 16 letters in four years. He participated in all four major sports—track, baseball, football and basketball. He was involved with coaching sports at the Warsaw city schools for 39 years. Thorn was inducted into the Indiana Football Hall of Fame in 1976. He received many awards over the years and in 1959 was honored as the first Chamber of Commerce "Man of the Year."

When Warsaw residents paid tribute to Thorn on June 11, 1963, at his retirement reception, he received numerous letters from other Boys' Club executive directors and local citizens. Then postmaster (and future mayor) Frank Rarick wrote: "No individual has ever served this community with a greater degree of integrity and sincerity. The true value of your services in connection with the guidance and training of our youth cannot be determined or adequately appraised, because your influence will continue to live and be reflected in

Wonder Bread and Kool-Aid were introduced in 1927.

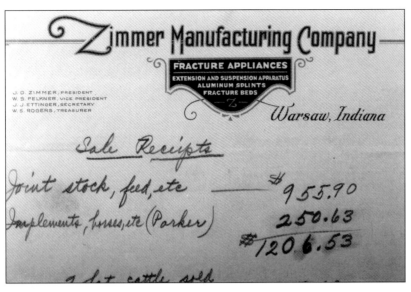

Original letterhead for Zimmer Manufacturing Company founded in 1927.

Justin O. Zimmer (1884-1951)

Reader's Digest began publication in 1922.

Zimmer Manufacturing Co.

Zimmer Manufacturing Company was founded in 1927 by Justin O. Zimmer and fellow DePuy employee Joe J. Ettinger. At age 43 following his 20-year career as national sales manager of steel wire mesh type splints for DePuy Manufacturing, Zimmer started his own business in the basement of Ettinger's house on Prairie Street. He developed a new line of aluminum splints and other orthopedic equipment.

He soon rented space in a building at the corner of N. Detroit and Arthur Streets to keep up with product demand. Zimmer entered the international market in 1929 when a Scottish surgeon ordered $1,200 worth of splints.

When J.O. Zimmer died while vacationing in Florida in 1951, Joe Ettinger became company president. In 1954 when Ettinger retired, Zimmer Manufacturing expanded into Plant 1 on Center Lake along Detroit Street, and Jim Hartle became president. During Hartle's 15 years at the helm, Zimmer sales grew tenfold, and in 1968, land was purchased in Boggs Industrial Park for further expansion. J. Alan Morgan, grandson of the founder, was named president in 1969.

The company was acquired by New York based Bristol-Myers in 1972, and Tom Hughes assumed the presidency in 1979, followed by Ron Davis in 1988. The Zimmer Corporate Headquarters between Main and Fort Wayne Streets was dedicated in 1992, and Ray Elliott has served as president since 1997.

In 2001, Zimmer, Inc. was divested from Bristol-Myers Squibb and became an independent, publicly held company known as Zimmer Holdings, Inc. With 3,200 employees worldwide, Ray Elliott was appointed chairman of the board and CEO.

Jewelry Stores

Fred S. Ward had a jewelry business at 118 S. Buffalo Street in the mid-1920s. Ward sold diamonds and watches, and provided jewelry repair. By the 1950s and through the 1960s, the business was located across the alley at 108 S. Buffalo Street.

Fitch's Jewelry was founded in 1927 by Dr. Fred G. Fitch, a local optometrist who also ground and fitted his own lenses. When Dr. Fitch wanted a business that would coincide with his optical practice, he decided to open a jewelry store in 1932. Since Fitch was not very knowledgeable

the lives and activities of these students and their families for years to come."

Judge Gene B. Lee wrote: "In your role as the leader of the Boys' Club, you have been the foster father, athletic director, psychologist, sociologist, economist, spiritual guide, family counselor and, more importantly, a true friend of our boys through more than two generations. You have treated 'your boys' fairly and equally to the end that they have learned to recognize and appreciate the admirable qualities of honesty, integrity, fair play, good sportsmanship in clean and hard competition, ambition, self-expression, self-respect and desire for self-improvement, while at the same time you have helped many of them through the most trying emotional disturbances of their young lives."

Pete Thorn was an Honorary Rotarian for 33 years and a life member of the Elks Club. A 32nd degree Mason, he was a 50-year member of the Blue Lodge Scottish Rite Shrine and American Legion.

Following Thorn's retirement, Robert W. Lichtenwalter then served as the director for 29 years, until Scott Wiley took over the helm in 1992. "Coach" Lichtenwalter recalls that when he became director in 1963, the organization had $4,400. When he retired in 1992, deposits totaling over $63,000 were earning interest to help pay for annual scholarships and operating expenses.

Local professional golfer Denny Hepler was instrumental in establishing a scholarship program when he started a pro am golf fundraiser. To date, the Baker Boys Club has given out over $20,000 for high school scholarships.

The letters at the far right show that this photo was taken from the second story of the Carter's Department Store on the southeast corner of Buffalo and Market Streets (c. 1940). Looking north on Buffalo Street, the various storefronts that existed before the bank expanded were: a drug store in the Saine building, Fitch Jewelry, Ward's jewelry store, The Hub men's clothing store, and First National Bank.

about the jewelry business, he hired Everett H. Hanft to operate the jewelry store.

The optometry/jewelry store was located in part of what was formerly Gilworth's department store at 110 S. Buffalo Street in one of the small storefronts to the south of the Indiana Loan & Trust Building. Mr. Hanft managed the store until 1965 when he was able to purchase the business from Dr. Fitch's daughter and grandson. When Mr. Hanft passed away in 1967, the operation of the store was passed to his son, Don E. Hanft.

The building at 110 S. Buffalo Street was sold in 1970 and the store was moved across the alley to 116 S. Buffalo Street, where it operated until 1994 when the retail part of the store was closed. Don and his wife, Beverly, still operate a jewelry repair and engraving service located in Winona Lake.

BPW & Altrusa Clubs

On March 4, 1927, the Business and Professional Women's Club of Warsaw (BPW) was organized as a network for working women. The first meeting was held at the public library with 58 charter members present. The first officers were: Mary Jane East, president; Olive Matthews, vice president; Helen J. Kyle, secretary; Lucia McRaven, treasurer.

The BPW's annual fish fry fundraiser and the sale of Abbott caramels allowed the club to award three or four scholarships to high school students each year, in addition to supporting other community projects. By the late 1980s, the majority of the membership consisted of older women. Attendance at meetings began to drop and the club was eventually dissolved.

The Altrusa Club of Warsaw was chartered November 30, 1973, with twelve members. Inez

The 2,448 mile long Route 66 was commissioned in 1926.

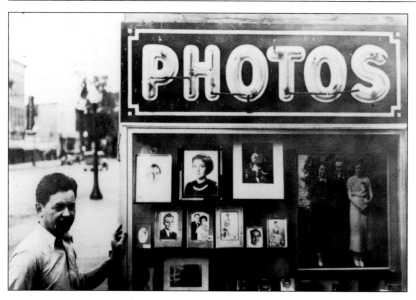

Lowell L. Blosser stands by a photo display near the stairs leading to his photography studio below the Lake City Bank building on S. Buffalo Street. The studio was at this location from 1927 to about 1946.

Charles Lindbergh made the first solo, nonstop, transatlantic flight in 1927 in his plane named "Spirit of St. Louis."

Devenney served as the first president. Altrusa is responsible for establishing The Beaman Home in 1985, a shelter for women and children who are victims of abuse. The club was also a moving force to establish CASA (Court Appointed Special Advocate), which appoints an advocate to speak on a child's behalf in abuse and neglect cases that occur in Kosciusko County.

Altrusa awards scholarships each year and supports Project Independence, a program through Combined Community Services that financially assists single mothers who are trying to go to college and other needy citizens. The Altrusa Club currently has 23 members.

Blosser Photography

In 1927, Lowell L. Blosser opened a photography studio in the basement of the Lake City Bank building at 114 S. Buffalo Street. About 1946, Blosser moved the business to a small building at 909 E. Center Street next to his home.

Following Lowell's death in 1976, the business was purchased by Fred Logan. Two years later it was sold to George Clement, who moved the business to its current location at 1002 E. Center Street, on the southeast corner of Center and Scott Streets. (The small building formerly occupied by Mr. Blosser's shop has since been demolished.)

In 1990, Tom Skaggs purchased the business, now known as Blosser's Camera & Video. Blosser's today is a full-service photography establishment, selling cameras and related equipment,

along with a large selection of picture frames and matting supplies.

The corner building currently occupied by Blosser's Camera & Video has had a variety of occupants over the years. Clarence and Roy Cox formerly operated Cox Brothers Grocery there from 1934 to 1942, followed by Walter's East Side Drug Store. In the early 1960s, Wesley and Ruby Moore operated Moore's Pizza and Broasted Chicken Carry-Out at the 1002 E. Center Street location, which was the first pizza restaurant in town. About 1968, the Moores moved their carry-out to 502 E. Winona Avenue, and the pizza business closed in 1972.

Dress Shops

The Marianne Shop, owned by Mrs. Grace M. Pierce and her daughter, was first located in a small store on Buffalo Street in 1927. Selling the latest styles and the highest quality ladies apparel, the business grew and in 1935 moved to the Widaman-McDonald Building at 115 E. Center Street. The Marianne Shop was purchased by Willard Greengard about 1952.

Mr. and Mrs. Roy F. Cox opened the Town & Country women's clothing store at 119 E. Center Street about 1951. The Coxes purchased the fixtures of the Toggery Shop, a former apparel store located across the street in the Arcade of the Elks Building. Their daughter and son-in-law, Diane and Lyle Shenefield, purchased the business in 1968, and the store closed following a fire in 1974.

The Hub

Roy Hatfield was proprietor of The Hub in the late 1920s. Located at 106 S. Buffalo Street, the men's clothing store carried Arrow shirts, Portis & Dobb's Hats, and McGregor, Wilson Brothers, and Hickok sportswear. By 1949, The Hub was owned by Grant Croy and his son-in-law, Homer A. Ring. Later, Ring was the sole proprietor until the store closed in the 1950s.

Funk Park

A proposal was made by Harry Crites to the City Council in 1928, that the city purchase the remainder of a triangle of property on Lake Street where Union Street meets Lake Street for a park. Gordon Rutter agreed to donate a portion of the triangle if the city secured a deed to the other land held by an estate. This is now known as Funk Park.

Lincoln Highway Marker

On September 1, 1928, the Boy Scouts set the Lincoln Highway marker in Funk Park on North Lake Street in recognition of Warsaw being located along the 3,300 miles of America's first coast-to-coast roadway.

Warsaw takes great pride in the fact that it is home to one of the few Lincoln Highway markers still in existence. In fact, it is the only marker in the State of Indiana in its original location and the last remaining marker known to exist along the 23 miles in Kosciusko County.

The Warsaw marker had been removed in the early 1990s during some roadwork, and the Warsaw Street Department saved the marker. On September 1, 1995—exactly 67 years after it was first set—the restored marker was reset and rededicated. The ceremony began with honored guests gathering on the east side of Warsaw and parading west in antique autos along the famed highway to Funk Park.

Among the guests were three men from Pierceton who were Boy Scouts in 1928 from Pierceton Troop #1, when the 3,000 markers were placed approximately one mile apart along the highway. That fall day in 1995, current Boy Scouts from Warsaw unveiled the refurbished marker as red, white and blue balloons lifted off to the sky.

A small group of interested persons, along with the Junior Historical Society and members of the Lincoln Highway Association, were instrumental in planning the celebration to recognize this special road. For many years before the four-lane U.S. 30 highway, the Lincoln Highway was the main thoroughfare east to west across Kosciusko County.

Bixler Park

In 1928, Sarah Bixler willed $10,000 to the City for a proposed William Bixler Hospital. However, after much debate and public input, the funds were used instead to purchase a strip of land owned by the State Bank of Warsaw on the east side of Center Lake near the current Kiddieland playground area, and Bixler Park was established. Each year many families enjoy having family reunions and picnics in this lovely park.

Power King Tool Corp.

Power King Tool Corporation was founded in 1928 by Theodore "Thede" Frazier, a prominent local businessman, and James P. Goodrich of

A ceremony was held at Funk Park on September 1, 1995 to rededicate the Lincoln Highway marker. Mayor Jeff Plank, center, is shown addressing the crowd.

This open chute in the railroad tracks allowed carloads of coal to be delivered to Warsaw Ice & Coal Company on E. Winona Avenue behind the former county garage building. Trucks would park under the railroad tracks and railroad cars stopped at the chute so a door on the bottom of the car could be opened and fill the trucks.

Indianapolis. The business was established on the ground floor of the two-story brick building on the southwest corner of Market and Detroit Streets (now Schrader Auto Parts). Power King manufactured quarter and half-inch electric drills.

Power King expanded to the second floor in 1929 when it purchased a line of portable electric hand saws from the Crow Saw Company. Business declined during the Depression, and in 1939 the

This horse-drawn cart was used to sell ice cream, cold pop, and peanuts. As noted at the top of the cart, it was operated by the "Frauhiger Boys."

An employee of Frauhiger Coal & Coke is shown with his truck before making a delivery.

An aerial view of the first buildings H.P. Frauhiger, Sr. constructed on Winona Avenue just east of the north-south railroad tracks. The railroad tower and interlocking are shown in the background.

company was purchased by Atlas Press Company of Kalamazoo, Michigan. A new line of woodworking tools was added, including electrically powered lathes, saws, jointers, shapers and drill presses for both the hobbyist and small building contractor. Power King also had a line of lawn mowers at one time.

In 1940, the company purchased property at Cleveland and Main Streets. A new, modern plant was constructed and additions were subsequently made to the facility over the next 13 years. In 1958, the management of Atlas Press moved its Clausing Lathe Division from Ottumwa, Iowa, to Warsaw, which turned the company's concentration to the production of metal turning lathes.

In 1942, Clausing employee Karl J. Heinzelman left the organization to start his own business in Warsaw named Union Tool Company. Clausing, Inc. was later bought by an out-of-state company.

Frauhiger Enterprises

Herman P. Frauhiger, Sr. was born in 1907 in Bluffton, Indiana. There were 12 children in the family, and the boys had a horse-drawn covered cart from which they sold ice cream, pop, and peanuts—the beginning of their business ventures. Herman Sr. also worked in coal yards as a young boy.

When he moved to Warsaw to live with his grandparents, Herman Sr. started his own business selling coal to the general public. Frauhiger bought his first train carload of coal in 1928 and sold it from a rented lot on S. Lake Street across from the railroad depot.

Frauhiger was soon able to buy property on South Street (now Winona Avenue) east of the intersection of the Pennsylvania and Big Four railroad tracks. At that time, the city limits ended at Detroit Street and South Street was a dirt road that ended at Scott Street. Business was good for "HP," as he became known, and he soon expanded his coal yards to Plymouth and Goshen. HP also began to build rental property along South Street on and around the coal yard to expand his business ventures.

His father-in-law, Ernest Clase, owned the Warsaw Ice Company. The businesses soon merged to become the Warsaw Ice and Coal Company. There were "ice rights" on Center Lake from where ice was cut and stored in large ice houses on the lake's south shore. The ice was sold from their offices on South Street.

Frauhiger expanded yet again by selling coal-burning furnaces and ice boxes. Adding to his rental properties, warehouse space was rented to the Coca-Cola Company. Al Hodges had a cement business on the south side of the Pennsylvania Railroad tracks behind the coal yard.

During World War II in the 1940s when the government started a program to subsidize lime applications to farmers' fields to supplement the growth of their crops, Frauhiger began selling and applying lime in the surrounding area.

The coal business began to decline in the 1950s. With technology changing and the introduction of electric refrigerators and other home appliances, Frauhiger changed with the times and entered the appliance business, starting Warsaw Appliance and TV. Business was good, and when Herman Jr. saw commercial laundromats in Muncie, Indiana, he convinced his father it would also be a profitable business to get into. Thus, during the 1960s the Frauhigers built and operated laundromats in eight Indiana cities.

The 1960s and 1970s saw significant growth as HP continued to purchase property on both sides of Winona Avenue. In 1974, Herman Sr. retired from the retail business, but then at age 67 he began to build the first public storage units in Warsaw on the grounds of the old coal yards, known today as U-Store Mini Warehouses. He eventually expanded that business to four Indiana towns with more than 750 individual storage units.

Frauhiger continued to build and develop property in and around Warsaw, including the Lake View Shopping Center, until well into his 80s. Following his death in 1993, his family's continuous involvement in the business has allowed the third generation of Frauhigers to add their mark to the ever-growing enterprise.

Unique Bakery

The Unique Bakery was started in 1929 by Anthony Mathia in a two-story building at 107 S. Buffalo Street. Mathia sold the well-known business in 1943 to Russell "Red" Smith and his wife, Helen.

Red had worked for a number of years with Merl Reiser at the Temptation Bakery located at 1228 E. Center Street (now site of Warsaw Health Foods). Smith bought the Temptation Bakery from Reiser in 1940 and operated that until purchasing the Unique Bakery in 1943.

These people are admiring the wonderful bakery items displayed in the Unique Bakery's large window on S. Buffalo Street.

The Unique Bakery made delicious sweets and desserts.

Some of the bakery's most popular treats were: painted cookies, long john and carmel rolls, rum cake, marble cake with chocolate fudge frosting, and a high yellow layered cake topped with whipped cream and cookie crumbs. Among many others, Frank Grose and Burleigh Burgh worked at the Unique Bakery in the 1950s.

Russell died in 1963, and Helen operated the bakery until she sold it in 1975 to Erly Grissell, who operated it until a fire in 1985. The fire not only affected the bakery, but also Helfrich's Women's Apparel and D&D Meats.

A one-story building was then erected on the former bakery site. Rod and Pat Teeple have operated their floral shop, Creative Floral Designs, at this location since 1987.

Walt Disney created Mickey Mouse in 1928.

The Chief Super Market held its grand opening April 21, 1939. This crowd of kids was excited about winning the bicycles and other prizes being given away.

When the Chief Super Market celebrated its 10th anniversary in April of 1949, owner H.B. "Doc" Lowery, right, asked Unique Bakery owners Russell and Helen Smith, left, to bake this 410-pound cake.

Looking east on Market Street in the 1950s, Warsaw's first shopping center was occupied by the Marsh Supermarket, Thornburg's Walgreen Drug Store, and Harvey's Dime Store.

Grocery Stores

Kroger, Warsaw's first large franchise grocery store, opened its doors in 1929 at 109 S. Buffalo Street. In 1942, Kroger moved to 114 W. Main Street (now the location of Reinholt's Town Square Furniture), and the store was managed by Martin Bauer.

By the 1960s, Kroger had moved to 1801 E. Center Street (current site of Auto Zone) and continued to thrive at that location until 1998. At that time, Kroger Company purchased the two Owen's Supermarkets in Warsaw and closed the 1801 E. Center Street store.

Horace B. "Doc" Lowery had operated the first Kroger store in Fort Wayne for 14 years before he came to Warsaw in 1939 and opened the Chief Super Market. It was located on the west side of the Courthouse Square in the north part of the former Oram Building (later occupied by Fred McKown and Bruce Petro's car dealerships).

The new, modern, self-service grocery provided special services such as the cashing of payroll checks, a lounge and sitting room with telephone service, "magic carpet" swinging doors, and music while shopping. The Chief Super Market was the first Warsaw grocery to install open-top deep freeze and self-service produce display counters.

Doc and Scharline Lowery had four children. Their son, Charles, was assistant manager at the store, and their twin daughters, Sharon and Shardene, and daughter Darlene also grew up helping with the grocery business. Doc's brother, Arthur, was manager of the meat department.

A newspaper ad for the Chief's grand opening Friday, April 21, 1939 included: bananas, six pounds for 25 cents; fancy Washington apples, five pounds for 25 cents; one dozen California Navel oranges, 10 cents; assorted Perfection cookies, 15 cents per pound. Breakfast bacon was priced at 15½ cents per pound, ground beef at 13½ cents per pound, and lunch meat at 11½ cents per pound. In addition, three pounds of pure pork lard could be purchased for 20 cents.

The Lowerys held an anniversary celebration in April of 1949. A giant 410-pound birthday cake, commemorating the Chief Super Market's ten years in Warsaw, was baked by Russell Smith, owner of the Unique Bakery, and decorated by his wife, Helen. The cake measured 4 feet in diameter, 4½ feet in height, and 9½ feet in circumference. Mrs. Smith spent over 20 hours decorating the cake which consisted of 105 pounds of cake flour,

90 pounds of egg whites, 50 pounds of sugar icing, and 48 pounds of creamery butter.

Within the cake were some 800 concealed capsules which contained notations of prizes, each valued up to $50. Each customer received a piece of cake, until it was gone, and those with a capsule were eligible for prizes noted in the capsules. The grand prize was $50 worth of groceries—the equivalent of six large baskets full. The celebration also included a Pet Milk quiz show.

In 1952, Lowery moved the grocery to 540 E. Market Street. He expanded the building to include a drug store and variety store, thus creating Warsaw's first shopping center. Marsh Supermarkets bought the Chief grocery in 1956 and remained at the 540 E. Market Street location. Doc Lowery still owned the building and when he died in 1958, his wife took over management of the property.

Marsh moved to a larger facility on the southwest corner of Winona Avenue and Buffalo Street in 1993. Sharon Clay, a daughter of the Lowerys, states that the grocery business was her life and she thoroughly enjoyed her work. She recently retired after 28 years with Marsh Supermarkets.

Kincaide's Bakery

Kincaide's Bakery, owned by Arden Kincaide, was first located at the corner of Lake and Washington Streets. It opened April 16, 1929, with a daily output of 260 pounds of bread and baked goods. The bakery moved to 926 E. Clark Street in 1930.

A few years later after extensive renovations and the installation of new equipment, the bakery had an open house June 12, 1938. A free cake was given away every half hour, and 2,103 people attended the open house. The new facility with the most modern automatic machinery allowed the daily output to be in excess of 2,200 pounds. The daily routine was all done by hand in 1929, but the new equipment installed in 1938 handled 85% of the work.

Kincaide's Bakery was the first small bake shop in town to place sliced bread on the market at the same price as unsliced bread. The staff of experienced bakers worked in shifts both day and night to service eight trucks that made deliveries throughout every town in Kosciusko County. Doris Kincaide Kesler recalls working at her father's bakery from 6:00 a.m. to 6:00 p.m. for $12 per week.

In 1941, Kincaide sold the bakery to Andy Goshert. The name was changed to Puritee Bakery

Arden Kincaide, owner of Kincaide's Bakery, poses by his panel truck in the 1930s before making a delivery.

Employees bake bread at the newly remodeled Kincaide's Bakery in 1938.

and they sold "Honey Bun" bread. When Goshert's sons had to leave for World War II, the bakery was sold back to Kincaide, who operated it for a short time thereafter.

Warsaw Plating Works

Brothers Guy H. and Russell "Dean" Aker, along with Paul Grimm, started a metal plating shop in 1929 known as Warsaw Plating Works. It is located at Jefferson and Lincoln Streets, and by 1961 was among the nation's largest consumers of nickel in the plating industry.

The business initially was devoted to plating and polishing surgical and orthopedic instruments. Just prior to World War II, however, it was involved in the plating of tubular steel furniture. Warsaw Plating Works then fulfilled defense contracts during the war, along with RCA's electronic plant in Marion, Indiana.

Grimm sold his interest in the business in 1945 to a third brother, Edward Aker, making it a single family held corporation. The firm went on to specialize in the polishing and plating of metal furniture, toys, orthopedic products, automobile and boating accessories.

Warsaw Plating Works continues to be owned by current members of the Aker family, although they are not involved in the management of the company.

Electric Motor Shop

Darryl Martin started an electric motor repair shop in 1929 on McClellan Street. The business moved in 1957 to the building at 710 McClellan Street formerly used by Bish Brown for various businesses. Martin's cousin, Lewis Rule, purchased the shop in 1964 and it became known as Rule Electric Motor Repair. The business was purchased in 1984 by Rule's daughter and son-in-law, Elaine and Ronald Reed, and the name changed to Reed Electric Motor Shop. The Reeds' son, Scott, is currently manager of the business.

In 1927, Gutzon Borglum began sculpting Mount Rushmore in South Dakota's Black Hills.

The Great Depression

Referred to as "Black Monday," October 29, 1929, was when the stock market crashed and started the Great Depression. The business bubble which had been expanding and glowing with optimism suddenly burst! People living in the cities were in dire need, as well as those in farming areas.

The Depression during the 1930s threatened people's jobs, savings, and even their homes and farms. At the depth of the Depression, over one-fourth of the American workforce was unemployed. To help local citizens, Warsaw provided about 15 acres near Arthur and Cook Streets, known as "Victory Gardens," where residents could grow vegetables. About 150 people applied for garden space.

A city garden on North Detroit Street was used to plant 600 cabbages. Dr. Clifford DuBois, then mayor, is credited with getting Warsaw through these trying years, and it is suspected that he used some of his own finances to help the city residents make it through that difficult time.

"Mac" Silveus remembers his father buying and selling wool and furs (mink and muskrat hides). Known as Silveus & Fawley, Curtis W. Silveus and Hubert Fawley operated their business at 105 N. Lake Street in the rear of the former Oram Building through the late 1940s. They had buyers in Ohio, Wisconsin, and Minnesota, and also sold to the Goldblatt's department store.

The American Legion Band and Company L, now known as the National Guard, marching east in the 100 block of Center Street on Decoration Day in 1929. Note the Interurban tracks in the middle of the street.

Chapter 10

Theatres & Drive-Ins

Strand Theatre

Grant S. Boice, had a photograph shop in Michigan City, Indiana during the late 1800s. In 1885, he started his first "magic lantern" shows where he would travel to area towns and put on still slide movie exhibitions. Grant and his son, John R. "Ralph" Boice, would hang a sheet up in a vacant building or on a large wall and set up benches for people to watch the show.

Soon silent movies were introduced and Grant Boice opened the first theatre in Elkhart in 1906. Ralph was operating the movie projector by age nine, which began his avid interest in "moving pictures." Following his return from the service, Ralph held projectionist positions at theatres in South Bend, Elkhart, and Mishawaka. In 1924, he opened his first theatre in Nappanee, The Boice Theatre. A year later he sold that theatre and returned to the Elco Theatre in Elkhart, before coming to Warsaw in 1931.

Although it is not known when the Strand Theatre at 110 N. Buffalo Street first opened, Louis J. Dunning owned the theatre in the 1920s. Ralph Boice became a projectionist at the Strand Theatre in October of 1931, and purchased the Strand a few months later in February of 1932. Councilman Jerry Patterson's mother, Barbara, sold tickets at the Strand and met her future husband, Max Patterson, there when he was a projectionist. Eugene Brown was also a projectionist.

The Strand was very small—just 22 feet wide and 132 feet long—with one middle aisle, five seats on each side, and a fairly small screen. At first the Strand did not sell concessions and had no restrooms. Patrons would go next door to the Mumaw Newsstand to buy popcorn and use the public restrooms in the Courthouse basement.

Randy Boice recalls that when he was fourteen his father spent $750 for a popcorn machine

The Strand Theatre was located at 110 N. Buffalo Street. Offices occupied the second story. In the early 1920s, the Carteaux Café was next door.

An admission ticket for the Strand Theatre.

Known as "Popcorn Annie," Mrs. Hansman sold popcorn at the Centennial Theatre. Her husband, John, who served two terms as mayor, was the ticket taker at the theatre.

and supplies. Weather permitting, Randy would wheel the cart outside on the sidewalk to sell five-cent and ten-cent bags of popcorn as people entered the theatre. It must have been quite a moneymaker, as he bought his first new car at age sixteen.

Admission for a Saturday afternoon movie was ten cents. Offices were located above the theatre, and at one time, the draft board was upstairs. The Strand Theatre was still operating in the late 1940s, but the building was converted into office space after it closed.

Centennial / Boice Theatre

Attorney John D. Widaman and Dr. Angus C. McDonald constructed the Widaman-McDonald Building in 1916 on the northwest corner of

Center and Indiana Streets. The Centennial Theatre opened in that building in 1917, and ventriloquist Charlie McCarthy was one of the first to perform there. A November 11, 1918, newspaper ad states that the Centennial was showing Sessue Hayakawa in *Secret Game*, a detective story between the Japanese and the American Secret Service officials. Admission was six cents and eleven cents, with shows at 7:00 p.m. and 8:30 p.m..

The theatre, which occupied most of the rear part of the building and had a balcony, was named the Centennial in commemoration of the centennial of our state in 1916. Over the years, various businesses occupied the front of the building. The Interurban Railway had a station on the northwest corner of Center and Indiana Streets, with a rail siding on Indiana Street to stop and pick up passengers.

Two-term mayor John Hansman was the ticket taker for many years at the Centennial Theatre. His wife, known as "Popcorn Annie," sold popcorn at a stand just outside the theatre lobby by the Interurban station. Nick Mallers managed the Centennial Theatre from about 1937 to 1948, and then built his own Lake Theatre on the northwest corner of Buffalo and Main Streets.

There were drawings on Saturday nights at the Centennial Theatre. Patrons wrote their names on pieces of paper that were put in a big chicken wire cylinder. Barbara Anderson recalls that the cylinder would become very packed with names because it was not emptied from week to week. Sometimes a name would be drawn for someone who had died. However, you had to be present in the audience to win. During the Depression, dishes were given away as prizes, and small amounts of money were given away in the 1940s.

Ralph and Gladys Boice, who owned the Strand Theatre on N. Buffalo Street, also took over management of the Centennial Theatre. The Boices acquired Dr. McDonald's interest in the building in 1948 from his estate, and by 1954 owned the entire property. At that time, Mayor Hodges had a contracting business and was hired to completely remodel the 550-seat theatre.

The Centennial's name was changed to the Boice Theatre and a new lighted marquee was added to the front of the building. The Boice Theatre showed *The Long Gray Line*, a story about the West Point Military Academy, for its grand opening on April 4, 1955. The Boice family operated both the Strand and the Boice theatres for several years.

The Centennial Theatre was in the Widaman-McDonald Building on the northwest corner of Center and Indiana Streets. It later became known as the Boice Theatre. The Interurban depot and newsstand was next door to the east.

A view of the Centennial Theatre lobby. The wooden double doors led into the theatre, and the stairs on the right led to the balcony. A Gene Autry poster hangs above the door.

Mr. Boice spent many hours each week taking movies of local events for the Boice Theatre "newsreels"—Rotary programs, sorority events, church events, school football and basketball games, the county fair, Pioneer Days, visiting dignitaries and natural disasters. Almost every Friday night he would film a ballgame and then spend the weekend processing the film in his basement. Ralph Boice also filmed every draftee that left from Warsaw during World War II.

His documentation on film during the 1930s through the 1960s varied from parades, farm activities and jitterbug contests to ice harvesting on Center Lake, sporting events, and visiting politicians. Max Patterson worked closely with Boice to take movies over the years and was also instrumental in helping record an outstanding history of our community. The newsreels were played only at the Strand Theatre prior to 1941 and were usually shown before the feature movies started. Local residents flocked to the theatre to see pictures of themselves and their children in the movies.

It should be noted that without the help of Mrs. Boice, the many, many movies could never have been made. Randy recalls that his father would use at least 100,000 feet of film per year. While Ralph worked in his basement laboratory at 710 N. Lake Street on Friday nights, Saturdays and Sundays to process the film, Gladys would oversee the operation of the movie theatres.

Mrs. Boice donated their collection of over 100 reels of 16mm films to the Kosciusko County Historical Society in 1986. The Society was awarded a grant to have segments of the films reformatted on videotape so they could be shown at the Jail Museum.

Max and Barbara Patterson leased the theatre from Ralph Boice from 1960 to 1964. For a number of years, the Pattersons also managed the Fairy Theatre in North Webster and the Pickwick Theatre in Syracuse. Their son, Jerry, was responsible for changing the Boice marquee each time the movies changed. Admission during the 1960s was 75 cents for adults and 25 cents for kids, and admission sometimes went up to $1 if a really good movie was showing.

In 1967, Ralph Boice offered to lease the theatre to Roger Vore for $100 per month for one year. Vore accepted, changed the name to Center Cinema, and opened Halloween Eve 1967 with a wildlife show. He took in only $35 the first weekend,

A view from the stage of the Centennial Theatre, looking out to the seating area.

A side view of the seating area of the Centennial Theatre.

and the first six months were difficult. However, Vore featured movies being shown on the national level, and with shows like *Woodstock* and John Wayne cowboy movies, business quickly picked up. With things going well, Vore leased the theatre for $350 per month the second year. *Walking Tall* was showing at the time a fire badly damaged the building on January 5, 1974. Randy Boice states that the fire department determined an electrical fire started in the wiring under the projection booth.

Following the 1974 fire, the Widaman-McDonald Building was purchased and renovated by Frank Saemann, and has since been known as the Town Center Mall. Tenants in 2001 on the first

The movie industry instituted the Oscar awards in 1929.

The Centennial Theatre often had live entertainment on Saturday nights. This group includes many members of the Brumfield family. Note the organ sitting on the floor at the front of the stage.

floor are: Key Bank and Zimmer-Rowland. Tenants on the second floor include: F.I. Saemann Foundation, Welborn & Associates, BABE, Health Care Foundation, Attorney Jim Butts, Financial Advisor Brad Skiles, GTP Financial Services, and the Indiana Institute of Technology.

At one time, Roger Vore owned 36 theatres and drive-ins throughout northern Indiana. Nick Mallers leased the Lake Theatre to Vore in 1974, which he operated until 1982 before building his own Center Cinema on the east side of town in the strip mall across new U.S. 30. Due to a construction problem, Vore requested the contractor put carpet on the walls in the theatre. That unplanned change worked out so well that he did the same in all of his future theatres. After managing the Lake Theatre, Vore also took over the Warsaw Drive-In for a short time in 1982.

Lincolndale Drive-In

When the Lincolndale Drive-In closed in Fort Wayne during the early 1980s, Max and Barbara Patterson bought the screen and moved it to the east side of Warsaw on the north side of U.S. 30. Max worked for NIPSCO and at that time NIPSCO was on strike, so he hired some of his fellow workers to help cut the large screen into sections, weld wheels on the pieces, and then pull them down U.S. 30 to Warsaw.

The NIPSCO workers also helped build the Lincolndale's log cabin concession stand. The drive-in had radio sound and two screens, and all of the projection equipment came from the Miami Open Air Drive-In at Peru, Indiana. The Lincolndale Drive-In only operated a few years in Warsaw, from 1982 to 1986. Bill Batalis has since constructed several buildings on the property.

Lake Theatre & Warsaw Drive-In

The Mallers brothers opened the Lake Theatre on the northwest corner of Buffalo and Main Streets in 1948. The first show on Friday, October 1, was *Up in Central Park*. After they opened the Warsaw Drive-In Theater in 1952 on Old Road 30 West, Nick split from the Mallers Brothers, who were already in business with other theatres in Fort Wayne, Muncie, Bluffton, and Lima, Ohio, and retained the Lake Theatre and Warsaw Drive-In.

The last movies to be shown on the drive-in "big screen" were *Star Wars: The Phantom Menace* and *Bowfinger* at the end of the 1999 season. The

A fire on January 5, 1974, damaged the Center Cinema Theatre and other businesses occupying the building at that time.

Windows in the Widaman-McDonald building were boarded up after the 1974 fire. The stairway along the east side of the building led to the basement where a pool hall, as well as several other businesses were located over the years.

screen was demolished May 26, 2000, with plans for a housing subdivision.

Now operated by Mallers' granddaughter, Elizabeth McMillan, the 52-year-old Lake Theatre was totally renovated in 1999 with stadium seating, Dolby Digital and DTS sound systems, and other hi-tech amenities. Mr. Mallers' daughter and son-in-law, Bess and Tom Joyner, opened their six-screen North Pointe Cinemas on Husky Trail in December 1996.

An aerial view in the 1920s of the park along Center Lake.

During the 1920s and 1930s, the beach at Center Lake Park was lined with benches.

Chapter 11

1930-1939

Tennis Clubs

In the early 1930s, there was a Warsaw group that played tennis at Plymouth, Goshen, South Bend, and the Fort Wayne Country Club. The group included Ralph and Kenneth Boice, George Bowser, Earl Fausnaught, Robert P. Gast, Bob Hall, James Hartle, Clarence Hartman, John "Red" Morse, and Reub Williams.

Howard Levin recalls that he was nine to 10 years old at that time. His father, Myer Levin, built a private clay-surfaced tennis court on N. Detroit Street by Center Lake Park. Howard made a deal with the guys that he would roll and line the court, and in exchange they would teach him to play tennis. Each player had different variations and strokes, and Levin became quite an accomplished tennis player, going on to play at Indiana University. The courts were turned over to the city in 1945 after World War II interfered with the club's activity.

Theatre owner Ralph Boice continued to be an avid tennis player, spending many hours each summer at the courts with the youth of our community. In fact, he met his wife on a tennis court in Elkhart. In the spring of 1947, he urged the high school to start a tennis team. At that time the IHSAA rules were very strict and all coaches had to be employed as teachers. The shop teacher was appointed the title of tennis coach, in name only, and Boice was given permission to form a team. The nine-member team consisted of Joe Beeson, George Carnegis, Herb Dye, Dan Gast, Bob Henderson, Ron Jacobs, Don Lora, Frank Luecke, and George Rosselot.

The 1947 tennis team remains the only team to go undefeated for the season. Unfortunately, the team was not recognized as a varsity sport and did not receive letters. In fact, they were not recognized in either the 1947 or 1948 school annuals. Five of the team members, however, went on to play college

For many years, the Warsaw Racquet Club held an annual tournament in memory of tennis enthusiast Ralph Boice. Winners of the 1983 Boice Classic Division I were, left to right, Carolyn Davidson, Elaine Glova, Susan Smith, Mrs. Gladys Boice, Louise Creighton, Millie Paton, and Fran Hampton.

Winners of the 1983 Boice Classic Division II tennis tournament were, left to right, winners Susan Smith and Louise Creighton, runners-up Martha Strayer and Alberta Montgomery, consolation winners Carol Sands and Mary Stamper, consolation runners-up Freida Helm and Ann Howe.

Avid tennis players Ralph and Gladys Boice pause on the tennis court by Center Lake about 1960. They owned and operated the Strand Theatre and Boice Theatre.

Oscar Mayer introduced the first Wienermobile in 1936 to promote its hot dogs.

tennis. Due to guidelines from IHSAA, the school board eliminated the tennis team after one season.

Joe Beeson was the Warsaw High School athletic director for a number of years, and in the spring of 1963 he started the first official tennis team. Joe recalls that Ralph Boice left a sum of money in his will to be used for an annual high school tennis sportsmanship award. Furthermore, the Northern Indiana Tennis Association held its organizational meeting in the basement of the Boice home on North Lake Street.

With his continued interest in tennis, in 1976 Beeson built the Warsaw Racquet Club north of Warsaw on State Road 15. He was the first pro/manager/janitor. For a few years they held the Gladys Boice Classic women's tournament there. Beeson sold the Warsaw Racquet Club in May of 1999 to Garry and Sherry England, who totally remodeled and updated the facility.

Biltwell Basket Company

Chester L. Hoover had worked at basket companies in Converse and Claypool, Indiana, and in the early 1930s started the Biltwell Basket Company in a large building on N. Detroit Street (currently the site of Instrumed Technologies). That building burned in the late 1930s and Hoover built a small factory behind his home at 326 N. Buffalo Street. When the family home was sold, he constructed a new building on the north side of W. Winona Avenue at the edge of town.

Biltwell Basket Company made all kinds of baskets, including clothes hampers, baby baskets, and market baskets, but production ceased when a fire destroyed the building in 1951.

H.J. Schrader & Company

H.J. Schrader & Company, consisting of a number of department stores in northern Indiana, including Warsaw, was purchased in 1930 by Everett Ridge who owned the Ridge Company in South Bend. Ridge focused the business on automotive parts and supplies.

In the 1940s, Schrader's occupied both the Biggs Building at 121 W. Center Street and the Hitzler Building at 123 W. Center Street. The adjoining buildings were filled with tires, batteries, furniture, paints, wallpaper, hardware, and auto parts. Alvin D. Brallier was the manager in 1947.

The automotive department was made independent in 1949. The Schrader name was retained and the business moved to a separate location at 201 W. Center Street. Rene Nine became manager of the automotive department at that time, and in 1953 acquired 25 percent interest in the automotive part of the business.

Schrader's housewares and furniture department remained at 121 W. Center Street, and in 1949 was managed by C.T. Zimmer. In the 1950s, Ivan Croy was general manager and Andy Goshert was the appliance manager.

By 1956, Schrader Auto Parts was outgrowing the building at 201 W. Center Street. Rene Nine purchased a larger building at 209 E. Center Street for the company and acquired the remaining interest of the automotive business. Schrader Auto Parts remained on E. Center Street for twenty years. In 1976, Nine purchased the two-story brick building at 314 E. Market Street (formerly occupied by Power King Tool Corp.) and moved Schrader Auto Parts to its current location.

Chester Hoover constructed this building on W. Winona Avenue for the Biltwell Basket Company.

Employees Ted Shull, Ledford Hensley, and Maurice Noble receive a delivery at Schrader Automotive, 209 E. Center Street (c. 1960). The sign on the front of the Arnolt Building to the left states that the U.S. Air Force and Civil Air Patrol offices were located next door at that time.

Clifford Scholl retired in 1990 after 40 years with Schrader's. His son, Kent "Butch," began stocking shelves at age 15 in 1966 and has been employed there ever since. For a time, Clifford Scholl and Marvin Evans were partners in the business with Rene Nine maintaining controlling interest. John Calhoun has managed the Warsaw store since 1988.

Nine retired in 1991 and sold the building and the business to Hoffman Brothers in South Bend. Schrader Auto Parts is the oldest continuous parts distributor and automotive machine shop in Kosciusko County. The business continues to handle auto parts and accessories of all kinds, in addition to tools and equipment, and has a well-equipped automotive machine shop.

Truman / Bartel Printing

Truman Printing originated in 1930 when Rev. Benjamin H. Truman and his son, Raymond "Bud" Truman, bought equipment to print things for their church. The work was done in the elder Truman's home on the southwest corner of Market and Columbia Streets. The Trumans then moved to the southwest corner of Center and Columbia Streets, where the business was located in their basement. Over time, they began doing more and more printing for others and the business grew.

When Rev. Truman died in the mid 1960s, his son-in-law, Jerry Laurien, took over the operations. In 1970, Wilmer Bartel, who had been in partnership with Laurien, bought the entire business and changed the name to Bartel Printing. It moved to

"The Star Spangled Banner" became the national anthem in 1931.

The Post Office was constructed in 1931 on the northwest corner of Lake and Market Streets. When the current Post Office was built in 1978, this building was converted to office space.

In 1932, E.A. Gast bought the Smith Coal Company and service station on the southwest corner of Market and Columbia Streets and changed the name to Rainbow Fuel & Service. Since 1938, Gast Fuel & Service has been at this location, although the gas station was removed many years ago.

The Empire State Building in New York City opened on May 1, 1931.

the rear of the building at 502 E. Winona Avenue, where Moore's Pizza and Broasted Chicken Carry-out occupied the front portion. When Moore's closed, Bartel Printing took over the entire building, until the family moved the business to 310 Cedar Street in 2000.

Post Office

In 1931, a limestone building was erected on the northwest corner of Lake and Market Streets for the new Post Office. In 1978, the Post Office moved two blocks west to the southeast corner of Market and Columbia Streets. The block where the current Post Office is located was formerly occupied by Johnson Lumber Company, a service station, and the Jif-O-Mat laundry.

Rainbow / Gast Fuel & Service

The property on S. Columbia Street known as Smith Coal Company in the early 1900s was purchased by Estil A. Gast in 1932. He then incorporated with two partners, Porter Brown and Arthur Bishopp, to form Rainbow Fuel & Service.

The coal facility had a track siding for eight railcars and bins located directly beneath to unload shipments of coal. Just north of the coal yard facing Columbia Street was Rainbow Fuel's Sinclair service station which also sold Goodyear tires. Mr. Gast bought out the interest of his partners in 1937; Stanley Kintzel was hired as general manager; and in 1938 the present corporate name of Gast Fuel & Service, Inc. was adopted. Gast Fuel was the last coal company in town.

Over the years, Gast Fuel has had service stations in surrounding towns. The Gast family interest was sold to Stanley Kintzel in 1969, and his son, David, is currently president of the company. The business office remains at 216 S. Columbia Street.

Pinky's 76 Station

In 1932, the Pure Oil Company built a gas station on the southeast corner of Center and Detroit Streets. There were three or four owners over the years, but Clarence Norris had it for many years until about 1958. Robert "Pinky" Eherenman owned the business from 1964 to 1998, and it was known as Pinky's 76 Service Station. When the business closed, the property was sold to D & D Oil Company in Rochester, and the building with a unique tiled roof was demolished.

The Buffalo Inn

In 1933, C.O. "Charlie" Gerard operated The Buffalo Inn at 204 S. Buffalo Street. He kept a sawed-off billiards cue stick behind the counter to keep the rowdy customers in line. Jerry Gerard recalls the Pekinese dog his grandfather had in the late 1930s. It was named "Billy Potts" after a man who hung around the Courthouse Square. Charlie would feed the dog ice cream at The Buffalo Inn. Billy Potts had his own bank account at the Lake City Bank, and a paw print would cash his checks. *Reader's Digest* even published an article about the popular dog.

In the late 1940s, Benjamin and Dorothy Turner purchased the business and changed the name to The Warsaw Grill. Merlin "Tip" Keener took over the bar-restaurant about 1952. Rex Watters then purchased the business in 1977 and changed the name to Rex's Rendezvous. It is currently operated by his son, Robin Watters.

Prior to 1933, the 204 S. Buffalo Street site was the location of Charles F. Nye's clothing store, and a tailor business was in the basement. At one time another bar, the Rainbow Inn, was next door at 206 S. Buffalo Street.

Dahms & Yarian

Herman C. Dahms founded his accounting firm in 1933, now known as Dahms & Yarian. The office was first located in the former Catlin house on E. Fort Wayne Street. For one year the office was on N. Indiana Street across from the Centennial Theatre. (There was a building with three small offices where the Lake City Bank park is now located.) In 1935, Dahms moved the office to his home in the 1000 block of E. Fort Wayne Street.

In 1938, the firm moved above the Fashion Shoe Store at 113 S. Buffalo Street (in The Globe Building). At that time, Claude Longfellow became a partner for a short period of time. The company became known as Dahms & Yarian when John Yarian joined the firm in 1940. George "Gordy" Bumbaugh joined his father-in-law's company in December of 1945, retiring in 1977. When Lake City Bank relocated from 114 S. Buffalo Street in 1962, Dahms & Yarian moved across the street to that location.

Due to failing health, Dahms retired in 1957. Yarian was a partner until his death in 1970. Alan Wuthrich joined the firm in 1958 and remains a partner to date. When DePuy moved its offices in 1975 to a new facility on U.S. 30, Dahms & Yarian made their last move to the northwest corner of Market and Columbia Streets at 110 S. Columbia Street.

Bodkin Abstract Company

In 1934, Herman M. Bodkin established Bodkin Abstract Company at 111½ W. Center Street. Until that time, Kosciusko Abstract and Guaranty Company (started in 1899) was the dominant local abstract company.

When the monthly rental fee of $6 was raised due to new owners of the building, Bodkin moved his business in 1939 to the second floor above the Central Shoe Company at 106 E. Center Street. The company was admitted to the Indiana Title Association in 1941. Competition arrived during the postwar years when Snodgrass and Williamson opened the Warsaw Abstract Corporation in the basement of the First National Bank.

When Mr. Bodkin died in 1946, his wife Lois, along with Thomas J. LeHew who worked as manager, continued the business and it was incorporated. Mrs. Bodkin held the position of president until the business was sold in 1979 to Bob and Sharon Sanders.

In 1983, Sanders acquired the Kosciusko County Abstract and Title Guarantee Company, followed by the purchase of Warsaw Abstract Corporation in 1997. The merger of these three companies has since become Kosciusko County's largest and most complete abstract company.

View of the northeast corner of Lake and Main Streets on the north side of the Courthouse Square in the early 1920s. The Smith Battery & Electric building is now a parking lot. Bodkin Abstract occupies the two middle buildings at present. The Chinworth building to the far right is currently the site of Reinholt's Town Square Furniture.

White Hill Manor

In the early 1900s, the property at 2513 E. Center Street was owned by Dr. John R. White, a dentist, and referred to as White's Hill. The large, elaborate home at that location, now known as White Hill Manor, was built in 1934 by Justin O. Zimmer, founder of Zimmer, Inc. Mr. Zimmer lived there for 12 years before selling it in 1946 to Frank Saemann, founder of Bourbon-based OEC International. Between 1972 and 1987 the property was owned by SYM Financial and used for offices.

Chuck Yeager Insurance was also located there, and it was during that time that Jerry Gerard used his artistic talents to design and install a stained glass window in an east bathroom on the first floor. In January of 1988 rooms began to be changed for the evolvement into a Bed & Breakfast.

Carm and Zola Henderson owned it for a few years before Bruce and Steve Shaffner purchased the property in 1998 to merge with the Wagon Wheel Playhouse and Ramada Plaza. This elite B&B offers a quiet, relaxing atmosphere. All eight guestrooms have their own baths, with two rooms having baths with original wall tiles and fixtures.

John Dillinger surprises Warsaw

At 1:00 a.m. on Friday, April 13, 1934, America's Public Enemy No. 1—John Dillinger and one of his henchmen—emerged from the darkness as Night Officer Judd H. Pittenger stopped at the

In 1935, Shirley Temple was the first child actor to win an Academy Award.

This cartoon, referring to when John Dillinger's gang was in Warsaw, appeared in the Fort Wayne News-Sentinel in 1936.

The live radio show of "The Lone Ranger" was broadcast from 1933 to 1954.

corner of Buffalo and Center Streets and began walking south on Buffalo Street.

They covered Officer Pittenger with two sub-machine guns, disarmed him when he offered resistance, then marched him two blocks to City Hall. As they walked to City Hall, Officer Pittenger was struck a severe blow on the back of his head with the butt of his own gun and was hit two more times on the head, but with less force.

Once upstairs in the police department, as the two bandits turned toward the ammunitions cabinet in the police room, Pittenger kicked the door shut and made his escape. He rushed down the stairs, falling most of its length, and dodged into an alley behind the Centennial Theatre, just in time to get out of the range of the machine guns as the men chased after him. Pittenger watched them get into a black sedan parked on Indiana Street and drive away to the north. It is reported that they stole three bulletproof vests and two revolvers.

Officer Pittenger rushed to Gill's Grill restaurant at 105 E. Center Street to report his experience, and within a few minutes the news was being flashed by telephone and telegraph to the state police, to nearby city and town authorities, and the entire world. Newspaper reporters and photographers began arriving as early as 3:30 a.m.

Mike Hodges (future mayor) was the fireman on duty at City Hall that night. He was aroused from his sleep by the noise made by the bandits as they rushed down the stairs from the upper floor. Frank Lucas was the chief of police at the time of the robbery and Phil Neff's grandfather, Ralph Liggett,

was an Indiana State Police officer.

Victor Hillery was employed at Earl W. Conrad's Garage just east of City Hall during the time that Dillinger and his cohort forced Officer Pittenger upstairs to the police department. A couple weeks later, Hillery was robbed at the garage and locked in the bathroom, and decided to quit soon after.

Dillinger's failed attempt at a holdup in his hometown of Mooresville, Indiana, on September 6, 1924, had put him in prison until his parole in May 1933. However, his days of crime after the Warsaw holdup were numbered, as he died just months later in July 1934, in Chicago.

Sears, Roebuck & Co.

Sears, Roebuck & Co. opened a retail store in Warsaw at 121 W. Market Street in 1934. The company started about 1886 and first catered solely to the farm trade, carrying fencing, poultry and dairy supplies, and other farm supplies. Sears then branched out over the years to include multiple lines of merchandise for both home and farm.

William E. Pearl was hired as the first store manager. Pearl remained with the Warsaw store until 1965 when he was transferred to Kentucky. Ray W. Kelley was appointed as the Warsaw manager, followed by Roger Peters.

After the downtown store closed in the early 1990s, Sears relocated to the Marketplace Shopping Center. At the time the Market Street building burned on September 27, 1998, it was occupied by The Butterfly music store. It remains a vacant lot today.

Dairy Farms

The Rife Dairy was started about 1934 by Chauncey Rife on the south edge of Warsaw at 652 S. Buffalo Street. The Rife Dairy was a competitor of the nearby Crystal Dairy. Dave Hillery recalls his uncle, Chauncey Rife, talking about a horse named Prince who quickly learned the milk delivery route and would automatically stop at each place without being directed. One day, however, a bad storm scared the horse and he took off with the wagon in tow—but without a driver—and ran through Oakwood Cemetery, scattering milk bottles everywhere. It took them several days to pick up all the bottles and clean up the broken glass.

Harmon Hillery, Dave's grandfather, also had a dairy farm on the south side of Warsaw. About 1935, seven cows on the Hillery farm were killed when they were struck by lightning during a torrential rain storm.

Hull's Transfer

In 1935, Stan Hull started Hull's Transfer, a local truck delivery business, in a building by the alley just south of M.M. Syphers, which was located at 110 S. Washington Street (now site of Tarkio Road bicycle shop). Stan was in his early twenties. He had a truck but no business, so he loaded the truck with empty boxes and drove around town to make people think he had business, until he finally did.

In the early 1940s, Stan kept getting deferred from the armed forces because his business hauled products for the Arnolt Corporation, which made numerous items for the war effort. Before he finally reported to the service, Stan sold the delivery business to Amos Myer. Unfortunately, Stan did not pass his physical, and just a day or so later returned to Warsaw without a job. It was then that he began working at his father's Warsaw Feed Store.

Hull's Transfer moved to its new facility at 2217 E. Center Street about 1939 (approximately now the site of Liquid Assets). In the mid 1950s, Amos Myer sold the business to O.J. Miller, who later sold it to Clyde Bair and Pete Burgh. A new building was constructed in 1964 at 2744 Old Road 30 West, and Bair was then sole proprietor until about 1982 when it closed.

Stan Hull's former wife, Mary Belle Latta, recalls the dapper uniforms the drivers wore with black leather ties. The men's clothes were neatly pressed and every morning they polished

Stan Hull started Hull's Transfer in 1935. It was first located in the 100 block of S. Washington Street, next to M.M. Syphers' ice cream and soft drink business.

These dapper men drove delivery trucks for Hull's Transfer. They are, left to right: unknown, Stanley Hull, Wilbur Tennant, Robert Hull, Pete Burgh, and Arden Hull.

Hull Transfer's fleet of trucks was lined up and ready to make deliveries.

Donald Weirick, right, in his Masonic Commandery uniform at the base of the stairs to the Courthouse, with his children, left to right: Jerry, Janet, and Mary Ann. The Weirick family lived in the Courthouse for 12 years when Donald was the custodian.

The Masonic Commandery during a parade (c. 1940), walking south on Lake Street in front of the Courthouse. Donald Weirick is carrying the U.S. flag, and Maurice DePoy is carrying the Commandery flag.

their boots before getting in their trucks. Stan and Mary Belle's son, Jerry Hull, was contracted with the Kosciusko County Convention & Visitors Bureau from 1990 to 1999 to fly the CVB's hot air balloon, which they referred to as their "floating billboard."

Kosciusko County REMC

A meeting was held at the West Wayne School on November 2, 1935, to discuss rural electrification, and the Kosciusko County REMC (Rural Electric Membership Corporation) was established. The first electric meter was set into place on the Clinton Whitney farm where Ettinger Road and Country Club Road intersect, and on December 21, 1938, the first Kosciusko County REMC light was switched on.

In 1945, no one had ever heard of "cherry pickers" or "bucket trucks." With an idea and $75, Maurice Salman, then line crew foreman for the REMC, built the first successful self-leveling aerial platform. The rig was used to trim trees and maintain electrical lines. In 1961 REMC was called upon by the Warsaw Fire Department to use the bucket truck to assist with a fire in a downtown multi-story building.

Family lived in Courthouse

In 1936, Donald C. Weirick was laid off from the Pango Milk Chocolate Company (later Litchfield Creamery) on Argonne Road. About that same time, the County Commissioners offered the job of courthouse custodian, with housing included. Don and his wife, Goldie, moved into the living quarters on the ground floor with their four-year-old daughter Mary Ann. Two weeks later, their daughter Janet was born in the bedroom on the first floor, and their son Jerry completed the family in 1937. The living quarters in the basement included the circle area, east hall, and about five rooms plus a bathroom in the southeast corner.

Don was responsible for climbing to the fourth floor to wind or set the clock in the dome. Steam heat for the courthouse was generated by coal stokers. Coal bins were on the north side of the first floor in three rooms, and coal was transported to stokers by wheelbarrow. Don swept the halls, emptied trash, and mopped where necessary every night. It was Goldie's job to keep the restrooms clean. Women could often be found visiting in the Ladies' Lounge, as in those days the courthouse restrooms were open most days and into the evenings.

Goldie hung her family's laundry in the hall on lines from the circle east. The children played on the courthouse lawn, and Jerry recalls playing with his toy trucks and cars and digging in the dirt around the northwest corner of the courthouse. He would sometimes ride his bicycle inside the courthouse on the ground floor, and kids would also rollerskate in the hallway. Jerry remembers the fair being held around the courthouse, and the Ferris wheel was located in the middle of the 100 block of S. Buffalo Street. Shows at the Strand Theatre cost 12 cents and you could stay all afternoon, which Jerry often did.

The Weiricks were the last family to live in the courthouse, as the basement was later used to store county records. When the Weiricks left in 1948, Don went into business at the DX service station across the street on Lake Street. Goldie was manager of the Greyhound Bus Station beside the DX station for many years. Don later managed the Mobil station on W. Market Street.

Litchfield Creamery Co.

Founded in the early 1920s in Litchfield, Illinois, the Litchfield Creamery Company opened a Warsaw branch in 1936 on Argonne Road with the purchase of the old Pango Milk Chocolate Company. Litchfield's main product was "Milnot," a canned milk product, which replaced Pango's chocolate milk. When the Canteen Company purchased the business, the name was changed to the Milnot Company.

In 1961, the company was reported to have been purchasing in excess of 72 million pounds of raw milk annually from its 1,150 farm suppliers. The company also manufactured cream, condensed milk solids and powdered milk which were sold to ice cream manufacturers in this area as well as the eastern seaboard, while most of the butter was sold in the New York market. By 1946 the business had grown to such an extent that a new million dollar plant was built, with the first raw milk processed through the new stainless steel facilities in early 1948.

Howard Thompson served as plant manager from 1938 to 1970, and was succeeded by Erwin Niemann, who had been the assistant plant manager since 1937. Long-time employee Rollin Knouff began as a general laborer in 1941, advanced to operating machinery, and was the maintenance supervisor when the Warsaw plant closed in 1977.

Endicott Church Furniture

Endicott Church Furniture Manufacturing Company was founded by Don Endicott in 1936 on Argonne Road. Started as a small cabinet-making business, the company grew to achieve the nation's number two spot for total volume of church furniture manufactured and sold throughout the U.S.

Pulpits and lecterns were the original products, which then led to the production of every type and

Don Weirick, Bill Sparks, and George Woodling stand beside new Studebaker taxis in 1954 at the Warsaw Cab & Bus Station. This small frame building was located on Lake Street across from the Courthouse. The County Clerk's office in the current Justice Building now occupies that section of the block. The building to the right was Don Weirick's DX gas station.

The Kinsey Coach Bus Lines, operated by Bill Kinsey in the 1950s, transported people to Fort Wayne and back to Warsaw. The bus station was on the west side of the Courthouse Square.

Don Weirick owned the DX gas station on Lake Street across from the Courthouse Square in the 1950s. Holding the dog is Weirick's son, Jerry.

Owner Emmalu Shideler takes a break to eat some ice cream at the Double Dip, 207 W. Center Street (c. 1945).

Hazen Shideler stands outside the Warsaw Double Dip which he and his wife operated. As shown on the window, two dips of ice cream cost a nickel (c. 1945).

The Warsaw Double Dip

After operating their Double Dip ice cream shop in Columbia City for one year in 1936, Hazen and Emmalu Shideler moved to town and opened the Warsaw Double Dip at 207 W. Center Street (current site of the Downtown restaurant), and the family lived upstairs. Ice cream cones with two scoops cost a nickel, and people would line up down the street waiting for a taste of the homemade ice cream.

One time at the Double Dip, a husband and wife stopped to buy sundaes to eat as they strolled through the downtown on a Sunday afternoon. Their routine stroll soon began to include a stop each week at the Double Dip for two sundaes. Thereafter for quite some time, one of the Double Dip's special treats was called "the walking sundae."

The Shidelers also opened a drive-in restaurant in 1953 across from the Warsaw Drive-In Theater on Old 30 West, which they operated for just two seasons. After closing the Double Dip in 1955, Mr. Shideler started Rocket TV in the same location at 207 W. Center Street.

Their daughter, Peggy Keeton, recalls the following businesses were located in the 200 block of W. Center Street in the 1940s: 201 W. Center was a doctor's office; at 203, Lyall and Peggy Stokes had The Donut Shop; Kenneth L. and L.W. Stokes had Stokes Tin Shop at 205; the Warsaw Double Dip was at 207; Mel's Luncheon was at 209; and George East's Dry Cleaners was at 211 W. Center Street.

Korth Furniture Company

After leaving the employment of Sears-Roebuck in 1936 and a brief partnership in a Milford wood-working business, Raymond J. Korth established Warsaw Furniture Manufacturing Company in 1937. It was located in the former Mayfair Furniture Manufacturing Company building in the 600 block of N. Detroit Street (since replaced by the former Zimmer facility now owned and occupied by Instrumedical Technologies).

Korth started with an order from Sears for 20,000 hardwood end tables. They were packed one to a carton and sold for 57 cents each. In 1939, Sears had run into problems with their source of low-end maple bedroom furniture. Therefore, Korth took over the 765 W. Market Street building to begin making bedroom furniture. The first three-piece maple bedroom suites sold for $24.95. The furniture business dropped drastically following

style of church furniture demanded, including pews, communion tables, altars, collection plates and baptismal fonts. Financial difficulties followed Don Endicott's illness in 1957, and the business was sold to Dalton Foundries, Inc. in 1959. During the 1960s, Endicott Church Furniture occupied eight buildings along Argonne Road.

Charles H. Ker and his son, Charles A. Ker, bought the business in December of 1974. A man from Elkhart purchased Endicott Church Furniture in 1983, and the business closed in 1985.

the bombing of Pearl Harbor in 1941, and the bedroom plant was closed in 1942. The buildings were leased to International Harvester for storage.

Mr. Korth moved a few key people to the 300 block of N. Detroit Street in the former Croop Bakery building (later used as a Zimmer warehouse). Production there was primarily devoted to war supplies, mostly for Zimmer. Korth Furniture made millions of basswood arm and leg splints at a cost of five cents each.

The property at 765 W. Center Street was sold to the Weatherhead Company in 1945. This was the site of the old Dundee Furniture Manufacturing Company, later occupied by Owens-Illinois Kimble Division, and then Kinder Manufacturing Company.

Toward the end of the war, Korth purchased a building on the southwest side of Pike Lake which was being used to raise chickens. He remodeled it and started again in the table business. There was an old icehouse across the street owned by John Lucas where he stored potatoes. With business growing, Korth bought that property, tore it down, and built a ramp over the street. When more room was needed, the adjoining old Lutz and Schram pickle house (also referred to as the Cruikshank pickle canning factory) was acquired to use as a warehouse.

Several other properties across the street were purchased, which then comprised the bedroom plant facilities at 208 N. Hitzler Street. Korth put up a water tower for fire protection. Many lumber shipments arrived via the railroad track siding that came from the former New York Central line servicing the canning factory and the bedroom factory. Ray Korth also purchased the old Camp Lucerne acreage (now Lucerne Park) along the west side of Pike Lake in order to prevent it from being developed into housing.

On December 31, 1955, Korth sold the business to the Grand American Furniture Company of Chicago, with the stipulation that he would not be involved in the furniture manufacturing business for five years. Ray's son, Robert, operated a top-line retail furniture business for a short period in Florida and then returned to Indiana and opened a store in Goshen for a time.

After that store closed, the former Kincaide skating rink at 800 S. Buffalo Street was purchased and a discount furniture store was opened. The Korths decided to get out of the retail business and re-enter the manufacturing business. Former employee Frank Keough and Ray Korth were talking

An aerial view in 1972 of Korth Furniture's manufacturing facility along the southwest shore of Pike Lake. The old Cruikshank pickle canning factory sat at an angle alongside the trees of Lucerne Park.

An aerial view of Korth Furniture's second manufacturing facility on S. Buffalo Street in 1972. This was originally the site of a quonset hut building constructed for a roller skating rink. Several additions to the structure were made over the years, but the rounded roof of the original building can still be seen.

at the Elks Club on New Year's Day 1961, and agreed to get back into manufacturing.

The business at that time was called Korth Furniture Manufacturing Company. There were numerous additions to the quonset type building over the years. The company produced multi-styled living room tables, record cabinets, bookcases, organ tables, and magazine racks, but primarily occasional tables. Sears was their primary customer, in addition to J.C. Penney and Gambles.

This Indiana Motor Bus is parked at the corner of Center and Buffalo Streets in August, 1958. First National Bank sponsored the bus, which gave free rides to the county fair.

Amelia Earhart was the first woman to attempt to fly around the world; after her plane left New Guinea in 1937, she was never seen again.

Grand American Furniture had leased the S. Buffalo Street property and in 1963 Korth took back the plant when Grand American went into bankruptcy. Barney Bannon left his sales manager position with a Peru, Indiana, furniture manufacturer to become sales manager of the Korth bedroom plant. He had already been sales manager for the table factory during the previous year.

The business grew and later in 1963 Perkins Trucking Company, Inc. opened a terminal in Warsaw for loading and delivering the uncrated shipments of bedroom furniture. Until 1967, Perkins' office was in the Korth facility, at which time Perkins built a warehouse north of town. At the height of production, the factory produced 300 bedroom suites each workday. Shipments were sent into most states east of the Mississippi River and about seven states west of the Mississippi.

Ray Korth sold both plants to G.L. Ohrstrom on December 31, 1968, and agreed to stay for three years, retiring December 31, 1971. Ray soon became chairman of the board and his son, Bob, was made president. The intent of Ohrstrom, a New York City-based investment company, was to put a large number of furniture businesses together (under the parent name of Dorset Corporation) and go public. The Dorset Corporation operated the bedroom factory through April of 1978 when it was closed along with five other Dorset companies.

The facility on South Buffalo Street ceased production in November 1978 and the property finally sold in the mid 1980s to Wildman Laundry. The 65,000 square foot Pike Lake facility was used by Dorset as a distribution warehouse for the two remaining Dorset companies through 1986. Bob Hardin was employed with Perkins when it came to Warsaw, then joined Korth Furniture in 1970, and stayed with Dorset until the property was sold to Steve Parker in 1989.

First National Bank

First National Bank of Warsaw opened its doors on May 22, 1937, on the southwest corner of Center and Buffalo Streets. With 44 stockholders, the bank had $62,500 in assets. There were five employees: A.I. Nelson, president; Dr. W. Bert Siders, vice president; Eugene T. White, cashier; and Evelyn Wood and Robert Hall, tellers.

Ten years later in 1947, deposits totaled over $4 million and the staff had increased to fifteen employees. By 1957, the bank had nearly $7 million in deposits and 22 employees. Over the years, the First National Bank acquired several area banks, including The Etna Bank in Etna Green in 1985, and eventually had 10 locations in the county.

In 1961, the First National Bank Building underwent a major renovation and received a new façade. Due to continued growth, the bank acquired the building at 108 S. Buffalo Street in 1966 for expansion. In 1972, the Sharp Hardware property on Center Street was purchased and demolished to make way for the bank's parking lot. Also in 1972, the Widaman Building on S. Buffalo Street adjacent to the bank was acquired and razed to construct a new addition which was completed in 1974.

A.I. Nelson served as president of First National Bank from 1937 until his death in 1963. At that time, Judge Donald Vanderveer was appointed president. When Vanderveer died in 1965, W. Robert Hall filled the position until his resignation in 1970 due to poor health. William E. Hadley followed as president until poor health required him to resign in 1974. At that time, Neal M. Carlson, a bank employee since 1955, was appointed president. When Carlson retired in 1990, Willis Alt filled the position.

Fort Wayne National Corporation purchased First National Bank of Warsaw in 1988. Alt was president until Fort Wayne National was acquired by National City Corporation in 1998.

For many years, the corner occupied by this bank has been used as a reference point for giving directions within the City. In the early 1900s, this corner was the site of a frame building for the F.P. Bradway and Sons grocery store. A brick building was then constructed for the Indiana Loan & Trust Company prior to being occupied by First National Bank of Warsaw.

Ford's Auto Supply

Harold "Dutch" Ford came to town in 1937 and opened Ford's Auto Supply on W. Center Street. In the early 1940s the business moved to 113 N. Indiana Street in the former Rabbit Brothers' livery stable building (now the parking lot south of the Jail Museum).

Former councilman Mac Silveus worked there before going into the oil business, and Bush Rice (Mayor, 1948-1951) also worked there for a time. Ford's Auto Supply was the only business in the county with tire recapping equipment, and also offered brake service and expert vulcanizing. The business closed about 1973 and the building was razed shortly after.

Carter's Department Store

After having opened Carter's Department Store in Wabash in 1919, Luther E. Carter opened the Warsaw store in 1937 in the Moon Building on the southeast corner of Market and Buffalo Streets. The business operated until the building was destroyed by fire in 1961.

Following the fire, George Bowser constructed a one-story building on that corner. This was the site of the men's section of the Kline's Department Store until it closed in 1996, followed by Fox Vog's ladies clothing store which closed in 1999. The Bowser family donated the property to the Kosciusko County Foundation in 2000 for its headquarters.

Phillips known as "Mr. Scouter"

G. Freeland "Flip" Phillips (1909-1998) was known as "Mr. Scouter" in the Warsaw community. Before his death, he had 77 years of continuous membership in the Boy Scouts of America. Flip was also active at the Baker Boys' Club and assisted Pete Thorn in establishing Troop 13.

Phillips worked with Troop 30 (now 730) at the First United Methodist Church, and served on

A view inside an unidentified automotive supply store. In the foreground is a stack of car tires wrapped in paper.

Carter's Department Store was located on the southeast corner of Market and Buffalo Streets from 1937 to 1961. This photo looking east was taken in the early 1940s. Note the stairway leading to a barbershop in Carter's basement. The three-story Opera House, by then known as the Moose Lodge, is at the far end of the block.

During World War II, many items were rationed and difficult to get. This line of anxious customers formed when Carter's Department Store received a shipment of women's silk stockings. The line began at Carter's door on Market Street, extended east in front of the Moose Lodge, and turned south on Indiana Street past Dr. Baum's medical clinic.

A view from atop the First National Bank building during the 1961 fire that destroyed Carter's Department Store on the southeast corner of Market and Buffalo Streets.

The aftermath from the 1961 fire that destroyed the Moon Block. It was occupied by Carter's Department Store at that time.

the District and Council levels. He received many honors in Scouting through the years and was Assistant Scoutmaster of Troop 34 that attended the first National Scout Jamboree that camped at Washington, D.C. in 1937. His tireless service to Scouting was a major influence to many young boys.

In addition to starting Union Tool Company in 1942 with Karl J. Heinzelman, Phillips was very active in the community. He was a Mason and Shriner, a lifetime member of The Salvation Army advisory board, and a 60-year member of Kiwanis. Phillips was also a City councilman, organizer for the YMCA board of directors, and was involved with the Chamber of Commerce.

Funeral Homes

An undated poster for the funeral homes of Kosciusko County lists the following fees:

City calls or a starting charge cost $3 plus 10 cents per driving mile, each way. Chairs delivered by the funeral director and called for by the same were 50 cents per dozen. A hospital bed with mattress cost $2 for the first week ($1 without mattress) and $1 per week thereafter. Wheel chairs were rented for 50 cents per week.

Burial fees for infants were: two-foot casket with box, no service, $15; two-foot casket with service, $25. Adult burial fees, including a service, were based on the length of the casket, beginning from 2'6" to 3'6" caskets at $45 and ending with 4'6" to 6'3" caskets at $75.

The Paul M. Bilby Funeral Home was established in 1937 at 122 N. High Street. After having worked there 1949-50, Gerald McHatton became a partner and the firm became Bilby-McHatton Funeral Home. In 1955, the business was split. Gerald started his own business, McHatton Funeral Home and McHatton Ambulance Service, at 929 E. Center Street. Ned Titus purchased the Bilby interest and started Titus Funeral Home at the southeast corner of Main and High Streets.

In 1971, Wendell Sadler teamed up with Gerald McHatton to form McHatton-Sadler Funeral Home. McHatton-Sadler moved to 2290 Provident Court in 1988. The Titus Funeral Home moved to its new location on the corner of East Sheridan and Harrison Streets in 1976. Both businesses are still in operation today.

Ringer Body Shop

Ringer Body Shop was started by Jake Ringer in 1937 at 211 N. Indiana Street. When his son, Paul, joined the business, they built a larger adjoining shop to the north (now occupied by Ab & Tom's Radiator Repair). Paul was well-known for frame alignment and had many out-of-state customers. When Paul died in 1982 his son, Mike, continued operating the business until his own death in late 1999. Mike spent many hours as a young boy at the body shop and painted his first car at age 10.

Owen's Supermarket

After having been involved in the grocery business working for Kroger and Jet White, Owen E. Emerick opened Owen's Meat Market in 1938 on S. Buffalo Street. Before long, he also owned one of the Jet White stores and Robinson's Market.

In 1959, he built a new facility for Owen's Supermarket at 302 W. Market Street. Emerick retired from active management in 1975, but was always ready to assist the new president, son-in-law Joe Prout, who took over the business after working with Owen for many years. A second store was built at the corner of Center and Harrison Streets in 1978, which then moved to a new building next door at 2211 E. Center Street in 1994.

Following the death of Owen Emerick, the Owen's Supermarkets were sold to Kroger Company in 1998. Both stores continue to be called Owen's Supermarket.

Playtime Products, Inc.

Playtime Products, Inc., founded by Bert J. Anderson in 1938, was the world's largest manufacturer of folding doll carriages and baby strollers. Playtime also made doll accessory items and other toys, along with houseware items such as clothes sorters and dryers, laundry carts, and tubular valets. It was located at 522 N. Detroit Street in the former Hugro facility, a long building that stretched a full city block south of the current Zimmer building that sits on the corner of Detroit and Arthur Streets.

At one time, Playtime had as many as 200 employees. H. Herman Jensen came to Warsaw in 1939 to be the plant manager for Playtime. Jensen had previously been employed with Junior Toy in Hammond, Indiana, which manufactured tricycles.

Playtime Products shut down production during the war due to lack of material, however,

In July 1937, Warsaw Troop 34 attended the National Scout Jamboree in Washington, D.C. Standing, left to right: Assistant Scoutmaster Freeland "Flip" Phillips, Argel Brallier, Ray Larson, John Ladd, Elvin Brallier. Kneeling, left to right: Bob Gast, Ralph Jackson, Billy Johnson.

Playtime Products on N. Detroit Street, shown in 1958, was the world's largest manufacturer of folding doll carriages and baby strollers.

the Army asked them to make field dental chairs and army cots. Playtime also made five-gallon gas cans to hang on the back of Jeeps and many tips for 30-caliber bullets. After the war ended, Playtime moved further north on Detroit Street to a quonset type building.

Arnolt Corporation employees operating threading machines in the machine shop.

A team of women comprised the inspection department at the Arnolt Corporation.

The Arnolt Corp. office staff in 1962. Front, left to right: Mildred Mote, Donna Mayer, Mildred Burgess, Evelyn Hoffer, Helen Tyner. Back, left to right: Bea Covol, Judi Blankenship, Gloria Shipley, Ruth Rice, Mary Lou Fitton, Elsie Wiest, June Jermeay, Phyllis Harris, Joan Plew.

Emmett Kelly, Jr. by an Arnolt-Bristol car. Stan H. Arnolt II enjoyed a friendship with Emmett Kelly, Sr. When Kelly died, his son quit his job as a salesman to become a clown. To this day, Stan Arnolt III keeps in touch with Emmett, Jr.

Anderson needed a manufacturer of spoked wheels for Playtime's doll carriages and tricycles, so in 1946 Ken-Jen Metal Products (later known as Sun Metal) was started. Bert Anderson's son-in-law, Bob Clarke, recalls that at one time the doll buggies and tricycles were sold to wholesalers at 50 cents each, 75 cents to retailers, and then sold in stores for 90 cents each.

In the early 1960s, Jack Chrisman was president of Playtime. The company was sold to a Michigan City firm in the mid-1960s that manufactured playground equipment.

Arnolt Corporation

Arnolt Corporation was founded in 1932 by Stanley H. Arnolt II (1907-1963) in Chicago with three employees, manufacturing automobile lubricating devices. During that time, Arnolt developed an inboard marine engine called the Sea-Mite, which was one-third lighter than other engines of equal horsepower. On the thick foggy morning of September 26, 1938, with one of his engines affixed to a 13-foot boat, Arnolt left St. Joseph, Michigan and headed for Chicago.

Fighting waves and fog, he made the trip in four hours. Boatmen along Navy Pier shook their heads in disbelief, stating that he had more nerve than they did. He was greeted through the still thick morning fog with, "Hallo there, Wacky!" The headline of an article that day in *The Chicago Daily News* read, "Wacky Comes Through in Fog; Crosses Lake in 13-Foot Boat" . . . and the nickname stuck. Thereafter, he was known as "Wacky" Arnolt.

Arnolt moved his operations to Warsaw in 1939, beginning in a residential garage at 320 N. Lake Street. In 1940, Arnolt formed the Atlas Steel and Tube Division for the production of tubular frames for casual furniture and dinette sets. By 1942, production had expanded to the point that the company moved to new manufacturing facilities on Argonne Road (now partially occupied by OEC Diasonics). Arnolt also occupied a sales office on the 30th floor of the American Furniture Mart building on N. Lake Shore Drive in Chicago.

During the war years of 1941-1945, a North Manchester plant was established to produce precision-machined parts for bombers and other war items. Arnolt Corporation also had a plant in Pierceton that required tight security due to its production of a variety of defense items for government contracts. Among its many other products, the company made boat trailers, fold-out travel campers, row boats and other marine items, in addition to the parts for B-47 bombers and other aircraft items. Later, primary business came from the Department of Defense when Arnolt was making the landing gear components and pilot ejection mechanisms for carrier-based aircraft.

Production had expanded by 1948 to include the Rol-R-Lift and Rol-R-Dolly, one-man material handling tools. Arnolt Corporation further diversified in 1950 by acquiring the Climax Machinery Company, a manufacturer of slicing machines and club smokers—an all-metal chromed ash receiver (some with glass holders)—which could be found in dining club cars or in Pullman accommodations on trains and in theatre lobbies.

In addition to being an industrialist, Arnolt was also a designer, builder and driver of racing cars. He designed a car, which he named the Arnolt-Bristol, with an MG chassis and exclusive Bertone or Turin coach works. The Arnolt sports car was introduced in 1952 in a race at Elkhart Lake, Wisconsin, and premiered at the International Motor Exposition in London in 1953.

S.H. Arnolt, Inc., an importer and distributor of foreign cars, was established in 1953 in Chicago. Arnolt obtained the Midwest distributorship for Nuffield Exports, Ltd. of England. His first order was for 25 MG cars and 20 Morris Minors, as well as six Riley cars. As the business grew to 30 dealers throughout the Midwest, other makes of cars were added to the line, including Rolls-Royce, Bentley, and Aston-Martin. The company's first advertisement for the Arnolt-Bristol sports car appeared in the premier issue of *Sports Illustrated* on August 16, 1954.

Arnolt also established Hoosier International Motors at 2307 E. Center Street (now site of Executive Office Products), a retail sales and service center for the world's largest builder of sports cars, British Motor Corporation. Hoosier International handled MG, Morris, Riley, Austin and Austin-Healy cars. In addition to new cars, Hoosier also maintained a good selection of used cars of European make. Autocessories, Ltd. was acquired for the manufacture of accessories for English MG cars, and Arnolt was also the sole distributor of Solex carburetors for foreign cars in the U.S.

Arnolt described his company as a "job shop." However, with such manufacturing diversification with products for the marine, automotive, aircraft, and furniture industries, in addition to focusing on

James C. Smith, executive vice president of S.H. Arnolt, Inc. in Chicago, passes the keys for a new Arnolt MG to James Morrow. The car was a prize won by Morrow in 1955 on the television quiz show "Feather Your Nest."

Stan Arnolt, right, hands the keys for a new Arnolt MG to 1950s musician Buddy Holly, who died in a plane crash in 1959.

Stan Arnolt, at right on the scooter, and the carrier with his race cars at Sebring, Florida.

A.C. Hively and manager Sam Lowman, right, at the Bashore Feed Store & Hatchery at 207 W. Center Street, with "Nip" guarding the doorway.

Sam Lowman, right, and his wife, Thelma, in the Bashore Feed Store (c. 1938). Note the mural on the back wall.

production of numerous items for World War II, by 1955 Arnolt's job shop had reached sales of nearly $8 million.

Wacky Arnolt was a vibrant, dynamic industrialist with a vision far ahead of his time. An unidentified newspaper article states, "While he was an engineering, sales and organizational genius—a serious-minded businessman who built an international industrial and sales empire, he never lost the boyish enthusiasm, the flair of showmanship, and the daring to try the unknown."

Ghean M. Arnolt became president and executive officer of the corporation after her husband's death in 1963. Their son, Michael, operated the business from 1976 until it was sold to a New York based firm in 1983.

Open Air Market

The Open Air Market was started at 955 N. Lake Street in 1939 by Russell and Ellen Gosnell. This was a wholesale-retail venture that trucked in fresh produce from as far away as Florida. The Gosnells also had a produce stand until about 1962 on the southwest corner of Detroit and Market Streets (by Schrader Auto Parts) during the summer, and they sold Christmas trees there each December.

Hans and Herta Voss and their son, Juergen, bought the business in 1978. The business discontinued providing fresh produce in 1986, but Juergen and his wife, Betsy, have operated their Open Air Garden & Greenhouse business at the N. Lake Street site since that time.

Bashore Feed Store

Claude I. Bashore had feed mills in North Manchester, Silver Lake, Akron, and Rochester. Sometime during the late 1930s, he decided to open a Bashore Feed Store in Warsaw on W. Center Street (where the Double Dip was located in the 1950s, and currently the Downtown restaurant). At that time, manager Sam Lowman transferred from the Akron store to the Warsaw store. The milling equipment was in the basement, which made the store on the street level very dusty and dirty.

The Bashore Feed Store & Hatchery moved to a larger facility on the northwest corner of Center and Columbia Streets in 1934. Dan Lowman recalls the long days his father worked there and states that if there was a small fire in the mill anywhere due to the corn cobs, grain and dust, his father didn't sleep much that night because he went back to the mill several times to check for more flames. Sam left employment at the Bashore Feed Mill in 1948 when it was purchased by Purina Mills, and the mill burned the following year.

Root Beer Stands

From about 1939 to 1942, Robert O. Chambers owned the Root Beer Barrel refreshment stand. It was located in the parking lot behind the building at 108 S. Lake Street. Glasses of root beer were sold from the small round structure that looked like a barrel, and a jukebox provided music for dances held in the parking lot.

Robert Lucas had two B & K Root Beer restaurants in Peru, when he decided to open one in Warsaw in 1954 on the northeast corner of Winona Avenue and Bronson Street. Mrs. Gale (Kate) Metzger began working there in 1956, and

bought the business in 1960. She developed "Kate's Spanish Sauce" for hotdogs, which she kept a secret. Bottles of her special sauce were sold for a time at the Jet White groceries.

The Metzgers' four children worked there through the years and gave up their lunch hours during school days to help at the restaurant during the busy lunchtime. Kate recalls that many young girls worked there over the years, and parents could always feel at ease when their daughters were at the B & K, because they were not allowed to leave the premises unless their parents picked them up or Kate took them home. The B & K was sold to Mark Pinnick in 1981.

Running Board Ride

In 1939, fifteen-year-old Louise Rife sustained back injuries when she jumped from the running board of a moving car to avoid being splashed as the car went through a large mud puddle. The accident

Parker Bros. introduced Monopoly in 1935.

The B & K Root Beer Drive-In's original building on the northeast corner of Winona Avenue and Bronson Street.

In the 1930s, this Texaco station on the northwest corner of Center and High Streets was owned by Raymond Kincaide, far left. Police chief Frank Lucas is standing by the car which was being used for a sales promotion.

The first NCAA Men's Final Four took place in 1939 with Oregon beating Ohio State.

occurred by the Center Lake Pavilion during the freshmen picnic. The car was taking classmates back to the picnic grounds from the ball diamond where they had been playing. Unable to crowd inside the car with the others, Louise rode on the running board. When the car headed for the water she jumped, falling on her back.

Admiral Byrd's Snow Cruiser

On October 31, 1939, a snow cruiser developed for Admiral Richard E. Byrd's third expedition came to Warsaw. The machine was 55 feet long, 15 feet wide, 16 feet high, and weighed 37 tons. It was to serve as a vehicular scientific laboratory and living quarters for members of the expedition.

The huge vehicle endured problems from the time it left Chicago en route to Boston's docks. It was involved in several highway accidents and had frequent mechanical troubles. When coming into Warsaw, the hubcaps had to be taken off in order for it to get across the Tippecanoe River at the Chinworth Bridge west of town.

The snow cruiser finally made it to Boston, but then World War II started and the expedition was cancelled before it could prove itself.

Streets Paved

Having been covered with brick since 1903, Center Street was first paved with asphalt in 1939.

Chapter 12

Candy Stores & Restaurants

Candy Stores

During the 1930s there were three stores in downtown Warsaw that were known for their homemade ice cream and candies. Brothers John N. and Angel N. Carnegis had Carnegis Confectionery in the Elks Aracade. Directly across the street at 119 E. Center Street was The Washington, which was started by Peter Karatzie from Chicago. The stores also sold sandwiches and light meals.

When Z.P. Sperou and James Klondaris came to Warsaw in the early 1900s, they started the Warsaw Candy Kitchen. The business was located on the southeast corner of Center and Buffalo Streets in the building referred to as Shane's Corner. In the early 1920s, James' son and daughter-in-law, John and Helen Klondaris, assumed ownership of the business.

A circa 1930s menu for the Warsaw Candy Kitchen lists 10 flavors of sodas. The cost, with whipped cream, was 10 cents each. There were

John Carnegis, left, and his brother, Angel, owned and operated the Carnegis Confectionery for many years in the Elks Arcade.

fourteen choices of sundaes, including the "Billy Sunday," that cost 10 cents. Add a nickel for sundaes with whipped cream and nuts, and "fancy" sundaes and parfaits were 20 cents. In addition, a quart of homemade ice cream or sherbet cost a quarter.

A Coca-Cola, Green River, Root Beer, or phosphate cost a nickel. "Stimulating" drinks such as Orangeade, a Boston Cooler, or Ginger Ale cost a dime, and fifteen cents would buy a Grape Juice High Ball. Patrons stopping by for lunch could get a variety of toasted sandwiches for 10 or 15 cents each. The Warsaw Candy Kitchen closed December 31, 1949.

Restaurants

A.F. "Gus" Carteaux operated a butcher shop with William R. Renier when he first came to Warsaw in 1898. The R & C Meat Market, located at 207 S. Buffalo Street, carried a selection of fresh and salt meats, and choice lard was a specialty. In the early 1920s, Gus had the Carteaux Restaurant at 105 E. Center Street. In 1929, the Carteaux Café was located at 112 N. Buffalo Street, and by 1936 it had moved to 118 N. Buffalo Street.

During the 1930s, there were also four restaurants within one block on Center Street between Buffalo and Indiana Streets. Gill's Grill and the Roxy Café were on the north side, and the Liberty Café and The Favorite were on the south side.

Gill's Grill, owned by Wilbur J. "Doc" Gill, was at 105 E. Center Street through the early 1940s. The restaurant was later sold to Lyle and Marie Stokes who called it the Chat-N-Chew. It was then owned by Forrest "Cherry" Parsons, who changed the name to Cherry's Café. For most of the 1990s, the Baskin-Robbins ice cream store occupied this building.

In 1886, John S. Pemberton cooked a batch of syrup as a headache remedy—which evolved into what is now the world's most popular soft drink, Coca-Cola.

The first location of the Liberty Café was on the north side of the 100 block of Center Street. The Liberty Café was owned by cousins George Stavropulos, center (in white), and Nick Gores, left (wearing bowtie).

The Liberty Café was located at 104 E. Center Street for many years until the early 1970s. Co-owner Nick Gores is shown at the left behind the counter with a bowtie. His cousin Louis Eliopulos, center, was the night cook.

An interior view of the newly remodeled Liberty Café at 104 E. Center Street in the 1950s.

The Liberty Café, owned by George Stavropulos and his cousin, Nick Gores, was started in the Rigdon Building on E. Center Street in the 1920s. The business later moved across to the south side of the street at 104 E. Center Street. George's daughter, Connie Stavropulos, recalls that another cousin, Louie Eliopulos, was a night cook at the Liberty Café.

The business was sold to Paul and Irene Kaufman when George died in 1961. The Kaufmans continued operation of the Liberty Café under the same name for 10 years. The business was then sold at auction, but closed about a year later. (The 104 E. Center Street location has been the site of Crownover Jewelry since that time.)

In the 1920s, Joe Foote owned The Favorite Café at 112 E. Center Street, followed by Bud Moon in the 1930s. In the early 1940s, The Favorite was owned by John W. Cook, followed by Charles L. "Tip" Welker and Frank E. "Doc" Harrison. (That location was then occupied by Shine Shoes from about 1950 to 1961, followed by Cox Studio, and was then the office for the Kosciusko County Solid Waste Management District until early 2001.)

About 1935, Leo Andrews closed The Washington candy store on the west side of the Centennial Theatre and opened the Roxy Café on the east side of the theatre. By 1947, George and Lois Nulf owned the Roxy Café. Warren Tatter recalls the time at age 17 he slipped in the back door of the Roxy Café and bought some beer and his buddies really thought he was a "cool dude" then.

The Roxy was eventually sold to Art Principi, who moved the restaurant to 522 E. Winona Avenue and changed the name to Club Oasis. The Club Oasis moved to 617 S. Buffalo Street and became a very popular place, especially on the weekends when patrons could dance to the music of live bands. The Smothers Brothers even appeared there once. The Club Oasis was operated for a time by Bill and Thelma Pittenger, followed by Bob and Bonnie Kissell in 1967 and 1968. For a few years, this location was occupied by the Thaddeus restaurant.

Wolfgang and Gerda Haack bought the business in 1981 and changed the name to Wolfgang's. Wolfgang played the organ in the restaurant until his death in 1989, and Gerda operated the restaurant another eight years before it closed in 1997.

The Blue Coyote Grill & Cantina has been at this location since April 1998.

It is reported that the Roxy Café downtown and the Hoosier Inn, owned by the Jonas family on the east side city limits along Center Street, were some of the first places in Warsaw to get beer and liquor licenses when prohibition ended.

The long-time Humpty Dumpty Grill at 114 N. Buffalo Street was started by Howard Peterson in 1947. Peterson sold the business in 1950 to John Klondaris and his son, Jim, who operated it until 1990. John's other son, Terry, also worked there for a few years. The building and restaurant was sold to Bill DeGaetano in 1990, who changed the name to Dig's Diner.

The two-story brick building at 114 N. Buffalo Street was originally a tavern and then became a liquor store owned by Julius Schubert. He moved the tavern during the Civil War era to the rear of the current Instant Copy building on the southwest corner of Lake and Center Streets. The business, known as Service Liquor Store, was then sold to Dick Underhill in 1961, who moved the store just south across the parking lot to 108 S. Lake Street. Underhill sold the business to Pat Likens in 1972.

Devon Smith built the Dog 'N Suds drive-in at 814 E. Winona Avenue in the early 1950s. Smith sold the business in 1960 to his nephew, Charles Smoker, who operated it for about four years. Charles' parents then ran the business for a short time until it was sold to Russell and Louise Sponseller in 1965.

The Sponsellers' seven children all helped at the restaurant. The Dog 'N Suds closed in the late 1970s, but Louise states that they still retain the Dog 'N Suds franchise. Their son-in-law, Warsaw Police Officer Randy Hart, enjoys the family get-togethers when his mother-in-law makes the special sauce and serves famous Dog 'N Suds chili dogs.

Devon Smith also operated other eating establishments in Warsaw over the years. He had the Calico Kitchen in the Opera House under the stairway leading to the Moose Lodge. Smith later had a delicatessen and coffee shop on N. Buffalo Street in the Menzie building, he owned the Cozy Cottage at 1821 E. Market Street for a few years, had the Lakeview Delicatessen at 2022 E. Winona Avenue for a time, and also owned the Candy Cane at 108 N. Buffalo Street.

The Humpty Dumpty Grill was opened at 114 N. Buffalo Street in 1947. Since 1990, it has been the site of Dig's Diner.

Horn's Sunnymede

By 1929 when the Depression hit, the Comstock Inn on S. High Street by the railroad tracks was rundown and the owner was getting old. It was timely then, when Milo and Emma Horn returned to Warsaw, that they were able to reopen the restaurant.

In addition to serving customers traveling through Warsaw by rail, the Horns also served Sunday dinner at the Comstock Inn to local patrons. Their son, Keith, remembers going with his father across the railroad tracks to the Farm Bureau Co-op on the southeast corner of Market and High Streets (now site of City Hall). Each Saturday the Horns bought live chickens at the Co-op, which they killed and processed to serve for their popular Sunday dinners.

Thinking that for the first time people would be traveling by motor car to the World's Fair in Chicago, the Horns bought a restaurant in Bourbon

The first Dairy Queen store opened in Joliet, Illinois, in 1940.

Officer Eugene Brumfield, left, and Mayor Mike Hodges, right, greeted the "Cisco Kid" when he stopped in town to eat at Horn's Sunnymede Restaurant in the early 1950s.

In 1955, Col. Harland Sanders began franchising his business, Kentucky Fried Chicken.

on U.S. 30 just west of the bank and named it the Bourbon Luncheon, which they operated from 1932 to 1934. (Knowing that Mr. Horn was a World War I veteran, the bank next door asked him to be a deputy because John Dillinger was robbing banks in the area at that time.) The Horns adopted their basic menu while in Bourbon: swiss steak, sugar-baked ham, and skillet-fried chicken. Chicken was only on the menu for Sundays and holidays.

The Horns returned to Warsaw in 1934 and opened the Mayfair Café in the 1800 block of E. Center Street (former location of Kroger, now Auto Zone). There had been a small brick Sinclair gas station with a service building next to it. The service building was remodeled to be a lunchroom, and then remodeled into a restaurant with tables and chairs. Milo Horn had a key to the filling station. When the city's only police car would run low on gasoline, the officer would stop and ask Milo to get him fuel.

Keith recalls the time his parents stayed up almost all night discussing whether to raise the price of a swiss steak sandwich with mashed potatoes

from 15 cents to 20 or 25 cents. They decided on 25 cents, since they had been losing money. Milo had been in the trucking business in Chicago before the Depression. Always loyal to their own, when the truckers found him in the restaurant along their travels, word spread and there were times the entire family was asked to help their father late at night when the semi-trucks would be parked for six or seven blocks each way along the street.

In 1937, the Horns traded the Mayfair Café for the Turner-Horn's Cafeteria in the 100 block of W. Center Street, formerly owned by the Turner family in Winona Lake. Keith remembers that during the county street fair his father would get a horse tank and put soda pop in it. The pop cost 60 cents for 24 bottles. Keith and his brother sold ice cold pop for a nickel a bottle (doubling their money) and received half the profit.

Howard Dillman built a restaurant attached to his Shell filling station about 1940. Having tried to run the restaurant with no success, he told the Horns that if they would buy the equipment on a payment plan and run the restaurant, he would rent it to them. Knowing what they knew best—

specializing in swiss steak, sugar-baked ham and skillet-fried chicken—Horn's Sunnymede Restaurant opened in the fall of 1940 at 2229 E. Center Street. Evangelists Homer Rodeheaver, Billy Graham, and Billy Sunday's widow were regular customers, along with many famous musicians who came to Winona Lake to perform.

World War II brought meat and sugar rations, and other problems. Milo had to get another part-time job as the family struggled through the war years. Milo Horn died in 1945 and his son, Peter, was killed going back to the naval base after his father's funeral. At that time, Keith was with the United Nations Relief in Europe and returned home. Emma continued to run the restaurant, baking pies that people still talk about today.

During the late 1940s, Keith Horn had a photography studio under the Corner Cigar Store on the northeast corner of Center and Buffalo Streets. When his mother passed away in 1952, the studio was closed so Keith and his wife could take over operation of the family's well-known Sunnymede Restaurant.

Keith attended the national restaurant show at Navy Pier in Chicago and saw a broaster machine. He inquired about a man who was mingling with the crowd and was told that the man was attempting to get people to try his fried chicken recipe. With the Sunnymede already having fried chicken on its menu, Keith was not initially interested—being in the lakes area, he was looking for a fish recipe.

Keith then attended the Indiana Restaurant Show the following fall in Indianapolis, where he saw that same man with a goatee wearing a gray frock coat. They engaged in a conversation and the man told Keith that he wanted to get 100 restaurants to put his chicken recipe on their menu and send him royalties of ten to twenty-five dollars so he could then retire. Although Keith was not too interested, he thought about the success of the chicken items on his current menu, and wondered if the guy really had something.

The following Thursday after the show, "that man" came driving up to the Sunnymede in a big, black Cadillac. He walked in and greeted everyone like he was an invited guest . . . and that is how Keith Horn met Colonel Harland D. Sanders, founder of Kentucky Fried Chicken. When Col. Sanders brought his pressure cookers in, one cook walked out and the other went to the far side of the kitchen to wash dishes. Keith had thought

Arden Kincaide purchased the Farmers' Restaurant at 118 W. Market Street from Fred Montel in 1921 and renamed it the City Lunch.

In the late 1920s, Arden Kincaide, right, owned the Court Café at 112 N. Buffalo Street. This building has been occupied by a newsstand since the late 1940s. The employee on the left is unknown.

The Dog 'N Suds drive-in was located at 814 E. Winona Avenue from the 1950s through the 1970s.

With flowers lining the counter, perhaps this photo was taken for a restaurant's grand opening. Note the man at the back with his arms crossed and holding a butcher knife.

An unidentified photo shows the interior view of a restaurant in the early 1900s.

80 orders of chicken on Sunday was big, but that first Sunday they sold 139 chicken dinners!

Keith began selling KFC in 1953 and fondly remembers his days with the Colonel. Sanders would stop by the Sunnymede on his way to see new prospects for the sale of his chicken franchise, and Keith sometimes had time to ride along. Keith recalls that in the beginning the Colonel slept in his car many nights to save money. When they first started, the recipe would be put together in the Colonel's kitchen the night before so it would be fresh for the prospective new franchisee. In the late 1950s, Sanders' nephew, Lee Cummins, became his driver. Cummins went on to form his own chicken franchise, Famous Recipe Fried Chicken, which became successful and was bought by Shoney's Restaurants.

About 1957 when U.S. 30 bypassed Warsaw, the tourist business slowed, but the Sunnymede still enjoyed a good local business. Keith went on to have restaurants in Michigan and had managers run the Sunnymede. A fire in April 1957 required some remodeling, at which time a carry-out area and party room were added. With the help of employees, friends and contractors, the restaurant was able to quickly reopen in June.

Keith states that Dave Thomas (founder of Wendy's restaurants) was employed by Phil Clauss (the author's great-uncle) in Fort Wayne at that time. When the Sunnymede had special promotions and could not keep up with the demand for chicken dinner orders, Thomas would bring Kentucky Fried Chicken from Fort Wayne to Warsaw.

Management problems led Keith to lease the restaurant in 1970 to Phil Clauss, owner of the

Hobby House Restaurants in Fort Wayne. When Clauss left in 1975, the business eventually closed and the building's roof collapsed after a heavy snow. The building was condemned in 1977 and was then demolished.

When Colonel Sanders set up his first corporation, Keith Horn was on the board of directors of the Kentucky Fried Chicken Company. In 1963, four franchisees (including Horn) went with the Colonel to England and Denmark to establish KFC franchises in Europe. Due to the acquaintance of many business friends over the years, in 1969 when Keith and his wife, Virginia, took a 30-day tour driving across the United States, they were alone only one night in the entire 8,000 mile trip.

One additional note: The author's father, Glenn "Bud" Clauss, worked side by side in the Hobby House kitchen in Fort Wayne with Dave Thomas. When they are in Florida for the winter, Bud and his wife, Jean, still occasionally meet with Mr. and Mrs. Thomas to reminisce.

Many Restaurants

Over the years, there have been many small restaurants located throughout Warsaw, especially from the 1930s through the 1960s. Although too numerous to include each one, the history of some locations has been compiled as follows.

Joy Munson operated Joy's Lunchroom at 116 W. Market Street. About 1949, she closed the restaurant and Robert Clendenen leased the property to open the Cozy Nook. The Cozy Nook was located across the street from the Sears store at that time, which helped attract many customers to the restaurant.

About 1954 when Munson decided not to renew Clendenen's lease, he moved two doors west to 120 W. Market Street, where he operated the Post Office Café until 1961. The License Bureau was later located in this building. From 1982 to 1986, Jack and Rita Simpson operated Lazy Jack's western store there. Jim Linton has managed the Allstate Insurance office at 120 W. Market Street since 1987.

The building at 209 W. Center Street was a popular restaurant location, with numerous owners throughout the years. In the 1940s, Henry Hartman had Hartman's Sandwich Shop at 209 W. Center Street. His son, Carl, later operated the restaurant. During the late 1940s, Donald O. Schaaf operated the restaurant as Schaaf's Sandwich Shop. Bob

The rear of Bledsoe Buick when it was first located in the former Oram Building on the northwest corner of Lake and Center Streets. Paul's Sandwich Shop can be seen in the background on W. Center Stree (c. late 1950s).

Clendenen bought the business about 1952 and renamed it Bob's Sandwich Shop.

Clendenen then sold the restaurant to Hartman's step-daughter and son-in-law, Pat and Paul Molebash, who operated it as Paul's Sandwich Shop for 28 years, from about 1953 to 1981. James and Kathryn Baumgartner then had a business there for several months that featured home-baked cinnamon rolls, blueberry muffins, and pies. In the mid-1980s, Rob and Nancy Gast operated the Southern Accent restaurant at that location for about a year and a half.

When Gordy Clemens bought the building at 205 W. Center Street in 1986 to start Gordy's Sub Pub, the Molebashes next door sold him their building at 209 W. Center Street. Gordy's Sub Pub moved to the corner of Buffalo Street and Winona Avenue in 1991, at which time Tom Clemens started the Downtown Eatery & Spirits at 205 W. Center Street. The single-story (former sandwich shop) building at 209 W. Center Street was demolished and is now used in the summer as an outside dining area for the Downtown Eatery.

Following more than 25 years in the restaurant business, in 1969 Bob Clendenen joined Penguin Point Systems as operations manager. He was promoted to executive vice president in 1971, a position he held until he retired in 1985. Coincidentally, Steve Devenney, now vice president of operations for Penguin Point Systems, worked at Clendenen's Cozy Cottage restaurant as a teenager.

Ray Kroc opened the first McDonald's restaurant in Des Plaines, Illinois, in 1955.

Bob's Sandwich Shop was located at 209 W. Center Street next to the Double Dip ice cream store. This building has since been demolished and is used for outside dining by the Downtown Eatery during the summer months.

The Cozy Nook restaurant was located on the north side of Market Street across from the Sears store.

A Family of Restaurants

Clarence Ira "Bish" Brown was a true entrepreneur. He started and conducted numerous enterprises in Warsaw and accomplished much of this with the aid of his wife and business partner, Becky.

The youngest of seven children, he earned the nickname "Bish" because his father thought he lacked ambition—which he disproved, as he not only had the ambition, but also creative ideas for new ventures. Bish met his wife in the mid-1920s when he entered a café in Brown County and asked her for a free cup of coffee. This business deal was the first of many negotiated between the two of them.

His business holdings were wide and varied from restaurateur, merchant, landlord, and excavator to owner of an auction house and property developer. During the Depression, the family recalls that Bish also operated a small coal company on the east side of town. Along with a pot of coffee, Bish always had a new project brewing on the back burner, while his wife was managing his last successful business venture and filling his coffee cup. With the help of Bish's five children—Arnold, Kendall, Leon, Susie and Mark—his business ventures succeeded.

With Warsaw factories booming during World War II, diners were a profitable business to be in, and brothers Russell and Bish owned many of the downtown restaurants at one time or another. Following Brownie's Restaurant, from the mid 1940s through the late 1950s, Bish and Becky Brown owned and operated numerous restaurants in Warsaw, including: Brownie's Sandwich Shop, 122 E. Market Street; The Square Deal at 110 E. Market Street, which was sold to Sam Cook in 1943; Cherry's Café, 105 E. Center Street; Bish's Steak House, 325 Argonne Road; and The Satellite Café at 822 E. Winona Avenue, from 1958 to 1961.

For a time, Bish owned and operated the Bish Brown Restaurant and Arcade in the Winona Lake Arcade. The arcade restaurant was later owned by Russell Brown, followed by Bish's nephew and niece by marriage, Jack and Carol Bilz, who changed the name to the Bilz Café. In 1953, Jack and Carol sold the arcade restaurant to an aunt and uncle, Clarence and Margaret Biltz. (Early Bilz generations spelled their name without the letter "t.")

Russell Brown owned Brownie's Restaurant at 113 E. Market Street during the 1930s. Russell's nephew, Jack Bilz, recalls earning his lunch during

An advertising promotion at Brownie's Sandwich Shop in the 1940s was tokens given out with change when diners paid for their meals. The reverse side says "Good in Trade."

Actual size of original photo.

"Bish" and Becky Brown owned and operated various restaurants during the 1940s and 1950s, including Bish's Steak House at 325 Argonne Road. Also shown is their daughter, Susie.

Russell Brown, left, with his children: Earl, Harold, Kate, Max, Bob, and Dorothy in front of one of their restaurants (c. 1940s).

Founded in Miami, Florida, in 1954, Burger King sold broiled hamburgers and milkshakes for 18 cents each.

his high school years in the mid-1930s by helping with the noontime crowd. He states that the popular hot beef sandwich with mashed potatoes and gravy was 15 cents, a price the average worker could afford. A plate lunch was also available for a quarter. The meal included meat, two vegetables, and fruit or pudding for dessert.

Jack's parents, John and Athol Bilz, bought the business in 1941 and it became known as the Bilz Café. Lois Eby Baker recalls the days when she was a waitress at the Bilz Café. By that time, a plate lunch cost 50 cents and coffee was a nickel. Ike Hire, manager of the A & P grocery on S. Buffalo Street, frequented the Bilz Café. He always wore his work apron and a flat-topped hat. Lois would sometimes carefully place a slice of bread on top of his hat, which often was still there when he removed his hat at the end of the day!

Jack recalls the time Max "Red" Brown was working the late night shift at his father's (Russell Brown) restaurant. Red had a habit of going to a back booth and napping when there were no customers. One night Officer Judd Pittenger came in for coffee and saw Red sleeping. He quietly picked up the cash register and sat it outside the door. Max sleepily awoke, got some coffee for Judd . . . and was shocked to see there was no cash register! That quickly cured his "sleeping on the job."

Mike Ragan, a grandson of Athol Bilz's sister, Jessie Brown Eby, operated the Silver Spur restaurant on Winona Avenue just west of the Dairy Queen from 1972 to 1975.

The last member of the Brown family to own a restaurant is Arnold's son, Steven R. Brown. Steve and his wife, Judy, constructed a building at the Lakeview Shopping Center on E. Winona Avenue in 1992 and opened the Lakeview Diner on Thanksgiving weekend. The restaurant's sign featured a 1957 Chevrolet and the interior was decorated with a 1950s theme. For a time, the diner was open 24 hours on the weekends. The Browns sold the business in 1996 and the diner closed a couple of years later.

Another restaurant location was a building at 1821 E. Market Street. It had fallen into disrepair by the early 1950s. About 1954, Max Brown bought the property, tore down the old structure, and constructed a new building for his restaurant. In 1960, the restaurant was sold to a man from Michigan City who closed it within about three months, and in 1961 Bob Clendenen purchased the property and opened the Cozy Cottage. He sold the restaurant in 1967 to Devon Smith, who also operated the Dog 'N Suds drive-in on Winona Avenue at that time. Although the Cozy Cottage has had several owners over the years, its name has remained the same.

Chapter 13

1940 to 1949

Lights Alert the Police

Terry Klondaris and Dick Heagy recall the time before two-way radios were available, in particular, the 1940s when the City had only four policemen. There were four lights posted throughout the downtown that telephone operators could switch on when a policeman was needed.

The officer would see one of the lights lit and go to the nearest telephone to find out where he was requested to go. There were lights in the center of the intersections at Center and Buffalo Streets and also at Market and Lake Streets. Another was on top of the courthouse, and the fourth light was reportedly near Breading's Cigar Store.

Electric Business

In the 1940s, Leedy Electric was operated by Devoe Leedy at 212 S. Buffalo Street. In 1947, the business was purchased by Leonard and Kathryn Wolford and known as Wolford Electric, until it was bought by Phil and Jean Ann Dennie in 1967 who changed the name to Dennie Electric Company.

Kate Wolford recalls that she and her husband lived upstairs during the time they owned the electric business. They remodeled the front apartment and bought new furniture from the Mellencamp's store. The Dennies purchased the building in 1973, and for the past 16 years the Dennie House Country Collectables has occupied the front portion of the building.

Soap Box Derbys

Soap box derbys were popular in the 1940s and 50s. The boys were given specific rules and guidelines to build their cars, but fathers were often responsible for most of the assembly and construction.

The Warsaw derbys began at the top of the hill on Indiana Street and went north toward Center Lake. The derbys were sponsored by Chevrolet dealers across the United States, and champions from the local races then met at "Derby Downs" in Akron, Ohio.

Owner Ray Kincaide, center, is shown at his Standard Oil gas station. The men in suits are salesmen of the Atlas Tire Company. On the right, Bob Devenney is kneeling in front of Harry Morgan. The two employees on the left are unknown.

Soap Box Derbys were popular in the 1940s and 1950s. They began at the top of the hill at the intersection of Indiana and Main Streets.

The Warsaw Locker Plant, located at 215 S. Buffalo Street, as it is being demolished in 1967 to clear the half block for a city parking lot. The section to the right with the back wall removed was the American Brattice Cloth building.

From Grocery to Locker Plant

Max Hull operated the East Side Market at 1314 E. Center Street in the early 1940s. Wayne and Phyllis Fribley, along with Paul Lichtenberger, owned the store from 1949 to 1954. Paul was responsible for the grocery business and the Fribleys were in charge of the meat department. They sold the East Side Market to Bob and Helen Bruhn in 1954 and bought the Warsaw Locker Plant at 215 S. Buffalo Street.

Wilbur J. Redick had operated the Warsaw Locker Plant for many years. The business provided butchering, processing, and curing of meats. Warsaw Locker sold all kinds of meat, including smoked hams and bacon and homemade sausage. Families could rent storage space at the locker to freeze not only meat, but fruits and vegetables as well. Lichtenberger did not like processing meat and was only involved with the Fribleys at the locker plant for a short time.

In 1967 when the city wanted to make the half block on the north side of the railroad tracks between Buffalo and Indiana Streets a parking lot, the Fribleys quickly sold their inventory before the building was demolished.

Their next business venture was to purchase Robinson's Market located around the corner in the former Opera House on E. Market Street. Unfortunately, the building burned in October of 1967, shortly after the Fribleys acquired the market, so they actually lost two businesses in one year.

Frank Capra's beloved movie "It's a Wonderful Life" was released in 1946.

Young Talent

As a ten-year-old boy, Doug Kehler collected records of Spike Jones and the City Slickers. When Spike finally got a band together, they wanted to have fun and wear outrageous costumes. They took the music of the day and made crazy arrangements with funny lyrics. Among their many silly novelty songs, their biggest hit was "Cocktails for Two."

Kehler memorized the songs, and by using a little creativity, he devised a microphone using the extensions and small brush from his mother's sweeper. In the fifth grade he was entertaining his classmates during show and tell by lip-synching Spike Jones' recordings. It went so well that during National Education Week the principal asked him to represent West Ward School at the high school and perform for all the teachers and kids.

From that point, Kehler began receiving phone calls asking him to entertain at local clubs and events. His mother bought a used tuxedo and hand-sewed yellow stripes on it so Doug could dress like Spike Jones. Jones wore bright, gaudy, striped tuxedo suits, and some even glowed in the dark. Doug recalls the night he performed at the Moose Lodge and was paid three whole dollars for a twenty minute act! In those days, that was a lot of money.

Kehler entertained at the Hotel Hays one evening when a barbershop quartet was also performing. He clearly recalls one particular song they sang, "Cruisin' in My Model T," but has never been able to locate the words for it. One year he had 14 bookings during the two weeks before Christmas, with a couple days having two performances.

In 1952, Kehler attended a show at the Quimby Auditorium in Fort Wayne and got to meet Spike Jones. Through his mother's involvement with the local Welcome Wagon, Doug appeared live on an Indianapolis TV show twice and also twice on the WSBT South Bend "Hoosier Favorites" TV show. Kehler went into "entertainment retirement," but was called back to the stage to entertain his Class of 1957 when they held their 40th reunion in 1997.

Goodyear Service Center

Gilbert C. Lewallen was manager of the Goodyear Service Center located at 112 E. Market Street in the 1940s.

In the mid 1960s, attorney Phil Harris and Ray "Pete" Strayer, Jr. purchased the former

Presbyterian Church parsonage on the northeast corner of Market and High Streets. After the house was demolished, a building was constructed and leased to Goodyear. Ed Davis was manager of the Goodyear Service Center from 1966 to 1967.

The building was then sold to J. Alan Morgan, who opened an antique store that featured a collection of his wife's elaborate dollhouses. This corner has been the site of Cox Studio since 1985.

Tractor Sales

In 1940, C.C. Kelley started Kelley Tractor Sales at Cleveland and Jefferson Streets. The business sold Allis-Chalmers and New Holland farm implements. Although it is not known how long Kelley was in business, a 1952 Warsaw Speedway program included his ad.

In the 1950s, Norman DeGood purchased a tractor business from Gerald Overmyer. DeGood Tractor Sales was located in the quonset building at 310 Argonne Road (now occupied by Ranger Materials), until moving in the 1960s to 2249 N. Detroit Street.

Center Lake Pavilion

Beginning in the 1940s, Carl "Chappy" and Mazie Chapman managed the Center Lake Pavilion for over 25 years (approximately 1940 to 1965) and oversaw the many celebrations, dances and reunions that took place there. The entire Chapman family was involved, including their granddaughter, Diane Grose, who remembers helping pick up glass pop bottles every morning which people had discarded throughout the park the previous day.

Warsaw Office Supply

During the 1940s, Homer L. Gooch repaired office machines in his house on E. Main Street. About five years after World War II, he opened a business in the basement of the Lake City Bank building on S. Buffalo Street. The business continued to grow, and in the mid-1950s Gooch moved Warsaw Office Supply to 208-210 S. Buffalo Street.

Homer's sons, Doug and Jim, were also involved in the business. When Homer retired in 1972, Doug and Linda Gooch took over management of the business until 1985. The Gooch family also had office supply stores in Wabash, Goshen and Elkhart.

Sylvan Schwegman owned an office supply business in Goshen for over twenty years. In 1985, he purchased the Warsaw Office Supply business

Dressed like his idol, Doug Kehler, left, was thrilled to pose with musician Spike Jones in Fort Wayne in the 1950s. The framed photo was taken several years earlier the first time Kehler met Jones.

Carl "Chappy" Chapman and granddaughter, Diane Derry Grose, at the Center Lake Pavilion (c. 1943). Chapman and his wife managed the pavilion activities.

Paul Lowman is assisted by two men to position his lion on a surfboard along the northeast shore of Winona Lake in the 1940s. Lowman kept the lion in a cage at Billy Botkin's Marina on Winona Avenue.

Paul Lowman straddles his lion as the two take a leisurely surfboard ride on Winona Lake in the 1940s.

and also bought the Wabash store. The stores operated under the same name for several years before Schwegman changed the name to NBS Office Supply in the late 1980s.

The two-story brick building at 208-210 S. Buffalo Street was built in 1890. In the 1930s it was owned by Charles O. Gerard, who then passed its ownership on to his sons, Hurley and Almon. In the 1940s, Hurley Gerard had a music store at 210 S. Buffalo Street called The Hobby House. The business sold pianos, radios, phonographs, records, sheet music, and musical instruments. Due to Hurley's poor health, the business closed in the late 1940s.

Bowling Alley

Royal R. Ruse, one of the first employees of the Winona Interurban and an excavating and hauling contractor for many years, operated Royal Alleys at 113½ W. Center Street above Sharp's Hardware in the early 1940s. About 1947, Ruse constructed a bowling alley at 1702 E. Market Street, known as Royal Recreation Alleys.

The business was sold to Harold "Dutch" Ford in 1954. Ford's Bowling Lanes was then purchased by Roger L. Clemens about 1960. The name was changed to Holiday Lanes, and the adjoining restaurant was known as the Holiday Grill. The business remained in the Clemens family through the late 1970s, when it was sold to Bob Gates and Lee Nichols.

In 1997, Kent Miller, Jamie Wright, and Delbert Robinson purchased the bowling alley, now known as Warsaw Bowl. Joe Wilson and John Nelson joined the partnership in 2001.

Warsaw Chemical Company

Warsaw Chemical Company was founded in 1941 on the northwest corner of Argonne Road and Durbin Street by Paul Grimm, Ed Stapleton, and William Funk. The business was first known as the G S & F Chemical Company, and the name changed in 1945.

The first product made by Grimm was a paste hand soap. Additional products were added and by 1961 Warsaw Chemical mixed and packaged over 70 different chemicals to use in the maintenance chemical field. Items included laundry and dish washing machine detergents, floor cleaners, polishes, insecticides, disinfectants, and a variety of other maintenance chemicals, both liquid and powdered.

Today their line of over 200 Warsaw Chemical brand products is marketed internationally, as well as under private label by hundreds of distributors throughout the U.S. Their car wash product line is ranked third in the nation in sales volume.

Acquisition and renovation of the Baughn & Zent building next door occurred in 1977. (The original Wagon Wheel Restaurant was a previous occupant of a portion of this property.) The company expanded its land ownership and building space in 1999 with the purchase and renovation of the former AMPI facility across the street.

The company is owned and operated as an Employee Stock Ownership Program (ESOP). Robert Steele and Ray Steenhausen guided the growth of the company for over forty years, until it was partially sold to the present management in 1992. Warsaw Chemical is now a 100% employee-owned company. The key management group today, with Donald Sweatland as president, consists of six people with a combined total of over 120 years experience at the firm.

Union Tool Corp.

Union Tool Corporation was started in 1942 by former Power King/Clausing employee Karl J. Heinzelman in a residential garage at 320 N. Lake Street (same site where Arnolt Corporation began). The business quickly grew and moved to 314-320 E. Market Street in 1943 (current location of Schrader Auto Parts). After several expansions, Union Tool purchased the former site of the Winona Railroad car barns on N. Detroit Street in 1951, which remains its current location.

With numerous acquisitions over the years, the diversification of Union Tool includes the early days production of air cylinders and air-operated devices; woodworking, metalworking and materials handling equipment; a line of jointers, saws and shapers; wood boring and chucking machines and sanders. Union Tool is currently operated by Heinzelman's son-in-law, Charles T. Simpson.

Gamble's, Inc.

Gamble's, Inc., headquartered in Minneapolis, Minnesota, opened a Warsaw store in 1942 at 118 S. Buffalo Street just north of Haffner's Five-and-Ten store. Harold Garwick was the managing partner at that time. Joe Arnold, who had been an employee since its start, became manager of the Warsaw store in 1961. Gamble's was at 110 W. Market Street in 1965.

In 1968, the business moved into Bill Chinworth's new building at 112-114 E. Market Street which replaced the Opera House that burned in 1967. (This building was later occupied by Kline's Department Store and is currently the Trust & Investments Division of Lake City Bank.)

Gambles expanded its inventory and offered everything from hardware, housewares, appliances and furniture to televisions, stereos, and health and beauty aids. The sporting goods department sold fishing items and fiberglass boats, in addition to boat motors. On the east side of the store was a large concrete patio which was used to display merchandise during good weather.

The Gamble's store closed in 1983 at the end of its 15-year lease.

"Old Betsy"

Following the desperate drive for scrap metal in the U.S. during World War II, the Mayor and Board of Works decided that "Old Betsy" could still be of service, only in a different way. In 1942, the City donated its fire truck known as "Old Betsy" to the war effort. She was turned over to the scrap metal committee to be melted down for ammunition.

Small piles of scrap could be seen in front yards along the streets of Warsaw. Among the interesting items turned in for scrap was a World War I aerial bomb complete, two gas masks, several radios, a Legionnaire's steel helmet, water tanks, copper boilers and other relics. Kosciusko County citizens answered the call with everything they had. Great interest was shown for a contest of $300 worth of war bonds donated by Warsaw manufacturer Stanley Arnolt. There were prizes for the seven individuals turning in the most scrap.

Jomac Products

In 1934, H. Howard Colehower and his uncle, C. Walker Jones, pooled their resources of $100 in Warrington, Pennsylvania, to buy a circular top knitting machine to make wash mitts. The men came to Warsaw in 1943 and bought Ed Lambert's glove company which was in a livery stable building across from the old high school on W. Main Street.

The name was changed to Jomac Products. The property at 1624 E. Winona Avenue was purchased in 1949 and an addition put on the building. The facility was expanded in 1954 with a two-story addition.

Japan attacked Pearl Harbor on December 7, 1941.

Owners Gus and Grace Tatter sit in front of the Warsaw Monument Works at 633 S. Buffalo Street (c. 1948).

The Flamingo, one of the first and most famous Las Vegas casinos, opened on New Year's Eve 1946.

An agreement was made with a company in England in 1958 to make plastic-coated gloves and rainwear. Jomac is a complete in-house operation, starting with knitting yarn into cloth, processing the material, and then cutting and sewing it for their terry cloth glove line. Jomac also produces polyvinyl chloride coated work gloves and protective raincoats.

Long-time employee Gordon Hackworth recalls that during the 1970s, production reached 10,000 dozen pair of gloves per week. Hackworth began employment with Jomac in 1950 and worked his way up to General Manager, retiring in 1996.

Cox Studio

Cox Studio was founded by Clarence and Lena Cox in 1944, and was first located in the basement of the Stephenson Building at 111 E. Center Street (now Allen's Designs). In addition to portraits and commercial photography, they sold Kodak and amateur supplies, and offered 24-hour service. Following the death of Mr. Cox in 1956, his daughter and son-in-law, Martha and Terry Klondaris, entered the business.

In 1962 Cox Studio moved across the street and above ground to 112 E. Center Street, with Mrs. Cox doing hand oils on black and white photographs and Terry continuing to gain valuable knowledge and expertise. Cox Studio was one of the first to use the new technology of "direct color photography" in 1967.

Terry and Martha's children, Michael and Cindy, joined the business in the 1970s. Cox Studio moved to its present location at 151 S. High Street in 1985 which also includes the Apollo Photo Center, providing one-hour photo and mini-portrait services.

Warsaw Monument Works

In the late 1800s, Warsaw had two "tombstone yards." All the work was done by hand with a chisel and wooden mallet, requiring 30 to 50 hours for each memorial. The two yards eventually combined into one. In the early 1900s, ownership of the company was under the name of Long & Pelton, followed by Skinner Monument Company, owned by Martin H. Skinner until his death. The business was located at 108 S. Lake Street (current location of Service Liquor).

In 1944, Gustav Tatter and Paul Oberli purchased the monument company from the Skinner estate. When Tatter became the sole owner in 1947, he changed the name to Warsaw Monument Works and built a new facility on its current site at 633 S. Buffalo Street.

In 1968, Tatter sold the business to Maurice J. Patten from Kalamazoo, Michigan, at which time Warsaw Monument Works and Patten Monument Company merged into one company. Patten Monument was started in Grand Rapids, Michian, about 1916 by Maurice Patten, Sr. and continued by his four sons. Maurice Patten, Jr. moved to Warsaw in 1975 and made it the main office for Patten Monument Company of Indiana.

Current owners Tony and Kathy Lloyd bought the business in 1983 after gaining eight years of experience managing the company for Maurice Patten. The Lloyds did extensive remodeling of the office facilities in 1995 and added a garage, followed by an exterior facelift of the building in early 2000.

Granites from all over the world are lettered in the Patten Monument plant. Even though modern automated sandblast equipment has replaced the chisel and wooden mallet of yesteryear, it still requires the meticulous attention of skilled craftsmen to permanently record the history of lives in stone.

Roller Skating Rink

During the summers of 1943 and 1944, Ray Kincaide set up a portable roller skating rink on S. Buffalo Street. A large tent covered the wooden floor. People could sit in their cars and not only watch the skaters and listen to the music, but hear the frogs and crickets, as well. In 1945, Kincaide and Norman Kelly constructed a quonset hut building at 800 S. Buffalo Street for a year-round skating rink. The sign above the entrance door read "Tunnel of Fun, Let's Skate."

Barbara Wolford remembers Ray's son, Weldon "Cy," skating around the rink and using a whistle to get the kids' attention to make announcements. Doug Kehler recalls attending a record hop in the early 1950s at the Kincaide roller rink. The hop was sponsored by the Fort Wayne WOWO radio station and emceed by its popular radio host, Bob Sievers.

The roller rink closed in 1952. For a time, the National Guard used it as their Armory and parked trucks inside. Over the years, the building was added onto several times for the Korth Furniture table plant. The property sat vacant for about eight to 10 years, but since 1985 has been the site of Wildman Uniform & Linen.

Although a roller skating rink was located on the east shore of Winona Lake for a time, the City of Warsaw was without a rink until 1981 when Joe Chester built the Eastlake Skate Center at 3010 Frontage Road.

Crownover Jewelry

Leroy Crownover had established a Crownover Jewelry store in Rochester in 1921. In the mid 1940s he opened a second store in North Manchester, Indiana, followed by the Warsaw store in 1945. When looking for a location in Warsaw, Mr. Crownover chose the first storefront location of the three-story, three-front building on the northeast corner of Center and Buffalo Streets (now known as the Saemann Building). This corner had housed a cigar store for many years. To obtain the lease on this location, Crownover bought the cigar store's lease, inventory and fixtures, including the famous wooden Indian that stood outside.

In the early 1960s, the third room of this building became available to purchase. Leroy and his wife, Sue Ann, bought this third room, which included the second floor and a right-of-way to the stairwell between the first and second storefronts. At that time, the third floor was titled to a non-existent organization, the Red Men's Lodge, and it was not until several years later that the Crownovers obtained title to the third floor and roof. The third room was remodeled, including

Ray Kincaide built the "Tunnel of Fun" roller skating rink at 800 S. Buffalo Street in 1945. The National Guard Armory used this building for a time, before Korth Furniture purchased it to manufacture living room furniture.

the second floor, and Crownover Jewelry was then located on the main floor.

Mr. Crownover died in 1969, and his wife continued operation of the business. In the early 1970s, Mrs. Crownover purchased the building at 104 E. Center Street (formerly occupied by the Liberty Café), and moved the jewelry store across the street. Andy Goar purchased the business in 1984, and Andy Garrett has managed Crownover Jewelry since 1988.

Swivlstool, Inc.

A partnership was formed in 1945 under the name of A & A Manufacturing Co. by Orval Alspaugh and his son, Waveland. The company was started in a small building at 1015 E. Market Street to make V-belt pulleys for coal-fed heating stokers. Its quick growth necessitated a move to a larger facility in 1951 along U.S. 30 East near Penguin Point. By 1948 the company had designed and began the manufacture of its popular Swivlstool.

The stools were originally made for the barber trade, but with their versatility, a design change was made to meet the demands of the dental profession.

The partnership was then incorporated in 1958 as Swivlstool, Inc. to principally manufacture dental equipment. By 1961, Swivlstool had introduced its "Work Simplification Unit," a completely mobile, easy-glide unit that could be moved about with ease by a dentist. The company was sold in the mid-1960s.

In 1947, Raytheon Corp. introduced the first microwave oven, which was called a "Radarange."

Members of the Warsaw Police Department are shown in 1947 with Mayor Frank Rarick. Left to right: Frank Juterbock, temporary officer Lester Ball, Clarence Teghtmuyer, Mayor Rarick, Paul Shull, Ralph Jay, and Eugene Kinch.

Ed Sullivan introduced his popular TV variety show in 1948.

Hodges Ready-Mix

Albert M. Hodges founded Hodges Ready-Mix Concrete about 1945. It was first located along the railroad tracks at 600 E. Winona Avenue just east of the north-south tracks. In the mid 1950s, the business moved to 812 N. Detroit Street (current site of Warsaw Automotive/NAPA). Hodges sold his concrete business to Fidler, Inc. in 1972, who moved the operations to County Road 200 West.

Ken-Jen / Sun Metal Products

Ken-Jen Metal Products (named after Playtime Products' founder Bert Anderson's son, Kenny, and Playtime employee Herman Jensen) was originally started in 1946 as a job shop to produce wire spoked wheels for Playtime Products' baby carriages and tricycles. It was first located in a part of the Playtime building on N. Detroit Street, but soon a quonset hut building was constructed further north on Detroit Street, its current site. The company name was changed to Sun Metal Products in 1948.

Recognized as the industry's largest fabricator of wire spoked wheels, by 1954 the company was manufacturing wheels for golf carts, shopping carts, strollers, lawnmowers, garden utility vehicles, hospital equipment, and many more items. Today their product line includes stationary bicycles and bicycle manufacturers like Schwinn and Columbia. Sun began producing alloy rims for high performance, off-road motorcycle racing in 1974, and by the early 1980s more than half the world's professional racers were using Sun's aluminum rims.

Sun expanded facilities in 1992 to include a facility in North Manchester to meet the increasing demand for alloy bicycle rims. In 1995 Sun expanded again to a manufacturing facility in China to build for the increased demand of low- to mid-level original equipment manufacturers' needs in the bicycle market. Sun Rims was recognized in 1996 as one of the world's best rim makers, with numerous victories in the World Cup, NORBA Nationals, and a silver medal in the Atlanta Olympic Games.

Sun Rims purchased Ringle Racing Components in 1997. Their products have helped athletes win countless mountain bike races, withstood some of the most complex BMX and freestyle events, navigated some of the most difficult terrain on world trekking expeditions, and were used by champions of the Tour de France.

Feed Company

K & M Feed Company was originally started by Lloyd Kesler and Earl McCoy in 1946. It was located on the northeast corner of Detroit Street and Winona Avenue. The business served Kosciusko and twelve surrounding counties with quality feeds.

When Kesler's son, Robert, returned from serving with the U.S. Marines during World War II, he went to work for K & M. Lloyd Kesler passed away about a year later, and Bob became co-owner for about 10 years until 1957.

At one time, the original building burned and a new structure was built. By 1965, Ed Doolin was operating the business as Ed's Feed Store. When his son-in-law, Tom Smithson, joined the business, it became known as Ed & Tom's Feed Store.

Smithson bought the entire business in 1977 and changed the name to Tom's Feed Store. He still owns the property today, but since 1993 Tom Lemon has operated the business as Town & Country Feed & Seed.

Home Furniture Mart

Thames L. Mauzy's father, Charles, worked at Ringle Furniture. Thames worked at Mellencamp's Furniture and then in 1946 started Home Furniture Mart with Charles L. McClellan. By 1950, Mauzy had bought out McClellan's interest in the business which offered nationally advertised furniture, carpet and appliances.

The store was originally on N. Detroit Street in the former Playtime Products building. Mauzy then built a quonset type structure in 1949 at 1503 N. Detroit Street. When it burned in February of 1959, a new building was quickly constructed that opened the same year in October. Home Furniture Mart closed its doors in 1992. The building is currently occupied by the Sherwin-Williams paint store.

Prior to his furniture career, Thames Mauzy was employed by Remington Arms as an exhibition shooter and traveled for the company to demonstrate the accuracy of Remington guns. Mauzy was elected in 1966 as an Indiana state representative, a position he held through 1987.

Sheet Metal Shop

In 1946, Richard Siefken and Don Baum purchased the Philpott Tin Shop business at 205 W. Center Street from Ernest Philpott. The name was changed to Warsaw Sheet Metal & Electric Company. Siefken became sole owner in 1949 and added the sales, service and installation of HVAC products to the sheet metal business.

In 1953, Siefken purchased Garpow Sheet Metal Works. A new building was constructed on the southwest corner of Winona Avenue and Bronson Street in 1953, and by 1956 the company's name had been changed to ComforTemp, Inc.

When Siefken retired in 1977, long-time employees Mirriam Paege and Jim Hileman purchased the business. Paege then retired in 1995 and sold her interest in the company to Hileman, who remains the sole owner of ComforTemp today.

Lake City Electroplating

Lake City Electroplating was incorporated in 1946 by president Robert E. Morgan, Keith Doran, and Justin O. Zimmer to electroplate and electro-polish medical equipment. The plant was located on State Road 25 on the west side of Warsaw.

The firm started custom electroplating orthopedic and surgical instruments, but with the

This quonset hut was built at 1503 N. Detroit Street by Thames Mauzy in 1949 for his Home Furniture Mart business. It burned in 1959 and Mauzy constructed the current building on this site.

Warsaw Sheet Metal & Electric Co. constructed this building on the southwest corner of Winona Avenue and Bronson Street in 1953. Since 1956, the business has been known as ComforTemp, Inc.

advent of stainless steel, Lake City Electroplating collaborated with a Columbus, Ohio, inventor to develop electro-polishing. The company held the number one patent on this process before it became widely used throughout the surgical and orthopedic fields.

By 1961, the company was handling an output of eight to 10 million pieces per year for manufacturers in Warsaw, Evansville and Chicago. Robert Morgan's son, J. Alan Morgan, was appointed president of Zimmer, Inc. in 1969 and Lake City Electroplating was then acquired by Zimmer.

This small building was located at 214 S. Buffalo Street for over 100 years. It was a doctor's office in the early 1900s, and then J.L. Baker operated his dental office there for almost 50 years. The building was demolished in 1996.

Penicillin, developed by Sir Alexander Fleming, was first available to the civilian population in 1944.

Doctor's Office for a Century

Although the small, white clapboard, one-story building that used to sit at 214 S. Buffalo Street is best remembered as Dr. Baker's dental office, its history started long before 1900. It is thought that when Francis A. Place came to Warsaw in 1879 he operated a photography studio at this location, where he specialized in baby portraits.

When Dr. T.J. Shackelford came to Warsaw in 1883, he operated his medical practice in this building and his wife, Emma, taught china painting classes in the basement. Dr. Siders also practiced medicine in this small building for 36 years. When the Shackelford home next door was later used as the Kelly Funeral Home, the front room of the office building was used to display caskets for sale to the public.

However, in 1947 Dr. James L. Baker purchased the small structure and opened his dental practice on St. Patrick's Day. He had served two years as an Army dentist and returned to Warsaw in 1946. Dr. Baker bought the dental equipment of Dr. Shipley who was closing his practice.

The longest practicing dentist in Warsaw, Dr. Baker kept up with the new technology over the years, but still chose to use his original drill, later air-powered rather than belt-driven, and his General

Electric x-ray machine, which was inspected by OSHA on a regular basis. In addition to several assistants over the years, Rachael Knouff Turner made and repaired dentures in the back room for 34 years. Dr. Baker retired in April of 1996, just before the building was demolished.

The Wonder Store

Clothing was hard to come by at the end of World War II. Clarence "Bish" Brown saw a need and found a way to profit from it. The Wonder Store, Warsaw's first discount store, was started about 1946 in a tent on McClellan Street. The business was based on selling job lots and discounted name brand men's, women's and children's clothing. The first stock, purchased from Phillipson's and Carter's Department Stores, was outdated clothing that the businesses had stored in their basements because they had not been able to sell the merchandise.

Bish built a temporary building, never intending to use it for an extended period of time. However, his new enterprise was such a booming success that people often waited in long lines just to get inside the store. On the north end of this building his oldest son, Arnold, opened a shoe store.

Searching for more items to sell, Bish began purchasing stock from Chicago-based companies that were going bankrupt and/or going out of business. As a promotional gimmick to draw attention to The Wonder Store, Bish had an oil well drilled not far from the business site. People would come from miles away to watch the drilling process. The well was down 385 feet when a part of the drill was lost and the drilling stopped. Bish's youngest son, Mark, remembers the huge truck that was brought in to remove the well casing.

In 1951, Bish sold the business to someone from Chicago, who continued its operation into the 1970s. Bill Nay Furniture later purchased the property, tore down the building, and constructed a new concrete block building at the same site.

After the war, Bish and his sons began constructing homes and commercial buildings along McClellan Street. In the mid-1940s, the Browns built the Country Club Grocery at 612 McClellan Street. The building next door at 710 McClellan Street was used by Bish at different times as an auction house, a car lot, and a tire company. His son, Kendall, then used it as a place to rebuild batteries.

Train Wreck

Sleeping residents were awakened about 5:30 a.m. on April 28, 1947, when the Pennsylvania Railroad's Golden Triangle passenger train derailed as it sped through Warsaw at about 90 miles per hour.

The engine remained on the tracks, but all eleven cars derailed as they passed through the interlocking switch where the Pennsylvania Railroad tracks crossed the Big Four tracks. The tracks were torn up and debris was strewn about for four blocks.

The crossing watchman was injured when his tower was demolished; however, none of the 147 passengers were killed and only nine people were injured.

Osborn Manufacturing

Osborn Manufacturing Corporation was founded in 1947 by Robert E. Osborn and is located at 960 N. Lake Street. The company was originally in the Secor Building on Argonne Road. Its purpose was to develop, manufacture and sell industrial safety equipment and tools.

Osborn's main product was a plier or tong made out of a soft but tough aluminum alloy to feed parts into and out of industrial presses and other hazardous industrial operations. The company went on to fabricate hundreds of other products designed for safety, including a "lockout" device used to lock out electrical switches while a machine is being repaired or adjusted.

Major customers include automobile manufacturers, metal stamping plants, the lumber industry, food processing plants and chemical plants. Osborn Mfg. used to purchase aluminum castings from the Warsaw Pittenger Foundry. Current owners are Jerry and Vivian Kelly, Virgil Hagy and Michael Hagy.

Lowery Sewing Center

In 1947, Arthur Lowery began repairing sewing machines in his garage on E. Market Street. The business grew and was moved to 119 E. Center Street under Strayer Insurance, and then to the basement of the Centennial Theatre building below the Town & Country Dress Shop.

The business was purchased in 1961 by Arthur's son, Harold, who moved the store to the 100 block of E. Market Street in the Opera House. In 1967, a fire destroyed all of the contents of the store. Lowery Sewing Center then moved to the

Four blocks of railroad tracks were torn up when a Pennsylvania Railroad passenger train traveling through Warsaw at 90 mph derailed on April 28, 1947.

Only 9 of the 147 passengers on a Pennsylvania Railroad passenger train were injured when a train derailed on April 28, 1947, while passing through Warsaw.

Lakeview Shopping Center. The store was purchased in 1974 by Lowery's daughter and son-in-law, Linda and Dean Harman. The Harmans constructed a new building in 1978 and moved the business to its present location at 707 E. Winona Avenue.

Today, this family-owned business is the only sewing store in town that sells several brands of sewing machines and vacuum cleaners. In addition to a wide selection of sewing materials and supplies, the Lowery Sewing Center also has a machine repair service.

The Laminated Rafters facility on N. Detroit Street in 1960.

Laminated Rafters, Inc.

Robert Gilliam and some business associates formed Laminated Rafters, Inc. in 1947 to produce laminated barn rafters and arches for commercial buildings. Gilliam had been a lumber dealer in Leesburg, but by 1947 was operating a farm implement business with William S. Felkner at 1421 N. Detroit Street (now site of Warsaw Masonry).

Original production lines were set up in a 60-foot x 100-foot building on N. Detroit Street and the administrative operations were conducted from his nearby implement business. Due to poor health, Gilliam sold the company in 1955 to Willis Barkey of Plymouth and his son Lowell, a Lakeville, Indiana, lumberman. The corporate name was then changed to Laminated Rafters Corporation.

The business expanded to cover more types of building construction requirements, and their laminated beams or timbers are used in many commercial buildings as well as homes. Now known as LRC Products, the business has been operated by Lowell's son, Phillip Barkey, since 1974.

Phil recalls when Harold Derry was constructing a body shop on the northwest corner of Smith and Bronson Streets. LRC wanted to haul the assembled rafters to the site but they were over the allowable length to transport on city streets. Mr. Barkey called Mayor Hodges to inquire how the rafters could be delivered to the site. Hodges asked how tall they were and Barkey replied 13 feet.

A team at Harvard University, funded in part by IBM, constructed the first automatic, general purpose computer in 1944.

Mayor Hodges had been trying to get United Telephone Company to raise some of their phone lines in town to 13-feet 6-inches because they were too low. Hodges told LRC it was okay to deliver the rafters and personally led the escort through town, going down streets where he knew the phone lines were too low. They knocked down 25 to 30 phone lines before reaching Smith Street. And in the end, the phone lines were raised.

Ice Storm Strikes

January 30, 1947, was the worst ice storm in the history of Kosciusko County. Freezing rain began Tuesday night and continued through Wednesday, followed by thunder, lightning and high winds on Wednesday night. Ice broke power lines and cut off electricity within a 100-mile radius of Warsaw. Most factories were shut down and many stores were closed, although the hardware stores were very busy selling flashlights and batteries. Candles, oil lamps and lanterns were evident everywhere.

When the emergency crews began attempts to repair local power lines, they soon realized the true importance of electricity. The service trucks needed fuel and there was not a single old-fashioned gravity-flow gas pump in town, as every filling station had pumps that depended upon electricity to pump gas. Pitcher-type pumps were quickly rigged to the storage tanks to fill the emergency service vehicles.

News wire services were completely cut off and the *Warsaw Daily Times* was emergency printed on a two-page mimeographed sheet.

Lake City Candy Company

The Lake City Candy Company was started in the late 1940s by Robert Breading, Sr. and his son, Lewis H. Breading. The wholesale supply business was located in the former Opera House on E. Market Street. In addition to candy and gum, Lake City Candy Company sold tobacco and cigars, paper goods, fountain and school supplies, and sundries. The business moved to 917 S. Buffalo Street (now Fisher Avenue) in 1954 and is currently operated by Lewis' son, Tom Breading.

Kimble Glass

Kimble Glass Company was founded in 1901 by Col. Ewan Kimble in Chicago to produce vials. The company pioneered many "firsts" in the production of vials, ampuls, graduated ware, test tubes, and other scientific and medical ware. In 1946, Owens-Illinois Glass Company acquired the assets of Kimble Glass and it became a wholly owned subsidiary of Owens-Illinois.

In 1947 the Warsaw Kimble Glass Plant was established at 765 W. Market Street for the purpose of manufacturing primarily for the pharmaceutical industry. A new facility on a 20-acre site in Boggs Industrial Park was constructed in 1969. The Kimble Warsaw Plant has expanded their market for tubing-made ampul and vial containers to the pharmaceutical and personal care industries across the United States, Puerto Rico and Europe.

WRSW Radio

Reuben and Ted Williams, owners of the *Times-Union* newspaper, wanted to keep the Warsaw community better informed, so in 1948 they started the WRSW FM 107.3 radio station in the basement of the Times Building. The 1480 AM station was added in 1952. After WRSW was purchased by GBC Media in May of 1999, the station moved to 216 W. Market Street.

A prominent figure in the early days of WRSW was the late veteran newsman William "Bill" Mollenhour, Jr. Mollenhour joined the *Warsaw Daily Times* as a "cub" reporter/photographer in the 1930s. His relentless campaign against gambling and drugs kept the community well informed. Bill's radio and newspaper exposé of teen drug use in the 1960s resulted in a congressional inquiry on the problem being held in Warsaw.

In the early 1950s, old-timers say, guards were posted outside the WRSW studios to protect

The first truck owned by Laminated Rafters, loaded and ready to make a delivery.

The Laminated Rafters facility was damaged by fire Christmas morning in 1973. "Happy Holidays" can be seen on the window.

Charles E. Bertsch, founder of Bertsch Vending, received the Ernst & Young Lifetime Achievement Award in 2001.

In 1943 during the war, ration coupons allowed car owners to purchase three gallons of gasoline per week; the national speed limit was 40 mph.

Mollenhour while he was naming those involved in the local gambling operations on his nightly radio news show. The gambling interests were reportedly angered by the newsman's "tell it like it is, no holds barred" approach to their illegal activities.

Bill Mollenhour was very active in the community. He was vice president of the Murphy Medical Center when Hazel Murphy was in charge of its operation after her husband's death and also served as a state aeronautics commissioner. In addition, Governor Mathew Welsh honored Mollenhour with the "Sagamore of the Wabash" award in 1963.

Well-known local radio personality Harvey Miller began his broadcast career in Warsaw in January 1958 as a broadcast engineer. In 1968 he began working in sales for WRSW and then became assistant manager in 1974. Miller was promoted to manager in 1978, a position he held until his retirement at the end of 2000.

Rita Price-Simpson has been with WRSW since 1959. Before "canned" music was used, most radio broadcasting was live. Rita recalls the times she sang with piano accompaniment and hosted live music shows from the Elks Lodge. Rita is best known for her play-by-play sports broadcasting of area high school ballgames during the past thirty years.

Norm Hagg accepted a night radio job with WRSW in the early 1960s. He wrote news reports for the early daytime programs and reported the local news in the evenings. About a year later, Reub Williams offered Hagg a job with the *Times-Union*. He started as a general assignment reporter and advanced through a number of positions in the editorial department. Now general manager and editor-in-chief, Hagg is approaching 38 years with the *Times-Union*. He also was the WRSW play-by-play announcer for Warsaw Tiger basketball for 10 years in the 1970s.

Bertsch Vending

Charles Bertsch founded Bertsch Vending Company in 1948 when he combined $20 borrowed with $20 of his own and bought two used vending machines to sell candy bars at five cents each. One was placed at a gas station and the other at a small manufacturing plant.

Bertsch started the business from his basement and expanded to the garage. He delivered candy and cigarettes while his wife, June, answered the phone and managed the paperwork. The business soon extended to an outbuilding that grew into the

beginning of the current facility on Parker Street. The building has undergone multiple changes throughout the years, including the addition of a bakery/commissary in the 1960s and a second floor in the 1980s.

Within two years Charlie had hired the first route driver, and within three years there were five employees. During the 1960s, the Bertsch Vending fleet included seven route vehicles and a maintenance/service truck. Today, over 70 routes blanket northern Indiana from six centers (Crawfordsville, Garrett, Lafayette, Valparaiso, Wabash, Warsaw).

The first company computer was purchased in 1977. Today, each vending machine reports sales activity via internal and handheld computer devices that are fed into the main system. Having changed the name to Bertsch Services in the early 1990s, the company offers a full line vending service, a complete coffee service program, a dining service division to operate in-plant cafeterias, and an on-site catering service.

Silveus & Bradway

James C. "Mac" Silveus went into business in 1948 delivering fuel oil and gasoline to homeowners and farmers. He used bulk tanks on the former Tinkey Oil property on W. Market Street. Mac had three commercial accounts situated along several highways. Each location had a small grocery, tourist cabins and a gas station.

Mac's brother-in-law, Ted Bradway, became a partner in 1951, and the business became known as Silveus & Bradway. Mac was first a Phillips 66 consignee, later Mobil and Sunoco, and most recently, BP. The business headquarters has been at the 1721 E. Center Street location since about 1954.

Board of Realtors

The Warsaw Board of Realtors was formed in 1948. The organization submitted for a new charter in 1965 to include a larger area and changed the name to Kosciusko Board of Realtors. Gary Salyer is the only signer of the incorporation papers to still be an active member. He was designated an Honorary Member in June 2000.

Salyer started Warsaw Real Estate in 1971 in the old Oram Building on the northwest corner of Lake and Center Streets. In 1972, Salyer bought the building across the street on the southwest corner. The business was located at 201 W. Center Street until 1989, when it moved to the south end of the block into the old Post Office which was converted into office space.

The Four Freshmen

Warsaw native Hal Kratzsch was the originator of the famous "Four Freshmen" quartet in 1948. He asked brothers Ross and Don Barbour to join him, along with their cousin, Bob Flanigan. Their first professional booking was September 20, 1948, at the 113 Club in Fort Wayne.

Their first two singles recorded with Capitol Records were not encouraging. However, in 1952 with the release of their third single, "It's a Blue World," they were on their way to a singing career. Kratzsch left the group after five years to join another singing group. Bob Flanigan remained with the Four Freshmen the longest of the original four, retiring in 1992 to become the group's manager.

The Four Freshmen are unique because of their "sound." They were the first male group to put the lead voice at the top of the chord and called their style "open" harmony because they spread their four voices over the area that a five-part group would ordinarily cover. Their unique musical phrasing is more like instruments playing rather than voices singing.

Betty Kratzsch, Hal's wife, relates that they lived out of a suitcase for 11 years and had three sons while on the road. She remembers ironing tuxes on dresser drawers turned upside down in hotel rooms. Although the Four Freshmen were considered a jazz vocal group, Betty noted that both the Lettermen and Beach Boys basically were started after hearing the sounds and arrangements of the Four Freshmen.

Kenny Rogers has been a fan of the group since its beginning, and Betty recalls that when the fan club had its 50th anniversary celebration in Las Vegas in 1998, one thousand people attended representing thirteen countries. Although the foursome has changed over the years, their sound remains very similar.

Betty added that the Four Freshmen was the first group chosen to be inducted into the Vocal Groups Hall of Fame in Pennsylvania. In addition, a plaque was set at the north end of Warsaw's Central Park a few years ago to commemorate this still popular group. The Four Freshmen last visited Warsaw in October 2000 in an appearance at the Wagon Wheel Theatre for a breast cancer awareness fundraiser.

Tri-State Advertising

William H. Kreicker, the son of a Chicago industrial advertising businessman, founded Tri-State Advertising Company, Inc. in the spring of 1948. Kreicker's son, William L. Kreicker, joined the firm in 1949 and, with a talented staff, built the agency into a nationally recognized multi-million dollar business-to-business marketing communications specialist. Clayton R. Kreicker, the third generation to head Tri-State Advertising, took over the presidency in 1996. He joined the firm in 1982.

The Four Freshmen's first hit in the early 1950s was "It's a Blue World."

Bob Richmond, center, sometimes sang with The Four Freshmen quartet when they entertained in Warsaw. Left to right are Hal Kratzsch, Ross Barbour, Richmond, Don Barbour, and Bob Flanigan (c. 1950). They were guests on Richmond's WRSW live radio program the first time they returned to Warsaw to perform at the Elks Lodge.

The groundbreaking ceremony in 1968 for Armstrong Products, the first company to build in the Boggs Industrial Park on the west side of Warsaw. Left to right: Freddie Boggs (property owner), Ray Steenhausen (Warsaw Chemical), Cecil Armstrong (founder of Armstrong Products), Mayor Mike Hodges, Chamber of Commerce director Sam Dungan, and Freddie's son, Jim Boggs.

The feature race line-up on July 4, 1950 at the Warsaw Speedway. The previous Saturday night Russ Brown, of North Manchester, had set a new track record with his lap of 19.28 seconds. This night he broke his own record by making it in 19.25 seconds.

Tri-State was first located on the second floor at 108 E. Center Street, and has been at 307 S. Buffalo Street since 1966. Right from the start Tri-State specialized in what was earlier referred to as "industrial advertising," but is now called "business-to-business marketing communications." In a business as volatile as advertising, it is rather unique to find a firm, under the same family management, continuing to flourish after more than half a century of operation.

Derry's Body Shop

At age 16, Harold Derry was employed at Hartsock's Studebaker dealership, where he worked in the paint department. He then worked at the Ringer Body Shop for a few years before venturing out on his own. Harold started Derry's Body Shop in 1949 at 110 S. Washington Street (now site of Tarkio Road), and his brother, Claude, had a refrigeration business in the front of the building.

The body shop business grew and about 1960 a quonset hut building was constructed on the northwest corner of Smith and Bronson Streets. Derry retired in 1973, and ComforTemp acquired the property .

Armstrong Products Co.

Armstrong Products Company was founded in 1949 by Cecil and Marie Armstrong to do research and development of thermosetting epoxy resin adhesives. The business was started in one room at 407 Argonne Road, but grew rapidly with engineering work for such industries as Allison jet engines, Delco-Remy starter-generators, and diesel engines for submarine propulsion.

Armstrong Products was the first to market a formulated epoxy adhesive in the United States. The acceptance was rapid and world-wide. Customers began bringing their adhesives problems to Armstrong. To meet their individual needs, Armstrong Products expanded its research efforts for the development of numerous adhesives, eventually developing over 200 formulations.

The epoxy adhesives research led to the development of other epoxy resin products. In 1960, Armstrong Resins, Inc., a separate entity, was established to produce and market powder coatings and application equipment.

In 1968 a plant was built in Boggs Industrial Park to handle the adhesives product line. Additions were made to this plant and eventually all powder coating production was moved to Boggs Industrial Park, while the administrative offices remained at the Argonne Road facility.

In 1982, Morton (best known for its table salt) purchased Armstrong Products Company. Morton Powder Coatings was formed in 1986 when Armstrong merged with the Polymer Corporation located in Reading, Pennsylvania. These two companies had independently held leadership positions in this new technology prior to the merger.

Morton Powder Coatings has three plants, the largest of which is located in Warsaw. This plant

Warsaw Speedway legend Freddie Boggs in 1949 with his first racer. Freddie's son, Jim, and grandson, Butch, also raced at the Warsaw Speedway.

Popular driver Archie Holle was the fastest qualifier on October 3, 1959, at the Warsaw Speedway.

Announcer Milo Clase, left, and track president C.E. "Hoot" Gibson on Season Championship Night October 19, 1959.

The Davis racing crew September 19, 1959, left to right: John Crum, Roy Norman, Jerry Clase, John Davis and his brother, Sam Davis.

employs 108 people and is capable of producing over 30 million pounds of powder coatings per year, making it one of the largest plants of its kind in North America. Morton International merged with chemical giant Rohm and Haas in 1999, making the combined company the world's second-largest specialty chemical manufacturer.

Warsaw Speedway

The Warsaw Speedway's quarter-mile dirt track on the shores of Winona Lake was built for horse racing in 1946 when the property was purchased for a fairgrounds. With auto racing an up-and-coming sport, the fairgrounds hired Phil Tyrrell as the managing director.

Tyrrell had spent 25 years in the entertainment business helping start such stars as Ginger Rogers, Martha Raye, Edgar Bergen, Morton Downey, and Guy Lombardo. He was a vaudeville booker and booking manager of the Radio City Music Hall and Center theatres in Rockefeller Center for three years.

He added "show business" style entertainment to the weekly Saturday night races that were full of exciting thrills, variety, and great media coverage.

The first Saturday night of racing took place June 11, 1949, in front of an estimated 4,000 spectators. News spread quickly and within a month the Speedway was hosting live broadcasts of midget races on both the Hoosier Radio Network and the local WRSW radio station.

The Speedway drew followers from all over the United States and Canada. Its popularity brought drivers on a regular basis for the midget races sanctioned by the United Automobile Racing Association of Chicago. Hot rod races were also added within the first year, which attracted many local drivers.

Rollen "Joe" Hamsher took over management of the speedway in 1951. He had started the New Paris Speedway in 1948 and managed both tracks during the short period of time he was the flagman, and Milo Clase and John Niccum were announcers.

In 1953, Claris E. "Hoot" Gibson took over as the promoter and general manager for the Warsaw Speedway. Over the next 25 years he dedicated his life to the weekly physical and managerial work. Justice of the Peace Milo Clase was the voice of the racing action from the early 1950s through the late 1970s. Using two microphones, he announced not only for the crowd on hand, but also announced a half-hour of the competition on WRSW radio every Saturday night. Now living in Florida, Clase recalls that in nearly thirty years of announcing, he never missed a race!

During stock car racing's heyday in the 1950s, many popular and talented drivers raced at the Warsaw Speedway. One of the most successful was Freddie Boggs, who won many races at Warsaw and throughout the Midwest in both the midget races and hot rod stock classes. In 1957 his success took him to the most famous stock car race of all, the Daytona 500.

In 1978, several racers became frustrated with the management, track operations, and pay-offs, so they boycotted the races on July 8. Four drivers then bought out the remaining two years of Gibson's contract and took over operations of the speedway. Racing resumed with Jim Bucher of Akron as track president and manager.

Bucher ran the Warsaw Speedway for 2½ years and added entertaining attractions such as the hot dog races and watermelon races, where drivers raced three laps, stopped to eat a hot dog or slice of watermelon, and then drove backwards around the track for two laps. He also had the first $1,000 demolition derby and brought the world-famous "World of Outlaws" to Warsaw on August 25, 1978.

When Bobby Grindle was hired as the speedway promoter in 1981 and 1982, he introduced many interesting attractions, including a track clown and city officials races. A color-lighted pond with three fountains was added in the center of the track.

In 1983, Monty Miller from Huntington became the Speedway manager and promoter, and many track improvements were made over the next six years. The sprint cars, late models, and street stock classes continued to be popular through the 1980s. At one point an agreement was made for the newer high-performance cars to use mufflers and that races would end by 11:00 p.m. However, nine Winona Lake property owners filed suit in 1989 to close the speedway due to noise and dust complaints.

An organization known as WASP (Warsaw Auto Speedway Patrons) was formed in the same year to promote family activities at the speedway and provide voluntary support where needed for the continuation of the speedway activities. The fair association leased the track for a time to two private individuals, Earl Gaerte and Dee Chapman, in hopes of generating more funds.

In the end, however, the Kosciusko County Fair Board conceded and signed a legal agreement that forever banned oval track racing at the fairgrounds. The last races at the Warsaw Speedway were on August 11, 1990.

Hoot Gibson's great-niece, Kimberley Baney, has gathered many photos and memorabilia. She also talked with a number of former drivers to compile information about the Warsaw Speedway and established an internet web site dedicated specifically to the speedway.

Jimmy Elliott was a popular driver at the Warsaw Speedway in the 1960s and early 1970s. Following three straight track championships, he was killed in a motorcycle accident in 1973. His son, Tony, has continued the racing tradition.

Driver Tony Elliott in 1979 at age 18 near the start of his racing career. He can be seen yet today on television racing USAC sprint cars, midgets, and dirt champ cars.

City Parks Department employee Larry Plummer, Sr. wins a race at the Warsaw Speedway (c. 1986).

Chapter 14

Community Servants

William Bramwell Funk was active and supportive of the advancement of Warsaw, and was very interested in the welfare of the overall community. He liked politics, fishing, and music, and took great interest in the affairs of his church.

In 1857, "Bram" Funk accepted the position of deputy auditor of Kosciusko County, holding that position until 1862 when he was elected county auditor. Funk held that position by re-election until 1871.

In 1872 he became associated with his brother, Joseph A. Funk, in the mercantile business which was conducted under the name Funk Brothers. For many years he was connected with the Kosciusko County Agricultural Society, serving as president and secretary. Bram also served several years as chairman of the Kosciusko County Republican Central Committee.

In 1880, he was elected to the office of county treasurer and served in that position until 1884. During the late 1880s, Funk was president of Lake City Bank.

Elmer B. Funk, like his father, became quite an esteemed civic leader in Warsaw. Elmer's interests during his early years included boxing and swimming. He perfected his swimming until he could swim the entire length of Winona Lake. Elmer had one of the first high-wheel bicycles in town. Bicycle clubs were organized and racing became popular. In fact, for many years Elmer rode a bike to work when he was employed at Lake City Bank.

Like his father, Elmer was fond of music. He played clarinet for the Fourth Regiment band in the Indiana National Guard. Elmer was a member of the First Methodist Church and became choir director in 1899, a position he held for 30 years. Funk was also the Sunday School superintendent for nearly as long.

Elmer Funk also became affiliated with the Winona Christian Assembly at an early age when he served as its first gatekeeper, and in later years he was a member of the Assembly board of directors. In addition to being a charter member of the Warsaw Kiwanis Club, Elmer was a board member of the Salvation Army for 50 years. For 25 years, he was also chairman of the County Vigilantes, a group of men under the sheriff who pledged to help during emergencies.

Elmer Funk's banking career began at age 19 in 1895 when he was a collector and assistant bookkeeper at Lake City Bank. Following in his father's footsteps, Elmer also was appointed president of the bank, and later served as chairman of the board of directors.

George A. Nye graduated from Warsaw High School in 1907 and became a well-known county historian. School records show that he taught math and science at the school in 1917-1918 and then from 1924 to 1943. Nye served two terms as the Kosciusko County Surveyor, then later as drainage clerk and in other capacities in the surveyor's office for a total of 60 years.

Nye married Theresa Kleckner in 1920, who died in 1940. In 1943 he married Gladys Ramsey, who died in 1965. He then married Marjorie Fisher Berry in 1966, who died in 1998. George and Theresa's daughter, Sarah Jane Nye Thompson, currently lives in Beech Grove, Indiana. Nye's step-daughter, Waverly Berry Conlan, lives in Winona Lake. Charles Homer "Bush" Rice, mayor of Warsaw from 1948 to 1951, was Theresa's son from a previous marriage, making him George Nye's step-son.

An organized man with set routines who made instant decisions, George Nye always carried a notebook to take notes as he talked with people

William B. Funk (1838-1920)

Elmer B. Funk (1876-1962)

Local historian George A. Nye (1889-1977)

Warsaw High School Coach George L. Fisher (1901-1968)

about the history of Warsaw. He attended all the community events and worked at a table in his living room where he would type his notes. Nye's daughter states that he would put his history writings away each evening and get them back out the next morning.

Citizens enjoyed his interesting articles in the *Times-Union* for many years, and Nye's history of Warsaw is documented in the 37 volumes of his typed notes in the research section at the Warsaw Community Public Library.

George L. Fisher was an Indiana University star lineman in football and Big Ten wrestling champion. He was employed at the Warsaw High School, where he taught biology and coached from 1926 to 1954.

Fisher has, by far, the longest stay as football coach at Warsaw and ended his career with a 103-95-15 record. He coached many outstanding athletes in football, basketball and track. In 1936 and 1937, Fisher coached the Warsaw basketball teams to the state semi-finals.

Coach Fisher was admired and respected by the entire community. His comments in the 1929 Tiger Annual state: "When a game is played for the sheer fun of playing it; when it is played whole heartedly and with abandonment, the physical, mental and social rewards are almost beyond calculation. There is an intense personal satisfaction in a clean victory, and the feelings of complete joy and satisfaction that come when we know that the cheering of the crowd is in honest and heartfelt admiration, can hardly be surpassed."

When the property on the south side of Center Lake known as "Rigdon Row" was renovated, two softball diamonds and a football/soccer field were built between Detroit and Indiana Streets. The football field was used as the Warsaw High School grid-iron and was later named "Fisher Field" a few years after Coach Fisher's school retirement. Fisher Field was removed in the early 1990s to build the new Central Park, and all softball games have since been played at the City-County Athletic Complex. The Fisher Field sign now hangs at the entrance to the school football field on Smith Street.

During the years 1935 to 1938, Jerry Gerard was the manager of all sports under the direction of Coach Fisher. Gerard recalls the bruises his leg received over the years when Fisher would get excited during a game and pound on Jerry's leg as he talked. Gerard succeeded managers Forrest Croop and Tommy Gilliam.

Following his teaching and coaching career, Fisher turned to politics and was first elected to the Indiana General Assembly in 1956. A Republican, he was never defeated and served a continuous eight years.

Charles O. Gerard (1869-1951) moved to Warsaw in 1890. He bought a lot of land and by 1901 had established the "Grand View Farm" south of town. In 1902, Gerard started the Nickel Plate Restaurant on W. Center Street. When Franklin D. Roosevelt ended prohibition in 1933, C.O. Gerard opened Warsaw's first tavern, The Buffalo Inn, at 204 S. Buffalo Street.

C.O. Gerard's "Grand View Farm" in 1901 was located south of Warsaw. The unique barn was constructed with bricks.

Charles and his first wife, Addie Jane Palmer, had two sons, Hurley and Almon. Almon contracted tuberculosis while at Wabash College. Back then, patients with tuberculosis were usually sent to a sanitarium, but Almon went to Asheville, North Carolina, and got a job as a minor league baseball umpire. He also was a sports writer for the *Asheville Times*. Al returned to Warsaw and started a shoe business inside Richardson's department store on S. Buffalo Street.

Al Gerard (1892-1973) married Allee Whittenberger in 1916, and they had one son, Jerry. In 1922, Gerard organized and umpired the "Warsaw Specials" baseball team. The "locker room" was in the basement of the Gerard home at 221 W. Center Street, where the boys dressed and showers had been installed. The team warmed up in the lot beside East Dry Cleaners before going to their games at Hillery Park on S. Buffalo Street, where the ballfield had a marble home plate. Future mayor Frank Rarick was the first baseman.

By 1925, Gerard had started his own business, Central Shoe Company, at 106 E. Center Street. Jerry joined his father in 1947, and it remained a family-owned store until Jerry retired and sold the 58-year-old business in 1983.

The Warsaw Specials baseball team at Hillery Field on S. Buffalo Street (c. 1921). Coach Al Gerard is in the second row, center, with the mustache. Frank "Slats" Rarick, far left with his arms crossed, was the first baseman.

Jerry Gerard, a 1938 graduate of Warsaw High School, was a sports manager under Coach George Fisher. He entered the Navy in 1942 and served during World War II. Gerard became an engineering officer on the USS LST 920, one of the biggest ships that carried tanks. After the war he was in the local Navy reserves for 13 years and returned to Indiana University at Bloomington for his master's degree in fine arts.

Jerry and his first wife, Maryella, had one son, James, who has a daughter, Isabelle. A former vice president of the Kosciusko County Historical Society, Gerard remains active in the organization and is responsible for preparing creative displays and artistry work at the Jail Museum. He resides in Warsaw with his current wife, Diane.

Virgil A. McCleary opened his optometry office in 1940 at 115 N. Buffalo Street (now Lavender Law Offices). His first patient was 86-year-old Amos Ringle, owner of the Ringle Furniture Store. "Doc" McCleary retired in 1985 as an optometrist, but continued his efforts of being an active public servant.

McCleary served as a city councilman from 1950 to 1953 and was a member of the Republican Precinct Committee for eight years. McCleary held a pilot's license from 1947 to 1981 and was a member of the Flying Shriners Club. As a member of the local Shrine Club, he initiated the idea of taking the county third graders to the annual Shrine Circus in Fort Wayne and served as committee chairman for three years.

Local historian Jerry Gerard volunteers at the Old Jail Museum, where his artistic talent is used to create interesting displays for photos and items throughout the museum.

Al and Allee Gerard on their 50th wedding anniversary in 1966.

Virgil "Doc" McCleary (1914-1996), shown with his wife Lucille, had an optometry office on N. Buffalo Street from 1940 to 1985.

The slogan for Ed Pratt's campaign when he ran for Wayne Township Trustee was, "I won't hound you for your vote."

McCleary was one of three men who reinstated the Junior Chamber of Commerce, later known as the Jaycees, in Warsaw after World War II. He also served as president of the Warsaw Senior Chamber of Commerce and received the prestigious "Man of the Year" award in 1991. In addition, McCleary was the first president of the Rozella Ford Golf Course (1960-1968) and served as a local Civil Defense Deputy for many years.

In 1952, McCleary initiated the Warsaw Little League and served as its first president (1952-1955). In the 1960s he served as the camping and activities chairman for the Kosciusko District of the Boy Scouts of America. In addition to local involvement, he also served on many state boards and committees through his optometry profession, the Elks Club and Kiwanis Club. McCleary was the only

All officers of the Kosciusko County Republican Central Committee were re-elected in 1974. From left are Miss Pauline Jordan, vice-chairman; Ed Pratt, chairman; and Mrs. Nellie Garman, secretary. Treasurer Kenneth McBride is not pictured.

member of the Kiwanis Club to serve two consecutive years as president and in 1991 was honored for over 50 years of perfect attendance.

A self-taught organist, for many years McCleary played the organ before each of the Kiwanis Travelogue Series programs. In 1985 he was the first performer in the Warsaw Community Development's bi-weekly entertainment series on the courthouse lawn. As an active member of the United Methodist Church of Warsaw, he was a Sunday School teacher and made five trips to Haiti to serve on health missions.

Doc McCleary was born on Friday the 13th in February of 1914. Following is an excerpt of his message to family and friends at his 80th surprise birthday party on February 13, 1994: "The first 80 years are the hardest. By the second 80, everybody wants to carry your baggage and help you up the steps. If you forget anybody's name, forget an appointment, or spell words wrong, you can explain that you're 80. If you spill soup on your tie or if your socks don't match, you are 80. Nobody expects much of you. At age 65 or 70, they expect you to retire, but if you survive until 80, everybody is surprised that you are alive, surprised that you can walk, and surprised that you can talk above a whisper. So relax—you have a perfect alibi!"

Dedicated Republicans

Edwin D. Pratt (1914-2000) served as the Kosciusko County Republican chairman for 10 years, from 1970 to 1980. When Pratt ran for Wayne Township Trustee in 1966, his campaign photo included his dog, with the slogan, "I won't hound you for your vote." He was re-elected Trustee multiple times, serving in that position from 1967 to 1995.

Mr. Pratt was very instrumental in the development and beginning operations of the Multi-Township Emergency Medical Service, which came to fruition in December of 1977. Ed remained active with the organization until he left the Trustee's office in 1995.

Miss Pauline Jordan was a hard-working woman involved with many organizations in the community. Her work ethics, more than likely, were instilled at a young age. Pauline's father, Charles E. Jordan, purchased the Outdoor Advertising Company in 1925 from Charles Knause and changed the name to Jordan Advertising Company.

The business was operated out of the family's basement and garage at 218 Fort Wayne Avenue. His wife served as president, and at age 13, Pauline became the bookkeeper and secretary of the business. Pauline continued to operate the company for many years after her father's death, and sold the business to Burkhart Advertising in 1978.

Jordan was actively involved in politics for over 50 years, with service to the Republican party and Kosciusko County government. She began her career as a volunteer polling her precinct and by 1940 was secretary of the Central Committee. Jordan was elected the vice chairman in 1950, a position she held for 30 years. In the 1940s, Jordan was employed as a deputy county clerk in the courthouse and later was elected to two full four-year terms as the first female county clerk (1952 and 1956). She then assumed the position as manager of the Warsaw Branch of the Indiana License Bureau from 1971 to 1980.

In addition to emphasizing the importance of politics, Pauline also gave of herself and her time to numerous civic and women's organizations. She was instrumental in starting the Lakeland Civic Music Association, Beta Sigma Phi sorority, and the senior citizen organizations, in addition to the Warsaw Business and Professional Women's Club. She was also a key force in organizing the Kosciusko County Historical Society.

In the late 1960s, Jordan was instrumental in starting the Kosciusko County Young Republican's group which consisted of 200 to 300 young people. Laddy Hoffer was president and Avis Gunter was vice president. It is said that without the enthusiasm and dedication of Pauline Jordan, the Republican Party in Kosciusko County would not have the strength it has today.

In January 1980, Republican chairman Ed Pratt and vice chairman Pauline Jordan announced together that they would not be seeking re-election. Pratt had headed the Republican Party for 10 years following the retirement of Giles Hoffer in 1970. Miss Jordan served her party longer than any other official in Kosciusko County history-holding the vice chairmanship for nearly 30 years. She assisted six different party chairmen during her tenure: Vere Kelly (Burket), Judge Gene B. Lee (Warsaw), Frank O. Rarick (Warsaw), Earl Himes (North Webster), Giles Hoffer (Warsaw), and Pratt (Winona Lake).

County Republicans held their annual dinner at the Shrine Building on November 20, 1969. The guest speaker was former State Senator Will Erwin. Pictured are Giles Hoffer, chairman of the county Republican organization; E. Mazie Alexander, president of the Kosciusko County Republican Women; Will Erwin; Pauline Jordan, vice chairman of the county organization; and Brooks Pinnick, city chairman.

Jordan always encouraged women to get involved in the political system. One of her most notable keepsakes is a letter from Nancy Reagan thanking her for helping "Ronnie" get elected President. Today at age 90, she resides at Grace Village Retirement Center.

E. Mazie Alexander has been very active in community, state and national programs. Her political career has included serving as president of the Kosciusko County Republican Women's Club from 1966 to 1968, precinct committeewoman, and Third District director of the Indiana Federation Republican Women's Club of the Northern Half of Indiana. She is a member of the National Federation of Republican Women's Club and is a sustaining member of the Republican National Committee.

In April of 1964, the GOP Women had a membership drive with a goal of 1,000. Mazie Alexander and Joan Kindle were recognized for having recruited more than 100 new members each, and total membership was brought to 1,200. The organization was the largest in the state of Indiana at that time and received the Diamond Award, the highest recognition the National Federation of Republican Women can bestow on its member clubs.

Alexander was elected to two terms as Kosciusko County recorder, 1967 to 1974. During that time she also served as corresponding secretary and legislative chairman of the State Recorders' Association, and was on the Budget Finance Committee of the Kosciusko County Republican Central Committee. In addition, Alexander was a member of the National Advisory Board, on the committee to preserve Social Security and Medicare, and At-Large Delegate Survey and Platform

E. Mazie Alexander

Pauline Jordan was an avid supporter of the Kosciusko County Republican Party for over 50 years.

A winning smile from D. Jean Northenor who attends and supports many community events.

The Republican Party was organized in 1854 by former Whigs and Democrats.

Committee. From 1975 to 1983, she was supervisory assistant, School Food and Nutrition for the State of Indiana, and also represented Indiana at the Federal level on school auditing.

Alexander helped organize and found The Salvation Army Women's Auxiliary in 1968. She served as both vice president and president, and also served on the Salvation Army Advisory Board. For a number of years, Alexander was chairman of the "Christmas Red Kettles." When she was honored by the Kosciusko County Foundation in 1998 and received the "Heart of Gold" award which included a $500 grant, she presented the grant to The Salvation Army.

Her other civic involvements include: legislative chairman for the Business and Professional Women's Club, BPW Auditing Committee chairman, past president of the Warsaw Arts and Crafts Club, and member of Altrusa Club.

In January 2001, Alexander received a Certificate of Dedication and Leadership from the Republican National Committee for helping to elect a Republican president, congress, governors and state legislators.

D. Jean Northenor has been active in the community and state in a variety of capacities. She has served on a number of boards and committees for the Indiana State Chamber of Commerce, the Warsaw Chamber, the Kosciusko County Sheriff's Department Merit Board, and Kosciusko County Foundation. Northenor was a past president and founding board member of the Kosciusko Leadership Academy in 1980 and past president and founding member of the Warsaw Community Development Corporation. She also served from 1986 to 1992 as

a commissioner of the Bureau of Motor Vehicles Commission for the State of Indiana.

Northenor was elected auditor for Kosciusko County from 1976 to 1983. She has played a vital part in the success of the Republican party and served as chairman of the Kosciusko County Republican Central Committee from 1980 to 1986. In 1984, she was named to the Republican Hall of Fame. Northenor is listed in *Who's Who of American Politics*, *Who's Who of Women Executives*, and *Who's Who in the Midwest*. In addition, she was recently named to a recommendation committee to appoint Indiana's U.S. attorneys and U.S. marshals, as requested by U.S. Senator Richard Lugar.

Northenor has been honored with a "Sagamore of the Wabash" award from Governors Bowen, Orr and Bayh, and is an Honorary Secretary of State, Honorary Lieutenant Governor, and Honorary Auditor of the State of Indiana. The Warsaw Chamber of Commerce honored her as "Woman of the Year" in 1983. In 1997, she received the Warsaw Chamber's first Athena Award and was included as one of the "100 Most Influential Indiana Business Leaders" by the Indiana State Chamber of Commerce. Northenor was also recognized as an "Indiana Trailblazing Woman" in 2001.

During her seventeen years at Lake City Bank from 1984 to 2001, Northenor held a number of positions. She was most recently Executive Vice President of Marketing, Human Resources and Facilities. Although retired from active service, she has joined the Lake City Bank board of directors, as well as the board of its parent company, Lakeland Financial Corporation, and continues her responsibility to acquire land and construct new offices as the bank continues its expansion.

Congressman John Hiler, Jean Northenor, and Senator Richard Lugar share a moment during a Republican event in 1986.

Chapter 15

1950 to 1969

Penguin Point

Penguin Point was originally founded by Wallace and Lloyd Stouder in June of 1950. They began with one Penguin Point restaurant in Wabash, which offered its most well-known sandwich called the "Big Wally." The present Penguin Point Franchise Systems corporation was founded in 1961 and operates 15 restaurants in the state of Indiana, with headquarters in Warsaw on U.S. 30 East. The company also has a successful catering service.

For many years, the first Warsaw Penguin Point (No. 2) operated on the south side of Lincoln Highway/Old Road 30 on the east side of town approximately where the Hampton Inn now sits. In 1972 it moved to its current location at 2401 E. Center Street. The location at 408 N. Detroit Street was the first of the sit down/drive-thru Penguin Point restaurants (1964). Their third Warsaw location is at 1115 W. Lake Street.

Lloyd and Heleta Stouder also owned "Play Acres" across the road from the No. 2 restaurant, with a go-cart track and miniature golf course. Long-time employee Priscilla Conley first worked at Play Acres and has continued her employment with Penguin Point for nearly 40 years.

In addition to the Big Wally ground beef sandwich, Penguin Point's fried chicken and french fries are also favorites. Wally's son, Wes Stouder, relates that many kids who go off to college or move away will ask their parents to send them a supply of tenderloins via express mail.

Marge Priser can attest to the popularity of Penguin Point's breaded tenderloin sandwich. When she visits her son in Texas, she takes him a bag of 10 Penguin Point tenderloins. When he is in Warsaw, he buys tenderloins three at a time so there is always at least one sandwich in the refrigerator.

Wallace and Lloyd Stouder opened the first Penguin Point restaurant in Wabash in 1950. The first Penguin Point in Warsaw was designated as No. 2, so noted on the upper-right corner of the building.

Lloyd and Heleta Stouder owned Play Acres across from the Penguin Point restaurant, which had a miniature golf course and go-cart track.

Judd Rexall Drugs opened in 1950 on the southeast corner of Center and Buffalo Streets. The Liberty Café was next door. This corner was previously occupied by the Warsaw Candy Kitchen for about 50 years.

Pharmacist Paul Gadson, right, started at Judd Drugs June 5, 1950, shortly after it opened. Also pictured is manager Gus Judd and Paul's wife, Ruth Gadson.

Drug Stores

Charles W. Judd from Akron had three drug stores in Elkhart. Judd opened store #4 in Warsaw on the southeast corner of Center and Buffalo Streets in March of 1950. The pharmacy was first managed by Charles' nephew, Gus Judd, and Paul Gadson was hired in June 1950 as a pharmacist. Soon after, Gadson was called to serve in the Korean War. When he returned in 1952, Gus Judd managed the Elkhart stores and Paul managed the Warsaw store.

As a pharmacist at Judd Rexall Drugs, Paul Gadson recalls the time Mr. Judd wanted to have a sale to get rid of fifty or more towels. Gadson suggested having Bob Richmond mention it on his weekly radio program. Although skeptical, Mr. Judd agreed. It was stated on the radio that Judd Drugs was having a penny sale and there would be no display sign and nothing in the newspapers. The towels were gone in record time!

Gadson stated that when he first started at Judd Drugs, Dr. Yoder's office was upstairs. Later the second story was occupied by the Randall Yeager Insurance Company. Gadson then worked at Brennan Pharmacy from 1962 to 1965, followed by his employment at Thornburg Drugs.

Judd Drugs operated in downtown Warsaw for about 10 years before moving to 1175 E. Center Street. Gene Zale bought the business in 1971 and changed the name to Zale Drugs. The popular lunch counter serves breakfast and lunch and offers classic desserts made with soda. Zale Drugs makes it own compounds from scratch, producing creams, lots of capsules, and individual medicines for hospice patients.

Gadson joined Hook's Drugs in 1975 when they opened a store on the west side of town behind Lake City Bank's drive-thru branch on Old Road 30. Hook's first Warsaw store was on the east side of town in the Lake Village Shopping Center. The west side store was their second Warsaw location, followed by the third store in the Lowery Shopping Center on E. Winona Avenue.

Paul Gadson retired in 1994, the week that Revco bought the Hook's stores. Revco has since been bought out by CVS Pharmacy. CVS then closed all of the branch stores and built a new facility on the northeast corner of Center and Detroit Streets (former site of the First Baptist Church), which opened in 1996.

Walter's Drug Store at 110 E. Center Street, owned by Tom Walter, was a popular place for many years with its soda fountain. Pharmacists Harry Mosbaugh and Joe Mendenhall worked at Walter's Drugs. They eventually became partners and bought the Walter's pharmacy.

When Mosbaugh moved to Fort Wayne, Joe Mendenhall opened a small drug store on the east end of the Lowery Sewing Center building on E. Winona Avenue. Shortly thereafter, Mendenhall sold the business to Kosciusko Community Hospital.

Republican Women's Club

The Kosciusko County Federation of Republican Women's Club was organized in 1950 with 96 charter members. Mrs. Ethel Rarick, whose husband, Frank, served as mayor from 1943 to 1947, was elected president of the organization.

The group met monthly in the beginning years, with 75 to 100 members in attendance. Some ladies, including Pauline Jordan and E. Mazie Alexander, occasionally took the train to Washington, D.C. for special meetings. In recent years, however, membership has diminished and the Women's Club does not meet on a regular basis.

Warsaw Printing Company

Charles R. "Chick" Lamoree owned Warsaw Printing Company on the southwest corner of Lake and Market Streets at 201-205 W. Market Street from about 1950 until 1967. In addition to the printing business, Warsaw Printing also sold items such as pens, stationery, and books. As a young girl, Barbara Anderson fondly remembers buying her collection of *Bobbsey Twins* books there.

Claude Beeson started the Westminster Press printing establishment in the basement of the Winona Lake Westminster Hotel in 1955. When Claude retired, his son, Joe, managed the business until two owners of Lincoln Printing in Fort Wayne purchased it in 1971. The former Westminster Press was moved to Warsaw on the northwest corner of Center and Lake Streets in the old Oram Building. Since Lamoree had previously closed his business, Lincoln Printing was able to reinstate the Warsaw Printing Company name.

At that time, Max Mollenhour was hired as manager and Chick Lamoree as salesman. When Lamoree retired in 1977, Barb Goon took over the sales portion of the business. Max Mollenhour retired at the end of 1985, just prior to the company being purchased in 1986 by Frank Hardesty, owner of Hardesty Printing in Rochester. The Warsaw

Peggy Shideler visits with a friend in Walter's Drug Store on E. Center Street (c. 1950).

business name was changed to Hardesty Printing, and in 1987 the company moved to its current site at 407 W. Market Street. Frank's son, Bill Hardesty, manages the Warsaw operation.

Cover-All Rental

Cover-All Rental, headquartered in Fort Wayne, opened a Warsaw branch at 1209 E. Smith Street in 1950. Bill Lemons was the Warsaw manager until he retired in 1980. At that time, 17-year-employee Max Fribley took over the management until he retired in 1986. Cover-All Rental was purchased by Indianapolis-based Mechanics Laundry in 1998. The uniform business then merged with Cintas Company, the name it retains to date.

Dairy Queen

The Dairy Queen on E. Winona Avenue was originally a small building where customers ordered at the window. It is thought that Walt J. Runyan started the business in the early 1950s. Dean and Nellie Musser owned the Dairy Queen in the 1960s, followed by Glenn and Alldene Wagner in the 1970s, who expanded the building to include a seating area. The Wagners sold the business to another person who then sold it to Dave and Sue Magnus. The Dairy Queen has been owned by Jerry and Jane Nolin since 1989.

Supermarkets

Laddie Hoffer started Hoffer's Supermarket in the early 1950s at 1095 S. Buffalo Street, later the site of Wholesale Electric. It was the first grocery in

"I Love Lucy" premiered October 15, 1951.

Ditto's grocery store was located at 811 S. Buffalo Street in the 1960s and 1970s.

sewn in the Columbia City plant. The fabric was cut in Columbia City and shipped by Blue Bell trucks daily to Warsaw and Nappanee, where women would sew it into the finished clothing.

Sewing and finishing units throughout the nation produced clothing for the entire family, including play and work wear, coveralls, bib overalls, shirts for both sport and work, and blouses for ladies and girls. Outer garments such as car coats, windbreakers and other styles of jackets were also added to their product line. The Wranglers and dungarees from the three northern Indiana plants went primarily into the Chicago and Detroit markets.

Blue Bell was first located upstairs above Sharp's Hardware on the south side of the Courthouse Square and employed about 40 women. In 1954, an additional unit was opened at 205 W. Main Street over the Hartsock Studebaker Agency on the northwest corner of Lake and Main Streets. When Frank Hartsock retired and closed his business in 1962, Blue Bell then occupied both floors of the building.

Roy Duncan was the division manager of the Columbia City, Nappanee and Warsaw plants. John Moyer was the first Warsaw plant manager, followed by Phil Neff about 1963, who then moved to Canada in 1965 to continue his employment with Blue Bell. Neff recalls that at one point the factory was making up to 300 dozen pair of jeans a day, and that employees could buy casual slacks for $1.50 a pair in the 1960s.

For a time, Blue Bell had an outlet store at one end of the main floor which was first available only to employees. The company later opened an outlet store at 120 S. Buffalo Street which was open to the general public. Twenty-year employee Joann Rowe, a supervisor by 1970, recalls that Blue Bell closed its doors in Warsaw in 1978.

County Historians

Marion W. Coplen was appointed Kosciusko County historian by the Indiana History Bureau and the Indiana Library Board in 1952. He taught government and world history at Warsaw High School and became interested in county history. Coplen wrote a thesis in 1944 titled "History of Kosciusko County to 1875" for his Masters at Indiana University, which was then published in book form. He also wrote historical articles titled "Our County History" that appeared each week in the *Times-Union*.

Swanson Foods introduced the first frozen prepared TV dinners in 1953.

town to be open on Sundays. About 1962, George Ditto bought Hoffer's business and built a new, larger grocery store across the street at 811 S. Buffalo Street and named it Ditto's.

When Mr. and Mrs. Ditto were killed in an automobile accident in the late 1970s, employee Jim Sarber bought the business. Sarber sold the property in 1981 and the building was used for a fitness center. Cardinal Center has owned the building since 1994 and uses it for office space.

Woodie Schramm had been operating a grocery store in Bremen for a number of years, when he decided in 1963 to open a Woodie's Supermarket in Warsaw at 801 N. Lake Street. The grocery closed in the early 1990s. However, since 1978 a trust fund established by Woodie and DeVota Schramm has awarded $25,000 in scholarships in the Warsaw community.

Bert Anderson erected the block building at 801 N. Lake Street in 1949 for a Nash automobile dealership. In 1956 and 1957 it was used by R.R. Donnelley & Sons as a training center while their plant was being built west of town. For nearly the next thirty years, Woodie's Supermarket occupied this site. The building has been used in recent years by JoKids Scratch & Dent Warehouse.

Blue Bell, Inc.

In the early 1950s, Blue Bell, Inc., the world's largest manufacturer of work and play clothing at that time, expanded its operations by adding a Warsaw plant. Headquartered in Greensboro, North Carolina, Blue Bell first started a Columbia City plant, followed by the Nappanee and Warsaw plants. Only western-style garments were cut and

George A. Nye was the local historian for many years.

Petro's Restaurant on N. Detroit Street in the 1950s.

George A. Nye was an "unofficial" county historian for many years, and 37 volumes of his typed notes are located at the Warsaw Public Library. Waldo Adams was the county historian for a few years in the mid-1980s. He wrote a lot about history, but none of it was ever published.

Ronald Sharp has served as county historian since 1989. Over the years, Sharp has published numerous books pertaining to Kosciusko County history. He wrote five books about the Civil War, five about the town of Syracuse, two books about area churches, and two about county history. Sharp also researched murders that occurred in Kosciusko County from 1840 to 1950 and wrote a book. In 1998, he published a collection of General Reuben Williams' writings.

Petro's Restaurant

Petro's Restaurant was built in 1952 by William Petro, Sr. at 937 N. Detroit Street overlooking Center Lake. It opened on Labor Day in 1952. Two years later, Petro's Motel was constructed adjacent to the restaurant.

Unfortunately, the restaurant was completely destroyed by fire on November 17, 1970. In 1973, Petro's daughter and son-in-law, Margaret and Glenn Lancaster, owned and operated the motel and decided to rebuild the restaurant, which once again opened in late 1974.

The Lancasters used the brown wood swinging doors from Glenn's mother's former restaurant to divide the dining room from the lounge in their newly rebuilt restaurant. (In the 1930s, Allie

Lancaster had operated the Lancaster Café in the 2300 block of E. Center Street.)

Later, Bill and Vi Storey leased the property and operated the business until it was bought by Bruce and Steve Shaffner in 1982. The restaurant was renovated and the name was changed to The Viewpoint. The motel was also remodeled and maintained a steady business. In 1998, the Shaffners moved The Viewpoint restaurant to the Ramada Hotel, and the motel on N. Detroit Street closed and was demolished.

Orion's Restaurant, formerly at Rozella Ford Golf Club, then operated at the N. Detroit Street location for awhile. When Maple Leaf Farms took over the ownership in April 2000, the restaurant's name was changed to Bistro 'A Lago, as it continues today.

G.I. Printed Tape Co.

Harold Irvine started G.I. Printed Tape Company in 1952 at 1000 N. Lake Street. The business made all kinds of self-sticking advertising tape. His son, Jerry, moved from Chicago back to Warsaw in 1975 to help with the family business. When Harold died in 1983, Jerry took over management of the business. Now known as G.I. Tape and Label, the company's major product is pressure sensitive labels.

City Hall

Prior to being the site of the present City Hall, the southeast corner of Market and High Streets had been occupied by the Kosciusko County Farm Bureau Co-Operative Association since the 1920s.

Color televisions were introduced for the Tournament of Roses Parade on January 1, 1954.

The Kosciusko County Farm Bureau Co-op building was located on the southeast corner of Market and High Streets. This building was demolished in the early 1950s for construction of the current City Hall.

An unidentified driver for the Farm Bureau Co-op. The Presbyterian Church can been seen across the street.

Guy Method, Sr. was the first semi truck driver for the Farm Bureau Co-op. This photo was taken in the early 1950s at their location on N. Detroit Street.

The Co-Op handled ground grain, feed supplements, fertilizer, farm chemicals, petroleum products, poultry and dairy equipment, and other items such as tires and batteries. When City Hall purchased the corner property, the Co-Op built a new elevator and store on N. Detroit Street just south of Union Tool.

City Hall was built in 1952 by Mayor Mike Hodges, who owned a construction business. City Hall originally had four large overhead doors for the Fire Department. What is now Fire Station #2 at 2204 E. Center Street was built in 1978, and the east part of City Hall was converted into the Council Chambers. Fire Station #1 at 109 E. Main Street was built in 1982.

By the mid 1990s, City Hall was experiencing growing pains and the Police Department was especially crowded. In 2000, the City of Warsaw purchased the former NIPSCO facility on E. Fort Wayne Street to be used for the Police Department. Following extensive renovations, the building is scheduled for occupancy by the Police Department in early 2002.

Centennial Fun

Wilbur J. "Doc" Gill was the festival production manager for Warsaw's celebration from July 4 to July 10, 1954, of being incorporated as a town for 100 years.

Festival committee members placed a mock jail on the courthouse lawn in April of 1954 when the town was preparing for the Centennial celebration. The jailhouse was to be used during the celebration to put any beardless man "behind bars" who failed to purchase a shaving permit. A yellow-painted casket containing a giant-size razor had been placed on top of the old Civil War cannon base at the courthouse following the razor burial ceremonies the prior weekend.

Permit buttons were sold for $3 each. Bearded citizens wearing "Brother of the Brush" badges were official entrants in the beard contest, a feature event of the celebration. In addition, ladies wearing "Sisters of the Swish" buttons were allowed to wear makeup during the festival.

During the night of April 28, 1954, the one-ton jail and the razor and casket mysteriously disappeared. Charles "Tip" Welker, owner of the Favorite Café, found the following anonymous poem posted on the restaurant window when he went to work the next morning:

The present City Hall was built on the southeast corner of Market and High Streets in 1952.

An open house was held in 1952 for the new City Hall. The four stalls for the fire trucks faced Market Street. When the fire station was built on E. Center Street in 1978, the City Hall building was remodeled and this area was converted into the Council Chambers.

Twas 68 days till the festival and all thru the streets,
Not a policeman was stirring on any one beat.
The festival jail rested on the Courthouse lawn,
And all was quiet and peaceful until early dawn.
Then all over town there rose such a clatter,
The city officials said, "Hey! What's the matter?"
A local innkeeper and bearded hash-slinger,
Came up with one that really was a dinger.
The festival jail house had been stolen that's sure,
And the cops had a headache without any cure.
Not a cop on the force was ever named "Kelly,"
But our Chief does have a little pot belly.
He hollered, "Up, Juterbock, Jay, Shull and Adams,"
"Come Brumfield, Tennant, Tuka, and Hall."
They all fell out in a state of confusion,
So pale they all could have used a transfusion.
"Get out on the street and quiet that wail!"
"And don't come back without that there jail."
Then squaring his shoulders and blowing his nose,
Our Chief stood there looking down at his toes.
But we all heard him say in a voice soft and light,
"I sure hope this town don't find out—
Where Reub and I spent last night!"

These Schrader Automotive employees grew beards for Warsaw's Centennial celebration in 1954. They are, left to right: store owner Rene Nine, shop foreman Maurice Noble, store manager Clifford Scholl, and head counterman Dean Rowland. Noble and Rowland have their Centennial buttons pinned at their waists.

Benches made with wood planks and concrete blocks were set up along
Center Street for the 1954 Centennial Parade. These eager citizens chose
their seats in front of Walter's drug store, Essig's Sporting Goods store, and
Al Gerard's Central Shoe Company.

Mr. and Mrs. Luther E. Carter, owners of Carter's Department Store, rode a
float in the 1954 Centennial Parade.

A large crowd of people gathered on the Courthouse Square to watch the 1954
Centennial Parade.

The 1954 Centennial Parade traveled west on Center Street in front of the
Courthouse. Note the paper hats donned by the young kids in the foreground.

Horses pulled a wagon west on Center Street during the 1954 Centennial Parade.

A steam engine followed the 1954 Centennial Parade route.

The next day, Doc Gill and Tip Welker traveled to Angola, Indiana, where they located the razor and its casket atop a root beer stand. The heavy jailhouse was found beside a garage on Mishawaka's Lincolnway East, and Howard Kring drove up there to return it to Warsaw.

The townspeople had a good time joking about the mystery. Police Chief Don Snyder insisted he went to bed that night about 10:00, but it was reported he was seen driving through town between 1:00 and 3:00 a.m. Chief Snyder and Reub Williams denied all accusations and maintained their innocence.

Warsaw Coil Company

Warsaw Coil Company was founded by Charles and Florence Joyner in 1954. This three-generation, family-owned business manufactures custom electrical coils and related assemblies. The company moved from its location on Segal Street to its current facility on State Road 25 in 1958.

The Joyners' sons, Sam and Tom, were involved in the business, followed by Tom's son and daughter, Brad Joyner and Diane Doran. Warsaw Coil began operations with 15 employees to primarily serve the radio/television industry and has grown to more than 200 employees supplying products to a variety of industries.

The Flagpole

Joe Johnson (Mayor, 1964-1967) purchased the property on the northwest corner of Winona Avenue and Bronson Street in 1954 and opened The Flagpole Drive-In. The small quonset hut building on the property had been built in 1948 by a man named Griffith. Johnson sold the business in 1973 to his son-in-law, Chris Reed, who then sold it in 1981 to Ted Franchino and his son-in-law, Dennis Reeve. Following the death of Franchino in 1990, Dennis and his wife, Shelly, took over full ownership of the business.

Many are familiar with the "Pig's Dinner" at the Flagpole, which consists of five scoops of different flavors of delicious frozen custard layered over sliced bananas and topped with syrup, nuts and whipped cream. During the Flagpole's early years, if a person ate the entire "Pig's Dinner" while at the Flagpole, they would receive a yellow button with red letters that said, "I was a Pig at the Flagpole." When ten buttons had been collected, hungry patrons could turn them back in for a free "Pig's Dinner."

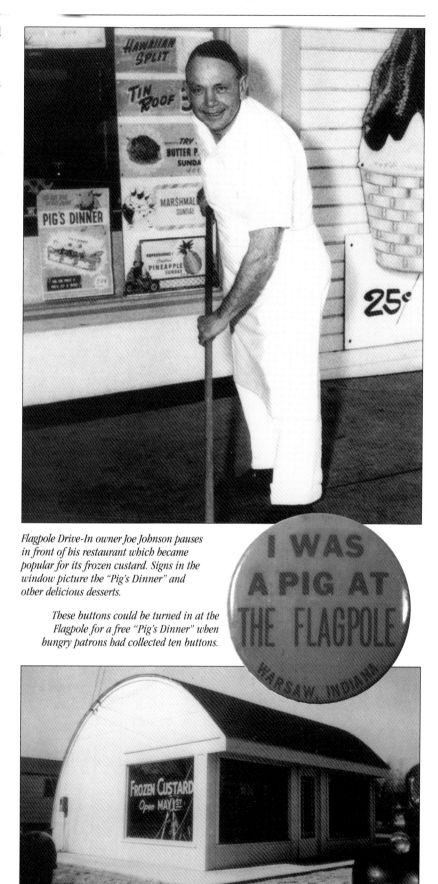

Flagpole Drive-In owner Joe Johnson pauses in front of his restaurant which became popular for its frozen custard. Signs in the window picture the "Pig's Dinner" and other delicious desserts.

These buttons could be turned in at the Flagpole for a free "Pig's Dinner" when hungry patrons had collected ten buttons.

The original Flagpole Drive-In on the northwest corner of Winona Avenue and Bronson Street.

Warsaw Business Equipment

After founding Business Equipment Company in Fort Wayne in 1945, Arden Ober established the Warsaw Business Equipment Company in 1954 at 110 S. Buffalo Street in one of the spaces on the street level of what is now known as the First National Bank Building. About 1961, Business Equipment Company moved to 123 W. Center Street in the Hitzler Building.

Ober leased the former Ringle Furniture building at 207 S. Buffalo Street from Ralph Henderson in 1971. The main floor housed the many office supply items the store held in inventory, and the second floor was used to display office furniture. In 1973, Ober's daughter and son-in-law, Elaine and Jim Bell, bought the building and then purchased interest in the business in 1981. Warsaw Business Equipment closed in 1991.

Since then, from 1996 to 1998, Jean Kuczewski operated TLC Gifts, Baskets & Candies at 207 S. Buffalo Street. Most recently, Horizon Pharmacy expanded its services to rent and sell home healthcare items at this location.

Champion Door Corp.

Champion Door Corporation of Indiana was established in 1954 by Donald C. Youse to make both interior and exterior pre-hung door units. Production lines were initially set up in a small leased space on E. Jefferson Street with six employees, but then moved to a much larger facility at 1506 N. Detroit Street.

The business grew to fabricate door units for both homes and commercial buildings, which were restricted for sale to building contractors only. Much of the company's automatic fabricating equipment was designed by Youse. The business was eventually sold and moved to another city.

Da-Lite Screen and Classic Car Centre occupied the Detroit Street facility after Champion Door moved out, prior to the current occupant, Rock Bottom Warehouse.

Cardinal Center, Inc.

Cardinal Center, Inc. originated when children with disabilities arrived at the home of Bob and Flora Overstedt in 1954 to receive educational training for the very first time in Kosciusko County. The group moved to the Methodist Church shortly after. In 1963, the Kosciusko County for the Retarded moved to its own building, a house at 304 S. High Street. The name Cardinal Learning Center was chosen and six students were served.

Diane Cleator was hired as the first Center director in 1964, and the Cardinal Center workshop was established in 1965, when Eugene Robb became the second Center director. The area Lions Club contributed heavily to aid in the purchase of the current 504 N. Bay Drive facility in 1966, when 21 clients were served.

A grant in 1967 funded the construction of an addition so the lunchroom, recreation area and workshop could be at one location, and Howard Wilson was appointed executive director. An educational wing was added in 1969 and Cardinal Center was designated as a Comprehensive Mental Health Center for Whitley, Huntington, Wabash and Kosciusko Counties, and classes for preschool children began.

The Special Olympic program began in Kosciusko County in 1972. In 1979, Michael Martin was hired as CEO, and the Urban Mass Transit Grant that funds the Kosciusko Area Bus Service (KABS) was obtained. The organization's name was changed to Cardinal Center, Inc. in 1980 and began providing Adult Basic Education to people 16 years and older without a high school diploma.

Steve Gerber was hired as CEO in 1984, and in 1985 Cardinal Center opened two group homes in community neighborhoods. By 1987, Supported Employment—the placement of severely disabled individuals into community employment—was started and long-term training and support was offered to individuals who qualified. Three additional group homes were developed in 1987, followed by three more in 1988. The last group home opened in Marshall County in 1992, totaling 15 group homes in a three-county area.

Cardinal Center purchased Big Boy Products in 1992, a manufacturer of trailer hitches, bicycle pumps and boat pumps, to generate an income to be used to assist the human services programs, to employ people with disabilities and to train people with disabilities in an integrated environment. Cardinal Center achieved its first national accreditation from the Commission on the Accreditation of Rehabilitation Facilities in 1993.

In 1994, a former daycare center building was purchased at 811 S. Buffalo Street. The building was remodeled to hold the infant, job placement, and supported living programs. Steve Gerber resigned in 1995 and Jane Greene was named

Disneyland opened in Anaheim, California, in 1955.

CEO in 1996. Cardinal Center became the new WIC (Women, Infant and Children) provider for Kosciusko County in 1997, and the Healthy Families program was started in 1998 to help prevent child abuse.

Rocket TV

After closing his Double Dip ice cream shop at 207 W. Center Street in 1955, Hazen O. Shideler and his son-in-law, Frank Coppes, started Rocket TV at the same location. Rocket TV sold televisions, radios and stereos. In 1963, the business moved to the current Instant Copy location on the southwest corner of Center and Lake Streets.

In 1967, they bought the building at 714 E. Winona Avenue, which was formerly a billiards hall and lunch counter. Rocket TV had sold RCA televisions since 1960 and began selling Whirlpool appliances when the store moved to Winona Avenue. Rocket TV & Appliance continued under the operation of Bruce Coppes, the third generation of this family-owned business, until it closed in June 2001.

Wagon Wheel Playhouse

Maj. Herbert Petrie, founder and co-owner of the Wagon Wheel Playhouse, spent his life in show business and in the educational and professional fields. After graduating from the American Conservatory of Music in Chicago, he studied trumpet with Edward Llewelyn of the Chicago Symphony and Max Schlossberg of the New York Philharmonic Symphony.

He taught music for four years and organized the famous Petrie's White Hussars, a concert brass ensemble which went into the professional field playing concerts all over the U.S., Canada and Europe. Maj. Petrie served on the faculty at Indiana University Music School and also organized and directed the Petrie Band Camp at Winona Lake for 10 years, which played before thousands of people every Sunday afternoon in the famous Billy Sunday Tabernacle.

During World War II he served his country as a major in the Army and was the Music Officer for the North African and Mediterranean Theatre. While on a special assignment, Petrie attended performances at the Penthouse Theatre in Fort Lawton, Washington, the first theatre-in-the-round in the U.S. He was so intrigued by the idea that he made his dream come true when he returned to Warsaw in 1955.

When Herbert Petrie started the Wagon Wheel Playhouse in 1956, a large tent was erected on the E. Center Street hill at the edge of town.

A reception for the entire audience was held on opening night at the Wagon Wheel Theatre in 1956 for Tri Kappa Night. Note the carpeting used to cover the dirt floor.

On property they owned on E. Center Street, Maj. Petrie and his wife, Mildred, along with her sister and brother-in-law, John and Kitty Butterfield, started the Wagon Wheel Playhouse. For several years, performances were held in a tent with a gravel floor and canvas chairs. Chicken coops were used as dressing rooms, a shop for building props, and for making costumes.

The Petries' first restaurant was the Chuck Wagon. It opened in 1949 in a log cabin style building on Argonne Road (now part of the Warsaw Chemical property). Marge Warren was a carhop at the Chuck Wagon. Within a couple years, a large two-story building was constructed on the hill on E. Center Street. The restaurant was moved to that location and the name changed to Wagon Wheel Restaurant. John Butterfield served as business manager and his wife supervised the smorgasbord restaurant during the summer.

The Wagon Wheel Playhouse was built at 2517 E. Center Street about 1961.

A crowd gathers in June 1962 to enter the Wagon Wheel Playhouse.

The Wagon Wheel Restaurant on E. Center Street in the 1960s. Now part of the Ramada Plaza complex, it is known as the 2517 Restaurant.

About 1961, the Playhouse was built at 2517 E. Center Street. For a time the Methodist and Presbyterian Churches of Warsaw held informal services each Sunday, June through September, in the Wagon Wheel Playhouse, with drama, dance interpretation, sermons in dialogue, and the traditional hymns and prayers. Mrs. Charlie (June) Bertsch, then known as "the cookie lady" by all the young people performing during the summers at the Wagon Wheel, was considered their "visiting mother."

Tom Roland, originally hired by Herb Petrie, was a long-time Wagon Wheel artistic director, continuing in that capacity until 1984. Tom also appeared as an actor in some Wagon Wheel performances, including *Fiddler on the Roof, Harvey*, and *On Golden Pond*. Roland developed the idea of bringing young college actors from Northwestern University, Indiana University, University of Cincinnati, and other schools.

Some of the early actors became well-known professionals: MacLean Stevenson (M*A*S*H series on TV), who played the lead in Wagon Wheel's *Music Man*; Ann Whitney, sister to MacLean Stevenson, played many seasons at the Wagon Wheel; and Faith Prince, now a very popular actress on Broadway, also played many seasons at the Wagon Wheel Playhouse.

In 1970, Petrie decided to retire. He called his next-door neighbor, Charles Bertsch, and asked if he would be interested in buying the Wagon Wheel Playhouse and Restaurant, plus the twenty acres of adjoining land that was undeveloped. Mr. Bertsch then called his friend, Blaine Mikesell, and after talking over the details, they agreed on a price which was accepted by Petrie.

Shortly after this, it was announced that the U.S. 30 Bypass would be built on the north edge of the Petrie property. The idea developed that this would be a good location for a hotel. It was determined that the Holiday Inn in Memphis, Tennessee, was interested in a Warsaw location, and they also discovered that more money would be needed to obtain the Holiday Inn franchise. Investors Larry Castaldi, Loren Miller, Bob Steele, Gay Robinson, Charles Bertsch and Blaine Mikesell became joint owners of the Warsaw Holiday Inn. Mr. Robinson owned the Holiday Inn in Wabash, Indiana, at that time. Petrie, although living in Florida, decided he would come out of retirement and invest in the Warsaw Holiday Inn. Robinson became the general contractor and the Warsaw Holiday Inn opened on June 1, 1971.

Petrie died in 1975, and in 1977 Dean White of Merrillville, Indiana, approached the remaining owners of the Warsaw Holiday Inn with an offer to buy them out. Arrangements were made to sell the Holiday Inn, but this group of original owners continued to own and operate the Wagon Wheel Playhouse until 1984, when five partners bought it: Bruce Shaffner, Tom Roland, Mike Hall, Bill Whitney, and David Willkinson. In 1995, Shaffner bought out the others' interests and was sole owner until his brother, Steve joined him in 1998. The Shaffner brothers currently own the Wagon Wheel Playhouse (now known as Wagon Wheel Theatre), the Wagon Wheel Restaurant (now known as the 2517 Restaurant), and the Holiday Inn (now the Ramada Plaza Hotel).

Carol Craig, a sister to Bruce and Steve, worked at the theatre as a teenager and fondly recalls the summer of 1960 when plays were still held in the tent. She has been business manager of the Wagon Wheel Theatre since 1989.

Today the artistic director is Roy Hine, who started at the Wagon Wheel as the set designer in the old chicken coop. The theatre now seats over 800 people and is the home of many different theatrical plays and musicals, as well as hosting various concerts and comedians. Considerable pride has been taken in the facility and the shows that have created lasting memories for residents and visitors alike at this theatre-in-the-round, "where you're never more than 10 rows from the stage."

Da-Lite Screen Company

Da-Lite Screen Company, the world's largest producer of slide and motion picture screens, was originally conceived in 1909 by Adele DeBerri, who owned a small Chicago theater. DeBerri began experimenting to find a highly reflective surface for best showing motion pictures. She mixed paints and chemicals, and was soon selling silver-painted projection screens—her paints on canvas.

An abandoned church was rented, and the DeBerri Screen and Scenic Company initially made backdrops for vaudeville shows and theater screens. As the motion picture industry grew, so did the need for larger, brighter pictures, and the company began using gold, silver, matte white and glass-beaded materials for its screens.

Guests relax outside Petrie's Chuck Wagon on Argonne Road (c. 1950).

Waitresses at the Chuck Wagon resstaurant wore Western style vests and skirts.

When DeBerri found that she needed more capital, attorney J.C. Heck invested in the company. They operated the business as a partnership, and eventually married. The business was renamed Da-Lite Screen Company, and J.C. Heck became the company's first president when it was incorporated in 1931. Property on Crawford Avenue in Chicago served as both plant and offices for Da-Lite through the Depression and World War II.

When Heck retired in 1947, his nephew, Chester C. Cooley, who Heck had hired in 1924, succeeded him as president. Cooley was instrumental in organizing the network of photographic distributors and dealers that helped make Da-Lite so successful. When the movie industry introduced sound on film, Da-Lite was first with a patented perforated sound screen. Cooley's son-in-law, George H. Lenke, Jr., joined the company in 1953 as an engineer.

Alaska and Hawaii became the 49th and 50th states of the Union in 1959.

Officers of the Warsaw Police Department in 1955. Front row, left to right: Frank Juterbock, Paul Shull, Ralph Konkle, Eugene Brumfield, Roy Adams, and Raymond "Fuzz" Neff. Back row: Wilbur "Dude" Tennant, James Tuka, Douglas Hall, Donald Snyder, Ralph Jay. Brumfield, Snyder, Jay, Adams and Neff at one time or another during their tenure served as chief of the department.

Mattell introduced the Barbie doll at the New York Toy Fair in 1959.

In 1955, Da-Lite bought 15 acres north of Warsaw, and all operations were moved to the new facility in 1957. George H. Lenke, Jr. succeeded his father-in-law as president in 1963, when Cooley became chairman of the board, a position he held until his death in 1975. At that time, Deborah Cooley resigned as treasurer to succeed her deceased husband as chairman. She held that position until 1984 when Heritage Communications acquired Da-Lite Screen Company.

Kosko Manufacturing Co.

Kosko Manufacturing Company was started on S. Buffalo Street in 1955 by William Chapel to provide such water treatment items as water softeners and iron, taste and odor removal equipment and neutralizers. William's father, Irvin C. Chapel, was also involved with the business.

Kosko was the only water treatment manufacturer at that time to use an Air Force type inspection of components with an electronic test panel to assure quality control. The business expanded into a plant at 800 S. McClellan Street, and the company's water treatment devices were sold to manufacturers and distributors by five salesmen who covered the entire United States, including Alaska. The business was sold about 1995 to Bob Blakely and eventually closed.

Warsaw Automotive

Russell Wilson started Warsaw Automotive in 1955 on E. Winona Avenue, and the business moved to

312 N. Detroit Street in 1966. Dick Witt purchased the business in 1973 and moved the store to its present location at 812 N. Detroit Street. Warsaw Automotive Supply Corporation is also referred to as NAPA Auto Parts. The building underwent a major expansion in 1999, which greatly increased the facility's size.

Hand Industries, Inc.

Hand Polishing was started in 1956 by William Hand in a building on the northeast corner of State Road 15 N. and County Road 350 N. to provide metal finishing for the orthopedic industry. The company soon became one of the largest outside processors of orthopedic prostheses in the United States. A new building was constructed and added on to as the business grew.

In 1972, part of the business moved to its current west-side location on Hand Avenue and the name was changed to Hand Industries, Inc. to reflect its diversification, which by then included the acquisition of a company named Dirilyte that now sells plaques and recognition awards nationwide. Hand also has aerospace metal finishing and agricultural divisions. The entire business moved to Hand Avenue in 1976.

William's son, Terry, became the company's president in 1984, followed by his nephew, John Hand (a 12-year employee), assuming the presidency at the beginning of 2000. With the emergence of the Internet in the 1990s, the company has utilized this technology to market many of its divisions, and has expanded into web design and programming for outside companies.

The Bunny Hut

In 1956, the Bunny Hut was just north of Home Furniture Mart on N. Detroit Street. Harry and Alice Batalis bought the building which had been damaged by fire and remodeled it. It opened briefly as a drive-in restaurant, complete with car hops, and soon became a regular restaurant. Although quite small, the high school team players and cheerleaders enjoyed going there after ballgames. The Bunny Hut closed in the late 1960s.

Mike Cox managed the Farmers Insurance Agency at this location from 1974 to 1983, until the property was purchased by Laminated Rafters Corporation to be used for office space.

Thomas Stamp Company

From an idea he saw in Kiplinger's *Changing Times* magazine in 1956, Paul "Lud" Thomas started the Thomas Stamp Company in his home at 214 W. Jefferson Street, where he made all kinds of rubber stamps. Thomas later moved the business into a house at 217 S. Washington Street.

Lud's wife, Martha, continued the business after he died in 1969. She later married Jim Osborne, who joined the business and added engraving to their services. Following Jim's death, Martha sold the business in 1998 to the Indiana Stamp Company in Fort Wayne.

The Grossnickle Doctors

After having completed service in the U.S. Navy as an optometrist during the Korean War, in 1957 Paul D. Grossnickle opened an optometry office on the northeast corner of Lake and Market Streets. He then bought an old home at 313 S. Buffalo Street in 1969 which was removed and an office building constructed (now site of the Chamber of Commerce). In 1976, Grossnickle joined a group of medical doctors and a dentist, and together they built the current office building near the hospital at 2255 Dubois Street.

Paul's oldest son, Dr. Steven P. Grossnickle, returned to Warsaw in 1978 to open his eye surgery practice in that building. His second son, Dr. Bruce P. Grossnickle, joined his brother in the ophthalmology practice now known as the Grossnickle Eye Center, with its state-of-the-art eye surgical facility.

Lakeland Art Association

The Lakeland Art Association was founded in 1957 by well-known artist and former Warsaw High School teacher Fred Olds. Fred invited artists to paint with him at the high school, which at that time was located on W. Main Street. The group initially met monthly in members' homes, and the annual spring shows to display their artwork done the previous year were held in the lobby of the Hotel Hays.

A 1935 graduate of Warsaw High School, Olds became a painter and sculptor. He sculpted a bronze bust of Thaddeus Kosciuszko—the Revolutionary War hero whose military genius contributed greatly to America's independence and after who our county is named—and presented it to the Warsaw High School Class of 1956. It has been on display at the Jail Museum since 1991.

Fred enjoyed painting western scenes and in the late 1940s, he painted western murals and sports scenes on the walls of the Humpty Dumpty Restaurant on N. Buffalo Street. When he moved to Oklahoma, he raised Appaloosa horses, taught at Southwestern State University, and donated his free time to teaching art at the government Indian schools in the area.

This bronze bust of Thaddeus Kosciuszko (1746-1817), a Revolutionary War hero, was sculpted by former Warsaw artist Fred Olds in the 1950s. It is currently on display at the Old Jail Museum.

Fred Olds published a book in 1999 titled "Just a Drop in the Bucket" which included a photo collection of his watercolor, oil paintings, and ink drawings. He did a show at the Cowboy Hall of Fame in Oklahoma City in May 2001.

Local artist Allee Gerard has a painting on display at the Smithsonian Institute.

Allee Gerard was a charter member of the Lakeland Art Asssociation. Allee's studio was located in her family's home at 1520 Country Club Drive, and she became quite an accomplished artist. Her one-man shows by invitation began in 1943 at the Hotel Hays in Warsaw, followed by the Fort Wayne Indiana Art Museum, and continued through 1980. Listed in *Who's Who in American Art* and *Who's Who of American Women*, Allee Gerard was a member of many state and national art organizations. Her participation at shows in Indiana, Ohio, Florida, and the National Gallery in Washington, D.C. earned her numerous awards, including 36 blue ribbons and six Best in Show. Gerard's "Plumes of Gold" Brown County, Indiana, hangs in the Fine Arts Room of the Smithsonian Institute.

Malcolm Landis, a 1948 graduate of Warsaw High School, is the only local charter member still living. He left the area in 1960 and returned in 1976 after serving in the army. Unfortunately, when Malcolm came back to Warsaw, he threw away all of his old paintings. Upon his retirement from R.R. Donnelley & Sons in 1995, Malcolm's interest in painting was rekindled and he once again joined the Lakeland Art Association. A trombone player himself, since retirement he has entered several paintings of jazz musicians each year in the annual spring show.

Over the years, the organization has sponsored exhibits in businesses, banks, hospitals, and nursing homes. The club met for many years at the Bowen Center and Cardinal Center, and held its annual spring show at the fairgrounds and the Bowen Center. The Lakeland Art Scholarship Program was established in 1980 to encourage talented young people to pursue a career in art.

Lila O'Connell became a member of the Lakeland Art Association in 1966. It was through her efforts that in 1993 the organization was able to locate in the north part of the old Oram Building on Lake Street across from the Courthouse Square. The group was then finally able to schedule ongoing art shows throughout the year. Serving as the director, Lila worked to incorporate the organization and obtain its not-for-profit status.

When the building was scheduled for demolition to make way for a new jail, the Lakeland Art Association, Inc. relocated to 116 S. Buffalo Street. Local artists display their works at the association's exhibits, and monetary, scholarship and ribbon awards are presented.

Senior Activity Center

The Kosciusko County Council on Aging, Inc. was founded in 1957 and incorporated in 1967 to determine the needs and problems of the 12,000 citizens over age 60 in our county. The organization is now known as Kosciusko Community Senior Services (KCSS).

The Pete Thorn Youth Center at 800 N. Park Avenue was initially built in 1979 for the Baker Boys' Club. For a time, the north end of the building was used as a children's daycare center. In 1991, Dane and Mary Louise Miller provided a financial gift to convert the former daycare area into the Senior Activity Center. The Center is open daily and serves as a place for senior citizens to socialize.

KCSS provides educational, recreational, and supportive services to senior adults. Many activities are held at the Senior Activity Center, including bingo, movies, card and board games, fitness and health programs. The agency also operates a van transportation program, and the homemaker program provides assistance a few hours each week to older persons or couples in their home.

In addition, KCSS administers the Mobile Meals program, where volunteers deliver meals to homebound elderly residents. The agency's nutrition program also provides low-cost nutritious lunches at the Center Monday through Friday.

Nursing Homes

Prairie View Rest Home, Inc. opened in May of 1957 at 300 E. Prairie Street. It was the first building in Indiana designed and built specifically to be a nursing home, and the facility initially had 63 beds, eventually expanding to 113 beds. Original incorporators were Grace Beaman, Don and Greta Shireman, Hazel Bradbury, James and Charlene Bradbury, Lucy Upson, and Allan Widaman. Hazel Bradbury served as the first administrator.

The facility enjoyed success for many years, but by 2001, Prairie View's financial difficulties had brought about the start of foreclosure proceedings. When the Hickory Creek Nursing Home on E. Center Street was closed in June due to structural concerns about the building, nineteen of its residents were moved to the Prairie View facility.

Hickory Creek was noted for caring for residents with Alzheimer's disease and some with mental or behavioral problems. Hickory Creek's specially trained staff was combined at Prairie View so all the residents can continue receiving their necessary care. The facility's name was changed to The Bradbury House. Both staff and residents seem pleased with the merger and look forward to a successful future.

Kline's Department Store

In 1957, Kline's Department Store started in business at 113 E. Market Street and also had a children's department west across the alley. About 1983, Kline's moved to the south side of the street into the former Gamble's location at 112-114 E. Market Street. The business later also expanded into the Bowser building on the southeast corner of Market and Buffalo Streets, for their men's and boys' department.

The Kline's Department Store closed in 1996, and both former Kline's locations are now occupied by departments of Lake City Bank.

Kimm Paint Company

In 1925, Henry Kimm bought a paint business in Muncie, and in 1936 Harold Edwards began his career with Mr. Kimm. In 1957, Edwards returned to Warsaw and purchased the Matson Paint store at 219 E. Center Street to open his own Kimm Paint store.

The business soon moved next door to 217 E. Center Street. Henry Kimm's daughter, Esther, married Harold Edwards, and they operated the business for 40 years. Kimm Paint sold paint, wallpaper, art supplies, and spray gun equipment. Long-time employee Joan Cox worked at the store from 1974 until it closed in 1997.

Furniture Store

Bill Nay started Bill Nay Furniture in 1969 at 520 E. Winona Avenue. Following his death in 1990, Jon Blackwood purchased the business and changed the name to JB's Furniture. The store continued operating on E. Winona Avenue for about four years. Blackwood then moved the store to 510 E. Market Street in the former Harvey's Dime Store location and later extended east to include the former Thornburg's Drug Store.

In June 2001, Blackwood expanded the business further when he opened the Downtown Mattress Showcase at 113-115 E. Center Street. This location was occupied for many years by the Compton Furniture store and later Anderson Furniture.

R.R. Donnelley & Sons

R.R. Donnelley & Sons, a large commercial printer with corporate headquarters in Chicago and many facilities around the world, came to Warsaw in 1958. A training center was established at 801 N. Lake Street (later Woodie's Supermarket) and began with 36 graduates of local area high schools. This site was used while their current facility was being built on Old 30 West. The Warsaw Division has grown into one of the largest rotogravure printing facilities in the world with almost 30 acres under one roof.

The facility houses a complete digital pre-press center, two modern gravure pressrooms, two high-tech binderies, and a complete mail and bulk shipping storage operation. By the postage

"The Andy Griffith Show" set in Mayberry, USA, debuted in 1960.

The Warsaw Optimist Club received its charter in 1958. The first officers for this service organization were, seated left to right: Robert Boley, vice president; John Logue, president; Fred Yohey, vice president. Standing, left to right: Richard Hamm, secretary-treasurer; directors Howard Mock, Max Greenland, and Paul Gadson.

In 1962, John Glenn was the first American astronaut to orbit the earth.

received from the third class mailing of catalogs, this facility makes the Warsaw Post Office the second largest post office in the state of Indiana based on revenue generation.

Now with employment of up to 1,850 people, the majority of the Warsaw Division's printing is catalogs and newspaper inserts. Some of its customers include: J.C. Penney, Radio Shack, Lands' End, Eddie Bauer, Chicago Tribune Sunday Magazine, Spiegel, Dayton Hudson, AARP, and this division prints the *NATIONAL ENQUIRER* and *Star* every week.

Warsaw Optimist Club

The Warsaw Optimist Club received its charter November 13, 1958, with 27 members. The "breakfast club" met at 7:00 a.m. each Wednesday at Horn's Sunnymede Restaurant. The first officers were: John Logue, president; Robert Boley and Fred Yohey, vice presidents; Richard Hamm, secretary-treasurer. Directors were: Paul Gadson, Max Greenland, Howard Mock, and Rev. Lee Rose.

The Optimist Club sponsors an annual triathlon and sells Christmas trees each December to raise money to support the youth in our community. The group has grown to 160 members and currently meets at the Shrine Building each Wednesday morning.

CVS Vending Company

Ed J. Shaffner started CVS Vending Company from his home on Country Club Drive in 1958. The

vending business at that time sold everything from candy and cigarettes to coffee and popcorn, and grew to the point that a warehouse was later built. In the early 1960s Ed's wife, Vivian, would get up in the early morning hours to make ham salad, chicken salad, and egg salad sandwiches for their first refrigerated vending machines.

Shaffner's biggest account was R.R. Donnelley & Sons, but he had numerous vending accounts throughout Kosciusko County. Around 1966, CVS Vending was bought by Bertsch Vending, and Ed worked at Bertsch Vending a short time before leaving the vending business entirely.

United Way

United Way of Kosciusko County, Inc. originated from a meeting the Warsaw Chamber of Commerce held in January 1958 with a representative from the United Fund to discuss the possibility of a local organization. The first officers were: president, Robert Ellison; vice president, Blaine Mikesell; secretary, John Widaman, Jr.; treasurer, Fred Stephens.

The purpose of organizing a United Fund was to eliminate multiple fundraising drives by all organizations. James W. McCleary was the first campaign chairman, and in the early years campaigns were conducted by professional fundraisers. Since then, however, campaign goals have been met and exceeded by the diligent efforts of volunteer speakers and fundraisers throughout the county.

In the late 1970s, Larry Castaldi, a local businessman deeply committed to community services, founded and became the first president of United Way of Indiana, whose purpose was to unite the efforts of all Indiana county United Ways and work for the good of all not-for-profit agencies in state government. In his name, the Castaldi Award for the state's most outstanding volunteer is given each year by the United Way of Indiana.

Ross C. McNamara of Pierceton died in 1972 without a life insurance policy to his name. "Mack" did not need a life insurance policy because he left an estate that earmarked him as a millionaire. One of Lincoln National Life's earliest investors, Mack invested the money he made repairing radios and electronic equipment and inheritance received from members of his family.

Following bequests to distant relatives and a few friends, the remainder of his estate was designated to the United Fund of Kosciusko County. For five years that money was held in a trust fund and only the net interest was available for use by the United Fund. So that the money could work for the community in the broadest possible way, the McNamara money was designated for capital improvements. By 1979, the trust had grown from $383,000 to $680,000.

The trust now produces about $50,000 per year, and to date $3 million in interest income and principal has been granted to United Way agencies for capital improvements and emergency operational needs, as well as special grants for non-United Way agencies and community projects.

United Way of Kosciusko County is the only United Way agency in the state with such an endowment. It is through this trust that 95 cents of every $1 contributed goes directly to helping our community, and only about five cents is used to cover administrative expenses.

Shirley Sadler was hired as a full-time director in 1981, and by the late 1980s the United Way of Kosciusko County was funding 22 member agencies. Sandra Mafera has held the executive director position since Sadler retired in 1993.

Gilliam Bowling Lanes

Fred and Marguerite Gilliam purchased property on N. Detroit Street in 1959 from Fred's great-uncle, Robert Gilliam, Sr., to build the Gilliam Bowling Lanes. Fred Gilliam served the community as a County Commissioner for 25 years, from 1963 to 1988.

A restaurant called Road 15 Fine Foods was added in 1970 to the north side of the building. Over the years, the restaurant changed names to Clipper Lounge, LaMadre, and finally, City Limits. In 1980, a major interior renovation and facelift took place at Gilliam Lanes, followed by a huge open house that featured pro bowler George Pappas.

The Gilliams' son, Michael, and daughter-in-law, Deb, have been involved with the family business since 1974, and took over its management when Fred passed away in 1988.

In an effort to keep the business modern and current, automatic scoring was added in 1991, and beer and wine were added in 1994. In 1996, about $10,000 worth of black lights was added, along with all new house balls to feature the X-Treme glow-in-the-dark bowling that is still very popular today.

After the City Limits restaurant closed in 1997, a state-of-the-art game room was added, and Gilliam Lanes continues to maintain its reputation of being a very family-oriented facility.

Senior Bowlers, left to right, Jeannine Cavell, age 72, Edna Evers, age 83, and Alpha Weirick, age 90, bowl each Wednesday morning at Gilliam Lanes.

As a side note, at age 90, Alpha Weirick is by far the oldest bowler, male or female, in Kosciusko County. Alpha still bowls one day a week at Gilliam Lanes. She is a member of the Wednesday Morning Ladies Koffee Klatch League and maintains a bowling average of 146.

When her family moved to Winona Lake in 1919, her brother had a job setting pins at a bowling alley in Winona Lake. Alpha started bowling at age 14, when it cost 10 cents a game, and has continued to play for 75 years.

Alpha still uses the 14-pound brown Brunswick ball her first husband, William Wedrick, bought for her in 1941. She bowled her best score of 268 in 1948.

Two other senior bowlers in the Koffee Klatch League are Edna Evers, age 83, who has bowled for 68 years and averages 139, and Jeannine Cavell, age 72, who has bowled for 60 years and averages 163. A unique trivial fact noted at the beginning of 2001 before Alpha's birthday was that these three women's ages total 244 and their number of years bowling total 203. The average age is 81 and the average years bowled is 68; added together this equals 149—the average of all three bowlers' averages!

Cruisin' in the Fifties

Doug Kehler fondly recalls his high school years during the late 1950s, when all the guys customized their cars. One of the cars Doug had was a 1954 Ford convertible with 1958 Lincoln headlights and 1956 Lincoln taillights. The car had Oldsmobile rear wheel wells, 108 louvers in the hood, and the door handles had been removed. Doug's "ride" was topped off with gold and white carpeting.

President John F. Kennedy was assassinated in Dallas, Texas, on November 22, 1963.

In the late 1950s, there were four identical 1957 Ford convertibles in Warsaw. The cars were owned by Bill Storey, Max Hay, Don Hanft, and Bob Blosser—known as "The Black Roses." This photo was taken when only one car had flames painted on the sides, but the other three were flamed soon after.

Dorothy Snyder and her son, David Hamrick, are shown with 114 boxes that were delivered in the fall of 1977 for their first Christmas season at The Party Shop. The boxes were unloaded from a truck and stacked on the sidewalk in front of the store. Double metal doors in the sidewalk covered a chute to the basement. Each box was placed in the chute and sent to the basement, where the merchandise was unpacked and carried back upstairs to the store.

A group of high school guys formed a car club called "The Duals," named for the power-pack exhaust introduced by Ford in 1956. All of the members had matching black corduroy jackets embroidered with "The Duals" on the back and their names on the front.

One year the club wanted to race a 1941 black Ford coupe at the Warsaw Speedway. However, it would cost $50 to get the car ready to race. Kehler asked "Bus" Bledsoe, owner of Bledsoe Buick, if he would sponsor the car. Bledsoe agreed, and the club's car, driven by Joe Cutler, raced all summer.

In the feature race at the end of the season, The Duals' car finished second to long-time driver Freddie Boggs, founder of Boggs Industrial Park.

Dreaming back to the 1950s era and the movie *American Graffiti*, some may remember when four young Warsaw men bought new matching 1957 black Ford convertibles with white tops. Bob Blosser, Max Hay, Don Hanft, and Bill Storey customized their cars to look identical. At that time, Doug Kehler worked at Russ Perry's Shell station on the northwest corner of Center and High Streets, which became somewhat of a "hangout" for the guys with cars.

Doug recalls the day one of the black convertibles had sat at the station all day. That evening about 7:00 a member of the Sheriff's Department saw the car sitting there and stopped to ask where the owner was. Doug replied that it had been sitting there all day and he didn't know. The officer got very upset because he thought Doug was trying to protect his friend, and said, "I just saw that car out west of town drag racing with another car! Where is the owner?"

Doug suggested the officer should place his hand on the hood of the black Ford. He did, and to his amazement it was stone cold. As he turned around with a puzzled look on his face, one of the identical cars went east and one went west on Center Street. Doug smiled and said, "There's four of them!"

The Party Shops

Two men from Griffith, Indiana, started The Party Shop in Warsaw at 110 E. Center Street about 1959. Phyllis Ross purchased the store in 1967, and Norm and Dorothy Snyder acquired the business July 1, 1978.

The Snyders added M.I. Hummel and Norman Rockwell figurines to the Hallmark store's fine selection of gifts and collectibles. In December 1984, The Party Shop added the Chalet Christmas Gift Shop, which included decorated Christmas trees, ornaments from around the world, collectible Hallmark ornaments, and musical Christmas decorations.

Walter's Drug Store was next door to The Party Shop for many years. Dorothy Snyder recalls that as late as 1990 people would still occasionally walk into The Party Shop and ask, "Where are the aspirins?" We are certainly creatures of habit!

There was a greeting card store that opened on Winona Avenue in July 1982. The Snyders purchased that business in October 1982 and moved the store to its present location at 703 E. Winona Avenue. They currently have five Gold Crown Hallmark stores—two in Warsaw, one in Plymouth, one in Rochester, and one in Columbia City.

The 1,200-square-foot downtown business was moved to the Lake Village Shopping Center in 1989. In 1998, the Snyders purchased a 15,000 square foot building along U.S. 30 East and added the Christmas & Collectibles Outlet to their many business ventures.

The Party Shop on U.S. 30 is the second largest Hallmark store in the state of Indiana, and its Hallmark Museum is the only one of its kind in the world. The museum has every Hallmark ornament made for sale since 1973 on display. The Hallmark Museum ships ornaments all over the world and attracts many out-of-state visitors to Warsaw.

Dorothy's son, David Hamrick, joined the business in 1987. He is president and general manager of the stores and is in charge of the museum. Son-in-law Cornell Vlot joined The Party Shop team in 1990 as vice president of operations. Norm and Dorothy still remain very active in the business, but are pleased to have the younger family generation involved to carry on the standards and principles that have made The Party Shop a one-of-a-kind Hallmark, gifts and collectibles store.

City Judges

Allan S. Widaman began practicing law in Warsaw in 1906, and carried on the law firm established in 1873 by his father, John D. Widaman. Allan's son, John D. Widaman II, was a member of the law firm.

Before 1960, elected mayors were automatically designated to also serve as judge of the City Court. As legalities became more involved and it was determined that judges should have a legal background, the state of Indiana implemented a statute in 1960 requiring city judges to have a law degree.

Having formerly been the Kosciusko County prosecuting attorney and later the city attorney, Allan Widaman became Warsaw's first city judge. Following Widaman's death, Robert Burner served as the city judge from June 1964 through January 1975. Burner was succeeded briefly by Michael L. Valentine, followed by Milo Lightfoot. County Courts were created and commenced on January 1, 1976. At that time, the City Court and County Justices of the Peace were discontinued.

Furniture Stores

Having previously worked for H.J. Schrader Furniture in Kokomo, Richard Glover purchased the H.J. Schrader Furniture business in Warsaw on the southeast corner of Lake and Center Streets in 1960. A couple of years later, Glover moved the store to the former Kroger location at 118 W. Main Street, naming the business Glover Furniture. Don Reinholt bought the business in January 1982, although the name was not changed to Reinholt's Town Square Furniture until about 1986. Don currently operates the store on Main Street with his sons, Keith and Brent.

Azar's Restaurant

Stan Hull constructed the building at 220 S. Buffalo Street on the north side of the railroad tracks in the early 1960s. Paul Cordell opened Gardner's "Mr. Big" restaurant there about 1964, complete with carhops who went to the parked cars under the canopy to take customers' orders. Cordell's daughter, Ronna, managed the restaurant.

After the Gardner's restaurant closed, Bob Murphy purchased an Azar's Big Boy franchise in 1969 and opened an Azar's restaurant. Murphy later sold the business back to the Azar's company, and Grover Martin managed the restaurant until it closed in the early 1980s.

This property was then converted into offices. It was occupied by a real estate agency for a time and several other small businesses. The Warsaw Housing Authority has been in the back of the building since 1989.

YMCA

The Kosciusko Community YMCA was incorporated in 1961. The YMCA was headquartered at 118½ W. Main Street, with Dr. Carl Schrader as the board president. Membership was 295 in 1963, and programs were conducted at the School Armory on Main Street, Lincoln School, and Lake City Bank.

Phil Harris was president of the board in 1964 when construction began for a new $130,000 YMCA Center. The location for the facility was determined after Mr. and Mrs. James Johnson and Mr. and Mrs. Norman Kelly combined to make a generous donation of land on E. Smith Street worth $25,000. The initial facility included a swimming pool, locker rooms, offices, and some meeting rooms.

Allan S. Widaman (1883-1964) was appointed the first city judge in 1960.

The Beatles first appeared on the Ed Sullivan Show in 1964.

The John Deere Farm Equipment business at 1403 N. Detroit Street was owned by Robert Gilliam and William S. Felkner. The building is currently occupied by Warsaw Masonry.

For many years, a gas station was located in the front of the former Oram's Wagon Works building on the northwest corner of Center and Lake Streets. The two buildings to the right were occupied by the Warsaw Bus & Taxi Station and another service station in the 1940s and 1950s.

The 630-foot stainless steel arch in St. Louis, Missouri, was completed in 1965.

Membership reached 1,600 in 1980, and a $1.5 million fundraising campaign began in 1985 for a capital expansion program. The expanded YMCA facility was completed in 1987 and included a double gymnasium, suspended indoor track, fitness center, and other amenities.

Under the leadership of executive director Don Enterline, from 1990 to 2000 the Y's membership tripled, more than $2-million was raised for capital improvements, and a major addition was made to the facility.

In 2001, YMCA membership is over 7,000. Pat Berkey has been the aquatics director since 1972, providing swim lessons for preschoolers, youth and adults. Other programs offered at the Y include gymnastics, soccer, volleyball and basketball, in addition to fitness classes, weight training and water fitness.

Executive Office Products

Executive Office Machines, Inc. was opened in 1961 at 205 W. Center Street by partners Len Wendt and Clete Couture. Several years later, the business moved to 108 S. Lake Street. It relocated in 1980 to the Lakeview Shopping Center and added a third partner, Dick Leutz. With continued growth, it was necessary to lease more space and the business moved to 1802 E. Winona Avenue (now site of Alternative Learning Center).

Dennis Couture joined the business in 1974 and with his parents acquired the other two partners' interest. Jon Couture joined the family as outside salesman from 1981 to 2001.

The name was changed to Executive Office Products, Inc. when the two Couture sons took over the business in 1987. In 1989, the Coutures purchased the property at 2307 E. Center Street (former site of Tractor Supply Co.).

Dennis is currently president and the sole owner of the business. Executive Office Products carries a full line of office furniture, equipment, and supplies.

Merry-Maker Corp.

About 1962, the Merry-Maker Corporation, a division of a New York company, made paper party supplies in the former American Brattice Cloth building (between Buffalo and Indiana Streets on the north side of the railroad tracks). Jenny Wilkins, one of only about a dozen employees, recalls that their specialty was items for New Year's and birthdays. The business closed about 1967.

Music Stores

Herbert A. Dye III started the Dye Music Center at 119 E. Center Street in 1963. The business carried a variety of brands of pianos, organs and guitars, and also offered lessons. The store later moved to 715 E. Winona Avenue and closed in 1982 when Herb went to work for the City Street Department. When he retired in early 2000, Herb again opened Dye Music Center on E. Winona Avenue in the Lakeview Shopping Center.

Jim Derry opened Derry's Music Store in 1964 at 215 E. Center Street just west of Kimm Paints. When the building burned in 1965, the store moved to 116 W. Market Street. About 1967 Derry's Commercial Sound moved to a concrete block building on Smith Street just west of his father's body shop (since occupied by the Cintas uniform company).

In 1970, Larry Engle bought Derry's Commercial Sound and the name was changed to Engle's Electronics. The business remained on the north side of Smith Street near the fairground entrance. Engle provided background music on 24-hour tapes for stores. He also did commercial sounds and store paging systems, in addition to selling sound equipment to bands. With his three employees, Engle also offered TV and radio repair.

Engle joined the Warsaw Police Department in 1976. After several years of working for the police department during the day and many late nights at the store, he closed the business in 1980.

Miller's Merry Manor

Miller's Merry Manor was founded in 1964 by Wallace T. and Connie Miller. Prior to this business venture, Mr. Miller was a banker and later a bank examiner for many years. Mrs. Miller was a registered nurse who enjoyed working with older people and recognized the need for another nursing home in Warsaw. In 1964, the Millers mortgaged everything they had to purchase the former Kosciusko County Home and its 158 acres on County Farm Road just south of Warsaw.

Within a short time, the 86 beds were filled and in 1966 the decision was made to add a new building on the same property for a combination retirement center and nursing home. The original structure was remodeled to serve as the corporate offices. Within several years, the Millers purchased a Columbia City nursing home. Miller's Merry Manor, Inc. has since evolved into a corporation that operates 31 nursing facilities and two assisted living facilities under the Miller's Health Systems name throughout Indiana.

Providing an array of services, Miller's Merry Manor continues to specialize in long-term restorative nursing care at each of its facilities. Recognizing the need for specialized services, Miller's Merry Manor also provides rehabilitative care, respite care, and adult day services.

The Millers' three sons (Wally, Jr., Richard and James) and two daughters (Beverly and Barbara) have all been involved in the organization. Prior to his death in 1998, Wally, Jr. served 20 years as the CEO and chief operating officer for the family's health care business. His dedication to the aging was found in the way he lobbied for the health care industry and in the numerous articles on health facility administration that he published. Today, Miller's Health Systems is managed by Lucas Management Services, LLC, and the other four siblings serve on the board of directors.

Tyler Machinery Co.

Claude Tyler started Tyler Machinery Company at 610 S. Detroit Street in 1964, where it remains today. His son, David, later owned the business, and the current owner is Larry Wettschurach.

As he was observing his 50th year as a musician, Gus Tatter's life-long dream of owning a pipe organ came true in June of 1964.

Tyler Machinery manufactures industrial wood cutting machinery.

Uniroyal, Inc.

In 1964, U.S. Rubber bought property on N. Detroit Street from North American and changed the name to Uniroyal, Inc. (Brunswick Boat built this facility in 1954 to manufacture fiberglass boats, but went out of business.) This plastic thermal forming plant made engine covers for trucks and later manufactured canoes, in addition to extruded plastic sheeting.

Boats, life raft cases, aircraft cargo containers, and some band instrument cases have been fabricated at Uniroyal over the years. From 1967 to 1989 the firm also had a department which made products for the military, including collapsible, temporary fiberglass fuel storage tanks which held up to 50,000 gallons.

Its main business today is flat plastic sheeting sold to the thermal forming industry where their customers form it into objects, and Uniroyal/Royalite continues to sell laminated flat plastic sheets to canoe manufacturers. The company was purchased by Spartech in 2000, and the name was changed to Spartech Plastics.

The Love of Music

Gustav Tatter owned the Warsaw Monument Works from 1944 to 1968. When Gus was a child, his father was a violin maker in Chicago. Members of the violin section of the Chicago symphony would

Vietnam War, 1959-1975.

The Warsaw Sporting Goods Store was owned by Ardel Hanna and Lee Hartle. It was first located on S. Buffalo Street and moved to E. Winona Avenue in the mid-1970s. Shown, left to right, is owner Ardel Hanna, manager Harold Brown, and employees Phil Sand and Jeff Stackhouse.

The first Super Bowl was held January 15, 1967, with the Green Bay Packers winning over the Kansas City Chiefs.

go to the factory to select the finest violins for themselves and choose others for their students. Gus began the study of piano at age six and by age 12 had begun taking organ lessons. At age 19, he was a choir director and organist.

In the 1930s, Gus formed the Baptist Singers, a group of 14 singers for which he was accompanist, and the group became quite popular in the Chicago area. He also sang with a famed mixed Chicago choir of 180 voices for several years. When Tatter moved to Warsaw, he became minister of music at the Evangelical United Brethren Church, a position he held from 1937 to 1960.

As he was observing his 50th year as a musician, Gus Tatter's life-long dream of owning a pipe organ came true in June of 1964. A church in Nappanee was being torn down and had to sell its 75-year-old organ. Tatter saw the advertisement in the Presbyterian national magazine and promptly made a phone call. Tatter's sons, Warren and Milton, helped dismantle the pipe organ and transport it to Warsaw for storage in their garage until a room could be built onto the family home at 635 S. Buffalo Street.

When Gus and his wife retired and moved to Florida, a room was built on to their double-wide mobile home for the organ. At Christmas time, he would open the windows and entertain the neighbors with Christmas carols. It didn't take long for neighbors to fill the Tatter yard with lawn chairs. When Gus could no longer play, the organ was given to a Baptist church in Leesburg, Florida.

A Visit from Gerald R. Ford

Mrs. Giles G. (Mary) Hoffer recalls the time when Gerald Ford visited Warsaw. Her husband was chairman of the Kosciusko County Republican party from 1958 to 1970. For the Republican dinner on October 28, 1964, Hoffer asked Congressman Charlie Halleck to find a guest speaker. Halleck contacted Gerald Ford, who agreed to come to Warsaw. There was talk of Medicare at that time and many physicians were against it, so the local doctors were anxious to meet with Ford to protest.

Hoffer, Congressman Halleck, and several doctors met Gerald Ford at the Warsaw Airport, and they took him to a local motel for a cocktail party. Hoffer then drove Ford to the fairgrounds for the Republican ham and bean supper, and the others traveled in separate cars. Halleck and Ford were at separate ends of the head table.

After the meeting, the Hoffers invited some of the people to their home at 715 N. Union Street, and Mrs. Hoffer and Ford's pilot hurried to the store to buy apple cider and doughnuts. The pilot and Mrs. Hoffer stayed in the dining room where the refreshments were served. After about an hour, Gerald Ford walked into the room and asked if he could leave by the back door. Mrs. Hoffer was able to nonchalantly get her husband away from the "party" in the other room so he could quietly leave and take Ford and his pilot back to the airport.

Later after Charles Halleck left the Hoffers' home, Mrs. Alvin Rockhill stated that while attending the cocktail party earlier that day she had accidentally walked into the room that Halleck was using as an office. He was talking to his aide in Washington, DC, and had just found out the evening paper stated that Gerald Ford was running for the position of Speaker of the House, the position which Halleck currently held. That was why Ford had tried to keep his distance from Halleck all evening and left without saying goodbye to anyone.

Gerald Ford served 25 years in Congress, from 1948 to 1973, including House Minority Leader from 1965 to 1973. Upon the resignation of Spiro Agnew in 1973, Ford became Richard Nixon's vice president, and then in 1974 he became president when Nixon resigned.

Sports Shops

Dale and Rose Nellans started Nellow Camp & Sports Center in 1965 in a building at 618 N.

Detroit Street. Bill and Judy Reneker bought the business in 1984 and changed the name to Reneker's Sports Shop. Over the years, the building has tripled in size and added a sideline of embroidered clothing and warm-up suits.

Paul "Bud" Lucas started the Sportsman's Center at 704 S. Buffalo Street in the 1960s. Warsaw police officer Ardel Hanna and Warsaw fireman Lee Hartle purchased the business in 1972 and changed the name to Warsaw Sporting Goods. Within a couple years, the store was moved to 720 E. Winona Avenue.

Boyd Walton had been with the Sportsman's Center for 10 years specializing in bicycle repair, and continued his work with the new owners. Warsaw fireman Harold Brown also worked at Warsaw Sporting Goods, until it closed about 1980.

Historical Society

The Kosciusko County Historical Society was founded in 1966 to collect, preserve and exhibit materials of history. The old Kosciusko County Jail, which was built in 1870, was vacated in 1981 when the Justice Building and larger jail were completed. County officials decided to turn over the former jail to the Society to serve as its headquarters and museum.

Volunteers give informative tours through the Jail Museum to many school children, organizations and clubs, and both local and out-of-state visitors. The Society has sponsored numerous special events, such as the Gingerbread Extravaganza, weaving and flint demonstrations, a doll display, and the annual Historic Homes Tour.

Past presidents are: Claude Stahl, 1966-1968; Ralph Brubaker, 1969-71; Ron Sharp, 1972-74; Suzanne Ware, 1975-79; Waldo Adams, 1980-83; Phil Holiday, 1983; Neal Carlson, 1984-86; Don Frantz, 1987-89; Ken Fawley, 1990-93; Mary Ettinger, 1994-96; Doug Mayer, 1997-1998; Laurie Smith, 1999-2000. Mary Ettinger is the current president.

Kosciusko County Foundation

The Greater Warsaw Community Foundation was organized on June 28, 1968, under the sponsorship of the Warsaw Chamber of Commerce. The founding board of directors included Georgia Kaufman, Robert Rasor, Joe Ettinger, Rev. Richard Anderson, and Richard Glover. Robert Gephart and Neal Carlson joined the board in 1972. At the encouragement of Don Frantz in 1973, the foundation was reorganized

All nine living past presidents of the Kosciusko County Historical Society gathered on October 12, 2000, for the Society's 35th anniversary celebration. Left to right: Neal Carlson, Don Frantz, Ken Fawley, Laurie Smith, Claud Stahl, Phillip Holliday, Mary Ettinger, Doug Mayer, Ronald Sharp.

and expanded to include the entire county, and was renamed the Kosciusko County Foundation.

The Foundation office was first located at 117-B E. Center Street with Neal Carlson as the organization's part-time executive director. The board was expanded to 24 members when the Foundation became involved with the Lilly Endowment, Inc. GIFT program (Giving Indiana Funds for Tomorrow).

Upon Carlson's retirement in 1995, Suzanne Light assumed the position. When George Bowser's one-story building on the southeast corner of Buffalo and Market Streets was gifted to the Foundation in 2000, extensive renovations were made for the organization's new offices.

The Kosciusko County Foundation provides a way for donors to realize their charitable dreams and goals, and provides grant funding to area nonprofit organizations, scholarships for students seeking a higher education, and assistance with community projects.

Shopping Center

The construction of the Lake Village Shopping Center on the east side of town began in 1968, and several additions were made over the years. Grant's department store and the A & P grocery were early occupants. K-Mart located in this shopping center about 1976, and in the mid-1980s expanded its square footage to include the former A & P grocery space. Tenants in 2001 include K-Mart, Pizza Hut, Dollar General, and the Maurice's and Fashion Bug clothing stores.

Xerox Corporation introduced its first office copy machine in 1968.

Gill's Motel, owned by Wilbur J. Gill, was located on E. Center Street between the Library and Knights of Pythias house.

A view looking north between the rooms of Gill's Motel in 1952.

Chapter 16

1970 to 2001

Warsaw Orthopedic

In the late 1950s, Joseph F. Carlin, manager of the Warsaw Airport, set up a small shop in a hangar to manufacture bone screws for the local orthopedic companies. The business was known as Carlin Manufacturing. His son, J.F. "Fritz" Carlin, Jr., took over the business in the mid-1960s and moved the business to a building at County Road 400 North and Monoquet Road.

In the early 1970s, Miles Igo became a partner and the name was changed to C & I Manufacturing. Igo bought the entire business in 1980. By 1982,

the name was changed to Warsaw Orthopedic, and Igo moved the company to a larger facility at 100 Publishers Drive in Winona Lake.

Two businessmen from Indianapolis acquired interest in Warsaw Orthopedic in 1983, and a few months later the company name was changed to Biotechnology, Inc. The sales office was moved to Memphis, Tennessee, and the manufacturing plant remained in Warsaw.

On May 17, 1984, a fire severely damaged the manufacturing plant. The fire destroyed all of the finished goods inventory, the quality control room,

Disney World opened in Orlando, Florida, on October 1, 1971.

An aerial view of Central Park, which was completed in 1995. Zimmer Corporate Headquarters is in the foreground.

The Warsaw Holiday Inn, which opened June 1, 1971, was founded by Mr. and Mrs. Herbert Petrie, who started the Wagon Wheel Playhouse, and six local businessmen. Standing left to right: Loren Miller, Gay Robinson, Charlie Bertsch, D. Blaine Mikesell. Seated, Larry Castaldi and Mrs. Mildred Petrie. Herbert Petrie and Robert Steele are not shown.

The first personal computers were introduced in 1974.

much of the raw material for the soft goods area, and a lot of work-in-process for trauma implants and instruments. It was a difficult time for the company, and the sales office in Memphis was closed.

In February 1985, Biotechnology bought a company named Danek Medical. Danek was a small soft goods manufacturing and sales company started by Alan Olsen about 1979. Olsen basically manufactured the products at night and sold them during the day. By 1985, he had a small sales force and a small sewing room specializing in patient restraints. In 1986, the company started working with some orthopedic surgeons on spinal products, and its first plate and screw system, the 803, was soon released.

On May 17, 1991, seven years to the day after the fire, Danek went public and shortly thereafter the name of the holding company, Biotechnology, was officially changed to Danek Group, Inc.

The company merged with Sofamor in 1993 and became Sofamor Danek Group, Inc. Then in 1999, Sofamor Danek Group merged with Medtronic and the name was changed to Medtronic Sofamor Danek. The company constructed a new facility on the northwest side of Warsaw along U.S. 30 in 2000.

Restaurants

Beecher Wiggins constructed a one-story restaurant, known as the Village Inn Pizza Parlor, on the northeast corner of Buffalo Street and Winona Avenue in 1970. A second story was added in 1976 for a steak house that offered fine dining. That restaurant was called Top of the Inn.

Bruce and Steve Shaffner bought the building in 1984. Shaffner's Tumbleweed Mexican Restaurant was located upstairs and the Pizza Parlor remained on the first floor.

Gordy Clemens had started Gordy's Sub Pub in 1986 at 205 W. Center Street. In 1991, he purchased the Shaffner property and moved his restaurant to that location. Since 1991, Gordy's brother, Tom Clemens, has operated the Downtown Eatery & Spirits at the W. Center Street location.

In April 2001, Gordy Clemens sold Gordy's Sub Pub to his brother, Roger "Rocky." The restaurant remains on the second floor. However, the first floor was turned in to a new, up-to-date arcade with numerous games. Known as Tokens-N-Tickets, the arcade is operated by John Burtoft.

Tri-Namic Printing Co.

In 1963, Mrs. Jo Kennedy started a mimeograph and typesetting service, known as Multi-Copy Service, in her home. The business quickly grew and in the early 1970s Jo and her husband, Larry, acquired a building at 1101 W. Winona Avenue and formed Tri-Namic Printing Company, Inc.

With continued growth, about 1989 the business divided into two storefronts. Printing Plus, which is operated by Mrs. Kennedy, is located on the northeast corner of Center and Buffalo Streets in the Saemann Building. Tri-Namic Printing Company is operated by Larry Kennedy and his son, Bob. The Paper Place, a party supply store, was added at the 658 S. Buffalo Street location in 1990.

Holiday Inn / Ramada Plaza

Seven local businessmen—Charlie Bertsch, Larry Castaldi, Blaine Mikesell, Loren Miller, Herb Petrie, Gay Robinson and Bob Steele—formed a joint partnership to build the Warsaw Holiday Inn on E. Center Street, which opened June 1, 1971.

With Dane A. Miller as a silent financial partner, Steve and Bruce Shaffner acquired the Holiday Inn in 1997. The property has since gone through many transitions and renovations, and today is the Ramada Plaza Hotel, which employs over 130 people.

In 1998, it was recognized through the franchise efforts that the Warsaw Ramada was the best renovated hotel. The Warsaw Ramada was nationally recognized in 1999 and received the "Outstanding National Award" for the plaza status in food and beverage, and was also recognized as the "Best Plaza Hotel in the U.S." Bennigan's restaurant was added to the complex in June 2001.

Downtown Revitalization

Frank I. Saemann founded OEC International in 1942, with headquarters in nearby Bourbon. Saemann sold the majority of his multi-continent, multi-million-dollar Orthopedic Equipment Company to Diasonics in 1983, a California-based manufacturer of medical imaging equipment. Biomet purchased the remainder of the business in 1984.

In the 1970s, Saemann began acquiring buildings on the block along Center Street between Buffalo and Indiana Streets, and by 1983 he owned all but two of the ten in that block. Now known as the Saemann Building, the three-story brick structure with a full basement on the northeast corner of Center and Buffalo Streets was built in 1883 by the same workmen who were then finishing the Kosciusko County Courthouse. The building has cherry and walnut interior woodwork done by R.F. Hitzler, who owned the Warsaw Hitzler Furniture Factory.

Once known as the Red Men Building, in 1883 it originally housed the Richardson & Moran dry goods store (with entrances on both streets), the Masonic Lodge (until a new Lodge was built in 1924), and law offices until 1952. It was also occupied for a time by Chris Gilbertson's Corner Cigar Store. Leroy Crownover purchased the building, and it housed his jewelry store by that name until the 1960s.

Groceries with bar codes were first scanned in supermarkets in 1974.

Looking east from the intersection of Center and Buffalo Streets in the 1930s. The Liberty Café sign is visible at the far right. The building on the far left is now known as the Saemann Building.

The building was then abandoned and fell into disrepair, sitting vacant for almost 10 years, until being purchased by Saemann. When the Saemann Building renovation was completed in 1982-83, Crownover Jewelry (by that time owned by Andy Goar), Taco John's, and Baskin-Robbins ice cream parlor were the first businesses to locate in the street-level stores.

The Eagles Building in the center of the block was built in 1930 with retail space on the first floor (occupied by different clothing stores over the years) and meeting rooms for the Fraternal Order of Eagles on the second floor. A ballroom was also on the second floor.

His next attention was given to the corner of Center and Indiana Streets. Once known as the Widaman-McDonald Building, the structure was built in 1916 with a 500-seat theater on the first floor, including a proscenium stage and fly loft. It was later owned by Ralph Boice and known as the Boice Theater, which was damaged by fire in 1974. Saemann purchased the building with plans to make a mini-mall shopping area, which opened in 1984 after its renovation.

The current Warsaw Community Development Corporation traces its beginning back to June 22, 1976, when a group of 10 Warsaw businessmen met to discuss what could be done to rebuild the Warsaw downtown business area. At that meeting, it was decided to form the Downtown Development Commission as a means to accomplish downtown renovation.

The Downtown Development Commission's first priority was fixing up the Saemann Block of storefronts, which at that time many were vacant and the movie theater was charred by fire. Five banks put together a $900,000 low-interest loan from the Downtown Development Commission. Under the 1981 Economic Recovery Tax Act, Saemann also received a 25% tax credit on the renovation cost because the buildings, being more than 40 years old, were certified historical structures.

In 1985, leaders in the area agreed to purchase an Economic Development Bond, of which Saemann could repay the tax-exempt funds over 20 years. Saemann Real Estate was the first to sign up for the County's tax abatement program, which gave them a tax break on the reassessed value of the building, although he still had to pay current taxes. The City Common Council pledged $100,000

The Edmund Fitzgerald iron ore carrier sunk to the bottom of Lake Superior during a storm on November 10, 1975.

in 1983 to rebuild city sidewalks in a cooperative project with downtown store owners. Volunteer committees also raised more than $50,000 for trees and benches.

Around July 1982 there were nearly 20 street-level retail locations vacant. Following Mr. Saemann's lead, other business owners in the Historic District used "restoration and design excellence" as their theme, and restored and renovated their facades. The whole block along Center Street between Buffalo and Indiana Streets is now on the National Register of Historic Places.

Saemann donated forty acres of prime property to Warsaw Community Schools for the present middle school. He donated one year's office space for some not-for-profit organizations and donated washing machines and dryers to the local American Red Cross. In addition, Mr. Saemann paid the County over $170,000 for the Menzie property at the corner of Buffalo and Main Streets in downtown to improve at his expense and then leased it to the City to be used as a downtown parking area.

Although he passed away in 1986, Saemann will be remembered as a most respected philanthropist. His commitment to downtown development reflected his deep desire to improve his hometown and willingness to experience a financial loss in order to bring great gains to the community after his lifetime. In all development decisions he opposed advice to "level and build new buildings" and chose to renovate, even if it meant a greater expense.

Mr. and Mrs. Saemann continue to provide benefits to the Warsaw community through the Franklin I. and Irene List Saemann Foundation which gives grants each year in their memory.

The City Limits and Beyond

Retired Detective Sergeant Jerry Laurien recalls that when he joined the Warsaw Police Department in 1973, the city limits were: south on Buffalo Street to the north side of the Eagle Creek bridge; west to the intersection where Market and Center Streets meet (Boggs Industrial Park was just beginning); north to Koors Amoco on N. Detroit Street; and east to the Wagon Wheel Playhouse, at the top of the hill.

He also noted that at that time the police department still had a ring of keys for downtown businesses, because the officers used to put coal in the businesses' furnaces during the cold winter nights as they made their rounds.

As a side note, Laurien has fond memories of his childhood and growing up in nearby Winona Lake. He related his memories of Billy Sunday, a professional baseball player during the late 1800s who became an evangelist. Billy Sunday moved to Winona Lake in 1911, where revivals were held during the summers and he would preach before thousands of people around the United States each week about sin and salvation.

Laurien's family lived on the corner of Park Avenue and 12th Street, and the Sunday home was at the top of the hill People often stopped by the Sunday home in hopes of getting a chance to talk to the highly respected, famous preacher. It got to the point that when Billy and "Ma" Sunday had gone away, before they returned home they would stop at the bottom of the hill and look up to see if anyone was sitting on their front steps waiting for them. If so, the Sundays would park their car and visit with the Lauriens on their front porch until the people at the top of the hill got tired of waiting and left.

Like Warsaw, Winona Lake also has a great deal of history. Over the years, many homes in the town of Winona Lake had deteriorated and were in disrepair. In the early 1990s, Winona Restoration was formed with the financial support of Dane and Mary Louise Miller and the interest and enthusiasm of town councilman Brent Wilcoxson.

The goal was to renovate and rejuvenate the town of Winona Lake. The partners "had a vision" and began by purchasing properties and renovating old houses. The town was placed on the National Register of Historic Places in 1993 and has since been transformed into a delightful community. In 2000, The Village at Winona opened its Artisan's Court with over 12 specialty shops and galleries. Visitors can also tour several museums, including the historical Billy Sunday home.

McDonald's

The first McDonald's restaurant in Warsaw was built in 1973 on the northwest corner of Detroit and Fort Wayne Streets. That building was torn down in 1999 and a new, more modern McDonald's was built in the same place. A second McDonald's was constructed in the early 1990s along U.S. 30 East.

Clothing Stores

In 1973, Johnson and Beulah Helfrich opened their women's clothing store known as Helfrich's at 109 S. Buffalo Street. The Jet White #1 grocery

Mrs. Betty Morgan, left, in 1988 with President Gerald Ford in Vail, Colorado. Her generous philanthropy over the years has benefited many local community services, including the United Fund, YMCA, and Kosciusko Community Hospital.

was to the south and the Unique Bakery was to the north. John Snell bought the property and constructed a new building, and Helfrich's expanded to include that store.

When Helfrich's closed in 1980, John and Mariam Snell opened Snell's Apparel, a ladies ready-to-wear shop. In addition to the street level store, Snell's had a basement store which carried a complete line of women's undergarments.

Sue Cole operated the Green Apple children's clothing store at 107 E. Center Street (now location of Merrill Lynch) from 1973 to 1984. She also operated the Cider Press women's clothing store next door at 109 E. Center Street (now site of Male Fashions) from about 1976 to 1992.

Girls' Basketball State Champs

In late February 1976, a sign at the south edge of town read, "Good Luck Gals, last fan out of town . . . please turn out the lights!" The entire community was engaged in "Hoosier Hysteria" when the Warsaw High School girls' basketball team captured the first ever girls' high school state basketball championship in 1976. It was more than just a game . . . it was a complete happening for the town of Warsaw.

An estimated 5,000 Warsaw fans were in attendance at the Indianapolis Hinkle Fieldhouse, and the Tiger Adult Booster Club provided orange handkerchiefs for the fans to wave during the

Oprah Winfrey launched her television talk show from Chicago in 1986.

The Warsaw High School girls basketball team won their first state championship in 1976. Front, L-R: Leisa Waggoner, Lori Neville, Anita Folk, Lisa Vandermark, Judi Warren, Kim Rockey. Back, L-R: Coach Janice Soyez, Assistant Coach Linda Croop, Kelly Smith, Marcia Miller, Cheryl Kachlik, Cindi Ross, Chanda Kline, Cathy Folk. Not pictured: Marge Lozier, manager, and Judy Reed, scorekeeper.

Atlanta hosted the Centennial Olympics in 1996.

games. The Lady Tigers rallied over East Chicago Roosevelt, 62-44 in the semi-final game and won the championship over unbeaten Bloomfield, 57-52. Judi Warren made five out of six free throws during the last moments of the championship game to clinch the state title. Sophomore Chanda Kline was the tourney leading scorer with 45 points. The team finished with a 22-0 record as the state champs. The starting five included: Cathy Folk, Chanda Kline, Cindi Ross, Lisa Vandermark, and Judi Warren.

A mile-long caravan followed the girls home from the state capital, and cars were parked along State Road 15 to welcome them back at one o'clock in the morning. The team was greeted with four blasts from the cannon on the Courthouse Square. Some 3,000 fans gathered at the high school gym and joined the celebration. It didn't break up until nearly 3:00 a.m. and it was shortly before daylight before the last of the celebration came to an end.

The impact of the first girls' tourney could be seen Sunday afternoon when most Warsaw residents were watching the replay of the title game on a South Bend television station. And a drive past the Marsh playground revealed a group of youngsters playing a pick-up game of basketball . . . they were all girls.

On Monday, students throughout the school system got a vacation from the books. School officials, along with local police and fire departments, organized a parade through the downtown, with the girls—always confident and never shy—riding atop fire trucks with their lone fingers held high. The parade ended at the high school where a crowd of Tiger fans packed the gymnasium for a pep rally.

Senior Judi Warren was named the first recipient of the Indiana High School Athletic Association's "Mental Attitude Award." Warren was the team's leading scorer the past four years and finished with a 21.9 average in regular season play. In addition, Judi Warren was named "Miss Basketball 1976."

The Warsaw High School girls' basketball team won the state championship two years later in 1978 when they ripped past Heritage, 61-38 in the semi-finals. During the early moments of the championship game, a television announcer stated that she could hardly hear herself think, as the Tiger fans "roared" throughout Hinkle Fieldhouse in Indianapolis.

Boys' basketball coach Jim Miller moved the excitement of the estimated crowd of 5,000 Warsaw fans to an even higher level as he performed somersaults, flips and other handsprings during a third quarter time out, when Warsaw was clinging to a 40-39 lead. Warsaw went on to defeat Jac-Cen-Del, 75-60 to win the state title. The team finished with a record of 22-0. Anita Folk was the leading scorer in the tourney with 49 points.

Scoring their career-bests in their final high school game, seniors Chanda Kline and Anita Folk led the Tigers with 29 and 28 points, respectively,

in the championship game. The starting five consisted of: Anita Folk, Chanda Kline, Claudia Kreicker, Cheryl Sands, and Pam Shively. In addition, Chanda Kline was named "Miss Basketball 1978."

The cannon on the Courthouse Square was fired immediately after the game on Saturday night. Sunday, with a cold wind and blowing snow, the noise began in earnest. Wailing fire trucks, with team members perched precariously atop, led a caravan of horn-honkers through the downtown area. An estimated 4,000 people greeted the champions that afternoon at a pep rally in the gymnasium.

The rumble at the high school did not reach its crescendo until coach Janice Soyez and assistant Mary Hurley ran through a mass of howling fans carrying the three-foot trophy signifying another state championship. Soyez told the crowd, "We did something I think will be in the history books. To win it once is something, but to win it twice is something else."

The Women's National Basketball Association began play in 1997.

The Warsaw High School girls basketball team won their second state championship in 1978. Back row, left to right: statistician Shari Bibler, manager Senita Waggoner, Pam Busenberg, Lynn Galichus, scorekeeper Anne Moorehead, Cheryl Sands, manager Rhonda Waggoner, Marcia Miller, Pam Shively, Claudia Kreicker, Leona Bruce, Chanda Kline, Renee Wildman, Anita Folk, assistant coach Mary Hurley, Sue Loher, Pam Teeple, Kim Rockey, assistant coach Linda Croop, athletic director Bob Huffman, and coach Janice Soyez. Front row, left to right: cheerleaders Martee Mitchell, Christy Beck, Joye Fuson, Sabrina Handgen, Deb Brown, Linda Pringle.

Kosciusko Community Hospital

Kosciusko Community Hospital opened its doors to patients in June of 1976. The 20-acre tract for the 113-bed hospital was purchased from the Beyer family by eight local physicians and donated to KCH.

The Kosciusko SurgiCenter with five operating suites opened in February 2001. The SurgiCenter provides patients with state-of-the-art medical technology, equipment and facilities. The following month, the Birthplace opened as Phase I of the new Kosciusko Women's Health Center. The maternity center includes four labor-delivery-recovery rooms, plus ten private rooms and an expansive nursery.

The Kosciusko Women's Health Center was completed in June 2001 and provides obstetrics, gynecology, surgical services, and imaging radiology services. Classroom and computer resources for health education are available, in addition to seminars and women's health support groups.

Othy, Inc.

Othy, Inc. was founded October 1976 in Warsaw. Located at the northeast corner of State Road 15 and County Road 350 North, Othy's mission was to provide orthopedic surgical instruments to the large orthopedic companies. Over the last 25 years, Othy has expanded to become the largest supplier of orthopedic instruments in the U.S.

In August 1996, Poly-Vac (Manchester, New Hampshire) was combined with Othy to offer cases and trays for surgical instruments. Also, Symmetry Medical, Inc. was formed as a holding company for Othy and Poly-Vac. By offering instruments and cases and trays together, the concept of "Total Instrument Solutions" was created.

Symmetry Medical Limited was formed as the European link to the Symmetry family of companies in November 1998. Located in Cheltenham, England, Symmetry Medical Limited provides surgical instruments to the European orthopedic companies from this UK base. To provide cases and trays in Europe, EuroSter (Lille, France) became another subsidiary of Symmetry Medical Inc. in August, 1999.

Corporate offices for Symmetry Medical Inc. moved to downtown Warsaw in April, 2001 at 220 W. Market Street.

East Side Development

The east side of Warsaw began developing rapidly in the 1970s after the four-lane highway was completed. J.C. Penney opened a catalog-only store in the Center-Center shopping area on the east side of U.S. 30 in 1976. The store moved to the Marketplace Shopping Center in 1988 with both a department store and catalog center.

Dick Allen established the Arby's Restaurant on U.S. 30 East in 1978, with restaurant manager Bill Aguilar. The second Arby's on N. Detroit Street opened in 1994.

Microsoft introduced its first Windows version for computers in 1987.

The founders of Biomet shown in 1980, left to right: M. Ray Harroff, Dane A. Miller, Jerry L. Ferguson, Niles L. Noblitt.

Gus Katris and his sons, Chris and Jim, opened the American Table Restaurant in October 1987 on U.S. 30 east of Warsaw in the former Waffle House building. This was a popular restaurant for breakfast, lunch and dinner, but a fire in 2000 caused the business to close.

The Bob Evans restaurant opened at 3100 E. Center Street along U.S. 30 in 1991. Further development in 1991 included Commerce Village and the Wal-Mart Shopping Center.

Biomet, Inc.

Biomet, Inc. was founded November 30, 1977, by former Zimmer employees Dane A. Miller, Ph.D., and Jerry L. Ferguson, and former Orthopedic Equipment Company (OEC) employees Niles L. Noblitt and M. Ray Harroff. Producing a line of orthopedic softgoods, the company recorded sales of $17,000 and a net loss of $63,000 during the first year.

Sales quickly gained momentum by using the softgoods business as a backdrop for the development of a line of orthopedic implants. In addition to molding its own polyethylene components, Biomet was one of the first orthopedic companies to use titanium alloy for its implants. Early in its history, Biomet also developed an innovative porous coating technology to promote bone growth onto the implant.

In 1984, Biomet purchased OEC, which had an established distribution network in Europe and manufacturing facilities in England and South Wales, Australia. This acquisition enhanced Biomet's product offering in trauma devices and operating room supplies. Additional company acquisitions over the years have allowed Biomet to grow quickly as a leader in the orthopedic marketplace.

Headquartered in Warsaw, Biomet has manufacturing and/or office facilities in over forty locations worldwide. The company's products are currently distributed in more than 100 countries.

All four founders are still active with the company. Miller serves as president and CEO, Noblitt is chairman of the board, Ferguson is vice chairman of the board, and Harroff serves on the board of directors. In fiscal year 2001, Biomet sales are projected to reach $1 billion.

Ramsey, Wilson & Wiggins, Inc.

Lawrence A. Ramsey, CPA, started his accounting business at 102 E. Winona Avenue in 1978. His brother, Burton A. Ramsey, joined the firm in 1979, and in 1980, with the addition of Robert Mannan, the firm became Mannan, Ramsey & Co. With the addition of Steven B. Wilson in 1982, the name changed to Ramsey, Wilson & Associates, and when current mayor Ernest B. Wiggins joined the firm in 1983, the business became known as Ramsey, Wilson & Wiggins, Inc.

Pizza Hut

Pizza Hut of Fort Wayne, owned by Richard J. Freeland, opened a Pizza Hut in Warsaw at 502 N. Detroit Street in 1978. Under the management of Bruce Shaffner, just two years later in 1980 the restaurant was recognized as the first Pizza Hut nationally to reach $1-million in sales. In 1982, the second Pizza Hut in Warsaw opened in the Lake Village Shopping Center. That same year, Shaffner left Pizza Hut to open the Viewpoint Restaurant with his brother, Steve.

Star Services

In 1978, Sheila Burner started a branch of Star Temporary Services in her home at 403 W. Winona Avenue. Many people seeking jobs entered her kitchen to discuss employment possibilities, and she states that her storm door and kitchen floor could attest to the amount of foot traffic her house endured during that time.

The business expanded to include full-time employment positions and experienced terrific growing pains. The name was changed to Star Staffing Services, and in 1986 she opened an office at 206 W. Fort Wayne Street. The business was later moved to the northwest corner of Buffalo Street and Winona Avenue. She began to plan her retirement in 1997, and sold her interest back to the corporation.

Ivy Tech State College

Ivy Tech State College first started offering classes in 1978 at the Warsaw High School, then located on E. Smith Street. Classes were moved to the old McKinley School for a time and later downtown to the second floor of the Saemann Building. In 1992, Ivy Tech moved back to Smith Street in a portion of the school, by then known as the

The first ticket for the Indiana Lottery was sold October 13, 1989.

Ed and Huldah Brandenburg, center, have donated $1,000 annually to the Multi-Township EMS for the past 22 years. Fireman and EMS volunteer Larry Baker, left, was present when EMS director Cindy Dobbins, far right, accepted the Brandenburgs' check in 2001.

The World Wide Web was invented in 1990, which evolved into today's Internet.

Lakeview Middle School. Ivy Tech offers technical and professional courses with a selection of computer, general education, and basic skills classes.

Donations to EMS

Ed and Huldah Brandenburg have no children. Therefore, they have chosen to financially assist local community services with special projects. Since 1979, the Brandenburgs have donated $1,000 each year to the Multi-Township EMS. Their generous contributions have helped purchase equipment not allocated in the EMS budget.

Together, the couple worked a total of 54 years at Creighton Brothers' poultry farm. In addition to their daily jobs, they farmed 80 acres, raised livestock, and grew a large garden each season. The Brandenburgs are well-known for helping people throughout our community. For example, they supplied nearly 8,000 pounds of fruits and vegetables to Combined Community Services in 1987. Although their garden has gotten smaller over the years, they still enjoy sharing candies, fruits and home-grown vegetables with their friends.

Instant Copy

Instant Copy was founded in the late 1960s by Jack Caffrey of Fort Wayne in a garage (before the emergence of copy machines) with ink presses and black ink. The business grew and in 1976 a store was opened in Warsaw at 203 W. Center Street.

When Warsaw Real Estate vacated the space next door at 201 W. Center in 1989, Instant Copy was able to expand.

Instant Copy continues to be a full-service print shop with walk-in customers and self-service copy machines. However, technology has expanded the service to include full digital copying, large blueprint copying, and digital full-color posters.

Little People Productions

City councilman and future mayor Jeff Plank teamed up with graphic artist Tim Kennedy to establish Little People Productions. In 1980, they published a children's book titled *Warsaw, Indiana is my Town!*

Word got around and soon Little People Productions was receiving manuscripts, poems, recipes—anything and everything that people wanted to publish—from all over the United States. The venture grew to such an extent that Plank and Kennedy, both still holding other full-time jobs, could no longer keep up with the demand. Therefore, Little People Productions ceased publishing and is currently inactive.

Explorer Van Company

The idea which brought about the origin of Explorer Van Company occurred in the summer of 1980. Robert H. Kesler was the owner-operator of a failing Ziebart rustproofing business. At that time, Bob's son, Steve, was driving RVs and vans for Coachman Industries.

Bob had been a traveling salesman for 20 years selling medical and dental equipment. With no automotive background and at that time in debt and nearly broke from the Ziebart operation (and despite a depressed economy at the time) Kesler began researching the idea of converting vans.

Explorer Van Company began in two stalls in the Mavron building on Zimmer Road in the fall of 1980 under the name of Bodor Corporation, which means Bob and Doris (his wife). Needing more space within about four months, the business moved to a building on Ellsworth Street. The company sold 60 vans its first year.

The business was growing and completing four vans per week; Explorer Van sold 300 vans in 1982. Steve had a teaching job at that time, which he quit to join the van business full time. In 1983, the company rented a building from Bill Hand on U.S. 30 East, which they thought they would never outgrow. At that time Explorer Van had two large customers (one in St. Louis and one in Columbus, Ohio) and still did not have a sales force. The first salesman was hired in 1984.

Also in 1984, Explorer Van moved to the 20,000 square foot Yeiter building on U.S. 30 West which, once again, they thought they would never outgrow. However, when the Keslers saw 37 acres for sale across the highway at the corner of Fox Farm Road and U.S. 30 West, they looked at it, bought it that same afternoon, and what is now Explorer Van Headquarters was built in 1985.

The current site of buildings includes the primary assembly plant with corporate headquarters, wood products shop, state-of-the-art painting facility, an injection molding facility, a service and parts facility, and additional buildings provide security, specialized storage and preliminary product manufacturing. More than 1,000 vans can be secured and stored on the fenced, paved lot with room for an additional 300 more on an overflow lot.

Three successful "sister" corporations have also been formed. Seats Plus, located in Elkhart, manufactures fabric van seating for Explorer; Olympic Manufacturing on the Explorer property is a fiberglass operation that manufactures all of Explorer's fiberglass products; and Haimbaugh Enterprises, located in the Airport Industrial Park, makes all the custom leather seating, shades and wiring harnesses used by Explorer. In addition, the Explorer woodshop is a fully equipped volume cabinet operation that produces all of their woodwork.

In the late 1980s, Explorer diversified to the retail automobile business. Its Lakeside Motors location on State Road 15 North is a Chevrolet/Geo dealer. Explorer also has a location in Sullivan, Illinois, in addition to a trucking company called Tiger Transport, which transports Explorer Vans to the over 350 dealers nationwide. The company produces the luxury passenger Explorer conversion van on Chevrolet, GMC, Ford and Dodge van chassis.

So what began on a $20,000 restrictive loan investment, has grown to an enterprise generating more than $100 million in sales annually and employing as many as 250 workers. Explorer Van Company grew from total production in its first year of 60 vans to the present 8,000 to 10,000 units per year. Robert H. Kesler currently serves as chairman of the board and Stephen L. Kesler is president.

Of special note is that a white Explorer van was featured in about six or seven episodes of the "Dallas" TV series around 1984. Some of the well-known people who have purchased specially ordered Explorer vans include: Eric Dickerson, Bill Gates, Reggie Jackson, Tommy LaSorda, Dan Marino, Wayne Newton, Shaquille O'Neal, Walter Payton, and Prince.

Justice Building

The Kosciusko County Justice Building was constructed on the southwest corner of Lake and Main Streets in 1981. (That corner had previously been the site of a two-story brick building occupied during the 1940s through the early 1960s by the Hartsock Studebaker dealership, and for a time the Blue Bell jeans factory was upstairs.)

County Auditor Jean Northenor was instrumental in coordinating the architect with county officials to plan and organize the combined court-jail project through its 18-month construction process. In addition to four courtrooms, the facility is occupied by the County Clerk's office, Prosecuting Attorney's office, and Probation Department. There is a large meeting room in the basement and a shooting range is located under the jail. A tunnel connects the Courthouse to the Justice Building.

Warsaw Health Foods

Brothers Steve and Mike Grill started Warsaw Health Foods at 1228 E. Center Street in 1981. The store offers a wide selection of vitamins and supplements, along with a variety of healthy snacks and foods. Although the property is still owned by the Grill brothers, the business has been operated by an out-of-state businessman since 1987.

Instrumedical Technologies

Anthony "Tony" Miller founded what is now known as Instru-Med in 1981. The business began as Miller & Sons Tool & Die, Inc. The name was later changed to Instrumedical Technologies, Inc. to better reflect the company's main focus, orthopedic machining.

Miller started his business in North Webster, but soon moved it to a rented building on U.S. 30 East. He then built a facility on Corridor Drive about 1988. The company grew over the next 10 years, and in 1998 Instru-Med purchased the former Zimmer manufacturing facility at 727 N. Detroit Street and moved to the shores of Center Lake.

The Rock & Roll Hall of Fame opened in Cleveland, Ohio, in 1995.

Ranger Materials

In 1982, Darwin "Poodie" Call purchased Don Dalton's Lawn Rangers business, which was started in 1977 as a lawn care service, and moved the business to 310 Argonne Road. He sold off the lawn care portion to concentrate on asphalt maintenance and paving. The name was changed to Ranger Materials about 1998. Prior to Ranger Materials, this site was formerly home to Wayne Love Motors in the 1960s.

Typing Services Unlimited

Typing Services Unlimited was started in 1983 by Michelle J. Bormet at 204 W. Fort Wayne Street in the former Bibler Funeral Home, which by then had been converted to various office spaces. Bormet provided secretarial services to small businesses and organizations, and prepared many résumés for job seekers. During that time, she typed speeches and other reports for Mayor Jeff Plank, which later led to her being offered the secretarial position at the Mayor's office in 1991. Bormet sold the business in 1988 and it closed a short time later.

Boys' Basketball State Champs

The Warsaw High School boys' basketball team won its first and only state championship in 1984. The Tigers defeated New Castle, 78-74 in the semi-final game at Market Square Arena in Indianapolis and took the championship with a victory over Vincennes, 59-56.

The Tigers made 59% of their field goals and clinched the game in the fourth quarter when they held the ball for more than a minute while leading by five points. When the Vincennes coach received a technical, Jeff Grose made both shots and put Warsaw ahead 39-38. A minute later, Grose added another free throw when a Vincennes player was given a technical, and Vincennes never regained the lead. After Scott Long's free throw broke a 56-56 tie, in the final closing seconds Steve Hollar made two free throws that won the state title for the Tigers.

The starting five included: Jeff Grose, Steve Hollar, Marty Lehmann, Scott Long, and Rob Randels. During the state tournament, Jeff Grose

Indiana University basketball coach Bob Knight was dismissed in 2000 after 29 years on the IU campus.

The Warsaw High School Boys Basketball Team won the State Championship in 1984. First row, L-R: Cheerleaders Jackie Leeper, Jodi Wilson, Patti Boyer, Krystal Gsell, Jodi Weirick, Teresa Miller. Second row, L-R: Chris Rhodes, Manager Scott Lee, Curtis Rhodes, Head Coach Al Rhodes, Jeff Tucker, Joe Sands, Rob Randels, Marty Lehmann, Jeff Grose, Scott Long, Steve Hollar, Assistant Coach Dennis Van Duyne, Assistant Coach Jerry Ryman. Third Row, L-R: Superintendent Dr. Larry Crabb, Athletic Director Dave Fulkerson, Principal Richard Kline, Mike Hall, Robert Johnson, Greg Marsh, Mike Lynch, Mike Norris, Tracy Furnivall, Assistant Coach Pete Smith, Assistant Coach Hal Gunter. Fourth row, L-R: Managers Chris Wheeler, Bill Miller, John Lee, Brant Bair, Rod Wilson, Brad Drudge, Greg Hall, Ford Olinger.

and Marty Lehmann each exceeded 1,000 points for their prep careers. The Associated Press named junior Jeff Grose the state finals' "Most Valuable Player." He scored under 20 points in only one tourney game, averaging 22.5 for the eight games. The team finished the season with a 26-2 record.

Saturday night after the Tigers won, several local residents gave the team a 21-gun salute with a miniature cannon in front of Breading's Cigar Store. Fans lined the streets and cars cruising the downtown area found themselves in a traffic jam.

Despite rain and sleet the next day, victory still showed in the hearts of the Tiger fans during the parade through town. Singer Janie Fricke, who was in town for a concert at the Wagon Wheel, even made a brief appearance at the Tiger Den that afternoon to help congratulate the state champs.

Jeff Grose went on to have an outstanding basketball season his senior year and was named "Mr. Basketball" in 1985. The following year, Steve Hollar played the role of Rade Butcher in *Hoosiers*, a movie about high school basketball starring Gene Hackman as the coach.

Paws and Claws

Janet Zimmer opened the Paws and Claws pet store in 1984 at 1302 E. Center Street, next door to the Warsaw Health Food store. The business moved to 1801 E. Market Street in 1989 and carries a wide selection of supplies for small pets, hand-fed birds, reptiles and fish.

Ice Cream Shop

Henry and Tina Schmidlin opened the Baskin-Robbins ice cream shop at 105 E. Center Street in 1984. Joe and Linda Schwartz operated the store for a time before Ron and Patricia Donkers purchased the business in 1992.

Baskin-Robbins closed in 2000, and in April 2001, Jim and Patti Thompson opened Kelainey's Ice Cream Shop at the same location. The business is named after the Thompsons' daughters, Kelsie and Laine.

Warsaw Engineering & Fabricating

Warsaw Engineering & Fabricating, Inc. was created in 1986 by Jim Weaver and Don Bice to provide custom metal fabrication and maintenance services to a mainly industrial clientele. The initial work

The Warsaw Biblical Gardens, completed in the late 1980s, is one of the largest and finest Biblical botanical gardens in the United States.

staff was comprised of the founders plus three employees. Today, the employee base has expanded to approximately 50 skilled tradesmen.

In 1998, the Warsaw Fabricated Systems was spun off with the purpose of developing a manufacturing center for gas-fired makeup air units, ovens and similar custom products. An additional facility was added to the original location to accommodate this expansion. The facility has remained at 2780 E. Durbin Street and grown from the original 6,000 square foot building to the present four buildings containing 90,000 square feet of production space and offices.

Warsaw Biblical Gardens

The Warsaw Biblical Gardens began in 1986 as the idea of one individual, Sara Lee Levin, and has since emerged as one of the largest and finest Biblical botanical gardens in the United States. It is located adjacent to Center Lake alongside State Road 15. The gardens include six micro-climates which represent the main environments of which the Bible speaks.

In addition, a large gathering area provides a place for information and for assembly. For those desiring a place of solitude, a sitting area with benches under the branches of two spreading oaks is provided in a more remote part of the garden.

The Warsaw Community Development Corporation oversees the annual maintenance of the Biblical Gardens.

In 1996, Madeline Albright became the first female Secretary of State.

The Lake City Skiers placed third in Division II at the 2001 national competition. Members of this pyramid are (left to right), bottom row: Keith Farmer, Mike Wilson, Jake Wilson, Mark Skibowski, Gary Hawblitzel and Ty Patrick; second row: Shanna Ewert, Angie Malcolm, Ericka Wilson; third row: Rachel Lehman, Tracey Patrick; top row: Ashley Wilson.

During the winter months the team practices in local gyms, barns, and community swimming pools to prepare for shows beginning in June. Each year the theme, music and costumes are changed. The team's water acts include high-speed barefooting, a beautiful ballet line, amazing jumping, graceful slalom swivel skiing, and awesome pyramids with as many as 24 skiers behind one boat.

Midwest Rake Company

Midwest Rake Company was formed in 1990 by Bob South and Steve Petty, who designed their own lightweight, aluminum landscape rake. They produced the rakes in a small garage in Akron and introduced them at the American Rental Show in Indianapolis, where 147 rakes were ordered by two buyers. More trade shows that year resulted in a total of 3,000 rakes sold in 1990.

In 1991, the business was moved into a leased space in the lower level of the vacated Free Methodist Headquarters building in Winona Lake. Land was purchased in 1995 in the Boggs Industrial Park for their current site at 1605 W. Center Street.

Bill Henthorn purchased South's company interest in 1996, followed by his brother-in-law, former mayor Jeff Plank, purchasing Petty's interest at the end of 1999. The new management team allowed the company to enter 2000 with a very positive outlook for their ever-increasing number of quality products. Midwest Rake produces numerous construction and maintenance tools for the professional sports, landscaping, asphalt, concrete, and floor coating industries.

Rock Bottom Warehouse

In 1990, Max Jones started Jones Furniture in the former Home Furniture Mart building, but soon moved across the street at 1506 N. Detroit into the former Champion Door facility. Now known as Rock Bottom Warehouse, the business sells furniture, appliances, and electronics, and is currently operated by five members of the Jones family.

Bob List Photography

Bob List started a photography business in North Webster and moved to Warsaw in 1987 to work with Blosser's Photography for several years. In 1991, he started Bob List Photography in the old State Bank building on the southwest corner of Buffalo and Market Streets. In 2001, List was named "Michiana Master Photographer of the Year" and was inducted into the Presidential Circle.

After many decades as 219, Warsaw's area code was changed to 574 in 2001.

Allen's Designs

Bill and Susan Allen had a private jewelry studio near Chapman Lake in 1974, and moved it to Lake Tippecanoe in 1983. The Allens came to downtown Warsaw in 1987 and opened Allen's Designs at 111 E. Center Street. Allen's Designs specializes in one-of-a-kind, unique designs created by Bill. Long-time employee Melanie Rooney has been with the business since shortly after its move to Warsaw.

Lake City Skiers

The Lake City Skiers, established in 1989 and formerly known as Kosco H2O Ski Show Team, is a competitive water ski show team. They produce weekly water ski shows free to the public at Hidden Lake on the northwest side of Warsaw. In 2000, the ski team had almost 60 members ranging in age from three to 50, who were from Kosciusko and several other surrounding counties.

The Dueling Elvises

The "Dueling Elvises" originated in 1992 at Gordy's Sub Pub on the northeast corner of Buffalo Street and Winona Avenue. During 1992, Gordy's became a popular place for karaoke, and restaurant owner Gordy Clemens often sang Elvis Presley songs. When Lonnie Witham was there for karaoke nights, he also chose Elvis songs to sing.

The two started singing together and one night someone asked them to put a program together for an auction benefit at the Elks Club. Before the night was over they had five more "gigs," and the Dueling Elvises were born.

Since they began, the duo has performed at various clubs and charity events throughout northern Indiana, including the Plymouth Blueberry Festival, New Year's Eve parties in 1995 and 1996 at the Wagon Wheel Playhouse, and New Year's at the Fort Wayne Elks Club in 1998 and 1999. The Dueling Elvises also sang at the Saks Fifth Avenue Christmas Party on Chicago's "miracle mile," and have traveled as far as Detroit and St. Louis to entertain.

Best Small Towns in America

In 1993, Norman Crampton ranked Warsaw 67th in his book titled *The 100 Best Small Towns in America*. Jean Northenor, then senior vice president of Lake City Bank and former county auditor, was quoted as saying, "I would describe Warsaw as a very young old town. Warsaw has been here a lot of years. Yet the people in Warsaw have never allowed it to become stagnant."

In his second edition of the book in 1995, Warsaw was ranked 42nd. Crampton stated, "It's my feeling in all these places you have a strong feeling of community pride and a large reservoir of volunteers. It goes back to fundamental values of this nation, the importance of people working together on behalf of community regardless of pay . . . to keep local institutions vital." These words speak volumes about Warsaw.

CCAC & Central Park

The Downtown TIF District (Tax Increment Financing) was established in 1993 during the administration of Mayor Jeff Plank. This resulted in construction of Central Park on the former site of Fisher Field and the Zimmer Corporate Headquarters between Main and Fort Wayne Streets.

Through the vision and leadership of Mayor Plank, our community's dream of a public sports

Lonnie Witham sings a solo during a performance by "The Dueling Elvises."

Gordy Clemens sings to a fan in the audience during a performance by "The Dueling Elvises."

The first season of softball and soccer played at the City-County Athletic Complex west of Warsaw took place in 1994.

The Courthouse dome can clearly be seen from the Gardens of Central Park.

facility became a reality. The whole project became possible because of the 65-acre land donation from R.R. Donnelley & Sons on Old Road 30 West.

City-County Athletic Complex was chosen as the facility's name. As the key force behind the plan, Plank met with many local businesses to explain the idea of a sports complex. More than one million dollars was generated by private pledges made as five- and ten-year financial commitments. Those funds have been used each year to pay off the CCAC's construction loan payment.

The two softball fields and soccer field formerly on N. Detroit Street were replaced by the eight softball fields and eight soccer fields at the CCAC. The first season of softball and soccer play at the City-County Athletic Complex took place in the spring of 1994. This facility serves more than 3,000 local participants in the community and hosts athletic tournaments with participants from other communities and states, as well.

Relocating the sports fields on N. Detroit Street paved the way for construction of Warsaw's beautiful Central Park along the shores of Center Lake. The grand opening night at Central Park on June 30, 1995, featured a free concert by "The Grass Roots" classic rock group. Some of the rock bands performing for annual concerts since have included: "Three Dog Night," "Blood, Sweat & Tears," "America," "Paul Revere and the Raiders," and "Herman's Hermits."

Central Park is the setting for many free entertainment events, such as the Friday Evening Performing Arts Series which features a different type of music each week, and the annual Country and Blues/Jazz concerts performed by popular bands and musicians.

And finally, through the Kosciusko County Foundation, Robert and Roma Maish visualized and set up a fund to build and maintain a beautiful flower garden on the northeast corner of Central Park alongside N. Detroit Street. The Maishes were recognized by the City at a reception in June 1998 held at the Gardens of Central Park, which has been referred to as "a treasure of living beauty."

Lake City Greenway

The idea of a community bike path began in the early 1990s with the construction of the City-County Athletic Complex (CCAC). A proposal was developed to construct a bike path along the railroad to provide a safe alternative for children and families traveling by bicycle to the CCAC. Unfortunately, the plan was not implemented and efforts for the bike path became idle.

In 1995, the need for establishing a greenway corridor was recognized again. Two students in the Kosciusko Leadership Academy (KLA) did a thorough study on the planning process for a bikeway. In 1997, another KLA project was aimed at creating a greenway system. This follow-up project proposed routes that would link schools, recreational opportunities, and other amenities of the community together.

Building on both KLA projects, a bikeway steering committee was formed in the summer of 1997 to explore the feasibility of establishing some of the proposed routes. The concept of the route is to build a bicycle wheel with Central Park as the hub and the proposed routes branching off will represent the spokes. Eventually, enough spokes will branch off of the hub to encircle the entire county—completing the bicycle wheel.

In 1998, a third KLA project, "The Lake City Greenway Master Plan," was completed to build on past efforts and set forth a blueprint for the community to use as a working document. The master plan estimates the cost of construction, identifies a series of potential routes, and indicates which property owners will be affected by the development of the bikeway.

The Lake City Greenway is a multi-jurisdictional project that will be an approximate eight-mile bicycle/pedestrian system that will begin west of Warsaw at the Chinworth Bridge. The greenway will travel past the City-County Athletic Complex, connect with Central Park and the Central Business District, travel through the Village at Winona, Winona Lake Park and the former Chicago Boys' Club, and terminate at Roy Street in the southern part of the Town of Winona Lake.

The City of Warsaw obtained a $1 million grant from the Indiana Department of Transportation. The city must match the total construction costs at twenty percent. The local community has been very supportive of the project, as indicated by the following contributors to date: National City Bank, $15,000; R.R. Donnelley & Sons, $25,000; Kosciusko County Foundation, $30,000; and Kosciusko County 21st Century Foundation, $50,000.

The project is currently in the design and engineering phase, with construction scheduled to begin in the Spring of 2002.

A view of the beautiful Gardens of Central Park.

The first concert at Central Park on June 30, 1995, featured "The Grass Roots."

Thousands of people attended the first free community concert at Central Park.

Courthouse Coffee

In 1997, Dave Bowman opened Courthouse Coffee at 108 N. Buffalo Street in conjunction with his wife Paula's interior decorating business called Kaleidoscope. Decorating accessories and gifts are displayed throughout the store, in addition to a Thomas Kincaide gallery, and the coffee shop is in the rear. In October 2000, the Bowmans expanded to the east side of town and opened Courthouse Coffee East in the Marketplace Plaza.

The 108 N. Buffalo Street location was occupied by a hardware store for about 100 years until 1966. It was later occupied by the Candy Cane restaurant owned by Devon Smith. The building then sat vacant about six years until DeVerl and Diane Baney operated the D & D Café from 1981 to 1991. Robert and Carolyn Rosbrugh had Mr. R's Café from 1991 to 1997, prior to the Bowmans' businesses opening in 1997.

Collector Plate

During Warsaw's Downtown Days celebration July 21-23, 2000, a 10¼-inch white porcelain plate was introduced to commemorate Warsaw's celebration as a city for 125 years and its 22 mayors since 1875. Michelle Bormet, secretary to Mayor Wiggins, contacted seven of the oldest businesses still in existence. They generously agreed to donate the funds to purchase 500 plates, which

were sold by the Kosciusko County Historical Society.

The sponsors were: *Times-Union* (1856), Lake City Bank (1872), DePuy (1895), Little Crow Foods (1903), Dalton Corporation (1910), Myer Levin & Sons (1914), and Zimmer (1927). Sketches of the early establishments of these businesses are depicted in chronological order around the rim of the plate, with a picture of the first mayor at the top and an early sketch of the courthouse in the center.

The production of 500 collector plates commemorating Warsaw as a city, 1875-2000, was sponsored by seven of the oldest local businesses.

It is my hope that future generations will recognize the significance of history and will strive to record it on a timely basis.

MJB

Jeff Plank, the only mayor elected to four consecutive terms (1984-1996), was presented a large Dirilyte plaque when he presided over his last city council meeting on February 17, 1997. Shown in front are council members J.C. "Mac" Silveus and Tammy Rockey. Left to right are councilman Jerry Patterson, Mrs. Jodene Plank, Mayor Jeff Plank, council president Ernie Wiggins, and councilman Porter Polston. Standing behind are councilmen Dewey Lawshe and Eugene Brumfield.

Chapter 17

Reproduction Postcards

Bird's-Eye View of Warsaw, Ind., looking North and Center Lake in Distance.

This early bird's-eye view looking north shows few homes along Lake Street as it extends alongside Center Lake.

Bird's-Eye View of Warsaw, Ind. looking Southeast.

An aerial view looking southeast from the Courthouse. The lower right shows the various buildings that sat along Center Street on the south side of the Courthouse. The Moon Block is on the southeast corner of Buffalo and Market Streets. A Bull Durham advertisement is painted on the west end of the Opera House on Market Street in the upper left corner.

The Winona Interurban trolley is stopped at the corner of Center and Lake Streets. It transported passengers between Warsaw and Winona Lake. Note the horse and buggies hitched in front of the Courthouse.

Colorful poster for M.M. Syphers, who established the first ice cream and soft drink business in the county in 1896.

The Elks Building in the 100 block of E. Center Street was completed in 1907. A wide hall with a marble floor extended through the building on the first floor. Over the years, the Elks Arcade was occupied by numerous businesses, including a barbershop and candy store. The Elks Lodge utilized the second and third floors.

Interior rooms of the Elks Building included a lounge, upper left; rooms for billiards and playing cards, upper right; and the ladies' reception room, at bottom, which was furnished with numerous ornate rocking chairs.

The trolley has just passed the intersection of Buffalo and Market Streets, traveling east to Winona Lake. The Opera House is to the right of the trolley. Phillipson's is on the left, with the Hickman & Neff real estate office upstairs. On the right is the W.R. Thomas store in the Moon building, with N.N. Boydston's real estate office on the second floor. Note the outside stairways for the multi-story buildings on all three corners.

A night view of the Moon Block, the three-story building on the southeast corner of Market and Buffalo Streets. The W.R. Thomas store was located there at the time of this photo in the early 1900s. The three-story Opera House is at the east end of the block.

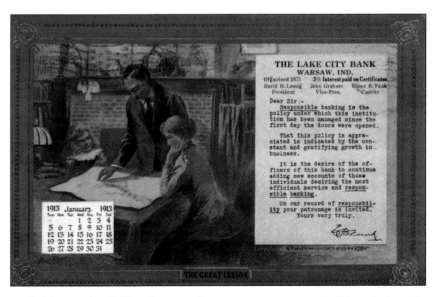

A colorful postcard mailed by Lake City Bank to customers in January 1913. This particular card is titled "The Great Lesson."

The Indiana Loan & Trust Building was on the southwest corner of Center and Buffalo Streets. Note the eagle atop the building, which signifies that the third floor was used as the Eagles Lodge for a time. There were five or six small storefronts along S. Buffalo Street for a number of years.

In the early 1900s, the 124-foot double-decker steamboat named "City of Warsaw" was navigated on Winona Lake. The steamer would travel along the Beyer Canal from the Winona Hotel to the Warsaw Depot where the Pennsylvania and Big Four Railroads crossed.

The State Bank was located on the southwest corner of Buffalo and Market Streets. Charles F. Nye had a clothing store next door on S. Buffalo Street.

The beautiful Hotel Hays was built by Elijah Hays in 1884 on the southeast corner of Center and Indiana Streets. The hotel closed in the late 1950s.

Center Lake offered a wooden toboggan slide and diving tower anchored off the shore for swimmers in the 1930's.

The Knights of Pythias Lodge in the 300 block of E. Center Street was demolished in 1954 so the Gill Motel could be expanded.

The 80-year-old First Baptist Church on the northeast corner of Center and Detroit Streets was demolished in 1995. The CVS Pharmacy now occupies this site.

The Big Four Railroad Depot was located on the south side of Market Street by the north-south tracks.

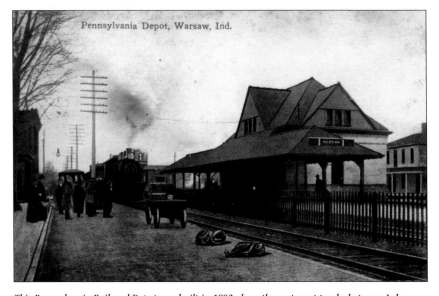

This Pennsylvania Railroad Depot was built in 1892 along the east-west tracks between Lake and Washington Streets.

Center Street looking East, Warsaw, Ind.

NO. 835

Looking east from Lake Street, a view of the buildings on Center Street across from the Courthouse. At far right is the R.H. Hitzler building; next door is the H.S. Biggs building. The 3-story building in the center was occupied by Rutter's Hardware.

Water Works and Electric Light Plant, WARSAW, Ind.

An early view of the Warsaw Water Works and Electric Light Plant on N. Buffalo Street by Center Lake.

BUFFALO ST. LOOKING NORTH, WARSAW, IND.

Buffalo Street looking north from the railroad tracks. A sign is visible on top of the Phillipson's clothing store on the northeast corner of Buffalo and Market Streets. The Western Union telegraph office to the far right was in the former Pierce Hotel.

Horn's Sunnymede Restaurant, which opened at 2229 E. Center Street in 1940 and operated until about 1970, was well-known for its chicken dinners.

A crowd enjoys sidewalk sales in the 100 block of S. Buffalo Street during "Pioneer Days" in the 1950s.

The limestone Post Office was built in the early 1930s on the northwest corner of Lake and Market Streets.

Index

239

The Kosciusko County Historical Society would like to thank the following for their support:

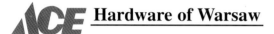

The Kosciusko County Historical Society would like to thank the following for their support:

The Kosciusko County Historical Society would like to thank the following for their support:

The Kosciusko County Historical Society would like to thank the following for their support:

The Kosciusko County Historical Society would like to thank the following for their support:

The Kosciusko County Historical Society would like to thank the following for their support:

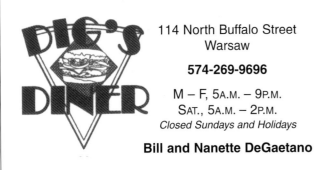